Low-Intensity Conflict

Westview Studies in Regional Security

Wm. J. Olson, Series Editor

Low-Intensity Conflict:
Old Threats in a New World,
edited by Edwin G. Corr and Stephen Sloan

The Military, the State, and Development
in Asia and the Pacific,
edited by Viberto Selochan

The Comandante Speaks: Memoirs of an
El Salvadoran Guerrilla Leader,
edited by Courtney E. Prisk

Uncomfortable Wars: Toward
a New Paradigm of Low-Intensity Conflict,
edited by Max G. Manwaring

U.S. Strategic Interests
in the Gulf Region,
edited by Wm. J. Olson

FORTHCOMING

The Emergency in Malaya, 1948–1954,
edited by John Coates

The U.S. Counterinsurgency
Campaign in Thailand,
edited by William Rosenau

Low-Intensity Conflict

Old Threats in a New World

EDITED BY

Edwin G. Corr
and Stephen Sloan

Westview Press

BOULDER • SAN FRANCISCO • OXFORD

Westview Studies in Regional Security

Published in 1992 in the United States of America by Westview Press, Inc., 5500 Central Avenue, Boulder, Colorado 80301-2877, and in the United Kingdom by Westview Press, 36 Lonsdale Road, Summertown, Oxford OX2 7EW

Library of Congress Cataloging-in-Publication Data
Low-intensity conflict : old threats in a new world / edited by Edwin
   G. Corr and Stephen Sloan.
     p.   cm. — (Studies in regional security)
   Includes bibliographical references and index.
   ISBN 0-8133-8593-8 (hc) : — ISBN 0-8133-8594-6 (pb) :
   1. World politics—1975-1985.   2. World politics—1985-1995.
3. United States—Foreign relations—1977-1981.   4. United States—
Foreign relations—1981-1989.   5. United States—Foreign
relations—1989-   .   6. Low-intensity conflicts (Military science)—
History—20th century.   I. Corr, Edwin G.   II. Sloan, Stephen.
III. Series.
D849.L69   1992
909.82'8 —dc20   92-17572
                                                                                    CIP

Printed and bound in the United States of America

The paper used in this publication meets the requirements
of the American National Standard for Permanence of Paper
for Printed Library Materials Z39.48-1984.

10   9   8   7   6   5   4   3   2   1

This book is dedicated
by Ed to his loving parents, Rowena and E. L. "Bert" Corr,
by Steve to Michael Joel Weiss, one of the best and brightest,
and to
the twenty million people who
have perished in low-intensity conflict
since World War Two.

Contents

Foreword

Your tale, sir, would cure deafness.
—Shakespeare, *The Tempest*

We have arrived on the shores of a brave new world after a dire and turbulent voyage. For more than forty years we have lived with the certainties of rivalry with the Soviet Union and the defining features of a policy of containment. Although it was a period filled with many cares and sorrows, there was a coherence and consistency of purpose that lent us reassurance on the often vexing question of how this country should determine its international role.

As a nation we have been most comfortable as a symbol or an inspiration to others. Believing in the soundness of our founding principles, initially we were mostly inclined to remain aloof from a world whose politics and intrigues we found distasteful. George Washington's familiar words to avoid entangling alliances were less an admonition to the fledgling nation than a reflection of a deep psychological element in the American character. Yet, as the world has grown more complex and fearsome since his day, the bent of our natures to remain aloof has undergone stress and change.

The world simply would not leave us in peace. Nor, ultimately, would our own native restlessness and sense of what is proper be reconciled to idle watching with the approach of World War II. Thus, when our sense of responsibility clashed with our sense of isolation, we chose, rightly, the former. It was never a comfortable decision, however, and it is one that has remained troubling.

The consensus that sustained our postwar containment policy was showing major fault lines in recent years, and it is only the collapse of the Soviet Union that has forestalled a crisis in U.S. foreign policy. Ironically, or perhaps inevitably, the disintegration of our former adversary has not postponed the critical review suggested by that decline. It has only deflected it into an area whose features are even harder to discern. Far from ending ambiguity or simplifying questions about our role in the world, the demise of our enemy presents us with even greater uncertainty as to the nature of the world we face and leaves us more unsure of what our purpose should be.

This present volume attempts to provide, if no final answer, a timely and true definition of the challenges we face and the course we should undertake. It is a partisan book. It clearly sides with the universal bent of our nature. It makes it clear that the world will be very much with us, demanding our attention. It also describes the nature that much of the threat is likely to take.

Today we face a range of contradictory challenges in distant jungles and urban environments. In many of these conflicts it is hard to discern or explain concrete U.S. interests that would justify our serious involvement. This was so when we still had the Soviet threat to validate our concerns. Now that underpinning, that imperative for action that subdued our inclination toward aloofness, no longer has the force to ratify the type, scale, or longevity of involvement that these situations require. It remains unclear just what the American public will support as an expression of its interests in the larger world or what use of U.S. power overseas it will sustain.

What challenge to our basic values and survival is posed, for example, by the *Sendero Luminoso* in Peru, however murderous and cruel they may be? What interest is at stake that should see us engaged in small countries such as El Salvador? With the demise of communism, what rationale is left for becoming involved in distant, obscure struggles? With so many concerns at home, what should we care for the squabbles of others?

This volume frames the issues for intelligent debate. The genius of the American people has always been in our pragmatic idealism, our willingness to take the measure of a problem and then get to work doing something about it. We have a bit more in our character of the reflexive than the reflective, and ambiguity troubles our collective soul. Clearly, however, we have serious issues that will demand our best efforts, both intellectually and materially. There are no easy answers, nor do we have the luxury of a clear and present danger around which to coalesce.

Ambassador Corr and Professor Sloan have assembled an impressive array of experts to provide insight into the answers to such questions. The chapters detail the nature of the challenge to our interests and to our inclinations. They suggest the basis for sound policy and the vision that must underpin our efforts. What principles should now guide the purposes of U.S. power in the world is one of the most vital questions of our day. The debate is one that we cannot avoid. This volume provides firm ground upon which to have a rational and timely discourse.

Wm. J. Olson
Series Editor

Preface

We live in a time in which our basic assumptions about geopolitics and military power have been rendered obsolete. Perhaps the greatest threat to U.S. national security is the danger that we will not change our thinking to coincide with the changes in the world around us. World leadership in the next century will depend upon a different set of assets and resources from those it depended on during the cold war era of superpower confrontations. In the national security establishment, where the primary focus had long been the Soviet threat, policymakers are searching for new strategies for a changing world.

That is why this much-needed book is so welcome. Ambassador Edwin G. Corr and Professor Stephen Sloan have brought together an eminent group of defense specialists who are devoted to new thinking. Their analyses of current challenges to U.S. security are clear and historically insightful. Most important, the contributors to this volume take an approach that mirrors the milieu of current U.S. foreign policy—pragmatic and nonideological.

One message is unmistakable: The end of the cold war–era conflict does not signal the end of all global conflict. Indeed, just the reverse will undoubtedly be true. The absence of the relatively straightforward bipolar struggle leaves a power vacuum, an unstable environment in which the potential for low-intensity conflicts is greater than ever before. Tribalism, extreme nationalism, religious fundamentalism, and hold-over Marxist ideology all provide fodder for small-scale wars—wars likely to be fought within existing states rather than between them.

Indeed, some now long for the "good old days" when the enemy was obvious and the terms of reference simple. They do not want to think about the nuances of a multipolar world. Instead, they turn to nostalgic and self-congratulatory visions of the "end of history," in which all nations, rich and poor, seek only material fulfillment—a strangely empty vision of peace and prosperity. Such visions, whatever one may think of them, are premature.

U.S. policymakers must now consider which potential low-intensity conflicts warrant our attention. What criteria should be used in deciding whether U.S. intervention in worldwide insurgencies and regional wars is justified? How do we weigh our own narrow national interests against a broader responsibility as a great power to promote international order and stability?

The definition of U.S. interests and power is clearly undergoing a fundamental transformation. For at least the past decade, international power has derived more from economic than from military sources. This trend will continue unabated, and, as one of the contributors to this volume asserts, we face a challenge to change perspectives.

Superpower involvement in both the Ethiopian and the Afghan conflicts heightened their significance on the world political scene. Later, both the United States and the former Soviet Union distanced themselves from those regional wars. Even the brutal Yugoslav civil war did not elicit a forceful U.S. response. Now, without the context of cold war ideology, the impact of the Yugoslav conflict on U.S. interests was called into question.

The United States must quickly come to an understanding of its changing interests in our post–cold war world. For the intelligence community, low-intensity conflicts will not be the only consideration to occupy our attention. Economic espionage is an area that will require both more resources and clearer policy guidance. Biological and nuclear arms proliferation, international drug trafficking, and terrorism must also be among U.S. intelligence priorities in the post–cold war world.

Critical to an adequate intelligence response to these concerns, as well as to specific low-intensity conflicts, is an increased emphasis on human intelligence. With shrinking military and intelligence budgets, human-source intelligence can provide higher quality and less expensive intelligence than technological collection systems. Fewer U.S. forces forward-positioned around the world make early warning of potential threats much more important. Satellite technology, particularly valuable for tracking large-scale military maneuvers, is far less useful for predicting or resolving low-intensity conflicts. Streamlining communication between military and civilian intelligence services and improving raw intelligence analysis will also make responses to regional conflicts more timely and accurate.

As low-intensity conflicts engage more of our military and intelligence attention, the U.S. government requires more sober evaluations of our military missions, capabilities, and strategies. Ambassador Corr and Professor Sloan's book is an outstanding effort to frame the new defense debate. As long as the United States intends to remain a leading power in a rapidly changing world, our policymakers must have the benefit of such thoughtful and thorough works.

Senator David L. Boren
Washington, D.C.

Acknowledgments

Admiration and thanks are expressed first to the authors whose knowledge, experience, analytical powers, wisdom, and many hours of thought and writing made this book possible. The University of Oklahoma, through the Henry Bellmon Chair, provided support for a secretary, a research assistant, a professional editor, and a planning session for the authors to organize the book to ensure coherence and valuable content. The Office of the Assistant Secretary of Defense for Special Operations funded travel of the authors to the meeting. The help of these two institutions is greatly appreciated.

Diana Brown did the typing, retyping, proofing, and organization of the authors' planning session contributions with persistence, accuracy, tact, and harmony. Sharon Vaughan expertly assisted in research and prepared the index, maps, face-sheets, and diagrams. Aileen Moodie, our professional editor, made all of us more articulate and our drafting consistent and contributed significantly to the manuscript's form and content. Sandra Rush skillfully made the final draft camera ready. Bill Olson, the series editor, and Peter Kracht, senior editor for Westview Press, were flexible and gave us guidance in our endeavor.

Finally, we are indebted to our wives, Susanne and Roberta, for encouragement, patience, and comprehension during the many hours we spent organizing, writing, and editing this volume. We and the authors alone are responsible for any errors of fact or judgment.

Edwin G. Corr
Stephen Sloan

PART ONE

The Challenge, the Concepts, and the Context

1

Introduction

Stephen Sloan

The disintegration of the Soviet Union has led to a fundamental and uncertain transformation in the international order. The former equilibrium based on the "balance of nuclear terror" by the superpowers is rapidly becoming a footnote in history, and the policy of "containment" that directed the formulation and conduct of U.S. foreign affairs has become an obsolete doctrine. As we move into the next century, the breakdown and reconfiguration of the Soviet empire, the assertion of an expanded and revitalized Europe, and the massive economic and concomitant political growth of Japan have invalidated a comfortable, if sometimes erroneous, base point from which to analyze the scope and direction of fundamental political, social, and economic movements. The changes rapidly unfolding before our eyes on the evening news ushered in what may become an epoch of great possibilities but even greater dangers. We have entered an era where uncertainty, unpredictability, and conflict have replaced the enforced outward stability of what was once a bipolar world.

While public attention will continue to focus on the profound changes within the former Soviet Union and on its periphery, such changes will probably be accelerated throughout the countries of the third and fourth worlds. Analysts still reeling from the dissolution of the Soviet empire will face a variant of intense "future shock" in those postcolonial countries throughout Asia, Africa, and the Middle East that became independent after World War II.

This "future shock" is partly the result of two changes, one associated with the monumental events taking place, the other a longer term development that is yet to be fully understood by both policymakers and academics. The first change is related to the end of the cold war. No longer can the states of the transitional area be primarily viewed as either pawns or surrogates of superpower

3

machinations. Neither classic "wars of national liberation," which are now part of a bankrupt ideology, nor "anti-Marxist insurgencies," which were largely a response to that discredited ideology, explain or justify superpower involvement in the often fragile orders of the developing states. What will happen in the ensuing years will not be conveniently identified as part of the global designs of Moscow or Washington.

The second change was often obscured but in the long term may be far more significant than the bipolar competition. Those policymakers and academics who focused on superpower competition often failed to recognize that in the long term it is regional and local factors—not necessarily related to superpower competition—that have determined and will determine the course of politics in the transitional area where the majority of the world's population live, and in many cases barely survive.

This transformation of the developing world is characterized by two often contradictory forces. On one hand, the so-called forces of modernization that preoccupied social scientists in the sixties and seventies did break down the arbitrary boundaries of the developing states. The result, however, was not the end of "primordial loyalties" in the form of tribalism or sectarian conflict that threatened the development of that outwardly "modern" community known as the nation-state.[1] Moreover, an uneven modernization process characterized by an information explosion did not necessarily lead to democratization in the new states. With notable exceptions, the bullet and not the ballot box still determined the course of politics.

Perhaps even more vexing to those imbued with the credo of modernization and democratization is the reluctant realization that in an expanded technological universe, it was primordial loyalties that not only survived but also grew, largely as a reaction to modernity and the supposed onslaught of the secular state. The assertion of the loyalties of the extended family, the clan and the tribe, the rise of Islamic fundamentalism, and the vitality of other old and deeply held beliefs underscore the fact that traditional forces are alive and well in the transitional area.[2] Such values will be intensified and fueled by current events in the former Soviet Union as nationalities and ethnic groups assert their independence from an increasingly impotent center.

Finally, had conventional thinkers looked beyond their prisms of modernity they would have been better prepared to understand, if not predict, the events now taking place in a discredited empire. The assertion of the Baltic states and the separatism of the Soviet republics are largely a manifestation of the fact that a former superpower is now reacting to the winds of change that have buffeted the social, economic, and political order of the new states since their independence. The disintegrated Soviet system is largely emulating the experience of the countries of the Third World.

Learning to Live with Ambiguity in the New Order

Faced with these profound changes U.S. policymakers must understand and formulate courses of action that can enable Washington to move beyond its essentially reactive posture to the instability that will probably increase in the immediate future. At the core of the new policies should be the recognition that international politics will be characterized by ambiguity, an ambiguity that will have some of the following elements.

On the global level, as noted earlier, the arbitrary equilibrium outwardly imposed by the superpower conflict and resultant accommodation will increasingly be replaced by regional and localized conflicts that by themselves will not have strategic geopolitical implications for the United States. Such conflicts will not fit into previous patterns of instability that were related to the bipolar competition of the past. They will largely be the result of internal factors ranging from inter-elite competition to the assertion of ethnicity in the forms of internal strife ranging from tribal conflict to separatist movements. Ordinarily U.S. security concerns will not be directly affected, and Washington's involvement will be minimal, other than offering diplomatic good offices to resolve conflicts, evacuation of U.S. nationals, and provisions for humanitarian assistance when requested.

Policymakers will be hard pressed to identify in these low-level conflicts those conditions that can lead to instability that can adversely affect U.S. national security, however. The ability to identify potential areas of escalated conflict in a confused and diffused arena of localized conflict will be crucial if the United States unilaterally, or preferably in concert with other states, can assist in defusing conflicts before they become regionally significant. Policymakers and planners will have to be particularly sensitive to the emergence of states that seek aggressively to become regional powers and to social or political movements that can threaten the stability of a particular area. Moreover, the ability to engage in preventive diplomacy will place a heavy strain on a national security apparatus that has tended to engage primarily in short-term crisis management.

In seeking to accommodate to a highly fluid international

environment, policymakers will be forced to define more clearly what constitutes U.S. national security interests. They will have to adjust to a range of concerns that go far beyond the past preoccupation with nuclear deterrence and the expansion of Soviet power. In effect, the "new world order" is already redefining major elements of security that are not amenable to either traditional diplomatic or military actions. The impact of the so-called war on drugs, concerns about technology transfer, proliferation of nuclear weapons, and the increasing political power of Japan and such newly industrialized states as South Korea will require those charged with policy to look beyond traditional adversaries or the immediate short-term threat of an "outlaw" state.

Finally, both civilian and military policymakers will have to accept the fact that in the new world order the line between peace and war will increasingly be blurred and ambiguous, that warfare itself, to cite the astute observation of Admiral James D. Watkins, will be "less coherent."[3] Although the possibility of conventional regional conflict like the Gulf War will remain, the prevailing environment will be more ambiguous. In this environment the uniquely American dichotomy that seeks to differentiate between peace and war must be replaced, and policymakers and their respective bureaucracies must seek to achieve a unity of effort instead of basing their role on an outdated concept of what constitutes both political and armed conflict.

The Challenge of Adjusting to Ambiguity:
Low-Intensity Conflict and Beyond

There is a body of policies, doctrine, organizations, and capabilities that can be a guide in meeting the demands of the fundamental global changes now taking place. The policies and associated doctrine come from an old tradition associated with fighting different forms of unconventional wars. More specifically, the "rediscovery" of the importance of the capability to engage in so-called uncomfortable wars provides a foundation to address the changing nature of conflict and national security requirements.[4]

This book focuses on what is now referred to as low-intensity conflict (LIC). The armed hostilities that have predominated in the Third World during the last half-century have been known by many names— small wars, regional wars, revolutionary war, the struggle for national liberation, guerrilla war, low-intensity conflict, prolonged peoples' war, insurgency, and protracted conflict, to name a few.[5] One student of the phenomenon compiled fifty-five such names.[6] None seems satisfactory. Currently in the Department of Defense there have been efforts to rename LIC either "peacetime engagement" or "forward presence operations." It is better that we halt the persistent controversy over what to call this kind of conflict, stick with the last iteration—"low-intensity conflict (LIC)"—and move on to conceptual models and organizational structures to enable the United States to cope successfully with low-intensity conflicts of the second and third worlds when our interests are at stake.

The authors of the respective contributions suggest that an understanding of the major characteristics of LIC, its politico-military dimensions, and its policy ramifications can be the basis for a proactive U.S. policy instead of a short-term reactive posture to the profound and long-term instability that will certainly mark the future direction of international politics.

Although there is not total agreement on a definition of LIC, the following one, after long and often very acrimonious debate, has been accepted by the military and has very significant implications for the civilian national security hierarchy.

> Low-intensity conflict is a politico-military confrontation between competing states or groups below conventional war and above the routine, peaceful competition among states. It frequently involves protracted struggles of competing principles and ideologies. Low-intensity conflict ranges from subversion to the use of armed force. It is waged by a combination of means, employing political, economic, informational, and military instruments. Low-intensity conflicts are often localized, generally in the Third World, but contain regional and global security implications.[7]

The genesis of the term and of associated concepts is deeply embedded in the history of warfare. Different forms of armed conflict ranging from guerrilla and partisan war, insurgency and counterinsurgency, unconventional war and protracted conflict have been practiced throughout history. The U.S. experience with such conflicts dates back to the Revolutionary War, but the desire to rely on conventional forces of arms has been the rule.

Despite some notable exploits in the unconventional arena during World War II, the end of that conflict and emergence of the cold war reinforced the reliance on conventional military forces and high technology. With U.S. involvement in Indochina, the Kennedy administration did recognize the importance of developing unconventional capabilities through its support for special operations and counterinsurgency programs, but the fall of South Vietnam raised serious questions concerning U.S. involvement in the Third World and relegated U.S. thinking about LIC and the special operations community to the back burners in U.S. military planning.

The failure of the hostage rescue force at Desert One in Iran in 1979 brought into sharp and painful focus the relative U.S. military decline under the Carter administration, provoked serious doubts about the ability of the United States to project its power globally, and more specifically raised questions about the capability of the armed forces to engage in special operations against terrorism and other forms of unconventional strife. The Holloway Commission Report succinctly presented the reasons for the failure of the rescue mission and made an exceedingly strong case for a reorganization and revitalization of the special operations community.[8]

With the initiation of the Reagan administration there were important changes. President Ronald Reagan reemphasized the importance of building up U.S. military capabilities to meet what was perceived at that time to be a serious and protracted Soviet military threat—the buildup of Soviet nuclear strategic capabilities and conventional forces arrayed against Europe, and Moscow's support of "wars of national liberation" in the resource-rich and strategically placed "choke points" in the transitional area. This assertion of U.S. political and military capabilities was to be tested in support of what were called "anti-Marxist insurgencies" in Angola, Mozambique, and Afghanistan, as well as in the particularly sensitive policy issues associated with Washington's support of the contra guerrillas in Nicaragua and military and political assistance programs to the endangered government of El Salvador.

The maturation of this policy was perhaps best enunciated in *Discriminate Deterrence*, a report of the Commission on Integrated Long-Term Strategy, in which U.S. involvement in the transitional area was stated as follows:

> To help protect U.S. interests and allies in the Third World we will need more of a national consensus on both means and ends. Our means should include:
> • Security assistance at a higher level and with fewer legislative restrictions to inhibit its effectiveness.
> • Versatile mobile forces, minimally dependent on overseas bases, that can deliver precisely controlled strikes against military targets.
> • In special cases, U.S. assistance to . . . insurgents who are resisting a hostile regime that threatens its neighbors. The free world will not remain free if its options are only to stand still and retreat.[9]

Despite the maturation of this policy, the willingness of both the civilian and military establishments to develop a meaningful capability to engage directly and indirectly in such operations has been long in coming. It took an act of Congress—the Goldwater-Nichols Department of Defense Reorganization Act of 1986—to force the armed forces to recognize the importance of special operations and develop an organizational framework in the form of the United States Special Operations Command (USSOC) to meet also the challenges of LIC.

Actual U.S. military involvement in both the Reagan and the Bush administrations unfortunately obscured and consequently lessened the concern of policymakers, the public, and the armed forces about the need to have the capabilities to engage in low-intensity conflicts. In Grenada, although special forces were employed, the conflict was essentially an invasion by an overwhelming conventional force in a very short conflict. In Panama the operation was also essentially an invading force involved in another short conventional conflict. The Gulf conflict went one step beyond: it involved the maximum use of conventional forces and high-technology weapons by a coalition that indeed did have impressive results against largely static and conventionally positioned and equipped Iraqi forces.

As a result, although there may have been an end of the "Vietnam syndrome" on questions associated with the ability of the United States to wage war, the victory in the Gulf reinforced the U.S. penchant to emphasize conventional responses to aggressive action. Euphoria over military victory there further obscured the importance of learning how to identify, and when necessary respond to, the particular complexities of the type of conflicts Washington will have to deal with most frequently in the future—LIC. It is ironic that the "Vietnam syndrome," which was a reluctance to develop the capabilities and policies to meet challenges to U.S. national security interests in the states of the transitional area, would be replaced by the "Gulf syndrome," which reinforced the penchant of civilian and military policymakers and the public still to rely on conventional responses in a rapidly changing and uncertain unconventional security environment.

The Audience for This Book—The Beltway and Beyond

The editors and contributors of this book, whose biographies are provided at the end of the book, share a number of common experiences and values. Some have come from the academic community and others from the policy and operational sector, but all agree that the remarkable changes in the international environment call for a rigorous and fresh analysis of how knowledge concerning LIC can be applied to meet as yet uncharted challenges to U.S. national security.

Because all the contributors to varying degrees have been involved in the public sector, we recognize that solid analysis of the future challenge will have little meaning unless it reaches those senior policymakers and mid-level bureaucrats both in and out of uniform who will be responsible for identifying and implementing national security objectives, however they are defined by this or any future political leadership. Based on their individual and collective experience, the authors know that their task will not be easy, for they must convey their message to those who work inside what is called the Beltway and yet breach the insularity of the Beltway to reach a broader audience.

The Beltway represents both a geographical designation and a state of mind. It is a series of highways that encircle Washington, D.C. Perhaps even more important is the fact that inside the Beltway are the national political leaders or senior members of the federal civilian and military bureaucracy who must make and implement policies based on the administrative constraints of large-scale organizations with their own vested interests. The perceptions of those within the Beltway are often quite parochial because their bureaucratic concerns do not necessarily mirror those on the other side of the Beltway—the rest of the United States. The concerns among inhabitants often appear to be disconnected to the rest of the country.

These differing concerns and insularity are ironically found among those who outwardly are concerned about global issues and more specifically national security affairs. Although they look outward, they are always turned inward to protect their designated bureaucratic turfs from the other inhabitants within the Beltway.

Despite its global concerns, there is a lack of unity of purpose within the national security apparatus. At the top level the president, buffeted by Congress, is served by a National Security Council and staff personnel who must translate the president's current policy concerns and accompanying rhetoric into general programs of action. Often those concerns use the analogies of warfare, changed to meet new political agendas. Thus, though the "cold war" has been rendered obsolete, there are still many wars to be fought—the "war against terrorism" and now the "war against drugs."

In this highly competitive environment the continuing turf battles within the Department of Defense have been intensified as each service or command seeks to maximize its share of a declining defense budget. The interservice rivalries are often eclipsed by the chronic competition between the Department of Defense and the Department of State, which despite its small numbers and resources seeks to maintain its primacy in the conduct of foreign affairs by the justification that everything short of conflict is in its domain. The competition is further heightened by the policy statements of the president. When the words of the chief executive can translate into a national concern and subsequent funding, the members of the national security and foreign policy hierarchy are well attuned to the latest slogans. Indeed, changing terminology may also reflect a sea change in foreign policy.

The term "low-intensity conflict" became such a phrase, modified to meet the changing requirements of presidential leadership. At first LIC focused on the terrorist threat and insurgency sponsored by the Soviet Union, and then it encompassed a counternarcotics role as part of the war against drugs. The bureaucracies responded to these changes to maximize their position in the constantly evolving definition of what constituted national security concerns and objectives. As a result, the long-existing turf battles have been exacerbated by a shrinking budget as well as a desire to find "living space" in a rapidly changing national security agenda. This competition is likely to intensify even further as the departments and agencies seek to redefine their roles to meet yet-to-be determined security requirements of the new world order.

It is precisely this escalating bureaucratic infighting that will lessen the ability of the United States to meet the monumental challenges that it faces with the breakdown of the Soviet Union. What are required now are imagination, vision, and long-term planning, not bureaucratic fragmentation.

The authors believe that there are specific lessons to be drawn from their individual contributions in the book. An even more important lesson is that recognizing the nature of LIC and the requirements for a unity of effort within the political leadership and the national security and foreign affairs bureaucracy can provide a foundation from which to deal effectively with the challenges of this post–cold war epoch.

Beyond that, the authors hope that opinion leaders and informed citizens beyond the Beltway will read this book to understand the challenge and to articulate effectively the concerns to those who do not live in the "federal village" known as Washington. By developing an understanding of LIC an informed bureaucracy and public can help to chart U.S. national security policies in the days ahead. In so doing they can assist in promoting a sense of common purpose among those on both sides of the Beltway who ultimately share common values as Americans. The challenge of meeting the accelerating changes in the international arena is profound but offers us opportunities as we as a people and a nation enter the next century.

The Manwaring Paradigm

In addressing the major aspects of LIC and how to take the initiative in or respond to it, the variable case studies use a common analytical approach based on a paradigm developed by one of the contributors—Max G. Manwaring.[10] The underlying premise of the paradigm is that "the ultimate outcome of any counterinsurgency effort is not primarily determined by the skillful manipulation of violence in . . . many military battles." Rather, the outcome will be determined by (1) legitimacy of the government, (2) organization for unity of effort, (3) type and consistency of support for the targeted government, (4) ability to reduce outside aid to the insurgents, (5) intelligence (or action against subversion), and (6) discipline and capabilities of a government's armed forces. These elements can be applied in understanding LIC environments that transcend different regions or stages of political economic development. Testing of the paradigm has shown that each of these dimensions is of the utmost importance in determining the effectiveness of response to a LIC situation.

The paradigm is equally applicable for focusing on crucial factors that will help to determine whether a threatened government and its allies can meet many-faceted challenges created by LIC or for assessing the ability of insurgents to achieve their strategic goals in a low-intensity conflict. The elements are not culturally bound in terms of Western values and goals. The paradigm can help to explain the dynamics of LIC not only in traditional and modernizing societies but also in industrial states facing the monumental changes unleashed by the breakdown of the former Soviet empire.

The Critical Factors

Legitimacy. The *single most important* dimension is legitimacy, the moral right to govern. The primary objective of an insurgent is to destroy the legitimacy of the incumbent government; therefore, the primary objective of that government must be to protect, maintain, and enhance its right to govern. The strategic center of gravity in this key struggle is the relative rectitude of the contending organizations. For the targeted government, the fight for legitimacy is the most critical factor for lasting success. It also becomes the primary concern for external power supporting the targeted government.

Organization for unity of effort. The ideal for this dimension is that all efforts are guided by a single strategic perspective and focused on the ultimate goals of survival, reconciliation of the conflict, and removal of the causes. Without adequate organization at the highest level to establish, enforce, and refine a national campaign plan embracing both civilian and military efforts and programs, authority is fragmented; and there is not sufficient unity of effort to resolve the myriad problems endemic in an insurgency. Government or insurgent failure to attain unity of effort is likely to cause defeat. Governments are often disadvantaged against the insurgency, particularly if the insurgents have seized the initiative in the conflict through superior organizational skills and clearly defined objectives.

Type and consistency of external support for targeted government. Long-term consistent support during and after a low-intensity conflict is critical to success. The paradigm underscores the fact that when material or nonmaterial support for the targeted government is either withdrawn during an insurgency or provided inconsistently, the possibility of success is significantly reduced. Conversely, when the aid was provided consistently over the long term, chances for success in a counterinsurgency were considerably enhanced. Likewise, failure to support an embattled government after military success in a guerrilla war was deemed to have damaged progress in the other five critical areas; in most cases the guerrilla war regained momentum, and the country continued to suffer.

Ability to reduce outside aid to the insurgents. The fourth dimension of the paradigm shows the need of the besieged government to separate the insurgents from their network of internal and external sanctuaries and from their external support, and the need of insurgents to maintain external material, political, and diplomatic support if they are to succeed. The analysis indicates that to ignore this aspect of the insurgent war as too difficult or too dangerous in its internal and external politico-military ramifications is simply to deny the military principle of the strategic offensive. The war against outside support is critical. When successful it provides a force multiplier in the fight in all other critical areas.

Intelligence. This dimension is vital to success for either targeted governments or insurgents. Intelligence is required by insurgents to economize the use of their normally smaller forces and to use the element of surprise. For the government it is essential to locate, isolate, and destroy or neutralize the insurgent leadership and organizational structure. No situation presents a more ambiguous problem to the strategic planner and policymaker than the indirect threat posed by an insurgency. If the appropriate intelligence apparatus and psychological instruments are not in place to find, eliminate, and discredit subversive actions, organizations, and revolutionary leaders, experience shows that the conflict will continue in one form or another indefinitely.

Discipline and capabilities of a government's armed forces. The last dimension concerns the ability of the government to influence positively the populace, through control of the armed forces' actions affecting the population. Similarly, the ability of the armed forces to engage and defeat the insurgents in military operations is critical. Analytical findings clearly show that the best intelligence and other countersubversion activities are of little consequence without troops who can decisively engage the enemy without alienating the citizenry. A primary goal of the insurgents is to provoke government forces into indiscriminate warfare, atrocities, and human rights abuses in order to destroy the government's legitimacy.

Acceptance of the notion of a multidimensional conflict requires that an insurgency be successfully engaged on several fronts. To provide a cumulative scorecard on the prospects for a specific country we must remember that each dimension of the counterinsurgent war must be positive to favor success by the targeted government. Furthermore, "to the extent that any one component is absent, or all or most are only present in a weak form, the government's success is not likely."[11]

Organization of the Book

The book is divided into three parts: the challenge, the concepts, and the context; case studies of seven selected countries; and the implications of and conclusions about low-intensity conflict for the United States in the post–cold war era.

In Chapter 2 of Part One, Ambassadors David C. Miller and Edwin G. Corr describe previous efforts of the U.S. government to cope with LIC, examine the current bureaucratic structure for dealing with the subject, and recommend actions that the president might take to improve policy formulation, agency coordination, and program implementation. Dr. Max G. Manwaring, the creator of the paradigm that provides the conceptual framework for this book, describes in Chapter 3 the strategic environment of the post–cold war era, defines the central strategic problem, and argues that the challenge is essentially social and political as well as military. General John R. Galvin discusses in Chapter 4 the need for and efforts by our government and armed forces to develop a new strategic concept to deal with a greatly reshaped and unstable world and outlines four major security mission areas.

Part Two consists of case studies selected to demonstrate particular aspects of LIC. In Chapter 5, Dr. Robert F. Zimmerman analyzes reasons for the Thai success in the 1970s when the government withstood a foreign-supported insurgency. Professor Caesar D. Sereseres's examination of Guatemala in Chapter 6 shows that governments without foreign supporters can defeat a strong insurgency and that there are some advantages in going it alone. Looking at the phenomenon from the insurgents' perspective, Ambassador James Cheek in Chapter 7 describes the Eritreans' and Tigrayans' long, successful struggle against the Soviet-supported Ethiopian government.

Narcotics trafficking and the attendant violence is another form of LIC. Professor David Scott Palmer in Chapter 8 outlines the difficulties in dealing with a fanatical, totally indigenous revolutionary movement that has made common cause with illegal drug growers and traffickers. In Chapter 9 attention focuses on yet another aspect of LIC. Sean K. Anderson examines the relationship of terrorism and Islamic fundamentalism. Dr. David C. Isby shows in Chapter 10 that superpower support could not overcome the lack of legitimacy of the imposed Afghan central government and that external support for the *mujahideen* rebels could not compensate for rebels' lack of unity and weakened legitimacy to enable the insurgents to triumph immediately after the Soviet 1989 withdrawal. Finally, in Chapter 11, Ambassador Edwin G. Corr and Colonel Courtney E. Prisk analyze the prospects for democracy and a lasting peace in El Salvador, where U.S. involvement was great and efforts were made to help Salvadorans transform their society as well as to defeat the guerrillas militarily.

Part Three suggests implications of LIC for the United States and draws conclusions about what might be done to cope successfully with this phenomenon in the post–cold war era. Dr. Thomas A. Grant in Chapter 12 describes U.S. attitudes and political constraints that affect the ability to respond to LIC. Professor John Norton Moore examines in Chapter 13 the international legal system and its effect as a deterrent to aggression, particularly in the LIC spectrum. Admiral William J. Crowe in Chapter 14 discusses the implications of LIC for future U.S. policy and strategy. In Chapter 15, I offer some final reflections as to what our nation must do to meet the challenge of LIC in the post–cold war environment.

The editors and contributors hope that this book can assist those concerned with developing policies, strategy, and doctrine to deal constructively with low-intensity conflict in a world where fundamental transformation is now becoming commonplace and armed conflict in its many forms is the rule and not the exception.

Notes

1. Clifford Geertz, ed., *Old Societies and New States* (Glencoe: The Free Press of Glencoe, 1963).

2. Islamic fundamentalism represents in the Western world those values often associated with traditional societies. There is, however, a sense in which the recent surge of Islamic fundamentalism is counter to traditional Islamic societies, which were more tolerant and less fanatical.

3. Admiral James D. Watkins, "Terrorism: An Already Declared War," *Wings of Gold* (Summer 1984): 19.

4. Max G. Manwaring, ed., *Uncomfortable Wars: Toward a New Paradigm of Low Intensity Conflict* (Boulder: Westview Press, 1991).

5. Ambassador Edwin G. Corr, "Preface," in *El Salvador at War: An Oral History*, ed. Max G. Manwaring and Court Prisk (Washington, D.C.: National Defense University Press, 1988), p. xxxiii.

6. William J. Olson, currently deputy assistant secretary of state for international narcotics matters, compiled such a list while he served as the acting deputy assistant secretary of defense for special operations and low-intensity conflict.

7. Headquarters, Department of the Army and the Air Force, *Military Operations in Low Intensity Conflict*, Field Manual 100–20, Air Force Pamphlet 3–20, December 1990, p. 1–1.

8. "Holloway Commission Report," reprinted in *Aviation Week and Space Technology*, 15,22,29 September 1980.

9. Commission on Integrated Long-Term Strategy, *Discriminate Deterrence* (Washington, D.C.: GPO, January 1988), pp. 2–3.

10. The Manwaring paradigm is based on empirical analysis of forty-three post–World War II governments that resisted or succumbed to an organized and externally supported insurgency. The analysis identified six interrelated, salient dimensions critical to low-intensity conflict. The research involved interviewing more than a hundred respondents who were involved in specified conflicts and academics who had witnessed the conflicts and written about them. Seventy-two variables were compiled that had made a difference in winning or losing the forty-three conflicts. A questionnaire was then developed from the seventy-two variables and given to more than two hundred respondents who had been involved in the conflicts. The model derived was submitted to multiple statistical tests against other models, using standard regression analyses and Probit analyses. The results revealed powerful predictive capabilities for the Manwaring paradigm. Results of the research were first published in "A Model for the Analysis of Insurgencies," paper prepared for the Small Wars Operations Research Directorate, U.S. Southern Command, 1987. The paradigm was later explicated in Manwaring, ed., *Uncomfortable Wars*, pp. 20–24. A more methodologically oriented version of this research, entitled "Insurgency and Counterinsurgency: Toward a New Analytical Approach," has been accepted for publication in *The Journal of Small Wars*.

11. Manwaring, ed., *Uncomfortable Wars*, p. 20.

2

United States Government Organization and Capability to Deal with Low-Intensity Conflict

Edwin G. Corr and David C. Miller, Jr.

Introduction

New elements in national security arise from a changing global situation. In addition to the collapse of communism in Eastern Europe, the emergence of independent states there, the disintegration of the Soviet Union, the move toward an integrated, economically invigorated Western Europe, and the growing economic and political might of Japan and East Asia, there has been a remarkable movement in Latin America, Eastern Europe, and Africa toward the development of accountable governments—typically multiparty democracies. It is also clear that the world, at least for the moment, is moving toward market economies. Many Third World leaders, disillusioned with statist command economies, see no alternative to capitalism, though they remain skeptical of its ability to resolve the tremendous economic and social inequities of the developing world.

The United States and its allies have prevailed in a struggle that began with the Soviet Union in the late 1940s, if not in 1917. We contained and defeated communism and knocked out nazism along the way. Our values, approach to governance, and economic system have increasingly been accepted around the world. Our system has shortcomings, but it works fairly well. Our major opponents' did not.

One might therefore think that our national security—notwithstanding the Iraqi War—should be a fading concern. However, reflection on the very large disparity in global allocation of income, the continued rapid growth of population in most developing countries with attendant degradation of the environment, the intensified religious and ethnic hostilities, the frustrations of minority groups in many countries, and the general inability of Third World governments to grapple successfully with these problems suggests heightened instability in many regions of the world. This instability poses and will continue to present serious security challenges to the United States.[1] The United States must continue to be concerned about governmental organization and capabilities to deal with security threats, including the challenge of low-intensity conflict (LIC).

While U.S. public attention was focused on the threat of nuclear war with the Soviets over the last half-century there was great turmoil and hostility in the Third World. A 1988 Defense Department report pointed out that more than thirty wars and about twice as many guerrilla conflicts had killed more than sixteen million people in developing countries during the previous four decades. Except for Greece, all the wars the United States has been directly or indirectly involved in since World War II occurred in what is called the Third World.[2] The *Economist* outlined twenty-five "big wars" going on in the Third World in March 1988.[3] By 1991, after the events in Panama and Iraq and conflicts in other areas, the number of dead from such wars was estimated to have reached twenty million.

In the new environment of the formerly communist world and in the developing world the resource base, both human and natural, is frequently limited. The political systems, even if democratic, are fragile; and in many cases the politico-economic structure is regressive. Armed hostilities are only the most immediately threatening of the many crises facing these societies. The challenge is, and has been, how to create justice and peace through restructuring societies to promote economic growth with equity and responsible legitimate governments.[4] As President José Duarte of El Salvador used to say, prolonged peoples' wars must be met with prolonged strategies for peace, constitutional government, and democracy.[5] This idea is consistent with U.S. values, tradition, and history.

The challenge we face is whether we are effectively organized to support a lengthy, limited, and indirect engagement in support of U.S. values and security interests. Will the existing bureaucratic and military structure enable and prepare the United States to respond to the range of actual threats to its national security? Are we preparing to fight the right wars? Are we organized to fight prolonged engagements to support constitutional government, democracy, and economic growth? The cumulative effect of a series of losses by governments favorably disposed to justice, democracy, and the market economy could create disorder and violence that eventually could alter significantly the U.S. security situation and leadership position in international affairs.

The international environment and Americans' way of life will be greatly affected by global economic growth or deterioration of the developing nations, Eastern Europe, and the Commonwealth of Independent States, as well as by that of Western Europe and East Asia. The dispersion of weapons of mass destruction and the acquisition of long-range delivery systems by irresponsible powers present a clear threat to U.S. interests. Refugees seeking freedom from repression and improvement in economic conditions cause problems not only for the United States but also for countries with whom we trade, cooperate, and share values. The cancer of narcotics trafficking is aided and abetted by hostile governments and unstable societies. Even the containment of contagious disease and of its dangers is related to the maintenance and expansion of economically vibrant democracies. LIC is a menace to national stability, democratic government, and expanding economies and therefore is in some cases a threat to our national interests.

In describing U.S. government organization and capability to deal with LIC, this chapter notes briefly U.S. involvements in past conflicts of this type and earlier bureaucratic coordinating efforts. It outlines executive studies and congressional actions that affect capabilities and analyzes attitudinal and policy constraints, as well as the impact of recent midlevel intensity conflicts. The authors describe the current bureaucratic structure in Washington and at the country team level and present recommendations for improving U.S. organization and capabilities.

U.S. Government Experience with Low-Intensity Conflict

Current efforts to comprehend LIC in the post–cold war era, to assess its import to U.S. security interests, and to determine how it should be dealt with in an emerging new world order are only the latest of numerous attempts to do so. U.S. involvement in LIC is marked by successes and controversy.

The most glorious success was when American insurgents combined unconventional and conventional military action in the War for Independence, 1776–1781. The United States Marine Corps raid on Tripoli in 1804, immortalized in the Corps' hymn, was an early victory through special operations or limited war. The political-military struggle against Mexico to incorporate Texas, California, and other

Western states that culminated in war with Mexico in 1845 had earlier contained elements of LIC. The Spanish-American War of 1898 set the stage for numerous U.S. interventions in internal wars and conflicts of Central America, the Caribbean, and the Philippines during the initial third of the twentieth century.

Support for partisan and guerrilla operations in Europe and Asia during World War II established a precedent for U.S. support to insurgents. The United States extended counterinsurgency support worldwide during the cold war and deployed in combat large numbers of troops during the Vietnam War. Though greatly discredited by defeat in Vietnam, involvement in low-intensity conflicts continued integral to U.S. national security policy and actions, as witnessed in the cases of Angola, Afghanistan, and Central America, to name only a few.[6]

The United States' support for these insurgencies and counterinsurgencies was inevitably overshadowed in the media and public consciousness by the more recent direct employment of U.S. forces in Libya, Grenada, Panama, and Iraq—the last two cases little related to the struggle with the Soviets and occurring in the post–cold war era. The success of and popular support for these direct military actions to some degree distorted further U.S. understanding of low-intensity conflicts and make more difficult the challenge of responding to them when U.S. national interests are involved.

Creating the Bureaucratic Structure: Earlier Presidential Efforts to Coordinate U.S. Agencies in Low-Intensity Conflict Efforts

Administrations since World War II have addressed low-intensity conflict situations with varying degrees of interest and success. President Harry Truman gained congressional approval for the 1947 National Security Act, which created the bureaucratic framework through which the national security strategy of containment would be implemented. Within this larger framework, Secretary James Forrestal created in the Defense Department the Office of Special Programs and gave it responsibility for unconventional warfare planning and psychological operations. The Office coordinated with the National Security Council (NSC), the Central Intelligence Agency (CIA), and the State-Army-Navy-Air Force Coordinating Committee. In 1949 the Office of Special Programs became the Office of Foreign Military Affairs. The same year, the Department of State established the interdepartmental foreign information coordinating Office for Political-Military Affairs. In 1952 a deputy assistant to the secretary of defense for international security affairs was created.

President Dwight Eisenhower established the Operations Coordinating Board to integrate implementation of national security policies, including covert operations and LIC. The Office of Special Operations of the Defense Department had responsibility for psychological warfare, unconventional warfare, and intelligence.[7]

The Kennedy administration merits special attention when examining previous government efforts to organize itself to cope with LIC. President John Kennedy came into office acknowledging the importance of unconventional forms of conflict and committed to reorienting the strategic focus. He was responding in large part to a statement issued by world communist leaders in a meeting of November 1960 and to Premier Nikita Khrushchev's address of 6 January 1961, which clearly expressed communist and Soviet support for "wars of national liberation."[8] President Kennedy involved himself personally in outlining a strategy for dealing with insurgency and subversion. His policies and the bureaucratic machinery established were then the United States' most comprehensive organizational effort to deal with LIC.

Kennedy began by stipulating in National Security Action Memorandum No. 2 (NSAM 2) that the armed forces place more emphasis on counterguerrilla units. He prodded the Departments of State and Defense to build up their LIC capabilities. Secretary of State Dean Rusk appointed a director for internal defense. Secretary of Defense Robert S. McNamara elevated and strengthened the Office of the Assistant to the Secretary for Special Operations and Deputy Secretary of Defense.

Kennedy was reportedly frustrated by the Department of State's reluctance to assert leadership in LIC. Seymour Deitchman, a senior Defense Department official during the sixties, wrote that the Department of State:

> . . . appeared to consider problems of internal conflict a diversion from their main interest of foreign policy and diplomacy, and something that would, if played down long enough, eventually be resolved in the normal course of international relations.[9]

Chester Cooper, a CIA official on the NSC and later a member of Ambassador Averell Harriman's negotiating staff, described the State Department as ". . . resigned to playing a reactive, even peripheral, role during the early 60's. The war in Vietnam, it was felt, was the Pentagon's business."[10] Perhaps if the State Department had played a more active and aggressive role in the management of the conflict the U.S. effort could have been more balanced and the results more favorable.

President Kennedy asserted leadership from the White House. He promulgated NSAM 124 in January 1962 to ensure a government-wide counterinsurgency effort. NSAM 124 declared subversive insurgency to be "equal in importance to conventional warfare." The memorandum established the Special Group (Counter-Insurgency) to integrate counterinsurgency into national security strategy. The Special Group consisted of the military representative of the president (chair), the attorney general (the president's brother, Robert), the deputy under secretary of state for political affairs, the deputy secretary of defense, the chairman of the Joint Chiefs of Staff, the director of Central Intelligence, and the special assistant to the president for national security affairs. Other department and agency representatives were invited as the subject under discussion required.[11] It is of interest that the State Department, nominally the lead player in foreign affairs, chose to be represented at a bureaucratic level lower than all the other participants.

The functions of the Special Group (Counter-Insurgency) were:

a. To ensure proper recognition throughout the U.S. government that subversive insurgency ("wars of national liberation") is a major form of politico-military conflict equal in importance to conventional warfare.
b. To ensure that such recognition is reflected in the organization, training, equipment, and doctrine of the U.S. Armed Forces and other U.S. agencies abroad and in the political, economic, intelligence, military aid, and informational programs conducted abroad by State, Defense, AID, USIA and CIA. Particular attention will be paid to the special training of personnel prior to assignment to MAAG's [Military Assistance Advisory Groups] and to embassy staffs in countries where counterinsurgency problems exist or may exist.
c. To keep under review the adequacy of U.S. resources to deal with actual or potential situations of insurgency or indirect aggression, making timely recommendation of measures to apply, increase or adjust these resources to meet anticipated requirements.
d. To ensure the development of adequate interdepartmental programs aimed at preventing or defeating subversive insurgency and indirect aggression in countries and regions specifically assigned to the Special Group (C.I.) by the President, and to resolve any interdepartmental problems which might impede their implementation.[12]

President Kennedy's intent was to establish a bureaucratic mechanism that could establish "broad lines of counterinsurgency policy . . . ensuring a coordinated and unified approach to regional or country programs, and verifying progress in implementation thereof."[13] The Special Group was sufficiently senior to make decisions on policy, but not so senior that members' responsibilities and demands prevented them from meeting.[14]

In August 1962, Kennedy issued NSAM 182, the Overseas Internal Defense Policy (OIDP) Memorandum. It asserted that the government would support friendly Third World governments threatened by guerrilla movements. NSAM 182 covered threat, objectives, and strategy and addressed strategy implementation. Methods of support for Third World nations in low-intensity conflicts included intelligence, land reform, civic action, community development, education, leader groups, and police. The role of multilateral organizations was touched on, and specific roles were defined for the Special Group (CI), the State Department, the Department of Defense (DOD), the CIA, the Agency for International Development (AID), and the United States Information Agency (USIA). A model country internal defense plan was included as an annex.[15]

The Johnson administration replaced the Special Group with the Senior Interdepartmental Group (SIG), composed of key departmental representatives at the deputy secretary level and other key agency heads and officials. Underneath the SIG were five Interdepartmental Regional Groups, chaired by assistant secretaries of state for those regions.[16]

Despite the efforts of Presidents Kennedy and Johnson to involve all relevant government entities and these presidents' repeated insistence on the importance of the "other war" to achieve political objectives of security for the people, good government, and the people's well-being, the government normally gave higher priority to immediate military and geopolitical objectives. The result was that, although articulated, the political, social, and economic goals were consistently overshadowed. The considerable progress made in Vietnam in certain developmental areas at the local level was undone by the absence of a functional and legitimate South Vietnamese government.[17] The 1969 Nixon Guam Doctrine, to be discussed below, recognized this fatal weakness, but by that juncture it was probably too late. Even if not, the U.S. people and Congress were not willing to meet the commitments made by the Nixon administration to the South Vietnamese government to ensure a successful Vietnamization program.

By the end of the Johnson administration the momentum for LIC had stopped. Military budgets for the activity were cut back; and economic and security assistance funds for Asia, Latin America, and Africa were reduced. Diplomatic missions and the numbers and kinds of U.S.

personnel assigned to embassies in Third World countries were curtailed.

Under the Nixon, Ford, and Carter administrations LIC received scant attention. Their bureaucratic structures related to LIC are not here described. In general, LIC issues were addressed on an ad-hoc basis.

The Reagan administration again elevated the importance of LIC, particularly as it related to insurgencies in Angola, Afghanistan, Nicaragua, and El Salvador. The bureaucratic arrangements and machinery established by President Ronald Reagan and by the Congress during his term remain, with slight alteration, the bureaucratic structure through which the Bush presidency deals with LIC. It will be described and analyzed in some detail later in the chapter.

Attitudinal Constraints on U.S. Government Capabilities to Deal with Low-Intensity Conflict

The bureaucratic machinery created during the Reagan administration was a marked improvement but still deficient in forcing adequate political and bureaucratic priority for countries where the United States was engaged in LIC. The weakness was particularly evident among the civilian agencies. Three former ambassadors to El Salvador identified coordination of policy and operations as among the most challenging problems during their tenures in that country.[18]

For the Department of Defense, doctrinally, LIC includes insurgency and counterinsurgency, combating terrorism (including narcoterrorism), peacekeeping, and contingency operations.[19] For the government as a whole, LIC goes far beyond this. It includes state building and the creation of legitimate political systems as set forth in the Manwaring paradigm. It implies functioning democracy, economic growth with an equitable distribution of wealth, and justice.

As in the Kennedy administration, the Reagan presidency tried to force the bureaucracy to cope effectively with LIC. The Congress joined the president and legislatively mandated the Pentagon—kicking, screaming, and with many of its generals and civilian executives leaving their fingernails in the door frame as they were dragged through it—to create a special operations command (one of only eleven commands headed by a four-star general) and an assistant secretary for special operations and LIC. Similar reorganization and priority for LIC were not imposed on civilian agencies. Unfortunately, with the end of the cold war in 1989 and the United States' greater focus on and apparent successes through direct military intervention in Grenada,

Panama, and Iraq, the momentum to implement organizational changes to manage LIC situations more effectively appeared to decline.

Why has the United States been so reluctant to deal with the challenge of LIC? The principal U.S. defense priority during the last forty years was rightly the prevention of nuclear war, with a primary focus on Europe, while, ironically, nearly all armed conflicts occurred in the Third World. Although it need not have been so, our preoccupation with preventing low-probability, high-intensity nuclear conflict detracted from our giving sufficient attention to and learning to deal efficaciously with existing low-intensity conflicts. We have been slow to adapt our thinking, organization, and resource allocations to high-probability LIC where our military's role is usually relatively small and indirect, and where extraordinary support is required for civilian authorities in their developmental efforts. Meeting this challenge becomes more important as we move toward a new world order of greater instability and lower probability of massive nuclear exchange.

Part of the difficulty in dealing with LIC has been caused by the "World War II syndrome," not just the "Vietnam syndrome." It was World War II that created for Americans an almost total unity and commitment with regard to war, and this experience set thought patterns that still strongly affect the way we think wars should be waged. During the great conflict from 1941 to 1945, the United States felt itself to be righteously, unconditionally, and totally in a crusade to crush fascist states and liquidate evil enemy leaders, and thereby permit the world to continue a natural evolution and progress toward prosperity and democracy. The perceptions of the simple culpability of leaders such as Hitler, Mussolini, and Tojo and the justice of their defeat were not confused by the stark reality of the Third World, where conflicts occur today and where the roots of hostilities are deeply embedded in historical, social, political, and economic inequalities. In those circumstances, the military resolution of conflict does not and cannot bring lasting peace, progress, justice, and democracy. Our struggle and defeat in Vietnam, over which there were tremendous national division and ambiguity, strengthened the World War II mind set.

This misperception of low-intensity conflicts was reflected by congressmen and groups of citizens visiting El Salvador who inevitably asked: "When will the war end?" Those who made this inquiry were usually envisioning the termination of the conflict along the lines of V-E Day in Europe or the signing of peace with the Japanese on the USS *Missouri*, whereupon hostilities came clearly and finally to a halt. In the prevailing form of armed conflict today, LIC, nothing is so neat and definitive. Sometimes there are peace agreements and clear-cut victories for the governments or insurgents, but more often conflicts smolder for decades. Armed conflict may be halted temporarily, but as long as the underlying social, economic, and political causes of the hostilities do not seem to be improving, the resumption of terrorism and insurgency is always a threat. With good fortune and solid programs insurgencies dissipate and end as the guerrilla cause and guerrillas themselves seemingly tire and finally die of old age. More realistically, however, they are reduced over time to a tolerable, manageable level as a result of government legitimization and responsible and effective government counterinsurgency measures.[20]

Professor Stephen Sloan, the coeditor of this book, argues that U.S. governments have failed to convey to the public that LIC in the Third World is generally long term. The British, for example, with a world-class armed force after World War II, and in a period when human rights were not the political concern they are today, required fifteen years to defeat Malaysian insurgents. Sloan suggests that quick strike and withdrawal operations, such as the Libyan raid, Grenada, and Panama have acted as a barrier to popular and governmental understanding that most low-intensity conflicts are not quickly resolvable. He further suggests that rivalry between the executive branch and the Congress over foreign policy prevents long-term commitments to engage in protracted conflict.[21]

The evolution of international law on wars, the development of our national defense and foreign policy organizations, our laws, and our national psyche are built largely on a clear distinction between war and peace.[22] Secretary of State George Shultz in 1988 spoke of new political complexities in "the ecology of international change" and noted that "In this decade, I believe Americans have come to recognize that we are not likely to face either an era of total war or of total peace."[23] Still, this increased understanding will have little consequence unless it is accompanied by changes in our priorities, the will to persist, a modified legal framework, and organizational structure to implement national policy.

Traditionally, just as we have defined war and peace as mutually exclusive states, civil and military roles and organizations within the government have been clearly separated. Our laws and budgeting process prohibit mixing of civil and military functions and thereby impede cooperation, coordination, and integration of U.S. military and civilian programs. Such is particularly the case in the implementation of foreign economic and development assistance in combination with security and military assistance. Another problem with protracted conflict is that without appropriate organization, Washington (as well as the U.S. public) soon tires, and the priority of a specific LIC situation drops. It degenerates to "in-box" issues dealt with in a routine, inflexible manner on personnel assignments, resource allocations, and response time to changing events and crises.[24]

Executive Studies and Congressional Actions
Affecting Low-Intensity Conflict Capabilities

There have been a number of important efforts to understand and to better government capabilities to deal with LIC.[25] Some of the significant studies and commission reports are as follows:

• Rockefeller Report	1958
• Draper Commission	1959
• Special Operations Research Office	1962
• Howze Board	1962
• Defense Science Board Report	1964
• Restricted Engagement Options	1973
• Holloway Commission	1980
• Joint Low-Intensity Conflict Project	1986
• Packard Commission	1986
• Long-Term Integrated Strategy	1988

The Rockefeller Report identified "concealed wars" as one of the most serious challenges facing the nation:

These conflicts raise issues with which in terms of our preconceptions and the structure of our forces we are least prepared to deal. . . .Our security . . . will hinge importantly on our willingness to support friendly governments in situations which fit neither the soldier's classic concept of war nor the diplomat's traditional concept of aggression.[26]

The 1958 presidential commission under William H. Draper evaluated U.S. foreign policy and aid in 1958 and 1959. The report suggested more aid for the internal defense of Third World countries, including funding for military education, engineering, and community services, to help countries cope with LIC threats.[27] The Special Operations Research Office was established at American University in 1962 and along with the Department of Defense's Special Warfare Directorate was asked to "facilitate and coordinate" LIC programs. Within the military, counterinsurgency courses were institutionalized at the Special Warfare School at Fort Bragg, North Carolina. The

Howze Board called for increased indoctrination of U.S. military in counterinsurgency and for doubling the number of special forces.[28]

The 1973 Department of Defense "Restricted Engagement Options" proposed the creation of "an integrated, multipurpose, low cost, low visibility agency" to deal with low-intensity conflicts. The agency would have been at the same level as the Departments of State and Defense and the CIA.[29]

President Reagan established the Packard Commission (the President's Blue Ribbon Commission on Defense Management) in 1985, and in June 1986 it suggested sweeping changes in defense policy and organization. President Reagan issued National Security Decision Directive No. 219 in April 1986 and subsequent executive orders to implement the commission's recommendations. Many of these affected LIC capabilities. Especially important were broader authority for the unified commands and flexibility for them to deal with situations in their regions. This change meant a greater focus on LIC for those commands in the Third World.[30]

The U.S. Army's Low-Intensity Conflict Project's two-volume report of August 1986 painted a bleak picture of U.S. LIC capabilities, stating that "As a nation we do not understand low-intensity conflict. We respond without unity of effort; we execute our activities poorly; and we lack the ability to sustain operations." The Joint Special Operations Agency (JSOA) was established to ensure the involvement of the Joint Chiefs of Staff in special operations, and a number of initiatives were taken by the Department of Defense to strengthen capabilities in this area.[31]

Congress decided that national defense and especially Third World contingencies were too important to leave in the hands of the president and the generals. The War Powers Resolution was adopted by the Congress in 1973. It reflected a struggle between the executive and legislative branches over the control of foreign policy and war-making and was seen by Congress as a safeguard against the executive's engaging the country in other Vietnam-like quagmires. The resolution requires the president to:

1. "In every possible instance" consult with Congress before committing U.S. troops in "hostilities or into situations where imminent involvement in hostilities" is likely;
2. Inform Congress within 48 hours after the introduction of troops if there has been no declaration of war;
3. Remove U.S. troops within 60 days (or 90 days in special circumstances) if Congress does not either declare war or adopt a joint resolution approving the action.[32]

The Congress also claimed power to end U.S. military involvement before sixty days by passing a concurrent resolution, which does not require the president's signature and therefore cannot be vetoed. This claim was found unconstitutional by the Supreme Court in *U.S. vs Chadha* in 1983, but the court has not ruled on the rest of the War Powers Resolution.

Every president since the resolution was adopted has questioned the resolution's constitutionality. Presidents have acknowledged the need to consult with congressional leaders before committing U.S. military forces. They also have submitted reports to the Congress but have fulfilled War Powers Resolution requirements only in part, and they always made clear implicitly or explicitly the view that the executive was not bound to render such reports.[33]

The Goldwater-Nichols Department of Defense Reorganization Act of 1986, drawing on the Packard Commission Report, endeavored to make the Defense Department more effective, including in the area of LIC. The act mandated additional guidelines aimed at enhancing LIC capabilities. The creation of the United States Special Operations Command (USSOC) was particularly significant.[34] As a follow-on to the Goldwater-Nichols Act, the Defense Authorization Act of 1987 created an assistant secretary of defense for special operations and low-intensity conflict.[35] The act also directed the president to establish a Low-Intensity Conflict Board within the National Security Council and recommended that a deputy assistant to the president for low-intensity conflict be designated.[36]

Many of the executive branch and congressional initiatives met resistance within the armed forces, the Defense Department, and the national security establishment as a whole. The warnings and advice of presidential commissions and important strategic thinkers over the last forty years have not been sufficiently heeded.

Policy Restraints on Coping with Low-Intensity Conflict

Two national defense policies or doctrines have had and continue to have an important influence on the U.S. approach and capabilities to cope with LIC. The Nixon (or Guam) Doctrine was enunciated in 1969 by President Richard Nixon as an outgrowth of events in Vietnam. Public and congressional opinion was moving strongly against the country's involvement in Vietnam and against U.S. intervention in other countries generally. The Nixon Doctrine emphasized that henceforth the United States would assist friendly nations but would require threatened nations to provide the manpower and be ultimately responsible for their own defense. The United States, when its national interests were at stake, would play a supporting role by providing political, economic, and military support.

The Nixon Doctrine was implemented in the "Vietnamization Program." Lack of pledged U.S. support and lack of legitimacy and will on the part of the South Vietnamese government permitted the North Vietnamese to triumph, however. The Nixon Doctrine nevertheless has become a cornerstone of U.S. policy on LIC.

The Nixon Doctrine implies that the United States will avoid direct combat involvement of its own troops in an insurgency, that there must exist indigenous civilian and military elements with real or potential strength that the U.S. government can support, that there must be enough time to train and equip indigenous forces for their self-defense, and that there must be sustained U.S. political and economic support to allow political, economic, social, and justice reforms to occur. This doctrine was again put to the test in El Salvador.[37]

The Weinberger Doctrine was enunciated by former Secretary of Defense Caspar Weinberger in a 1984 speech to the National Press Club. He outlined six major criteria to be met before the United States would commit military forces abroad:

- Vital interests of the United States or its allies must be at stake
- We must be willing to commit enough forces to achieve our objectives
- We must have clearly defined political and military objectives
- We must subject our involvement to continuous reassessment
- Prior to deployment of troops, there must be reasonable assurances of public support
- The use of combat power should be a last resort[38]

The main purpose of these criteria, Weinberger said, was to keep the United States from being gradually pulled into a combat role.

Whereas the Nixon Doctrine serves to prevent overinvolvement of U.S. military forces and to place the major responsibility for countering insurgency on the supported government, the Weinberger Doctrine has been regarded by many as inhibiting all involvement in low-intensity conflicts. This impediment resides chiefly in interpretation of the requirement for U.S. public support, which many see as prohibiting involvement in Third World conflicts.

The Impact of Mid-Intensity
Conflict on Low-Intensity Conflict

On top of these two policies or doctrines must be put the effect of U.S. combat experiences in Libya, Grenada, Panama, and Iraq. The euphoria that much of the U.S. government, military, and public felt over the apparent successes of these actions had an impact on thinking, or lack of thinking, about LIC. The impression left to the casual observer was that these types of conflicts—what some would refer to as mid-intensity conflicts (with some debate as to whether Iraq was not closer on the continuum to high-level intensity conventional warfare)—would be the future wars of the emerging new world order. The greater attention that had been given to LIC during the cold war and Reagan years faded as proxy wars in the Third World with the former Soviet Union were less likely. Americans elatedly projected fighting the kinds of wars that the armed forces and the public prefer—a superiority of U.S. firepower and technology, short duration, and few casualties.

Presentations to the Congress by Department of Defense spokesmen during 1991 acknowledged impending cuts in the armed forces but stressed military might as the principal solution to future contingencies. General Colin L. Powell, chairman of the Joint Chiefs of Staff, was quoted as saying "We have overwhelming power, and we have demonstrated a willingness to use it."[39] Army Chief of Staff General Carl E. Vuono, describing restructuring plans for the 1990s, wrote "the preponderance of the Army will be based within the continental United States and will be focused on the projection of land combat power quickly and massively anywhere in the world."[40] An Air Force presentation stated that in "this new world we are rapidly moving into plays to Air Force strengths—rapid, deployable, long-range, flexible, and lethal capabilities, which can deter, provide a tailored response or punch hard when required."[41] Congressman Les Aspin, chairman of the House Armed Services Committee, said ". . . whenever you use military force it has to be quick and low in casualties."[42]

Respected analyst Colonel Harry G. Summers, Jr., argued in the *New York Times Magazine* after the Iraq War against dismantling the victorious U.S. military machine, called for building up strategic air and sealift capacity, and lauded high technology. He suggested that in the new world order the United States may be forced into the role of world policeman. The Marine Corps, he said, should be given the rapid deployment function; and the Army should assume its rightful role in the "armor dominated modern battlefield" as the decisive U.S.

military force, "the only one capable of destroying an enemy and its will to exist."[43]

Nonetheless, President George Bush in his 2 August 1990 speech at Aspen, Colorado, used the term "peacetime engagement," saying that the United States would remain "every bit as constant and committed to the defense of our interests and ideals in today's world as in the time of conflict and Cold War."[44] Department of Defense official documents, in contrast to some of the selected citations above that suggest less attention to LIC, interpret "peacetime engagement" to include "strategy missions and activities in all environments short of large-scale conventional and nuclear war; that is, ranging from peacetime up through major contingency operations but not including general war."[45]

The March 1991 Joint Chiefs' "Military Net Assessment" says military planning has moved to regional contingencies, such as renewal of Iraqi hostilities or a North Korean attack on South Korea. The report also indicated more attention to lesser regional contingencies and to counterinsurgency as well as to terrorism and counternarcotics operations.[46]

Secretary of Defense Richard Cheney in testimony to the Senate on 21 February 1991 noted that the ". . . cooling of superpower rivalry decreases the chances that a regional conflict will escalate into global war. . . " but that there also ". . . is a risk that the end of the bipolar world could unleash local, destructive forces that were previously kept in check." He said that ". . . we face the sobering truth that local sources of instability and oppression will continue to foster conflicts small and large virtually across the globe," and that "Separate and apart from the broad regional conflicts . . . there is another set of demanding threats. They are low-intensity conflicts, including insurgencies, terrorism, and drug trafficking."[47]

Speaking before the House two weeks earlier, Secretary Cheney said the following:

> To help deter low-intensity conflicts and promote stability in the Third World, we must have innovative strategies that support representative government, integrate security assistance, and promote economic development. Our approach for doing this is "peacetime engagement"—a coordinated combination of political, economic, and military actions, aimed primarily at counteracting local violence and promoting nation-building.[48]

The Department of Defense officially is aware of and officially gives priority to LIC.

The Current Organization of the
U.S. Government for Low-Intensity Conflict Engagements

After thirty years of efforts to organize the executive branch to manage effectively LIC engagements, insufficient progress has been made. Aside from the congressionally mandated changes of the Goldwater-Nichols Act and subsequent defense authorization acts, President Bush is left with the same lack of structure and coherence that President Kennedy found in 1960. The principal government actors today in LIC situations in which the United States is involved are the NSC, the Department of State, DOD and the armed forces, the CIA, AID, USIA, the Department of Justice (DOJ), the Department of the Treasury (DOT), the Department of Commerce (DOC), the Office of Management and Budget (OMB), and embassy country teams.

The problem is that overall responsibility for LIC does not belong to any one agency, there is no continuous center of authority, and it is very difficult to sustain an integrated effort.[49] Washington's lack of responsiveness to some urgent requests from one of the authors of this chapter while he served as ambassador to El Salvador is testimony to Washington's organizational and operational difficulties.[50] Officials who have been involved in managing LIC situations feel that interagency coordination is inadequate.

A certain amount of bureaucratic rivalry is part of the U.S. system and is constructive. Excessive competition by some agencies, combined with neglect and stone-walling to defend turf by others, has an adverse impact, however. Loyalties to office, bureau, service, agency, and department sometimes dominate over comprehensive government objectives. Differences in bureaucratic cultures and institutional orientation often lead people to avoid rather than seek coordination with other agencies. Such differences may result from clashes between those having technical or functional responsibilities and those charged with regional or country-specific responsibilities.

There is also the problem of differences in approach between the soldier and the diplomat. By training and experience the soldier seeks certainty and emphasizes victory through force. The diplomat is accustomed to ambiguity and emphasizes solving conflicts through persuasion. The soldier's principal expertise is in operations, and the diplomat's is in persuasion.

The dynamics of government and bureaucratic behavior are deeply ingrained in our culture and political system. It seems highly unlikely and probably undesirable that competitive tensions should be eliminated from U.S. bureaucracy. Nonetheless, to the degree that agency rivalries and lack of coordination are dysfunctional, preventing the United States from coping effectively with LIC, corrective actions should be taken.[51]

During 1990–91 the NSC conducted a review of government procedures and structure to meet the threats of LIC, both prevention and resolution. Ambassador David Miller, one of the authors of this chapter and the then special assistant to the president for national security affairs, and senior director for Africa and international programs, led the review. The purpose was to examine how the government formulates, coordinates, provides resources for, and implements national strategy and policy toward countries threatened by or engaged in LIC. In addition to extensive reviews with Washington agencies and meetings with outside experts, an interagency team visited key embassies involved in implementing U.S. policies in LIC situations.

A major issue of the review was interagency unity of effort, one of the elements in the Manwaring paradigm. The review team concluded that the existing array of actors and of interagency coordinating arrangements is inadequate to respond to unusual and urgent requirements for economic, developmental, informational, and military assistance either in anticipation of a growing conflict or over a sustained period. The need for coordination from the NSC level down through country teams was stressed. The underlying problem was defined as twofold. First, there existed no interagency forum to address generic issues irrespective of geographic location (e.g., training of U.S. personnel to work together in a low-intensity conflict situation and on nation-building procedures). Second, there existed no interagency forum below the level of the Deputies Committee of the National Security Council that could identify and ensure provision of functional expertise and a coordinated flow of resources to country teams for country or region-specific programs, especially in times of crisis. Given the workload of the Deputies Committee it is unrealistic to expect it to provide the needed support on a sustained basis.

Unity of effort among departments and agencies is also a function of intradepartmental structure. As long as geographic boundaries and functional responsibilities among departments and agencies are roughly equal, coordination is facilitated. When not, as is frequently the case, it is impeded. Unfortunately, agency structures are often incompatible.

Within the Department of State the five regional bureaus are effectively in charge of counterinsurgencies in their regions. Narcotics control is under the assistant secretary for international narcotics matters, who reports to the under secretary for political affairs. Counterterrorism is the responsibility of the coordinator for counterterrorism, who reports to the deputy secretary. Security assistance is handled by the assistant secretary for political-military affairs, who reports to the under secretary for international security affairs. Economic policy is handled by the assistant secretary of economic and business affairs, who reports to the under secretary for economic and agricultural affairs. Economic assistance is administered by AID, which is a separate bureaucratic entity but reports to the president through the secretary of state.

In contrast, the Defense Department has an assistant secretary for special operations and low-intensity conflict who is responsible for counterinsurgency and counterterrorism, but not for international narcotics control or security assistance. Regional policy is managed by the assistant secretary for international security affairs. Fortunately, both report to the under secretary of defense for policy.

The differences in organizational structures between Defense and State are paralleled by similar organizational incongruencies with the CIA, USIA, and AID. The offices responsible in the executive branch for aspects of LIC such as insurgency, terrorism, and narcotics control should be closely aligned. Moreover, the offices responsible for these matters also should be structured for easy access to offices of departments and agencies that deal with judicial reform, law enforcement, economic and trade policy, as well as economic development.

Comments and Conclusions

Given the thirty-year track record, it seems unlikely that any president alone would be willing to pay the political and bureaucratic price to overcome the powerful bureaucratic inertia and interests that would be required to reorganize comprehensively agencies that help formulate and implement U.S. policies and programs in low-intensity conflict situations. Further comment and cursory evaluations will be offered on specific agencies and their current disposition toward and effectiveness in responding to LIC, followed by recommendations for improvement.

The National Security Council. The NSC review conducted in 1990–91 is simply the latest example of the inability of an interagency effort to overcome bureaucratic inertia. Further, and probably correctly, the NSC is most definitely not in an "operational" mode following the Iran-contra scandal. The most important accomplishment of the NSC during the Bush administration has been the inclusion of nontraditional players, including law enforcement (DOJ), financial (DOT and OMB), and private sector (DOC). Another very concrete, positive achievement was the placement of counter-terrorism, counternarcotics, and low-intensity conflict in a single NSC directorate, International Programs.

Although the NSC should get credit for broadening the interagency group and for placing many of the LIC components into a single directorate, it gets relatively low marks on forcing fundamental rethinking or reorganization. The Deputies Committee of the NSC, in compliance with the Cohen-Nunn Amendment to the 1987 National Defense Act, finally and reluctantly assumed the responsibilities of the Board for Low-Intensity Conflict. The NSC also approved the Low-Intensity Conflict Board Sub-Group, chaired by the senior director for international programs and composed of functional experts, to serve as the Policy Coordinating Committee (PCC) for the Board. This arrangement, with good leadership, can be made to function but could certainly be improved.

The Department of State. If LIC is that ambiguous area between conventional war and peaceful relationships among nations, in one sense the Department of State has been managing LIC fairly successfully in the normal conduct of diplomacy since World War II. Nonetheless, with respect to specific countries where high levels of violence and insurgency prevail, the Department of State, where for many the lead for managing LIC properly belongs, is poorly organized, understaffed, and lacking in resources.

Regional assistant secretaries maintain their status as primus inter pares, and the assumption remains that the ambassador should turn to the regional assistant secretary for coordination of support from Washington. The assistant secretary theoretically accomplishes this coordination through a regional Policy Coordinating Committee (PCC) constituted by his regional bureau and other pertinent departments and agencies. For a multiplicity of reasons, the PCCs, although effective bodies to develop policies, are not effective bodies for the management of resources to support the policy. In addition, the regional PCC typically will be managing policy toward many countries and be supporting country teams in a number of crises simultaneously.

Competent and experienced ambassadors seldom have problems in achieving good country team coordination and effort "in-country" toward commonly agreed U.S. objectives. The ambassador's authority is fairly well established and recognized by his staff regardless of their parent agency, and the close proximity and sometimes dangerous circumstances within which U.S. officials work in low-intensity conflicts help to mold them into a single team. The ambassador's challenge is to obtain promptly and consistently from Washington via the Department of State the kinds of staffing and correct mix of resources needed to do the job.

Both authors feel strongly that the mechanism for development of LIC policy is good but is only the preplanning stage of a sixty-minute game, the success of which depends on team work and execution. This team work means effective management and coordination of personnel and resources from an array of often competing agencies that frequently have predetermined agendas. In effect, between the Deputies Committee and the country team—a bureaucratically long distance— the United States government has no effective mechanism to manage and support LIC efforts.

Bureaucratically, as described earlier, internal State Department lines of authority and organization for LIC are lacking. There is no consistent overall direction, coordination, or coherence. Thus, for example, on a complicated LIC engagement such as counternarcotics, which has components of regional policy, military assistance, and counterterrorism, the Department of State rarely presents a unified position unless matters for decision reach the deputy secretary level.

The Department of State is chronically short of personnel for the responsibilities assigned, is slow to make personnel assignments, does not order people to post without great difficulty, and is frequently limited in the awards that can be offered to personnel assigned to high-threat countries. The contrast between State and Defense Department abilities to assign people rapidly was stunningly illustrated in the Andean region counternarcotics effort, where the uniformed services produced on a moment's notice a wide range of personnel who were apparently enthusiastic about their assignments. Although this contrast is inherent in the difference between military and civilian organizations, the civilian agencies must find the personnel resources and procedures to become more responsive. Moreover, depending on the U.S. armed forces for the bulk of the advisory manpower and expertise to help local democratic leaders move toward a civilian-dominated government ironically undermines the very concept of military submission to civilian authority.

The Department of Defense. The Defense Department and armed forces reluctantly have accepted important organizational changes, such as Congress's creation of the United States Special Operations Command and the Office of the Assistant Secretary of Defense for Special Operations and Low-Intensity Conflict. The strength of the Department of Defense and the armed forces in the management, coordination, and execution of U.S. resources in a LIC situation resides in the regional command structures and their greater amount of personnel and resources. The regional commanders, in some ways analogous to the assistant secretaries of state, do in fact have command and control over all military resources dedicated to the effort. The assistant secretaries of state do not have adequate control over all civilian resources. If the regional commander gives LIC a high priority, he is far better equipped with the needed resources and personnel than any other U.S. government official.

The Defense Department and the armed forces as a whole, nevertheless, appear less than enthusiastic about a type of warfare that requires relatively limited resources and manpower (compared with mid- and high-intensity conflict), that seldom permits U.S. military forces a direct combat role, and in which the lead department is normally State rather than Defense. The enthusiasm for LIC is further tempered by the ambiguous environment of such hostilities and the lack of clearly achievable objectives and neatly won victories.

Discussions with armed forces personnel and the emphasis of some of their public comments cast doubts on their seriousness and commitment to LIC and whether the Defense Department and armed forces have escaped from their half-century of almost exclusive focus on nuclear deterrence and high-intensity conventional warfare. One is reminded of the Kennedy-Johnson years when there was much talk about the preeminence of political, economic, and social goals over military and geostrategic ones, but in the end the latter goals appropriate for U.S.-Soviet confrontation monopolized attention and resources.

The Central Intelligence Agency. In many ways, the CIA under Presidents Reagan and Bush should get some kudos for stepping up to the plate on two major "operating" LIC accounts—counterterrorism and counternarcotics. For these areas the CIA created "fusion centers" to bring together the operational and analytical sides of the institution. In addition, on counternarcotics, the director has actively exercised his role as the leader of the intelligence community, although there remain problems of sharing and integrating intelligence from the traditional intelligence organizations and from police organizations, such as the Drug Enforcement Agency (DEA) and the Federal Bureau of Investigation (FBI).

The Agency for International Development. Essential to the success of Third World governments against guerrillas and to earning legitimacy and popular loyalty is extending the host governments' presence, programs, and services into conflict areas. This function greatly transcends the U.S. military's "civil-military operations" and demands a better U.S. government civilian effort in support of Third World governments' development programs, including projects for conflict areas. It entails the creation of a skilled corps of civilian officials who can provide a continuous, though limited, presence in support of a government under attack, but who do not themselves make decisions and execute programs. Through training, advice, and provision of resources they would ensure that host country development projects in contested areas are effectively and honestly implemented.

AID employees as a whole do not enter the agency with the idea of working in perilous LIC situations, and AID procedures are not tailored for this environment. The ambiguous nature of neither war nor peace calls for a blending of military and civilian development programs. Although this mix might be accomplished through AID, it is worthwhile considering the creation of a small development agency dedicated to dangerous LIC situations, as will be proposed in the recommendations.

Many of the trends within AID over the last two decades have been counterproductive to effective LIC management. The current Foreign Assistance Act was enacted thirty years ago, in 1961. When originally passed it gave the president the necessary authority and flexibility to address the critical problems of that period. Over time, the budget has shrunk. During the early 1950s foreign economic assistance constituted about 11 percent of our federal budget. Today it is about one percent. Moreover, legislation has expanded AID's purposes to encompass some thirty-three distinct and often conflicting objectives. Congressional reporting requirements and restrictions coupled with AID's internal rules and regulations have become so onerous that providing cost-effective assistance to foreign countries is difficult, especially those in a low-intensity conflict environment.[52] In essence, AID programs in Tanzania and Zimbabwe were managed under the same policies and rules as in El Salvador.

The House Foreign Affairs Committee produced in 1988 a major reform package, known as the Hamilton-Gilman bill. Based on this bill, President Bush sent to Congress his proposed International Cooperation Act of 1991 to meet the needs for more flexible and rapidly available economic, military, and humanitarian assistance. Action by Congress on the proposed legislation would greatly enhance the government's capacity to cope with LIC situations.

The Department of Justice. All the countries visited by the NSC LIC study team indicated that our support to the judicial systems of the countries under attack was poor to nonexistent. Although insurgency frequently attacks police and courts to undermine the legitimacy of the existing government, we are severely constrained, both financially and by congressionally mandated restrictions, in the area of justice.

Of great importance is the urgent need to remove restrictions on U.S.

assistance to police, which is vital for improving Third World governments' police and judicial performance. Effective law enforcement is a critical element in legitimizing governments, which includes a heavy component of human rights training. It is probably time to recognize that only the Department of Justice and its agencies can provide effective support in this area over time, although police training might be conducted by another U.S. civilian agency, for example, by the Department of State or AID (as it was prior to 1974). Both the Drug Enforcement Administration and the FBI (and Customs under Treasury) should be challenged to develop more innovative and creative programs to provide law enforcement assistance to developing country governments.

Furthermore, to engage effectively the U.S. legal establishment to support governments under siege, the active involvement of the attorney general will be necessary. The attorney general is in a unique position to provide leadership, whether it is with the Judicial Conference, the Association of American Trial Lawyers, the American Bar Association, or U.S. law schools.

The Department of Commerce. At the Cartagena drug summit in 1989 it was striking that all three Andean presidents, led by Jaime Paz Zamora of Bolivia, agreed that one of the key components to winning the drug war over time was the development of effective investment and trade programs. President Bush responded with a series of measures, which culminated in the Enterprise for the Americas (EAI) program. A component of this is the Andean Trade Preference adopted by congress in December 1991. The Corr Report, prepared by an interagency team headed by one of the authors, further emphasized the critical role of economics and trade in offering alternatives to and removing the root causes of LIC and illicit drug production.[53]

When a low-intensity conflict places an economy under siege, often the first to withdraw are foreign nationals and foreign capital, frequently key players in the development of the modern sector of a developing country's economy. Again, though little thinking has been done on this subject, a single point of leadership in the Department of Commerce to provide encouragement to and support for U.S. industry to maintain or increase its presence in a country under siege could be of critical importance.

The Office of Management and Budget/Department of Treasury. Although OMB and Department of the Treasury must provide responsible fiscal oversight for U.S. government activities, innovative responses to economies under siege can be critical. In particular, concepts such as tax credits for U.S. investors in countries facing a low-intensity conflict (also recommended in the Corr study) should be considered.

Recommendations

It seems likely that any major effort to restructure the management of LIC will have to come from a joint effort by the president and the Congress. There are, however, five actions that could be implemented by the executive branch.

First, the Department of State should consider organizational changes to incorporate into one bureau the Coordinator for Counterterrorism (S/CT), the Bureau of International Narcotics Matters (INM), the Politico-Military Bureau (PM), and the functional offices and programs that deal with judicial reform and assistance to police. Because congressional consent for such changes might be difficult to obtain, a less comprehensive change is suggested so that the Department of State can provide the management and leadership required when the United States is engaged in LIC situations. The deputy secretary of state's office should be given oversight responsibility for this matter. This would prevent the department's conducting "business-as-usual" for those situations requiring prolonged, continuous attention and rapid, flexible programming. A very senior and experienced officer attached to the deputy secretary with a small staff could exercise the kind of department-wide authority and coordination needed to get the Department of State to sing from the same sheet of music and lead the interagency effort with NSC support.

Second, and clearly second, given the desire not to militarize LIC, it may unfortunately be true at this point that only within the Office of the Secretary of Defense are the required management capability and will to manage effectively a LIC program. If the Department of State is unwilling or unable to assume the role, it is worth examining whether the under secretary of defense for policy, to whom the current assistant secretary for special operations/low-intensity conflict reports, should be given the mandate for managing and marshalling the resources necessary to support ambassadors and their country teams involved in these situations.

Third, given that the NSC should not assume an operational role, it is worth examining whether a small institution within the executive office should be created to provide oversight of LIC engagements because only at the White House do all the required players effectively come together. This office could report directly to the national security adviser through the Deputies Committee (acting as the Low-Intensity Conflict Board), while maintaining a distinct identity from the NSC. It would be staffed by a very small number of career professionals (probably fewer than fifteen) who have the requisite field and Washington bureaucratic experience to provide effective support to the ambassador and Department of State.

Fourth, the president might wish to give an even higher priority to persuading Congress to act on his proposed International Cooperation Act of 1991. He could request unique authority for a unit within AID, or the creation of a small agency, dedicated exclusively to managing assistance for hostile zones in a limited number of countries engaged in LIC, the countries being approved through consultation with Congress. Among the changes needed is the legal authority to provide assistance to foreign police forces. Until something is done to enable the government to act more efficiently and effectively in the assistance area in environments that are neither at war nor at peace, the United States will be limited in its capacity to cope with this phenomenon.

Fifth, and finally, the president could, utilizing the Department of State's Foreign Service Institute, implement a multiple agency (including the uniformed services) training program for agencies' personnel who are being assigned to countries facing a LIC. This concept received wide support from many of the missions visited by the NSC review team in 1990–91, when it was pointed out that "on-the-job training" is a high-risk, inefficient way to prepare personnel to understand and cope with LIC.

These five proposals are not a substitute for a major restructuring of our government to deal better with low-intensity conflicts that affect U.S. interests, but we believe they would be an important step toward making the existing bureaucratic machinery operate better. The recommended actions are within the power of the presidency to implement.

Notes

1. Ambassador David C. Miller, Jr., "New Elements of National Security" (speech to the Seventeenth Annual Wirth Washington Seminar, Washington, D.C., 26 April 1991), pp. 1–2.

2. Commission on Integrated Long-Term Strategy, Report by the Regional Conflict Working Group, *Supporting U.S. Strategy for Third World Conflict* (Department of Defense, June 1988), pp. 1–6; and Commission on Integrated Long-Term Strategy, *Discriminate Deterrence* (Washington, D.C.: GPO, January 1988), p. 13. General Paul Gorman, former commander in chief, Southern Command, was the leader and principal author in the Regional Conflict Working Group.

3. "The World's Wars," *Economist*, 24 March 1988, pp. 19–22.

4. Ambassador Edwin G. Corr, "Preface," in *El Salvador at War: An Oral*

History, ed. Max G. Manwaring and Court Prisk (Washington, D.C.: National Defense University Press, 1988), p. xxxiv.

5. Ambassador Edwin G. Corr, "The Salvadoran Report Card" in *El Salvador at War*, p. 452.

6. Todd R. Greentree, "The United States and the Politics of Conflict in the Developing World," Center Paper no. 4, Center for the Study of Foreign Affairs, Foreign Service Institute, U.S. Department of State, October 1990, p. 24.

7. *Strategy and Policy Background: Umbrella Concept for Low-Intensity Conflict*, vol. 1 (prepared by Booz-Allen & Hamilton, Inc. for Headquarters, U.S. Special Operations Command, May 1989; finalized by Headquarters, U.S. Special Operations Command, August 1989), p. A–1.

8. Ibid., pp. 2–19.

9. Seymour J. Deitchman, *The Best Laid Schemes: A Tale of Social Research and Bureaucracy*, 1976, pp. 86–87, as cited in *Umbrella Concept for Low-Intensity Conflict*, p. 2–3.

10. Chester L. Cooper, *The Lost Crusade: America in Vietnam*, 1970, p. 255, as cited in *Umbrella Concept for Low-Intensity Conflict*, p. 2–4.

11. *National Security Action Memorandum No. 124 (NSAM 124)*, the White House, 18 January 1962, declassified on 11 August 1978, p. 1.

12. Ibid., p. 2.

13. Ibid.

14. Ibid., Annex.

15. *National Security Action Memorandum No. 182 (NSAM 182)*, the White House, 24 August 1962, declassified on 5 January 1980, pp. 1–31.

16. *Umbrella Concept for Low-Intensity Conflict*, p. A–3.

17. Greentree, "United States and the Politics of Conflict," p. 18.

18. Manwaring and Prisk, ed., *El Salvador at War*, pp. 111, 244, 245, 399, 400, 485, 486, 489.

19. The Joint Staff, *Doctrine for Joint Operations in Low-Intensity Conflict* (Joint Test Publication 3–07, which was staffed with the military services and ready for evaluation in the field, October 1990), p. I–1.

20. Corr, "Conclusion," in *Uncomfortable Wars: Toward a New Paradigm of Low-Intensity Conflict*, ed. Max G. Manwaring (Boulder: Westview Press, 1991), pp. 127–129.

21. Stephen Sloan, "The Reagan Administration and Low-Intensity Conflict: An Enduring Legacy or a Passing Fad?" *Military Review* (January 1990): 42–29.

22. A.J. Bacevich, James D. Hallums, Richard H. White, and Thomas F. Young, *American Military Policy in Small Wars: The Case of El Salvador* (Washington: Pergamon-Brassey's, 1988).

23. Secretary of State George Shultz, "The Ecology of International Change" (speech before the Commonwealth Club of California, San Francisco, 28 October 1988).

24. Corr, "Conclusion," in *Uncomfortable Wars*, pp. 129–130.

25. This list is adapted from *Umbrella Concept for Low-Intensity Conflict*, p. 3–1. The "Rockefeller Report" and the "Restricted Engagement Options"

were added; the former taken from *Supporting U.S. Strategy for Third World Conflict*, p. 6, and the latter from Greentree, "United States and the Politics of Conflict," pp. 39–40.

26. *Supporting U.S. Strategy for Third World Conflict*, p. 6.

27. Ibid.

28. *Umbrella Concept for Low-Intensity Conflict*, pp. 3–4, 5.

29. Greentree, "United States and the Politics of Conflict," pp. 39–40.

30. *Umbrella Concept for Low-Intensity Conflict*, p. 3-8.

31. U.S. Army Joint Low-Intensity Project: Final Report, vol. 1, *Analytical Review of Low-Intensity Conflict*, U.S. Army Training and Doctrine Command, 1 August 1986, as cited in *Umbrella Concept for Low-Intensity Conflict*, p. 3–11.

32. Glen P. Hastedt, *American Foreign Policy: Past, Present and Future*, 2d ed. (Englewood Cliffs, N.J.: Prentice Hall, 1991), p. 102.

33. Ibid., pp. 102–105.

34. Corr served as a member of one of the advisory Red Teams created to help the USSOC Commander organize his command.

35. *Umbrella Concept for Low-Intensity Conflict*, pp. 3–8, 9.

36. Ibid., p. 1-2.

37. Barbro Owens, "Military Power and Low-Intensity Conflict—Can LIC's Be Licked Without the Use of Threat or Force" (individual study project for the U.S. Army War College, Carlisle Barracks, Pennsylvania, 18 March 1989), pp. 4–6.

38. Ibid., p. 9.

39. Don Oberdorfer, "Strategy for a Solo Superpower: The U.S. Plans to Keep Its Powder Dry," *Washington Post National Weekly Edition*, 27 May–2 June, 1991, pp. 8–9.

40. Ibid.

41. Ibid.

42. Ibid.

43. Col. Harry G. Summers, Jr., "How to Be the World's Policeman," *New York Times Magazine*, 19 May 1991, pp. 40–46.

44. President George Bush, "United States Defenses: Reshaping Our Forces" (speech at the Aspen Institute, Aspen, Colorado, 2 August 1990).

45. Office of the Assistant Secretary of Defense for Special Operations and Low-Intensity Conflict, "Peacetime Engagement" (working paper from the Peacetime Engagement Conference sponsored by the assistant secretary of defense and hosted by the Army-Air Force Center for Low-Intensity Conflict, 10–12 July 1991), p. 1.

46. Oberdorfer, "Strategy for a Solo Superpower," p. 9.

47. Secretary of Defense Richard Cheney, "Conflicting Trends and Long Term Defense Needs," prepared statement to the Senate Armed Services Committee, 17 February 1991, in Department of Defense, *Defense Issues* 6, no. 6:4,5.

48. Secretary of Defense Richard Cheney, "U.S. Defense Strategy and the DOD Budget Request," prepared statement to the House Armed Services

Committee, 7 February 1991, in Department of Defense, *Defense Issues 6,* no. 4:3.

49. This section draws heavily on the initial draft of Joint Publication 3-07.1, *JTTP for Foreign Internal Defense,* April 1991, pp. II–7 to II–20.

50. It took two years to fill a vacant legal officer position vital to country team efforts in the area of human rights. The United States armed forces required almost eighteen months to send an urgently requested mobile training team for counterintelligence and two years to provide a Spanish-speaking army adviser to help the Salvadoran armed forces restructure their irrational recruiting, pay, and reenlistment systems.

51. Greentree, "United States and the Politics of Conflict," pp. 36–37.

52. It took about eighteen months for Ambassador Corr to overcome AID resistance to implementing the highly successful Municipalities in Action program that bypassed the central government and began the implementation of small projects in conflict zones.

53. "Recommendations and Findings for Expanding Andean Agricultural Production and Trade," prepared by Ambassador Edwin G. Corr, leader of Inter-agency Team on Andean Trade Initiative Agricultural Task Force, USTR document, 31 January 1991.

3

The Threat in the Contemporary Peace Environment: The Challenge to Change Perspectives

Max G. Manwaring

In an era when East-West tensions are considerably reduced and there is supposed to be a "peace dividend," it becomes important not to let enthusiasm or appearance run away with judgment. Although the improvement of East-West relationships is a welcome occurrence, a relaxation of superpower tensions has not created a peaceful world. On the contrary, as this chapter is being written, one out of every four nation-states on this earth is involved in some sort of serious conflict.[1] Moreover, the end of the so-called cold war has not resolved a host of other problems that can profoundly affect the vital long-term interests of one international political actor or another.

The concerns most likely to dominate international politics in the years ahead reflect an extremely dynamic world. They include the emergence of multipolarity, the problems of opposing nationalisms in an increasingly interdependent world, the changing nature of conflict, and the problems of governance because of an increasingly universal yearning to hold governors accountable to the governed. These concerns are compounded by other factors that further challenge the ability of governments to govern justly, to provide meaningful social and economic development, and to manage the range of external and internal security problems that confront them. Examples include "low-intensity" conflicts, the illicit multinational narcotics industry, international terrorism, ideologues at the extremes of the left-right spectrum, and other destabilizing elements. The result is a vicious downward cycle that manifests itself in a number of disparate activities in which the lowest common denominator is instability.

As important as the consequences of instability might be in the international threat environment, it is only a symptom—not the threat itself. Rather, the threat in the contemporary situation results from a lack of understanding both of the causes of instability and of the ways and means of dealing with the conflicts generated through the various manifestations of political, economic, social, and military disequilibrium. The more traditional threats that center on proximity of potentially unfriendly forces to national territory or other vital interests (in other words, strategic access or denial) must also be addressed in terms of causes rather than effects.

Carl von Clausewitz reminds us that "the first, the supreme, the most far reaching act of judgment that the statesman and commander have to make is to establish . . . the kind of war on which they are embarking; neither mistaking it for, nor trying to turn it into, something that is alien to its nature."[2] Determining the nature of conflict is thus "the first of all strategic questions and the most comprehensive."[3] Thus, it is imperative that senior decision makers and their staffs correctly identify the central strategic problem and the primary political objective (logical end-state) associated with it; prioritize the others; and link policy, strategy, force structure and equipment, and coordinated political-economic-psychological-military campaign plans to solving the central strategic problem. This linkage encompasses Clausewitz's "forgotten dimensions of strategy" and what Sun Tzu indicates is the indirect approach to conflict.[4] The idea is that there are other—more effective—ways to "render the enemy powerless" than to attack his military force.[5]

To identify and deal with the central problem, it is necessary to (1) define the strategic environment; (2) isolate the primary strategic problem within that milieu; and (3) postulate a conceptual framework within which comparisons and judgments may be given meaning. Such an exercise can provide a beginning from which to help change perspective and achieve the vision necessary for success in the contemporary unstable peace environment.

The Strategic Environment

The most fundamental characteristic of international politics is that of anarchy. There is nothing to check the international political actor except the power of other actors. The resultant security environment is not necessarily predictable or benign. The primary characteristics that further define the contemporary security arena are (1) multipolarity; (2) interdependence; (3) the changing nature of contemporary conflict; and (4) governability.

Multipolarity. From a structural point of view, the world is becoming multipolar. In addition to the United States, France, and other well-known international actors, little-noticed regional powers are emerging as well. As an example, India is a potential nuclear power and has been developing the fleet, the air force, and the army to make that country an extremely important military force in South Asia.[6] Other emerging powers that should be noted include North Korea and the so-called tiger ministates on the Pacific Rim, Brazil, Israel, Iran, Pakistan, and South Africa—to mention a few. Additionally, non-state actors such as the Palestine Liberation Organization (PLO), Algeria's Islamic Salvation Front, and other terrorist and militant ideological and religious groups cannot be ignored.

At the same time, the various poles exert different types and levels of effectiveness of power—military (the former Soviet Union), economic and financial (Japan and Germany), demographic (China and India), and military and economic (the United States).[7] Moreover, psychological opinion-making power belongs to any state or non-state actor willing and able to gain access to the mass media. Its effectiveness is limited only by the qualitative and quantitative efforts of the individual political actor.

Traditionally, military, economic, political, and psychological actions were intended to change material circumstances to influence decision makers. They were direct actions. Present-day actions are meant to change the perceived or apparent situation for the people as well as for decision makers. The process is one of education or inculcation of values or manipulation of people's views regarding a situation or set of situations. It is more indirect action, and perhaps more effective over the long term. As an example, Peru's *Sendero Luminoso* (Shining Path) has consistently labeled its military actions "armed propaganda." Tactically, Sendero has tended to operate in small units with political, psychological, and military objectives—in that order. Examples of these objectives would include assassinations, kidnappings, terrorism, destruction of transportation and communications nets, and the establishment of control over specific areas. All these actions are aimed at lessening regime credibility in terms of ability and willingness to govern and protect the citizenry and at providing the freedom of movement and the security necessary to further the revolutionary cause.[8]

Another complexity in the contemporary multipolar world involves questions such as what relations are going to develop among the various actors; what institutional links they will establish with others; and what "their relations with the rest of the world, in a context of vigilant, demanding and often turbulently mobilized masses" will be.[9] How stable might any of these relationships be, given the power of the psychological instrument? A multipolar world, in which one or a hundred actors are exerting differing types and levels of power within a set of cross-cutting alliances, could conceivably be a more volatile and dangerous one than the previous bipolar situation.

Interdependence. The second characteristic that contributes much to the current "peace environment" is that of interdependence. Jaques Maritain argues that the purely economic interdependence of nations does not necessarily lead to peace. The current interdependence is not a politically agreed-upon, willed, and rational interdependence. Despite wishful thinking, interdependence may in fact lead to war. His logic is compelling. "An essentially economic interdependence can but exasperate the rival needs and prides of nations; and the industrial progress only accelerates the process (toward) *la guerre totale*. Thus it is that we have the privilege of contemplating today a world more and more economically one, and more and more divided by the pathological claims of opposed nationalisms."[10]

Regarding clashing nationalisms, the hard evidence over time and in a variety of places clearly indicates that violence is all too often considered an acceptable option in attempting to achieve internal as well as international goals. The stark reminders of the strengths of tribalism, feudalism, and fundamentalism and the ubiquitous obstacles to change—lack of awareness, absence of preparedness, inadequacy of commitment, retention of privilege for a few, and corruption—are all very much a part of the cultures of a majority of countries in the world today.[11]

Nation-states, extreme nationalists, irredentists, ideologues, religious fundamentalists, militant reformers, civil and military bureaucrats, and demagogues have at their disposal an awesome array of sophisticated conventional and unconventional weaponry not to dissuade, but to be used—even against their own people. Violence is a normal and accepted way of dealing with problems—changing what needs to be changed or keeping things the way they have always been. Furthermore, these actors do not pay a whole lot of attention to cost-benefit analyses of their actions.

The resultant instability is pervasive in much of the world. It manifests itself in "unstable peace"—that is peaceful to those who are geographically removed from the problem, but usually extremely violent to those who are involved.[12] Approximately two-thirds of the forty or more conflicts that are ongoing in the world today involve revolutionary movements and/or internal suppression. The capability to wage conventional mid-intensity or high-intensity war is generally limited to the more affluent or larger countries of the world. Those nation-states—or groups within them—that are weak or do not want to risk the possibilities of nuclear war but who want to change things must resort to a more indirect form of conflict.[13]

The changing nature of contemporary conflict. The lessons of the Persian Gulf War, the Falklands/Malvinas War, and any of the hundreds of conflicts that have taken place since the end of World War II are not being lost on the new powers emerging into the contemporary multipolar international security arena. Ironically, strategies being developed to protect or further the interests of a number of political actors are inspired by the dual idea of evading and frustrating superior conventional military force.[14] The better a power, or government, has become at the operational level of conventional war, the more a potential external or internal opponent has turned to the more political-psychological conflict at the bottom of the warfare ladder. B. H. Liddell Hart saw all this in the early 1960s: "Thus, the concept of 'cold war' is now out of date, and should be superseded by that of 'camouflaged war.'"[15]

Normally, the primary aim of such a war is to gain control of a population—not simply to gain some sort of political or economic concession from a given government. The outcomes of these kinds of conflicts are not determined exclusively or primarily by the results of battlefield clashes. Instead, winning these wars depends on a long-term, protracted, multistage use of moral power to gain control of a society and its political system. This struggle for legitimacy and allegiance on the part of the existing regimes and their illegal opponents is more fundamentally political and psychological than military. Thus, the stakes in these conflicts are total from the standpoint of both the eventual winners and the losers.[16]

It is not only this type of war that must be taken into account when assessing the contemporary strategic environment, however. Border problems, territorial disputes, terrorism, migration and refugee flows, sanctuaries, foreign military advisers, and large-scale drug operations are also of consequence. The French experience in Africa during the 1980s and 1990s is instructive. "The threat confronted is never the same from one (low-intensity conflict) operation to the next. Opposing forces may range from weakly equipped detachments to cohesive units possessing tanks, missiles, radars, aircraft and naval assets, and having external support."[17]

In this environment of "unstable peace," issues of political legitimacy—aggravated by religious, ethnic, racial, and ideological differences—coupled with easy access to armaments and external state and non-state support mean that constant, subtle struggles for power dominate national life in many countries today. This state of affairs prevents virtually any chance of the national consensus and internal stability that must accompany sustained, realistic development in those parts of the world that remain "underdeveloped."[18] To exacerbate the problem, foreign debt accumulates while economies disintegrate further; infrastructure decays perceptibly; and pollution, famine, and disease make lives more miserable by the day.

Several of the ongoing or foreseeable situations could become an opportunity for exploitation by virtually any political actor—large or small—in the world. Even though many actual or potential conflicts are not now taking place in locations of vital interest to the United States, there are enough to cause concern. In the context of multipolarity, interdependence, and the destabilizing problems associated with the problem of governability, it is only a matter of time before one political actor or another will be mortally threatened.

Governability. The fourth and last element having important consequences for international politics is that of governability.[19] More than half the countries of the world have been brought to the point of economic and political collapse by corrupt and/or incompetent leadership. The gravity of the problem is hard to exaggerate. Almost all the nonindustrialized countries of the world are in an apparently permanent depression and have poor prospects for social or economic improvement. In the widespread demoralization, corruption becomes an omnipresent plague. Lack of faith in improvement makes reform difficult if not impossible. More specifically, there have been food riots, protests, strikes, looting, and violent demonstrations. Examples are in the news virtually every day, with Algeria being one case in point.[20]

There are not many options for improvement. Hundreds of thousands of people have voted with their feet and have been emigrating, creating new problems as refugees in other countries. Hundreds of thousands have become a part of the illicit drug industry. As only two examples, it is estimated that more than 250,000 and 300,000 people are employed in some part of the illegal narco-industry in Bolivia and Peru, respectively.[21] Those millions of people who have been unable to leave their countries or otherwise improve their lives through involvement in the black or gray economies, or drugs, tend to isolate themselves mentally from their governments. Others become revolutionaries—or at least tacit supporters of those who promise change. In most of the poorly governed and impoverished countries of the world—North and South—there are not many people left in a given society willing to provide their time, treasure, or blood to the state.[22] The susceptibility to upheaval and the resultant instability can only benefit former friends as well as established enemies.

History clearly shows that a population properly governed is an immense natural resource and an incomparable source of accomplishment. On the other hand, wretchedly poor people without basic necessities—or the hope of attaining them honestly and peacefully—turn upon themselves and others with distressing results.[23] Under these conditions, people can easily be turned into pawns on the global chessboard.

The Central Strategic Problem

A campaign that does not respond to the legitimate aspirations of peoples and deals only with "enemy" military capabilities is ultimately destined to fail. North Vietnamese General Vo Nguyen Giap understood that a type of legitimacy was the central strategic problem and the key to success in the Vietnam conflict. He argues that "The Vietnamese people's war of liberation was victorious because it was a just war, waged for independence and the reunification of the country, in the legitimate interests of the nation and the people and which by this fact succeeded in leading the whole people to participate enthusiastically in the resistance and to consent to make every sacrifice for its victory."[24]

It was also recognized early in the El Salvadoran conflict that the political-moral dimension would determine the success or failure of the participants. Speaking for the insurgents, Guillermo M. Ungo identified the legitimacy of the incumbent regime as the primary strategic problem in El Salvador.[25] President José Napoleón Duarte understood the issue and countered with a program designed to nullify the efforts of the insurgents. His argument was simple: "If the Christian Democrats demonstrate in El Salvador that a democratic system can bring about structured changes peacefully, then the polarized choice between domination by the rightist oligarchy and violent revolution by the Left will no longer be valid."[26] The fact that this conflict reached a temporary impasse indicated that neither side had found a way to convince the Salvadoran people of the validity of their respective actions.

The contemporary strategic environment requires a new people-oriented model. Every policy, program, and action—military, political, economic, opinion-making—must contribute directly to the maintenance or enhancement of political legitimacy. As much concern must be focused on preconflict and postconflict periods as on the conflict itself. If the situation is understood and adequate human and physical resources are allocated to the problem during the so-called preconflict period, chances are that an instance of instability may not develop into any kind of serious conflict. Even if it should, however, the conflict will still be primarily political-moral.

The task. In averting the threat and consequences of trying to make a conflict into something that is not, the task is to incorporate the "forgotten dimensions" into a strategy for success. Clausewitz defined three elements as intrinsic to war. This "remarkable trinity" includes the political objective, popular passions, and the operational instruments.[27] The success of the operational instruments is dependent on the other two elements of the trinity. The first element is the credibility of the political objective, and the resultant political motivation of a society. The second element—willingness of the populace to endure the sacrifices necessary to pursue a conflict to a successful end—is closely connected to the first.[28]

In the past, military officers have complained that a given war had been "won" militarily but "lost" politically—as if these dimensions were not completely interdependent. The 1954–1962 Algerian war against France for independence and the 1975–1979 "dirty war" in Argentina are cases in point.[29] Operational and technical factors must now become subordinate to the sociopolitical struggle. If that effort is not conducted with skill and based on a realistic analysis of the societal situation in question, "no amount of operational expertise, logistical back-up or technical know-how could possibly help."[30]

The challenge. The challenge, then, is to come to terms with the fact that contemporary conflict—at whatever level—is essentially a "social" conflict. In this connection, we postulate that legitimacy constitutes the central strategic problem that is the hub of all power and movement on which virtually everything in the contemporary international environment depends. This umbrella concept focuses on the moral right of a government to govern. Popular perceptions of right and wrong, poverty, and lack of upward mobility elaborate the right—and the ability—of a given regime to conduct the business of the state. Until it is generally perceived that these and other basic issues concerning popular sovereignty are being dealt with fairly and effectively, the threat of subverting a targeted political system is real.

The challenge is to change perspectives. The threat is that unless we recognize what is happening at the highest strategic level and reorient thinking and actions to deal with it, "the problems of the next

twenty years will eat us alive."[31] More specifically, President
François Mitterrand of France has argued that the disequilibrium in
the strategic environment in the post–cold war era could well
precipitate world war.[32]

Toward a Conceptual Framework Defining
National Security Priorities in the Current Peace Environment

Once the emphasis is put on the avoidance of large-scale military
violence and rests more on political-moral instruments of power, the
problem of conflict resolution appears in a changed light. In ironic
philosophical rhetoric, the experience of contemporary international
politics has turned the common wisdom concerning war upside down.
War is not an extension of politics; politics is an extension of war. The
tendency is for it to be at the lower end of the conflict ladder,
multidimensional, and total.

The first step in developing an appropriate response to the problems
noted above is to wake up to the implications of world disequilibrium
and popular sovereignty and to begin to deal with the relationship of
instability to legitimate governance. The second step is to realize that
whether one likes it or not, or whether one is prepared for it or not, a
populace-oriented model appears to be the best way of addressing the
problem.

By isolating the key analytical commonalities that play in the
strategic arena, one should be able to infer what conditions and general
actions may be required for a holistic approach to achieve success in
any given conflict situation. In Liddell Hart's terms, that success is
defined as the achievement of a relatively "better peace."[33]

The most salient variables of this conceptual framework have been
elaborated elsewhere.[34] It is based on the fact that the ultimate
outcome of any effort to deal with a given conflict is not primarily
determined by the skillful manipulation of violence in the many
military/police battles that might take place once a war is recognized
to have begun. Rather, control of the situation is determined by (1) the
degree of legitimacy of the government; (2) the organization for unity
of effort; (3) the type and consistency of external support for a targeted
government; (4) the ability to reduce outside support to an illegal
opposition; (5) the effectiveness of intelligence; and, (6) the level of
competence and discipline of a government's security forces.

To the extent that these six highly interrelated factors are strongly
present in any given situation, they favor a political actor's success in
controlling it. To the extent that any one component is absent, or all or
most are only present in a weak form, success is not likely. Thus, a

better peace is dependent on a balanced effort across the board. Another version of the conceptual framework—which graphically portrays the interrelated variables—is shown in Figure 3.1.

The primary implication here is that the various factors outlined above constitute a possible set of simultaneously waged wars within a general conflict. In becoming involved in a modern conflict—camouflaged or not—one is not engaged in a simple war of attrition in the classical sense of destroying an enemy. Rather, as Clausewitz explained, there may be various centers of gravity within a given conflict, and the primary center of gravity may change as the situation changes.[35] As a consequence, the problem of preparing specifically for "camouflaged" or "conventional" operations is moot. The problem is to create the ability to deal with warfare as a whole.[36] The ability to react appropriately to changing political-psychological-economic-military circumstances is an important key to ultimate success.

In sum, a political actor must meet its contemporary security obligation in two basic respects. The first is a conceptual requirement—it must understand the basic strategic problem. The second is an organizational and operational effort—the actor must adhere to the principles of unity of effort and the political objective. The necessary organization must be created to coordinate and implement an effective unity of political, economic, diplomatic, sociological, psychological, and military effort against those who would supplant a given regime. At the same time, the political actor or state must accomplish these tasks and still govern in a manner acceptable to those governed. Sun Tzu argues: "Those who excel in war first cultivate their own humanity and justice and maintain their laws and institutions. By these means they make their governments invincible."[37] In these terms, all efforts are focused on the ultimate common goal—survival in an anarchical world.

Implications

The primary implications of this analysis are clear. The ability of any political actor to control and protect its own destiny and the daily lives of its citizens is severely threatened in the contemporary international security environment. A populace-oriented model focused on legitimacy reflects the reality of contemporary life. Unless the trends of the cold war era are reversed and perspectives changed in consonance with the present manifestation of international reality, the forces that have produced the inequities of the old order will continue to pose insurmountable obstacles to the processes of reform, regeneration, well-being, and relative peace.

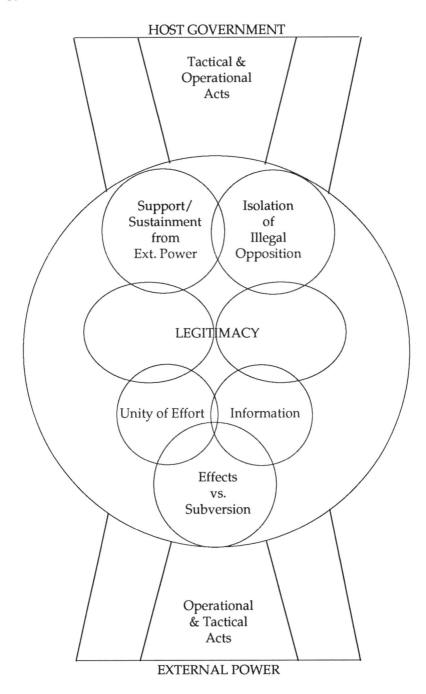

Figure 3.1 Key Aspects of Contemporary Conflict

The first definitive task in accepting the challenge to change perspectives has got to be the full consideration of the entire situation and the various aspects implicit in it. Subsequent tasks would be to plan, organize, and implement a strategy that will define security in terms of the central strategic problem. If pursued constructively, a holistic strategy for the achievement of stability with justice will also achieve a level of international security far exceeding that attained during the period since the end of World War II.

Albert Camus reminds us that "he who dedicates himself . . . to the dignity of mankind, dedicates himself to the earth and reaps from it the harvest that sows its seed and sustains the world again and again. Finally, it is those who know how to rebel, at the appropriate moment, against history who really advance its interests."[38]

Notes

1. A few examples would include Yugoslavia/Croatia/Serbia/Slovenia in Europe; Israel, Iraq, and Lebanon in the Middle East; Afghanistan, Burma, and Sri Lanka in Southeast Asia; Cambodia, Laos/Thailand, and the Philippines in Western Asia; and El Salvador, Guatemala, and Peru in Latin America.

2. Carl von Clausewitz, *On War*, ed. and trans. Michael Howard and Peter Paret (Princeton: Princeton University Press, 1976), p. 88.

3. Ibid., pp. 88–89.

4. See "The Forgotten Dimensions of Strategy" in Michael Howard, *The Causes of War* (London: Temple-Smith, 1981), pp. 101–115, and Sun Tzu, *The Art of War*, trans. Samuel B. Griffith (London: Oxford University Press, 1971), pp. 77–79.

5. Clausewitz, *On War*, p. 75.

6. See *The Military Balance, 1975–1976* through *The Military Balance, 1990–1991* (London: International Institute for Strategic Studies, 1975 through 1990).

7. Stanley Hoffmann, "A New World and Its Troubles," *Foreign Affairs* (Fall 1990): 121.

8. See "El Discurso del Dr. Guzman" in Rogger Mercado U., *Los Partidos Politicos en el Peru* (Lima: Ediciones Latinamericanas, 1985), pp. 85–90; and *Desarrollar la guerra popular serviendo a la Revolucion mundial* (Lima: Comite Central del Partido Comunista del Peru, 1986). Also see, in English, David Scott Palmer, "The Sendero Luminoso Rebellion in Rural Peru," in Georges Fauriol, ed., *Latin American Insurgencies* (Washington, D. C.: National Defense University Press, 1985), pp. 67–96.

9. Hoffmann, "New World."

10. Jacques Maritain, *Man and the State* (Chicago: The University of Chicago Press, 1963), p. 190.

11. These and subsequent assertions are based on more than a hundred interviews with civilian and military experts who were involved in the forty-three small wars examined by Max G. Manwaring, in "A Model for the Analysis of Insurgencies," a paper prepared for the Small Wars Operations Research Directorate, U.S. Southern Command, 1987. The research and analysis were further described in Manwaring, ed., *Uncomfortable Wars: Toward a New Paradigm of Low Intensity Conflict* (Boulder: Westview Press, 1991). A more methodologically oriented version of this research, entitled "Insurgency and Counterinsurgency: Toward a New Analytical Approach," will be published in *The Journal of Small Wars* in the near future. The interviews were conducted in the United States, Europe, and Latin America over the period 1984–1987 by Manwaring and Col. Alfred W. Baker, USA. More recently, more than eighty additional interviews were conducted in 1989–1990 by Manwaring. A paradigm was developed on the basis of the interviews. This paradigm presents the product of connecting and weighting those six most salient dimensions of power within the context of the win/loss outcomes of a sample of these forty-three insurgencies/civil wars that have taken place over the past forty to forty-five years. The model predicted an impressive 88.37 percent of the cases examined. Moreover, the estimated R2 (a standard Goodness of Fit test) equals .91. This shows very strong correlations between the dependent variables and the results of the conflicts examined. Finally, the model as a whole is statistically significant at the .001 level. That is to say, the chances of it explaining so well by chance or accident are one in 1,000.

12. Ibid.

13. B. H. Liddell Hart, *Strategy*, 2d rev. ed. (New York: Signet, 1974), pp. 320; 360–370.

14. As examples of Argentina's new approach to recovering the Falklands/Malvinas Islands, see Vice Admiral D. Jorge Alberto Fraga, "Malvinas: Existe el Paraguas de Soberania?" *Revista Argentina de Estudios Estrategicos*, no. 11 (julio–septiembre 1989): 41–53; Lt. Col. Mario Horacio Orsolini, "Islas Malvinas: Una Estrategia para su Recuperacion," *Revista Militar*, no. 722 (julio–octubre 1989): 16–24; and General D. Osiris G. Villegas, "La llamada doctrina de Seguridad Nacional," *Revista Militar*, no. 721 (enero-julio 1989): 22–26.

15. Liddell Hart, *Strategy*, p. 367.

16. Interviews.

17. Lt. Col. Michel L. Castellon, "Low-Intensity Conflicts in the 1980s: The French Experience," *Military Review* (January 1986): 72.

18. Interviews.

19. William J. Olson, "Low Intensity Conflict: The Challenge to the National Interest," *Terrorism* 12:76. Also see Michael Howard, "The Springtime of Nations," *Foreign Affairs* (America and the World 1989/1990): 17.

20. See, for example, the *New York Times* during the month of November 1988 and the *Economist*, 26 November–2 December 1988; and 10–16 December 1988. Then, see the *New York Times* again during June, July, and August 1991.

21. Interviews.

22. Ibid.

23. Ivan L. Head, "South-North Dangers," *Foreign Affairs* (Summer 1989): 84.

24. General Vo Nguyen Giap, *People's War, People's Army* (New York: Frederick A. Praeger, Publisher, 1962), p. 34.

25. Max G. Manwaring interview with Dr. Guillermo M. Ungo in Panama City, Panama, 11 December 1987.

26. José Napoleón Duarte, *Duarte: My Story* (New York: G. P. Putnam's Sons, 1986), p. 279; and Max G. Manwaring interview with President Duarte in San Salvador, El Salvador, 20 November 1987.

27. Clausewitz, *On War*, pp. 80–81.

28. Howard, *Causes of War*, p. 103.

29. Interviews.

30. Howard, *Causes of War*, p. 109.

31. *U.S. News & World Report*, Special Double Issue, 26 December 1988/2 January 1989 (vol. 105, no. 25), p. 51.

32. James Reston interview with President Mitterrand, reported in the *New York Times*, 4 June 1981, p. 23.

33. Liddell Hart, *Strategy*, p. 353.

34. Manwaring, *Uncomfortable Wars:*, pp. 19–28.

35. Clausewitz, *On War*, p. 596.

36. Frank Kitson, *Warfare as a Whole* (London: Faber and Faber, 1987).

37. Sun Tzu, *Art of War*, p. 88.

38. Albert Camus, *The Rebel* (New York: Vintage Books, 1956), p. 302.

4

Conflict in the Post–Cold War Era

John R. Galvin

In August 1986, I wrote some notes one night after a talk with a Latin American general who had spent his career, his life, fighting in low-intensity conflict. Here is part of what he said:

> We are in a new kind of war, [he said]. There have been guerrillas, irregulars, from the beginning of time, but still this kind of war is new. And we are fighting it in the old way. And we are losing. . . . We don't have a doctrine. . . .
>
> The enemy knows us and knows how to use us against ourselves.
>
> We don't even have the right equipment. Our soldiers' weapons are for long-range, open warfare, but a big part of the war is in the urban area. Bullets shot at a terrorist go through six houses and kill children. . . .
>
> We don't have the training. The soldiers are not prepared. They don't know how to deal with the people, our own countrymen. We don't have the intelligence network, the system, the institution. We're suspicious of everything. We don't understand the day-to-day situation. We don't understand the mix of politics, economics, religion in this war. . . .
>
> The enemy is willing to "work in the vineyards" for a long, long time. We don't sustain anything. . . .
>
> They are not fighting just in this country, but in the others around us. They are unified and we are not. Regardless of our victories, we can be defeated in the long run. It's very possible and for the other countries, too. One by one we will go down. . . .

This general was talking about a kind of warfare we have known about since the beginning of human history, but we still tend to think of it as something new. It is new only in that we have never given it the attention and priority it deserves. Now, in the post–cold war era, it will be more important than ever to understand this kind of warfare, which is known as low-intensity conflict or LIC.

The New Emphasis on LIC

In the shadow of the relatively few gigantic wars of the past there have been literally hundreds of small conflicts in which fear and death and violence and destruction were as brutal and ugly as always. There has been a recent emphasis on a concept of low-intensity conflict or LIC as a level of warfare with its own characteristics, quite apart from mid- and high-intensity and not a derivative of these; a concept that, highlighted by the scores of small conflicts, has gradually assumed a more definite position in the hierarchy of politico-military responses. The amount of attention that military and political leaders were willing to devote to this part of the spectrum of war has grown, providing an understanding that this kind of conflict has its own strategy, doctrine, operational concepts, and force structure.

"Low-intensity conflict" is not simply the other end of the totem pole from the dramatic warfare we saw in Desert Storm; there is a lot more to it than that. We are always in the process of finding a title for this level of warfare, although naming some phenomenon does not necessarily mean we understand it. I remember someone saying "If we're going to talk about low-intensity conflict, let's not spend all our time coming up with new names for it, or new definitions." Like other forms of warfare, low-intensity conflict musters all aspects, all agencies of the government that fight it and those who help.

Marxism is gone, but no one believes that we have seen the last of low-intensity conflict. In the immediate future we will see the same causes of low-intensity conflict we have found in the past, including weak national administrations, lack of political infrastructure, economic stagnation, historic problems of disfranchisement for large parts of the citizenry, corruption and mismanagement, and difficult military-civil relationships. In other words, such widespread conditions leading to unrest are the structural weaknesses in national and regional security arrangements that still allow low-intensity fighting to smolder on. As if that were not enough, drug traffic is fueling the fires.

Many nations in transition today that are dedicated to achieving political pluralism, rule of law, minority rights, and the other principles and aims of liberal democracy are hounded by the problems of change and vulnerable to every kind of instability. This means that the United States and the other nations in a position to help must be able to assess the situation of the afflicted country in all its ramifications.

Will we be prepared to handle the lower end of the spectrum of conflict in the new world order that is emerging after the collapse of communism? Now that the world has changed, are we developing our new strategies and new force structures in a way that will give us the greatest flexibility to deal with all eventualities? My assessment is that we are moving in the right direction, but we have a long way to go. The new strategic concept of the United States, if fully implemented, will allow us to deal with crises across the range of possibilities. If we are successful in restructuring our defense capabilities the way our strategy demands, the mechanisms necessary for responding to LIC situations will be in place to meet the security requirements of the twenty-first century. As I said, there is still plenty to do. The focus of any successful strategy for the future must be on crisis management, and many of the crises with which the United States will be involved in the future will start at the lower end of the conflict spectrum.

The Transition to a New Era

What will the world look like as communism fades into history and the broad European landmass is the focus of our concerns? This is the central question as we move to redefine our security requirements. We have lived for an entire generation under a monolithic threat of a radical superpower with an expansionist ideology that promised to bury us and subjugate the world. That threat is now gone. Yet, the century coming to a close has been the bloodiest in human history, with more than sixty-five million dead in two enormous wars and untold numbers killed in all the smaller conflicts. Even "peace" in the last several decades has been a rather violent state of affairs; for example, between 1946 and 1989 the United States responded to crises of one kind or another 187 times, and there has been no slackening of the pace.[1]

The first half of the century saw the defeat of the fanatic right, the forces of fascism, but also the rise of the radical left, communism. The result was a sustained tension and indeed conflict in many parts of the world—a half-century of protracted crisis that we came to know as the cold war. With the extremes of the political spectrum defeated and discredited, the world sees itself on the threshold of an unprecedented opportunity for peace, democracy, and prosperous free enterprise. Arms control and confidence and stability measures have produced the lowest levels of tension between East and West since the end of World War II. Nonetheless, forces are also at work in the world that make it clear that the end of the cold war offers no respite from protracted conflict, much of it low-intensity, as the world reshapes itself.

The year 1991 has gone down as a time to be studied for more than the lessons of the Gulf War (although that event certainly would provide enough); in addition, the Western democracies have responded to six other crises with deployments of forces. The North Atlantic Treaty Organization (NATO) sent forces to Turkey in response to the Gulf crisis because under Article Five of the North Atlantic Treaty, that ally asked for support. In addition, several nations deployed naval units to the Gulf under control of the Western European Union. Besides these deployments, eight nations placed forces under the United Nations (UN) for humanitarian assistance for the Kurds, and there were individual nations that moved some of their NATO-assigned forces, such as the U.S. Patriot air defense missiles sent from Germany to Israel to protect against Iraqi SCUD missiles. Then there was the deployment of troops by France and Belgium to Zaire for evacuation of foreign civilians. The United States committed airlift support for this combined operation. Finally, the European Community and the UN responded to try to settle the crisis in Yugoslavia.

The Security Challenges of the New Era

As the threat of war between superpowers fades, nations are beginning to focus on all the other uncertainties that have always been there but were kept in check by the East-West nuclear standoff. Confrontation between the superpowers was accompanied by a prudent unwillingness to trigger an explosion of war. These conditions tended to keep countries both large and small from acting militarily to redress perceived injustices—although even under these restraints there were many conflicts. The passing of this "bipolar order" allows the upsurge of new possibilities for conflict as regions of the world redefine their strategic aims. Unfortunately, the timing of this development coincides with the extraordinary proliferation of powerful modern armament, including nuclear weapons; and this combination paints a picture of a future world with greater possibilities for crisis.

By the year 2000, at least twenty nations will own ballistic missiles. Thirty countries will have chemical weapons, and ten may be about to deploy biological weapons as well. Eight more nations are close to acquiring nuclear capabilities. Underlying problems of poor human conditions, growing poverty, greater gaps between "have" and "have not" countries, rapid population growth, faltering economic conditions, and cumulative ecological damage feed discontent in many regions of the world.

Other security challenges growing from the aftermath of the cold war have created a situation even more complex than that of our recent experience. Despite notable progress in destroying several classes of nuclear weapons, the possibility still exists of nuclear devices being acquired by unstable Third World nations. In addition, there is little doubt that the conditions and potential for terrorism will grow. In Iraq, UN inspection teams discovered a nuclear weapons program far more advanced than the West had perceived. This shows not only the reality of the risk, but also the difficulty of monitoring and enforcing nonproliferation.

Reduction of nuclear and conventional weaponry under arms control treaties has helped lower the level of confrontation in Europe—but also has changed worldwide force balances, making non-European nations relatively stronger. Large standing forces with modernized equipment backed up by significant industrial capability remain to shape the post–cold war period. The residual military capabilities of the Russian Republic alone need to be assessed by the rest of the world. Russia today appears to be contemplating further military reductions but still possesses 75 percent of the former USSR's strategic nuclear forces, 50 percent of all maneuver divisions, and 85 percent of major defense industrial facilities. Barring extraordinary change, Russia, though not a world superpower, will continue to be militarily the strongest nation in Europe.

The aftermath of the cold war has given us an inheritance of Third World states armed far beyond minimum defensive levels. These states, as Iraq has recently demonstrated, have the capability to wage intense war on short notice. Ten nations in this region are known to possess a total of twenty-five thousand tanks. Acquisition of chemical, biological, and nuclear weapons would enable these or other countries to threaten levels of violence incomprehensible in the past.

Emigration will put considerable pressure on many states in Western and Eastern Europe as well as the Third World. Reemerging ultranationalism, religious fundamentalism, ethnocentrism, and terrorism have caused masses of dislocated people, many without prospects of full assimilation into host societies.

The U.S. Strategic Response

The U.S. response to the end of the cold war requires reflection on lessons learned, appreciation of the multiple dimensions of risk across the operational continuum, and the application of recent experience. "Fortress America" or neo-isolation in any form is completely contrary to everything we have learned and is an inadequate response to security challenges at all levels. President George Bush set the U.S. direction in August 1990 with these words:

> What we require now is a defense policy that adapts to the significant changes we are witnessing without neglecting the enduring realities that will continue to shape our security strategy—a policy of peacetime engagement every bit as constant and committed to the defense of our interests and ideals in today's world as in the time of conflict and Cold War.

He also singled out aspects of low-intensity conflict for emphasis, with recognition that "Even in a world where democracy and freedom have made great gains, threats remain. Terrorism. Hostage taking. Renegade regimes and unpredictable rulers. New sources of instability. All require a strong and engaged America."[2] The evolving U.S. defense policy stresses active engagement in international matters bearing on U.S. interests. The national security strategic shift mirrors shifts in NATO and is a move away from flexible response (with its strong reliance on the U.S. nuclear arsenal) and toward a new strategy of crisis management. Deterrence, discriminate response, and collective action have become the national security strategic centerpieces to protect peace and promote stability. Implications for change extend to the national military strategy, where forward deployments (large numbers of combat units stationed abroad) and rapid reinforcement have given way to forward presence (positioning of more limited military capabilities overseas) and crisis response. Fundamental to this stance is the selective nature of its application.

Running through all aspects of the evolving policy are utilization and coordination of the national effort, not only internally but also externally in support of coalitions for stability and security. When it comes to implementation of national strategic aims, the Defense Department and supporting intelligence agencies certainly should not be lonely in the future: all government agencies have been committed to the furtherance of the strategy. Providing common direction to these agencies is the imperative to promote peaceful democratic prosperity, free enterprise, and human rights. This international team effort should result in major U.S. contributions to international stability, orderly transition of nations, and greater world community consensus.

Given all the change in the post–cold war world, U.S. strategic interests and objectives have remained relatively stable—which is not surprising because these national goals have been with us from our beginnings. U.S. security means the survival of the United States as a free and independent nation with its fundamental values intact and its institutions and people secure. Along with a healthy and growing U.S. economy and cooperative and politically vigorous relations with allies and friendly nations, we want a stable and secure world where political and economic freedom, human rights, and democratic institutions can flourish.[3] Interagency efforts will be channeled into four security mission areas. Shaping the U.S. security environment in ways beneficial to our interests will be accomplished through support for diplomacy, precrisis activities, force projection and crisis response, and postcrisis activities.

U.S. Military Means for Strategic Response

The fading of the gigantic and stark East-West confrontation of the last half-century makes the possibility of global war very remote. Regional contingencies, on the other hand, are more likely now than before. In recognition of this change, U.S. national military aims have been laid out in five areas. First is the imperative to deter or defeat aggression in concert with allies. The next two objectives are closely related: to ensure global access and influence and to promote regional stability and cooperation. There is a correlation between the final two objectives, which are to stem the flow of illegal drugs and to combat terrorism. Overall, these objectives provide a foundation for addressing the wide range of future security challenges.

Strategic concepts that will guide national preparation for future conflicts include readiness, collective security, security assistance, arms control, maritime and space superiority, strategic agility, power projection, technological superiority, and use of decisive force when required. These concepts promise the development of a capable, credible posture for dealing with low–intensity issues.

Four military force "packages" constitute the base force, which is a new structure and not simply a derivation from the old one. Two packages have regional orientations, one for the Atlantic and one for the Pacific. Strategic forces will shoulder the nuclear deterrence mission, probably for decades to come. Contingency forces based in the United States are to reinforce forward-deployed forces in a crisis, and this is where the bulk of military special operations forces will be. Flexibility of this force structure ensures military capabilities for the whole range of future challenges and wisely avoids overspecialization of organizations, relying on inherent flexibility.

The base force makes U.S. support for multinational units and ad hoc coalitions possible. Forward-presence forces overseas, as well as units in the United States, may be moved in response to crisis. Air and sea mobility assets, prepositioned equipment and supplies, forward bases, host nation support, and reserve forces capabilities support this force array. Of high importance to U.S. coalition-building strategy will be NATO's immediate reaction forces, whose multinational show of support in a crisis can deter an aggressive state. Implicit in our strategy is the demand for crisis prevention and management. We do not lack experience in this: in effect the cold war was a forty-year exercise in crisis prevention and management.

LIC Capabilities in the New Era

The United States is coming out of the cold war with better capabilities in the field of low-intensity conflict than many critics are willing to concede. The mechanics for dealing successfully with the low-intensity end of the operational continuum are in place to make their contribution to overall security policy for the twenty-first century. Capabilities have been much enhanced; major issues are identified; solutions are being pursued. What must be done now is to push progressive development of response capability across the political/diplomatic, economic, informational, and military elements of national power in situations beyond peacetime competition. We also need proactive response capability before a situation goes beyond the bounds of peacetime competition.

Current national security and military strategies provide excellent overall guidance to shape our defense posture for the post–cold war era. The problem lies in translating the strategy into resources and commensurate capabilities. The U.S. defense posture in the cold war was characterized by vigorous debate on resources. At the upper end, for example, nuclear deterrence has had the leading role because the consequences of conflict were so catastrophic that risks there had to be dealt with first. The world has changed as the superpowers and their allies move toward peace and partnership, but the threat of nuclear weapons lingers on and probably will broaden through proliferation. The rapidly evolving multipolar world is driving changes in the way the United States deals with low-intensity conflict within a broader strategic concept. The lower end of the scale of military response cannot be given "lower end" consideration and resourcing. Security requirements of the twenty-first century can be met only with a carefully balanced security program in which low-, mid-, and high-intensity capabilities are fully resourced and balanced. Current circumstances have made it increasingly obvious that low-intensity conflict is part of the mainstream of security affairs.

We should come to agreement on an action agenda for low–intensity strategy, operational concepts, force structure, readiness levels and standards, training, and budget. We need, first of all, committed talent: experts and specialists in combat skills, but also people like medical and agricultural professionals and judicial systems advisers. We need a new look at structural and organizational development within special operations forces. Exercises that develop understanding and confidence among civilian and military leaders are needed.

The military leader who takes part in support for a nation encountering instabilities must have a knowledge not just of the military doctrine and tactics of low-intensity combat, but also of domestic aspects as varied as free economy, land reform, workers' rights and responsibilities, local traditional values, democratic pluralism, and demographic issues. One such issue is the movement of rural populations to the large metropolitan areas, with attendant "ring cities," or groupings of slum areas without proper organization that lack utilities, services, and political administration. Out of communication and set apart as pariahs, these slum areas become sources of disaffection, disturbance, and urban violence. Military leaders must also understand what kind of suppression "internal stability" has meant in some countries, partially through the misadventures of militaries and governments. Military-to-military contact can help in nation-building and lead to the development of apolitical military institutions in developing states. The aim of all countries should be always to have an effective, professional military force that is apolitical and subordinate to civilian control in every way, as well as integrated into the government structure. It must be principled in its conduct, ethics, and morality, and it must be supportive of national development.

The U.S. military, for example, has always been involved in national development. It produced the first engineers when the country had no engineers. It built the railroads across the nation and opened the West, but the military never governed the territories in the West. It established the Mississippi River flood control system and still runs it today, and it does the same for many other rivers. It controls six hundred lakes and supervises the dredging of ports. It is an apolitical military that supports peace and stability and contributes to crisis management through its contacts with armies, navies, and air forces around the world.

Our leaders will need all the tools we can give them, not only to deal with crisis, but also to be able to move up and down the conflict spectrum quickly in a well-practiced and coordinated way. Under budget pressures, military and political planners often oversimplify the essence of conflict at the lower end of the spectrum and even deemphasize the spectrum itself. The world is in a state of metamorphosis as not only the former Soviet Union but also the Muslim countries and to a lesser degree the European Community and the Far East face great changes that will affect all the rest. We need to sense the thrust of the future, the directions of change, and especially the possibilities of inherent instabilities and conflicts that such vast transitions may bring. We can hedge against the risks involved by developing an architecture of security institutions, concentrating on ways to manage crises, and building the broad coordination and the national force structures necessary for a responsive mix of politico-military capabilities to deal with all eventualities.

Austere times and a focus on domestic issues will make the establishment of military priorities a very difficult game on a field full of competition and conflicting interests. This puts a premium on a balanced, realistic game plan.

A plan that creates imbalances in our security posture is unacceptable. Our greater mastery of low-intensity conflict has to reflect a growing understanding of the dynamics of conflict at *all* levels and how all this comes together. National values have shaped our defensive posture, and we need a responsive mix of forces to enable us to respond to multidimensional aggression. To be ready to operate at the lower end of the conflict spectrum, we do not have to change everything. Many facets of U.S. intelligence operations, to provide a single example, are in good shape to make contributions during low-intensity conflict. The concept of the centralized joint intelligence center, concentrating analytical capability, has worked well and has good promise for the future. We will be able to rely on intelligence derived from, analyzed with, and distributed by the most modern technological means. Hardest to find and most in demand is always "HUMINT"—information from human sources. Growing understanding of the nature of low-intensity conflict and its greater likelihood has helped create understanding for why intelligence direct from human sources must be enhanced in the years ahead.

Harnessing governmental agencies to work more closely together is a task that will continue to demand attention. We need a stronger effort to synchronize organizations addressing low-intensity conflict; the top echelons need to see the gaps that exist. Enhanced interagency coordination is also necessary to support further progress in another dimension: continued development of U.S. capability to coordinate initiatives for low-intensity conflict with friends and allies. The key question in the future will increasingly be "How can the United States support resolution of low-intensity conflict?" rather than "How can the United States resolve low-intensity conflict?" Capabilities of host nations, allies, and friends must be integrated with those of the United States in the future, and this is not always a smooth process.

Means of measurement are essential if improvements are to have practical meaning. First, we need to see to what degree low–intensity conflict resources match our concerns in that area. When key leaders and their staffs incorporate low-intensity programs into daily considerations without the insistence of advocates, we will be well on our way. We can expect that most of the crises of the future will begin at the lower end of the spectrum of conflict, and it is there that we will have to act to deal with them. Our current strategy addresses this reality, and we are seeing the evolution of an international structure that will be better equipped to focus on stabilizing measures; therefore, it follows that holding low-intensity concerns to a rear rank behind those of mid- and high-intensity is an inadequate response to the demands of a multipolar world full of unpredictabilities. Balancing of all capabilities and levels ensures the full range of options essential for response in peace, crisis, and war. Any alternative to this is unthinkable.

Notes

1. Adam B. Siegel, "U.S. Navy Crisis Response Activity, 1946–1989: Preliminary Report" (Alexandria, Va.: Center for Naval Analysis, 1989), p. 1.

2. President George Bush, "United States Defenses: Reshaping Our Forces" (speech at the Aspen Institute, Aspen, Colorado, 2 August 1990).

3. The White House, *National Security Strategy of the United States*, August 1991 (Washington, D.C.: GPO, 1991), pp. 3–4.

PART TWO

Selected Cases of
Low-Intensity Conflict

THAILAND

COUNTRY DATA

Area 198,114 sq. miles (about the size of Texas).
Capital Bangkok (population 6 million).
Population 54 million (1987 est.).
Per Capita Income $771.
Ethnic Groups Thai 84%, Chinese 12%, other 4%.
Religions Buddhist 95%, Muslim 3%, other 2%.
Literacy 89%.
Work Force (21.4 million) Agriculture 58.9%, Industry, commerce, and services 26.35%, Government 8.18%.
Infant Mortality Rate 45 per 1,000 live births.
Life Expectancy 64.2 years.
Government Constitutional monarchy.

UNIQUENESS OF CASE STUDY

Thai government effectiveness and withdrawal of aid for insurgents by their major external supporter ensured that another domino did not fall in Southeast Asia.

CHRONOLOGY

1961 Communist Party of Thailand (CPT) adopts Maoist armed struggle.
1965 CPT guerrilla attacks in northeast Thailand; Thai government (RTG) establishes Communist Suppression Operations Command (CSOC).
1967 CPT expands to northern Thailand.
1969–1970 Insurgency spreads in southern Thailand.
1971 Chinese People's Liberation Army troops of hill tribe descent infiltrate North Thailand.
1973 University students overthrow RTG; democracy established.
1975 North Vietnamese triumph in Indochina.
1976 Military coup; students join CPT.
1978 Amnesty policy.
1979 Vietnamese invasion of Cambodia splits CPT; Chinese cut support; mass guerrilla defections.
1980–1981 Student leaders surrender.
1982 RTG overruns major CPT camps.

5

Thailand: The Domino That Did Not Fall

Robert F. Zimmerman

Introduction

Following the communist seizures of ruling power throughout Indochina in 1975, Thailand confronted an increasingly dangerous combination of communist pressures from outside the country's borders and a recrudescence of several externally supported communist insurgencies within its frontiers. Communist insurgents were active in the mountains of northern Thailand, in the rice paddies and low hills of the northeast, and in the jungles and mountains of the south, while much smaller communist armed groups totaling perhaps only fifty to a hundred men existed in central Thailand.

These forces all received varying degrees of assistance from external communist sources, primarily China and North Vietnam. In addition, communist Pathet Lao, North Vietnamese, and Cambodian military forces dominated Thailand's borders to the north, east, and southeast; Malayan Chinese communist terrorists held sway along the southern Thai frontier on the Malay Peninsula; and Burmese rebel groups, including some communists, moved freely on much of the western frontier. These circumstances led many observers to conclude that Thailand, too, would eventually succumb to communist insurgency and brought the much-debunked "domino theory" back to life in the perceptions of Thai and other noncommunist Southeast Asian leaders.[1] Most opponents of U.S. involvement in the Vietnam War derided this theory even though Vietnamese Communist Party doctrine had established this scenario in 1951 when the Vietnamese Party "reserve[d] the right to supervise the activities of [its] brother parties in Laos and Cambodia. . . ."[2]

The problem of communist insurgency was further complicated by the instability of internal Thai politics after the successful student uprising of October 1973 against the old military dictatorship. The Thai were trying to build a new, democratically oriented political system, but the period of transition was fraught with difficulties. Free parliamentary elections, for example, produced a plethora of new political parties and unstable coalition governments whose positions were increasingly undermined by political polarization between Left and Right. This polarization led to a coup in October 1976 that produced an ultraconservative government whose intention was to reestablish the "stability" of the pre–1973 political process with all the political power in the hands of the military and civilian bureaucrats. This government fell one year later, however, in another coup led by some of its own military leaders who realized that Thailand had no choice but to continue on the road to a more democratic political process. Partly as a result of the unstable political climate, the communist leaders of Vietnam, Laos, and Cambodia and their rival big-power backers, the Soviet Union and China, appeared to expect Thailand to fall. The Chinese government, for example, described the situation as "excellent."

In addition, the Soviet-assisted North Vietnamese and their Laotian allies tried to strengthen their influence over the communist insurgents in northeastern Thailand, while the Chinese, increasingly concerned about the close North Vietnamese ties to the Soviets, commanded a stronger influence among the Meo and other insurgents among the hill tribes in northern Thailand. The Chinese and Soviets were also simultaneously vying with each other in efforts to woo leftist elements among the student population of Bangkok as well as to cultivate relations with the established Thai government.

Nevertheless, the Thai "domino" never fell. Indeed, by 1985, the Thai Communist Party and its insurgent forces were reduced to no more than nuisance status. What happened? This paper will address the Thai experience with communist insurgency using the elements of the Manwaring paradigm for low-intensity conflict (LIC): organization, military and other support to a targeted government, intelligence, discipline and capabilities of the armed forces, reduction of outside aid to the insurgents, and legitimacy.[3] Application of this paradigm, however, requires some preliminary history of the nature of communist insurgency in Thailand.

The History and Nature of
Communist Insurgency in Thailand

History

Although armed communist insurgency in Thailand appeared first in 1965, communist political activity and influence were introduced into the country as early as the middle and late 1920s, primarily among Thailand's Vietnamese and Chinese ethnic minorities. In 1928, Vietnamese communist leader Ho Chi Minh began organizing Vietnamese communities in Thailand to support his revolutionary movement in French Indochina. These efforts were the beginning of the Indochinese Communist Party, which was formed in 1930.[4]

For their part, Chinese communists had been active in Thailand since the mid–1920s, their activities initially being restricted largely to the "overseas Chinese" community. Then, after the start of World War II in Asia, the Chinese Communist Party (CCP) in December 1942 organized a branch in Thailand, which set up a "Thai Section" to carry on propaganda and organizational work among Thai nationals of Chinese descent and others. The Chinese branch party largely dominated the communist movement in Thailand until October 1946, when the repeal of the Thai government's Anti-Communist Act of 1933 (the price for obtaining Soviet acceptance of Thailand's admission to the United Nations) prompted the formation of a separate Thai party. This party initially called itself the Thai Communist Party but changed its name to the Communist Party of Thailand (CPT) in 1952.[5]

As late as 1976, the CPT still depended on the leadership of the same fifty-five Sino-Thai members who had formed the Central Committee in 1952. The party drew its ideological inspiration from both Chinese and Vietnamese sources, however. Although the CPT decided as early as 1952 that it must adopt armed struggle and go to the jungle, the communist movement in Thailand remained essentially urban-oriented until the early 1960s.[6] Then, however, the emphasis began to shift, and the first armed clash between communist insurgents and government forces occurred in August 1965 in northeastern Thailand. Thereafter, the number of insurgents and the frequency of armed clashes and assassinations of local government officials and villagers grew slowly but steadily in various parts of Thailand, with the CPT finally declaring itself at the end of 1966 to be the manager of the revolution in the countryside.[7]

The Geography of the Insurgency

Armed insurgents in northern Thailand numbered approximately 2,800 in 1976 and were located primarily in the provinces of Chiang Rai, Nan, Uttaradit, and Phitsanulok, along the Thai-Lao border. Most of the insurgents were from the local hill tribes; however, according to Thai sources, there were at least 150 to 200 former Chinese People's Liberation Army (PLA) troops of hill tribe descent who infiltrated from southern China as a unit in 1971 and were subsequently ordered to remain permanently in northern Thailand.[8] Although the insurgency in the north was as much an ethnic rebellion as a communist-inspired "people's war," it was led primarily by Sino-Thai or Thai communist political cadre.[9]

The communist-led insurgency in the border region of northeastern Thailand had the most potential. It had a relatively high degree of political organization and orientation, with the most organized area in Na Kae District of Nakhon Phanom Province. The primary insurgent bases were in the Phu Phan mountains in Nakhon Phanom and Sakon Phanom provinces. Armed insurgents also operated in Loei, Ubon Ratchathani, Kalasin, Udon Thani, and Nong Khai provinces. In 1975, their overall number throughout the northeast was approximately three thousand, including village militia, not all of whom were necessarily armed.[10]

The insurgency in the northeast also had some ethnic orientation. The predominantly Lao ethnic population in all of the Mekong River border provinces adjoining Laos provided a base for irredentism and hence a potential cause that the communists could exploit with the objective of detaching the Lao portions of the northeast from Thai rule.

The insurgency in southern Thailand was the most enigmatic in that it involved bandits, separatists, and communists. The known communists fell into two categories: those under the leadership of the CPT and another group identified with the Communist Terrorist Organization (CTO). In 1975, the CPT commanded some fifteen hundred armed insurgents operating primarily in the midsouthern provinces of Surat Thani, Nakhon Si Thammarat, Krabi, Trang, and Prachuap Khiri Khan.[11] Unlike the CPT, the CTO was composed primarily of Malaysian Chinese communist guerrillas driven across the Thai border from Malaysia during the emergency crackdown in the 1950s, and its activities were largely oriented toward Malaysia. These guerrillas numbered approximately fifteen hundred.

In central Thailand, communist insurgency never presented a serious problem. As of 1975, there were fewer than 100 known armed communist insurgents in the entire area surrounding and immediately north of Bangkok. The city of Bangkok itself, however, always had the potential to become a hotbed of communist activity far more serious than even the insurgency in the northeast.

The Causes of Insurgency

The basic causes of communist insurgency in rural Thailand included limited access by the rural population to substantive political participation; restricted social mobility; the gap between popular expectations and government performance in providing improved conditions; economic disparities and inequality of opportunity; corruption in both the governmental and commercial sectors; poor treatment of villagers by some government officials; and ethnic, land, and citizenship anomalies.[12]

By contrast, the insurgents in the northeast offered those who were willing to become communist adherents an active part in decision making at the local level and new opportunities for attaining leadership roles. Their sophisticated social-political organization provided opportunities for exceptionally broad peasant participation, social mobility, and status achievement.[13]

Whatever the underlying causes of social discontent in the different regions of Thailand, however, there had been in the past a remarkable absence of active antigovernment opposition in rural Thailand. This absence clearly indicated—as Roger Darling pointed out—that the insurgency was not a spontaneous uprising by an outraged constituency protesting its dissatisfaction over nondevelopment and neglect, but rather the consequence of some elements "of a generally unproductive rural citizenry" having been "awakened to a new view of a deficient condition." The agency of this awakening in those areas where the communists had influence, Darling stated, was a leadership skillful in "manipulating causes" to the point where:

> . . . adherents [had] come to accept the credibility of the [Chinese Communist] idea of "putting a new man on earth," of the peasant's role in society, and [of] the injustice of contemporary governmental systems as explained in Communist terms of contradiction.[14]

Communist Resources

Although the communists—aided by the mistakes and ineptitude of the military-dominated regimes of the 1960s—managed to increase their manpower and even to score some substantial military successes, these gains would have been impossible if they had not received significant external support. This support came in various forms. For its initial conceptualization and subsequent ideological and strategic guidance, the CPT relied primarily on the Chinese Communist Party model of revolution.

There appear to have been several external support systems backing up the Thai insurgency. According to Somchai Rakwijit, the Chinese ran one system out of the southern Chinese province of Yunnan to support the hill tribe insurgency in northern Thailand and another through Hong Kong to channel financial support to the CPT Central Committee in Bangkok. A third support system, primarily North Vietnamese-run, moved weapons and ammunition into northern and northeastern Thailand via Laos.[15]

The Failure of Communist Insurgency in Thailand: The Manwaring Paradigm

Communist-led insurgency failed in Thailand for many of the reasons explained by the Manwaring paradigm. All six elements of the paradigm came together during the decade after the collapse of the U.S. effort to prevent a communist victory in Vietnam—yet the Thai and U.S. government counterinsurgency agencies involved were able to have a significant effect on only three: organization, external support to the targeted government, and intelligence.

Organization

The Thai government in 1965 established the Communist Suppression Operations Command (CSOC) to coordinate and support all counterinsurgency political and military operations. CSOC combined civilian, military, and police agencies' staffing at all levels. It was responsible for "providing guidance, policy, and support for all Civil-Police-Military (CPM) programmes particularly in the field of civic action, psychological operations and security."[16]

The Thai counterinsurgency doctrine addressed the insurgency in three different dimensions: political (essentially good government administration), basic police operations (including intelligence for dealing with the CPT's organizational structure and personnel), and military operations against armed insurgent groups. Direct military operations were not the primary focus. Rather, the objective was to win over the people by responding to their needs with good government, development projects, and effective police support for basic law and order, with the army ready to act as a reaction force and conduct operations as requested by the civilian authorities.[17]

An Operations and Coordination Centre (OCC) handled day-to-day operations while different committees—civil, psychological operations, intelligence, and so forth—"serve[d] to coordinate the activities of their respective independent civil, police, and military units, and present[ed] advice on their areas of responsibility to the CSOC Commander." In June 1974, in response to adverse public criticism of the CSOC's alleged narrow focus on "suppression," it became the Internal Security Operations Command (ISOC).[18]

The more important Thai counterinsurgency programs included efforts to improve rural infrastructure (rural roads, potable water systems, schools) under the Accelerated Rural Development Program (ARD), the training of district officers at the Nai Amphur Academy under the direction of the Department of Local Administration (DOLA), and to some extent the Self Defence Volunteer Programme.[19] The last program had two objectives: to train and advise villagers so that they could improve their lives politically, economically, and socially, and to ensure that villagers received the training and capability to defend their own communities.[20]

Despite the impressive organizational structure and a basically sound counterinsurgency or CI doctrine, the record clearly shows that CSOC never attained the capacity to command and control CI planning and operations intended by its founders. From its organization in 1965 through at least the early 1980s, CSOC was unable to "coordinate" the Royal Thai Army (RTA) or any other military branch, the Ministry of Interior (police and the DOLA), the Ministry of Agriculture, or other competitors for power and resources in the CI arena.

The U.S. perception of the flaws in Thai counterinsurgency effort were enumerated in November 1972:

- CSOC has no command responsibility; the RTA will not accept such a role for CSOC;
- The Thai National Police Department is incapable of providing law and order in the countryside and is rife with corruption;
- The RTA is incapable of pursuing the CT (communist terrorists) and conducting sustained operations and consolidating such successes as they do achieve;
- Intelligence is uncoordinated and not targeted on the CT;
- Organizations created to foster coordination among the Royal Thai Government (RTG) agencies in rural development instead compete with regular ministries;
- The RTG has no national psychological operations (psyops) effort to try to win over the people;

- There is no set of agreed priorities for allocating personnel, training, and other resources for CI; and,
- Leadership is very weak at all levels of government.[21]

A CSOC RTA general in a briefing for the U.S. ambassador on 13 November 1972 confirmed some of this critique. General Surikij observed:

> CSOC can't be a second government. It can't allocate resources. It can't plan. . . . The army (RTA) plans and each other government agency plans and contributes resources to CI according to *their* individual plans. All CSOC can do is try to act as a coordinating body.[22]

General Saiyud Kherdphol, who commanded CSOC and ISOC throughout the 1970s, provided another candid assessment in a document (circa 1975) entitled "A Blue Print for Reform":

> Perhaps the greatest drawback in the government's response to the insurgent threat has been its failure to recognize the basic political nature and seriousness of the struggle. This has been manifest in the direction and control of government internal security plans and operations, which have invariably been the responsibility of military staff officers and bureaucrats, operating under the aegis of the Internal Security Operations Command (ISOC). . . . Some civil and police services have occasionally withheld their full support, leaving it to the military services to staff ISOC and policies and operations, which they (the civil service, the police, and to lesser extent, the army) thereupon have failed to carry out, mainly because no one was willing or able to force them to do so.[23]

Although the Thai can be given some credit for trying to provide organizational coherence through CSOC and ISOC, this dimension of the Manwaring paradigm was not a major factor in the demise of communist-led insurgency in Thailand.

U.S. Military and Economic Support

Manwaring suggests that "the best possible use of 'foreign' military personnel in a Third World internal conflict is one variation or another in the relatively unobtrusive 'train the trainer' role." Moreover, "all support—military, economic, or political—to a target government must be consistent to be really effective."[24]

The United States tried to contribute to the Thai CI effort by providing economic and military assistance in support of the CI program and by trying to maintain a close relationship with planning and operations in CSOC through the joint U.S.-Thai Counterinsurgency Committee (CIC). It is difficult, however, to measure the impact of this support because throughout the CI effort from the 1960s to the 1980s, the Thai seemed always to have a different perception of the nature of the threat and a commitment to retain control of whatever CI program emerged from any joint U.S.-Thai planning. If anything, the U.S.-Thai relationship on CI issues was either strained or characterized by considerable mutual toleration of the other's "weaknesses" while each tried to cooperate on the margins.

Robert Muscat calculated that Agency for International Development (AID) and Thai government counterpart funding for security projects between 1960 and 1974 totalled $131 million, while socioeconomic and administrative projects received $223.8 million.[25] He notes that J. Alexander Caldwell, by drawing on the individual project narratives, "came up with a figure of 55 percent ($141 million) of the total gross obligations from 1965 to 1970 ($257 million) as devoted 'specifically for counterinsurgency purposes.'"[26]

The United States provided considerable support to two projects in particular: Mobile Development Units (MDU) and Accelerated Rural Development (ARD). MDUs were civic action teams of up to 120 military and civilian officials whose purpose was to demonstrate RTG interest in those rural areas where the insurgents had made normal government presence dangerous. This program eventually died for lack of Thai government financial and personnel support.

The largest single element in the history of the AID program in Thailand went to the ARD project. This Thai initiative was inspired by Prime Minister Sarit Thanarat in 1962. This effort also focused on rural infrastructure but had a decentralization aspect because projects were carried out directly by provincial authorities. Between 1964 and 1977, AID put $75.3 million into this program. This aid purchased construction equipment, trained Thai engineers, and supported planning and management programs at provincial level. ARD began with a staff of 65 and grew to a 10,000-person organization. AID trained the entire core staff of 101 and provided 40 percent of total funding to the RTG's 60 percent.[27] Although it was unlikely ARD would ever have grown without U.S. aid, the Thai retained effective control over all aspects of the program.

Assistance to the DOLA in the Ministry of Interior was the third major area in the U.S. effort to support Thai programs to bring stability to insurgent-affected provinces by improving the relationship between the central government and the villagers. Caldwell and Muscat give this institution-building program high marks. Moreover, as noted above, the graduates of the Nai Amphur

Academy (district officers) helped serve the objectives of the ARD program.

It is not possible to assign a direct cause and effect relationship between U.S. assistance to Thai programs that may have had some impact on the insurgency. Many experts argue both ways, sometimes depending on their personal ideological predispositions.

As the chief of the research program in the United States Operations Mission (USOM) Program Office I was involved in the planning and evaluation of many of these aid programs. I believe that they helped expedite the Thai government's own efforts at least to compete with the insurgents. This presence helped reinforce the Thai villager's predisposition to favor the central government and possibly bought time for other factors in Thai culture, coupled with the impact of major external events, to cause the remission of communist insurgency in Thailand. This aid helped the Thai government in its nation-building and economic development effort.

The impact of other U.S. military, intelligence, and political support for the Thai counterinsurgency effort is easier to assess: It was marginal to nonexistent. The Thai organizational competition and conceptual disarray was paralleled on the U.S. side. Moreover, the U.S. interest in and commitment to the Thai CI effort were inconsistent throughout the relationship.

The U.S. Mission counterinsurgency support effort always seemed to include bureaucratic struggles between the various sections and agencies of the embassy, particularly in the sharing of information and intelligence on the insurgency or on the activities of different Thai government agencies.

From December 1972 through February 1973, the U.S. Mission worked on the Fiscal Year 1975 aid program. In a draft of the Mission Strategy Memorandum[28] connected with that effort, a section entitled "U.S. Program Deficiencies" noted:

> Perhaps the most serious weakness in the U.S. effort stems from the quality of U.S. advisory input, particularly in the field. The fact is that the skills required to advise Thai on counterinsurgency—including language, area knowledge and sufficient level in an advisory role to gain RTG confidence—are scarce and it has not been our policy to develop them or to encourage successful practitioners to stay indefinitely until the job is done.[29]

There is, in sum, little if any evidence that U.S. military, training, and advisory support to Thai counterinsurgency programs over the years was a decisive factor in the defeat of the insurgency. Moreover, the advisory effort was itself plagued by as many different views of the problem and proper remedies as there were advisers—*very* few of whom could even use the Thai language to find a hotel room, much less help government forces find insurgents in the jungle fringes.

This is not to say that U.S. support was of no value. Clearly, there were benefits at least in terms of buying time for the RTA to gain experience, for new district officers to have an impact, or for the external supporters in the communist world to pull the support lines to *their* comrades in the field.

Intelligence

Logic certainly supports Manwaring's contention that "If the appropriate intelligence apparatus and psychological instruments are not in place to find, eliminate, and discredit subversive actions, and revolutionaries are free to exploit societal and institutional weaknesses, history shows that a conflict will continue in one form or another indefinitely."[30]

U.S. and RTG officials always seemed to have differing perspectives on and priorities for the CI effort. Probably the most constant concern of the U.S. embassy's counterinsurgency committee was how to resolve the intelligence gap. The RTG did have functioning intelligence offices in all branches of the military, the police (Ministry of Interior), and the CSOC. The most impressive work, however, was that of the twelve-person team directed by Dr. Somchai Rakwijit under a contract with CSOC that began in 1971. This research project organized all existing knowledge and research on the insurgency, including more than forty-four hundred files on interrogations of captured insurgents and ralliers, all captured documents of the CPT, recordings of CPT radio broadcasts, foreign research on the Thai insurgency, and interviews with RTG interrogators and village informants. It also reinterviewed captured insurgents and ralliers with priority for the highest ranking and conducted extensive interviews of RTG officials at all levels and village leaders.

Somchai's research produced a study entitled *The Jungle Leads the Village,* a revised version of the RTG CI handbook, an interrogation handbook, and a computer program to organize all collected and future data. AID helped provide funding for translation of the study into English in 1973.

Unfortunately, Somchai's efforts were often in search of adequate funding and were not always appreciated by elements in the Thai bureaucracy outside of the CSOC command staff. Indeed, many officials resented some of Somchai's findings, particularly if they implied criticism of certain programs. During a USOM seminar in February 1973, for example, Somchai had criticized some aspects of the ARD program, particularly the emphasis on infrastructure projects with large expenditures on equipment.[31] Somchai's research had found that the most important concerns for villagers were basic social justice, honest government, and opportunities for personal advancement. He did not find evidence that the RTG's development and psyops programs were having much impact on the insurgents.

Somchai was a strong advocate for the principle of knowing your enemy. There is little question that his research provided his government with enough strategic intelligence and analysis to make judgments about the nature of the threat facing them. It was clear that the RTG did not face the type of threat posed by the Vietcong in Vietnam. In retrospect, it may very well have been that the Thai authorities did know their enemy better than the U.S. experts did, a possibility that explains why their priorities seemed less intense than we thought advisable.

In the end, the RTG had enough intelligence to deal with the threat they faced. Communist weaknesses in recruitment and retainment of quality cadre, however, contributed to the RTG's intelligence successes at least as much as the organization and quality of the intelligence effort.

Discipline and Capabilities of the Armed Forces

Manwaring's next element calls for a "well disciplined, highly professional, motivated security force, capable of rapid and decisive actions designed to achieve political and psychological, as well as military objectives."[32] The evidence does not show that Thai security forces ever attained this ideal.

In the early years, the army's approach totally ignored the established Civil-Police-Military Programmes (CPM) concept. In a 1977 speech to the Ninth Special Forces Seminar in Bangkok, General Saiyud attributed the origin of CSOC's limited capacity as an administrative, planning, and coordinating agency to late 1967, when the RTA:

> suddenly and unexpectedly was ordered to take over operational responsibility for counterinsurgency from CSOC. At the same time, the Second Army (in the Northeast) was ordered to take over CSOC's CPM Advanced Headquarters for the Northeast at Sakon Nakhon. From that moment, the emphasis shifted towards military operations of the Vietnam type. As a result, the whole village security programme in

eleven target areas in seven provinces, covering 200 villages, was neglected. . . . This blunder was finally recognized . . . later in 1971 when the number of communists in the Northeast had increased to over 2000.[33]

The RTA returned to CSOC's CPM approach between 1971 and the student uprising in 1973. During this period, CSOC was also able to begin the Volunteer and Self Development Programme (known as Aw Paw Paw). Still, communist insurgents by early 1974 had reached 6,500—2,400 in the northeast, 2,100 in the north, 400 in the central region, and 1,600 in the midsouth. From October 1973 to October 1976, while Thai government and military leaders were trying to establish the new democracy, RTA and CSOC operations against the insurgency were unable to contain the growth of the insurgent forces. They reached 9,000 by the end of 1976—4,000 in the northeast, 2,800 in the north, 1,800 in the midsouth, and still 400 in the central region.[34]

The ineffectiveness of the RTA was apparent enough to have once even caused the king to challenge an RTA assertion that during Operation Phu Kuang in 1972 they were facing a thousand insurgents armed with AK–47s. His Majesty reportedly "read the riot act to General Surikij and other commanders after examining the spent cartridges of the insurgents. . . . He told them that groups of 10 insurgents were holding off RTA companies and changing their positions frequently to make the RTA think they were facing large numbers of 'CT'(communist terrorists as the RTG referred to the insurgents)."[35]

My own journal on 14 January 1973 contained a brief list of "notes on the insurgency" that suggest how wide the gap might have been between Manwaring's criteria and the actual performance of the RTA:

- Contractors in Nan and Tak provinces, with full RTG knowledge and acceptance, continue to negotiate with the CT for permission to continue road construction through CT "controlled" areas;
- The RTA in northern Thailand took no action against three CT base camps that had been found by Thai Long-Range Reconnaissance Patrols;
- The RTA's Joint Training Exercise (JTX) #16 has switched from a policy of military offense to containment of CT in the Tri Province area around Hin Long Khla; and,
- A CT attack on a district town in Na Kae Province and twenty-four assassinations in November 1972 (compared to eleven in October) have lowered RTG morale in the northeast.

The performance of the RTA on JTX 16 was particularly telling. This operation was supposed to be a major counterinsurgency operation, not a training exercise. RTG budget allocations for CI operations were so limited that training funds had to be used, with operations therefore designated as training exercises. One RTA general officer, according to the U.S. consul's report, said "CT body counts are less important than friendly count." The U.S. consul interpreted this statement to mean that the RTA's aim was "not to kill CT but to get them to rally on the assumption that they are only misguided." Other observers reported that orders had gone out not to take heavy casualties in CI operations—hence the switch from offense to containment. RTA casualties were too politically costly.[36]

Even in 1980, after fifteen years of communist military activity and more than twenty years after the establishment of the CPT, the RTA had hardly begun to approach Manwaring's criteria. In a February 1980 speech to the Bangkok Rotary Club, Saiyud noted that the spread of subversion had reached the majority of Thailand's provinces. He concluded that:

> The government's response to armed insurgency, which first broke out in 1965, has been an American-supported doctrine of resource allocation to rural areas coupled with integrated civil, military, and police operations. But the results have not been entirely successful. Resources have often been misapplied and there has been an inability on the part of vertically oriented government agencies to coordinate the counterinsurgency effort.[37]

Although the discipline and capabilities of the Thai armed forces never reached the Manwaring standards across the board, there were successes. In 1979, the RTA decidedly crushed the major communist base of Khao Khor and followed this with a highly successful operation against insurgents in the Banthat Mountains in central-southern Thailand.[38] The RTA's performance continued to improve in the 1980s, along with a new government amnesty policy established in 1978–79 aimed at students who had fled to the jungle in 1976. The amnesty policy led to the return of several leading personalities in 1979–1981, including former student leader Seksan Praseartkul. Mass defections began in 1982. The RTA claimed total victory in October 1983 after destroying all major insurgent bases. By 1984 the insurgents reportedly totalled less than two thousand—a remarkable decline from the level of nearly ten thousand in 1979.[39]

Nonetheless, the overall performance of RTA and other RTG counterinsurgent forces never reached the standard set by

Manwaring. Perhaps, as in other parts of the paradigm, the real nature of the communist threat did not require such high performance standards.

Reduction of Outside Aid to the Insurgents

There is no question that this dimension of the Manwaring paradigm was a major factor in the demise of the insurgency in Thailand. Nevertheless, this reduction of support was due far more to external political factors in Southeast Asia—including decisions made in Beijing and Hanoi—than to successful interdiction by the RTG's security forces.

The death of Mao Zedong set in motion a series of events that finally led to the cessation of Chinese material, organizational, and propaganda support for the CPT. As the Chinese government broadened its ties to Western governments to gain access to technology and aid, it lessened its active support for insurgents throughout Southeast Asia. It also wanted closer ties to the governments in this region. Finally, Vietnam's alliance with the Soviets, coupled with the Vietnamese invasion of Cambodia, demanded full Chinese cooperation with its Southeast Asian neighbors to contain Soviet-Vietnamese influence. These efforts to improve relations with other Asian countries were paralleled by a reduction in ties to insurgent movements in the region.[40]

The notable exception was China's massive aid to the Khmer Rouge forces, who were resisting the consolidation of Vietnamese power in Cambodia. For this effort, the Chinese needed the cooperation of the Thai government. This consideration was so vital that it overrode support for the Thai insurgents, even though the CPT had finally papered over its internal differences to take the Chinese side in opposition to Vietnamese control in Cambodia.

William K. Heaton neatly summarizes the remarkable decline in the CPT's fortunes:

[T]he CPT in 1975 was unified and self confident and had both Beijing's and Hanoi's support. By 1981 it was split, pessimistic about the future, and had diverged from both Hanoi and Beijing. It was seeking to negotiate a truce—most likely at Beijing's urging—with the central government but with little success. . . . Not only did China repeatedly express . . . support for Thailand in the latter's dispute with Hanoi, but openly supported the government of Prime Minister Prem Tinsulanon during the April 1981 coup attempt. . . .Thus, China increasingly demonstrated support for the Thai government and lack of interest in the CPT, a policy that had a decisive impact on the CPT.[41]

The Vietnamese were in no position to replace the Chinese support. They were bogged down in Cambodia, and the spectacle of communist warfare in that country would be even more politically damaging for the CPT among the Thai.

Legitimacy

As Manwaring contends, legitimacy is the most important single dimension in a war against subversion:

> The thrust of a revolutionary program relies on grievances such as political, social, and economic discrimination as the means through which the government is attacked. This is the essential nature of the threat from an insurgency, and it is here that a response must begin. A campaign that fails to understand this and responds only to enemy military forces is likely to fail.[42]

The cultural environment. Certain values and patterns of behavior that the communists could not "delegitimize" or otherwise overcome actually helped prevent the insurgents from gaining the momentum they needed before the government could mount its own counterinsurgency effort. The Thai cultural environment was notably resistant to communist efforts to mobilize a militant following—just as it, for that matter, impeded the efforts of Thai leaders to build a more broadly based system of parliamentary democracy.

Thai traditional political culture includes a general attitude of deference toward central government authority. The Thai peasant villager has traditionally regarded political matters as the business of the central government, viewing himself as a "phuunooj"—a little person without power and unable to initiate political action, especially action against the government.[43]

Deference to central government authority is closely related to the absence of a tradition of village-level political organization and involvement. The Thai village has never had an autonomous political structure of its own comparable to that of its Vietnamese counterpart, which traditionally had its own village council, tax register, and communal land.[44]

The lack of a tradition of local political participation in Thailand also stems in part from the strength of Thai individualism and from a social system whose functioning "is ultimately dependent on 'the quid-pro-quo nature' of Thai social relationships."[45] The Thai villager is jealous of his individual freedom, and when he enters into relationships with others and does things for them, he does so in the conscious expectation that they will respond in kind. When they do not do so, he feels free to terminate the relationship at any time. This trait does not make for stable political group affiliations of the type a strong insurgency network—or a political party—demands.

Thai Buddhism also impeded communist mobilization efforts. Thai Buddhist philosophy has traditionally stressed personal contemplation and detachment from mundane affairs rather than social-political activism. Thai Buddhism teaches that the ultimate goal of life is the attainment of nirvana, a state of spiritual perfection that can be achieved only through the personal acquisition of wisdom. Thus, it is a religion that did not provide a motivating force for social or political revolution, particularly in more tradition-oriented rural areas.

A democratic alternative. The second major legitimizing factor in favor of the Thai government was the unexpected success of the 1973 student uprising and the impact it had on the Thai political process. The fall of the Thanom-Praphass government in 1973 created an opportunity for new—and some old—political leaders to lay the foundations of a democratic parliamentary system of government that could provide a viable and more attractive alternative to the communists' blueprint for a violent revolution. A political process that permitted and encouraged many political parties to engage in open, legal competition for power on the basis of popular balloting directly undermined one of the communists' major propaganda themes—that the Thai government was undemocratic and illegal.

The post–1973 political process in Thailand was no longer the exclusive preserve of the elite. The old cliques of the Thanom era could no longer rule Thailand or dominate parliament on their own terms, although some elements thereof never stopped trying.

Such an attempt was the coup on 6 October 1976. This coup was an effort by the remnants of the Thanom-Praphass era to turn the clock back. Fortunately, the adverse trends set in motion by the 6 October 1976 coup were stopped short of full fruition after one year by a second coup on 20 October 1977. The second coup's leader, General Kriangsak Chomanon, had become concerned about the repressive policies of the government and rejected the Kraivichien government's twelve-year timetable for a return to democracy as "unrealistic and dangerous."[46]

Despite the apparent political instability, the general objective of all these changes was to find a more representative political system that would expand political participation and stimulate economic progress. There was no evidence that rejected leftists were effectively attracted by communist ideology, organization, and discipline. Though some student leaders fled to Laos after the 1976 coup, they had all returned by 1982 in response to an amnesty offered by the leaders of the

1977 coup. The liberal and leftist parties still enjoyed considerably greater opportunity to develop power bases among the people than they did under the pre–1973 political system. Thus, there is no question that democratically oriented objectives were being achieved. By the end of the 1980s Thailand had become one of the most successful newly industrializing countries (NICs) and had the freest political process in Southeast Asia.

The role of the king. The third—but no less important—factor working for the government in the contest for "hearts and minds" was His Majesty the King. Moreover, in this case the king was much more than a traditional institution. King Bhumibol Adunyadej is a special man. He is an active participant in the political process. Indeed, were it not for this king and the reverence in which he and the institution are held, the 1973 student uprising could very well have been the beginning of an era of violence and political disintegration in Thailand.

During the months of student activism before October 1973, the king was known to be sympathetic to their cause: democratization of the political process. He also, however, represented Thai tradition and opposed violence. Both the students and the military leaders still looked to the king—indeed, even vied—for his legitimizing support. In the end the king played the key mediating role because he retained the respect of both sides.

A fundamental fact of political life in Thailand is that no political leader or political force can hope to gain or hold power without at least the implicit—yet widely recognized—support of the king. For the Thai masses, the king is the key legitimizing force. The Thai Communist Party and its insurgents relied on Mao Zedong and Ho Chi Minh. They were always seen as threats to the king—and therefore the kingdom of Thailand. The king had always been at the apex of political leadership in Thailand and remains the single most widely accepted manifestation of the Thai nation.

The consequences of communist victory in Indochina. Perhaps one of the greatest ironies of the success of communist political warfare in Vietnam, Laos, and Cambodia was its delegitimizing impact elsewhere in Southeast Asia, especially Thailand. The aftermath of these victories exposed for all to see that the communists could not live up to their own promises for economic well-being, peace, equality, honesty in government, and justice. The Vietnamese communists who captured the nationalist banner in their struggle against the French and who for so long had used the promises of democracy, good government, and justice instead brought economic disaster, more violence, no justice, and death. Worst of all for their comrades in

Thailand, communist victory in Indochina initiated an endless stream of hundreds of thousands of refugees who would rather face death in the South China Sea or by Thai pirates than live one more day under the new governments in Vietnam, Cambodia, and (to a lesser extent) Laos.

The refugees from Indochina, the Thai intellectuals' experience with communist rule in Laos, the continuing warfare in Cambodia, and the increasing evidence of economic failure and political repression in Vietnam all combined to *delegitimize* the communist cause in Thailand. Whatever the continuing weaknesses of the Thai political process, including especially the weakened but still strong influence of traditional Thai political leaders and bureaucrats, the RTG and the existing political process actually regained some legitimacy in the eyes of many of its strongest critics.

Communist Weaknesses

Finally, in addition to the impact of the paradigm's six dimensions on the communist insurgency in Thailand, the Communist Party itself suffered from certain internal weaknesses. These need to be addressed in this analysis because they help to explain how the Thai could appear to have dealt so effectively with the insurgency even though performance on all of the six dimensions of the Manwaring paradigm fell short of the standard required.

Lack of Ethnic Thai Cadre

The most important of these weaknesses was the inability of the Communist Party to recruit an adequate body of rural political cadres from among the ethnic Thai. This weakness was directly related to the generally apolitical cast of rural Thai society, particularly the absence in the rural areas of a dissatisfied and politically conscious intellectual stratum from which the communists could draw key organizational cadres as they were able to do in Vietnam.

Moreover, few CPT cadres or, for that matter, communist sympathizers among Thai academics and intellectuals have relished the thought of life in the jungles or rice paddies of rural Thailand. Indeed, many Thai communist leaders, as well as other dissidents among the intellectual and political elite, preferred exile in Paris or in China to life in the Meo hill tribe country of the north and northeast. Dr. Somchai Rakwijit attributed the CPT's lack of cadres qualified to carry on mass mobilization work and guerrilla operations in the countryside directly to the cadres' reluctance ". . . to desert their easy livelihood and careers in town for the hardships of living in the rural areas."[47]

The CPT's Strategy and Tactics

Perhaps the CPT's second most important handicap was the party's revolutionary strategy and tactical line. The seizure of power by violent revolution against "feudalism," monopoly capitalism, and "imperialism" for the eventual installation of a "people's democracy" was not an effective rallying cry because these goals were not relevant to the value structure or actual political situation in Thailand. Thai Buddhism generally ties the society together and works against violence-oriented, uncompromising political creeds. In addition, the profound loyalty of the vast majority of Thai to the monarchy, particularly the current king, deprived the communists of a nationalist cause. Whatever the communists may have claimed, Thailand was never a colonized country; nor has any government—much less any since 1973—ever been either feudalistic or a harsh, fascist dictatorship.

Chinese and Vietnamese Links

A third and particularly exploitable weakness lay in the CPT's ties with the Chinese and Vietnamese communists. These external linkages belied the party's claim that it stood for Thai nationalism and that its interests were coincident with those of the nation. An additional drawback, in the eyes of the ethnic Thai majority, was the CPT's alliance with rebellious non-Thai in the northeast, where the communists tried to base some of their appeal on the ethnic Lao character of the population.

From the ethnic standpoint, the makeup of the CPT leadership itself was another handicap. At least through the 1970s, the members of the party's top echelon as well as its leading cadres were predominantly Chinese or Sino-Thai. As indicated earlier, the CPT had not been able to recruit large numbers from among the ethnic Thai. Moreover, the party failed to produce a Thai equivalent of Vietnam's "Uncle Ho" who might have won the sympathy and support of many noncommunist Thai.

The Support Base

The communists' internal resource mobilization process remained subject to a fundamental weakness: it rested on a peasant base that was generally less committed and disciplined than the core groups of communist adherents. As we have seen, the behavioral patterns and attitudes of the Thai peasant, heavily influenced by Thai Buddhism, were not conducive to clandestine, rigorous, and sustained commitment and effort to achieve transcendent, long-term goals. The villager remained more concerned with his subsistence-level existence than with social movements or causes that he did not perceive as bringing about an immediate improvement in his personal well-being. Thus, the villagers who had to be relied upon to support the insurgents with food, money, and shelter did not actually provide a reliable and stable support base.

This weakness was further aggravated by the Thai villager's strong individualism and his propensity to break off a relationship whenever he feels that it no longer serves him. The communists had long had problems with rural recruits, and even with cadres, who deserted from the insurgents' jungle strongholds for such reasons as personal disagreement with a group leader, restrictions on love life, or merely the hardships of life in the jungle, which is simply not "sanuk" (fun)—something that the Thai value very highly.

Conclusion

This chapter has placed considerable emphasis on the role Thai political, religious, and social culture played in the ultimate failure of communist insurgency in Thailand. Thai culture gave the Thai government—and the emerging new political process—a legitimacy that the communists were never able to challenge effectively. The importance of this culture has been demonstrated by the fact that the communists were never able to capitalize on the new correlation of forces that appeared to create so many opportunities for them in the 1974–1979 period. One conclusion that seems warranted by the evidence is that a communist insurgency in Thailand drawing almost exclusively on an indigenous resource base and receiving little more than propaganda and limited material support from outside sources would always have posed little threat to the Thai body politic. There is much to suggest that the CPT, given its internal weaknesses, was far more dependent on outside communist support than most other communist insurgencies or movements in Asia. If this judgment is correct, the final answer to the question of whether or not the communist insurgency in Thailand would succeed or fail appeared to depend as much on the intentions and capacities of Hanoi, and possibly of Peking and Moscow as well, as it ever did on the intentions and ambitions of the CPT.

An important question in retrospect is what were the real intentions of Hanoi before the new insurgency in Cambodia became the overriding priority. Did Hanoi really want to effect a communist takeover of Thailand or of parts of Thailand? Or did it merely want to keep Thailand in a position where it could not challenge Hanoi's pretensions to a dominant position in Southeast Asia?

The answers may be irrelevant today. If there is indeed a new "domino theory" at work in Asia today, the ones that are falling are the dominoes the communists built themselves—based on clever propaganda, deceit, violence, noble-sounding promises that drew on the appeal of Western democratic values, and exploitation of others' wealth rather than creation of their own.

Notes

1. Louis E. Lomax, in his *Thailand: The War That Is, The War That Will Be* (New York: Vintage Books, 1967), was among the first to suggest that Thailand was "another Vietnam in the making," but he was joined by others during the mid-1970s.

2. Arthur J. Dommen, *Conflict in Laos* (New York: Praeger, 1964), p. 72.

3. Max G. Manwaring, "Toward an Understanding of Insurgency Wars: The Paradigm," in Max G. Manwaring, ed., *Uncomfortable Wars: Toward a New Paradigm of Low Intensity Conflict* (Boulder: Westview Press, 1991). My analysis also draws on a previous article of mine that appeared in *Problems of Communism* in 1976. By coincidence, that article addressed the Thai insurgency using several of the elements in the Manwaring paradigm—in particular, the impact of legitimacy issues for both the government and the insurgents, external support for the insurgents, and an aspect not addressed by Manwaring—the impact of insurgent weaknesses. See Robert F. Zimmerman, "Insurgency in Thailand," *Problems of Communism* 25 (May–June 1976): 18–39.

4. Communist Suppression Operations Command, Royal Thai Government, *Communist Insurgency in Thailand* (White Paper), Bangkok, 1973, pp. 1–2. (Henceforth cited as White Paper.)

5. Ibid., p. 3.

6. This decision was taken after the Phibun Songgram government intensified repressive action against the communists, including mass arrests of alleged party members in Bangkok. The party then decided to spread its cadres out into the rural areas and establish a "Thai Liberation Organization" to prepare for armed struggle. See Donald P. Weatherbee, *The United Front in Thailand: A Documentary Analysis* (Columbia, S.C.: University of South Carolina Press, 1970), p. 61; and White Paper, pp. 3–4.

7. Weatherbee, *United Front*, p. 62. This monograph provides an excellent historical survey of the communist movement in Thailand.

8. See White Paper, Annex A: "Case History of PLA Defector," p. 41.

9. Somchai Rakwijit, *The Jungle Leads the Village*, trans. Ms. Race Chumsri, ed. Robert F. Zimmerman, Chief, Research and Evaluation Staff, USOM, Thailand, March 1974, p. 229. This report was prepared under the auspices of the Thai government's Communist Suppression Operations Command (CSOC) and contains a series of case studies on CPT operations in various parts of Thailand. It remains probably the most detailed analysis ever made of the communist political process in Thailand. See also "How the Communists Get Their Support," *Bangkok Post*, 6 April 1975.

10. George K. Tanham, *Trial in Thailand* (New York: Crane-Russak Co., 1975), p. 57.

11. Theh Chongkhadij, "Surat Thani, Where It's 'Just Like Vietnam,'" *Bangkok Post*, 11 November 1975.

12. Roger Darling, *Analysis of the Insurgency in Thailand and U.S./Royal Thai Government Counterinsurgency Strategy and Programs*, as summarized and interpreted in a separate unclassified report by Robert F. Zimmerman, USOM Research Office, Bangkok, 1973, pp. 4–5.

13. See Somchai Rakwijit, *The Jungle Leads*, pp. 14–221, for an illuminating description of this organizational structure and process.

14. Darling, *Analysis*, p. 3. It is important for the reader to bear in mind that the process described applied primarily or perhaps only to communist insurgent adherents—those who became active party members and fighters—and not to mere village supporters.

15. "How the Communists Get Their Support," *Bangkok Post*, 6 April 1975, p. 11.

16. Gen. Saiyud Kherdphol (Ret.), *The Struggle for Thailand: Counterinsurgency 1965–1985* (Bangkok: S. Research Co., Ltd., 1986), p. 29.

17. Ibid., p. 43.

18. Many observers, including General Saiyud, believe that this anti-CSOC campaign was a rare example of effective CPT "psyops" or psychological operations. The campaign's objective was the elimination of CSOC, but its only achievement was the name change.

19. For an extensive description and general evaluation of these programs and the U.S. contribution to them see Robert J. Muscat, *Thailand and the United States: Development, Security and Foreign Aid* (New York: Columbia University Press, 1990), pp. 147–184.

20. Saiyud, *Struggle*, p. 85.

21. Robert F. Zimmerman, personal journal notes dated 25 November 1972, Bangkok, Thailand. At the time I served as one of the Agency for International Development (AID) representatives on the Mission Counterinsurgency Committee.

22. Ibid., 16 November 1972.

23. Saiyud, *Struggle*, pp. 227–229.

24. Manwaring, *Uncomfortable Wars*, pp. 21–22.

25. Muscat, *Thailand and the United States*.

26. Ibid., pp. 158–159.

27. Ibid., p. 161.

28. Prepared under the direction of the Development and Security (D/S) Section.

29. The last four words of the first sentence should have been left out. The fact is that the U.S. advisory effort in the field was never intended to be extensive and in any event was tolerated at best by the Thai—as it properly should have been under the circumstances. Neither the RTG nor the United States would have gained from even the appearance of U.S. "direction" of Thai CI programs. My own feeling at the time was that the director of the D/S Section did not want to include himself within the meaning of the sentence—though many others in the Mission ardently so believed.

30. Manwaring, *Uncomfortable Wars*, p. 22.

31. The USOM Seminar Program was an attempt to engage Thai and U.S. officials and scholars in discussions of Thai political and administrative culture and patterns of action to understand their impact on implementation of assistance programs. A total of ten seminars were held over a two-year period in 1972–1973.

32. Manwaring, *Uncomfortable Wars*, p. 23.

33. Saiyud, *Struggle*, p. 116.

34. Ibid., pp. 118–120.

35. Zimmerman, journal entry of 16 December 1972. The source of this quote was an expatriate who was very well regarded within the RTG.

36. Zimmerman, journal entry of 17 February 1973.

37. Saiyud, *Struggle*, p. 153.

38. Ibid., p. 160.

39. Muscat, *Thailand and the United States*, p. 157.

40. William K. Heaton, "China and Southeast Asian Communist Movements: The Decline of Dual Track Diplomacy," *Asian Survey* 22, no. 8 (August 1982): 780.

41. Ibid., p. 786.

42. Manwaring, *Uncomfortable Wars*, p. 20.

43. See Herbert J. Rubin, "Will and Awe: Illustrations of Thai Villager Dependency upon Officials," *Journal of Asian Studies* (May 1973): 433; and Somchai Rakwijit, *Village Leadership in Northeast Thailand* (Bangkok: Military Research and Development Center, 1971), p. xxxii.

44. See R.B. Smith, "Thailand and Vietnam," *Journal of the Siam Society* (Bangkok, July 1972).

45. Herbert Phillips, *The Thai Peasant Personality* (Berkeley: University of California Press, 1975), p. 23.

46. During a private dinner with the author and Gen. Saiyud Kherdphol on 6 June 1977, General Kriangsak was surprisingly candid in stating his concerns that the Kraivichien government was actually playing into the hands of those leftists and communists who wanted to turn Thailand into a socialist state. He cited the flight of students to the jungle and to Laos.

47. Somchai Rakwijit, *Village Leadership*, p. xxxii.

GUATEMALA*

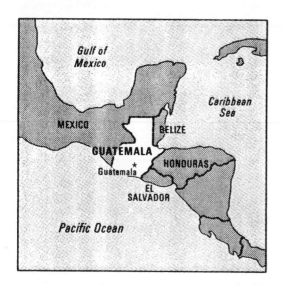

COUNTRY DATA

Area 42,000 sq. miles (about the size of Tennessee).
Capital Guatemala City (population 1.8 million).
Population 8.4 million (1986 est.).
Per Capita Income $1,000.
Ethnic Groups Ladino (Westernized), Indian.
Religions Roman Catholic, Protestant, traditional Mayan.
Literacy 48% of the population.
Work Force Agriculture 50%, Industry and commerce 27.1%, Services 12.1%, Construction, mining, and utilities 4.7%, other 6.1%.
Infant Mortality Rate 79 per 1,000 live births.
Life Expectancy 55 years, 44 years (Indian Population).
Government Constitutional.

UNIQUENESS OF CASE STUDY

A government that "went it alone" against insurgents, effectively improving their military and using civilian defense forces and socioeconomic programs in zones of conflict. Focus is on 1978–1985.

CHRONOLOGY

1954 U.S. supports overthrow of Jacobo Arbenz.
1960 Defeated officers in failed coup form insurgent groups.
1962 Guerrillas begin military actions.
1966–1972 Insurgency strong in northeast and urban warfare in capital.
1968 Guerrillas cleared from northeast.
1972 Guerrillas militarily defeated in city and countryside.
1978–1985 Insurgency covers northwest, north, and capital.
1980 Guatemalan National Revolutionary Unity (URNG) formed to unite four guerrilla armies.
1982 Junior officers coup. General Efrain Rios Montt heads military government; implements comprehensive counterinsurgency.
1984 URNG beaten militarily and confined to isolated and Mexican border areas.

Source: The map and some of the country data are from State Department "Background Notes."

6

The Guatemalan Counterinsurgency Campaign of 1982–1985: A Strategy of Going It Alone

Caesar D. Sereseres

Guatemalans have been at war with each other for decades. For thirty years, since the ill-fated military coup attempt on 13 November 1960, an organized guerrilla insurgency has existed in Guatemala. During this era there have been two periods of sustained, violent, and costly counterinsurgency: 1966–1972, when the insurgency fully emerged in the country's northeastern region of Zacapa and ended with urban warfare in the capital; and 1978–1985, when fighting covered most of the Indian highlands' northwestern region, the north, and the capital.

Thirty years of internal war have cost Guatemalan society the lives of more than fifty thousand inhabitants (the majority noncombatants), the kidnapping and disappearance of thousands, millions of dollars of damage to the economy and society, the capital flight of millions of dollars, and the departure of hundreds of thousands who sought safety in exile. For critics, the government—especially the armed forces— earned a deeply negative reputation for the abuses, violence, military domination of politics, and draconian approach to counterinsurgency. For others, Guatemala is an example of what is necessary in dealing with a guerrilla insurgency.

This paper examines the roots and character of the insurgency from 1972 to 1982; the major changes in the counterinsurgency strategy after the 23 March 1982 coup; Max Manwaring's six criteria for successful counterinsurgency as applied to the Guatemala case; and the lessons to learn from a government that "went it alone" in a war against a guerrilla insurgency.

The Evolution of Insurgency in Guatemala

Since the 1944 revolution, Guatemala has faced three serious leftist threats. The first was purely political. President Jacobo Arbenz (an army colonel) instituted domestic and foreign policies that Guatemalan conservatives and officials in the Eisenhower administration viewed as dangerously radical and leftist. The United States supported the overthrow of Arbenz in 1954.[1]

The second leftist threat was primarily military. The threat took the form of an insurgency that grew out of an aborted 1960 coup. These insurgents, who would come to call themselves the *Fuerzas Armadas Rebeldes* (FAR) and the *Movimiento Revolucionario 13 de Noviembre* (MR–13), later formed an alliance with the Guatemalan Communist Party, the *Partido Guatemalteco del Trabajo* (PGT).

It was, however, military officers, not Marxist radicals, who laid the foundations for the post–1960 insurgency. These were the officers who decided to continue their fight against President Miguel Ydigoras Fuentes after the 1960 military revolt failed. They selected for their operations the mountains of northeastern Guatemala, a rugged area between the capital and the Atlantic coast. In February 1962, they began military activities against villages, military commissioners, and the Atlantic highway.

For several years these officers-turned-guerrillas maintained contacts with their former institution and with political parties. Until Ydigoras fell in a 1963 military coup, the guerrilla leadership followed an insurrectionist strategy, hoping to obtain the support of the armed forces and political parties to remove him. Colonel Enrique Peralta Azurdia's military coup on 31 March ended the prospects for a successful insurrectionist strategy, however. Then the 1966 presidential elections removed the last possibilities for an alliance with non-Marxist political forces. With all political options closed, the guerrillas kept fighting. Their rejection of newly elected President Julio Cesar Mendez Montenegro's offer of amnesty completed their radicalization.

In November 1966, the Guatemalan army began major counterinsurgency operations in Zacapa. Within two years, the northeast was cleared of an organized guerrilla insurgency.[2] The FAR guerrillas continued to battle the army until 1972, when they were defeated militarily in both the cities and the countryside. Just as the FAR and MR–13 insurgency—which never amounted to more than five hundred armed insurgents—was quelled, the third leftist threat emerged in the densely populated Indian highlands.

The Second-Generation Insurgency

While the Guatemalan security forces (and civilian allies) were learning conflicting lessons from the successful Zacapa counterinsurgency campaign, the surviving FAR and PGT guerrilla cadres went through a searching self-criticism concerning their intellectual, political, and military assumptions of the 1960s.

After several years of travel to Cuba, Vietnam, and other nations that had experienced revolutionary war, a handful of survivors of the 1960s, joined by a cadre of new revolutionaries, formed the nucleus of the *Ejercito Guerrillero de los Pobres* (EGP) in the remote northeastern Indian region of Ixcan. Beginning with a cadre of twelve in 1972, the EGP eventually grew strong enough to operate as a military and political force in six highland departments by 1980.

The politico-military leadership of the EGP guerrilla organization initiated the highland-based insurgency with a revolutionary strategy different from that of the 1960s. This second-generation guerrilla leadership was more sophisticated than its predecessor about its opponents, its opportunities, and its capabilities.[3] The second-generation guerrillas immediately rejected the *foquista*-insurrectionist strategy of revolutionary warfare. Although this model had worked for Cuba's Fidelistas in the late 1950s, it had since produced a series of failures throughout the hemisphere.[4] By 1975, the EGP had established itself as the leading edge of the renewed guerrilla struggle in Guatemala.

The Guerrillas' New Strategy

The second-generation insurgency adopted a comprehensive politico-military strategy based on:

- *Prolonged popular warfare.* The guerrillas anticipated a long war requiring the mobilization of the population and the establishment of a virtually self-supporting infrastructure. The revolutionary vanguard not only relied more extensively on the indigenous population for recruits, but also believed that success depended on putting as much of that population as possible between government forces and guerrilla military actions.[5]
- *Popular front organizations.* During this prolonged struggle, another key to success was developing a heterogeneous set of participants and supporters. The insurgents needed either to create organizations or to penetrate existing ones. These organizations must be pluralistic, seeming to go beyond one ideology and class.

- *An "internationalized" war.* Success in armed struggle was thought more likely if Guatemala's internal war could be internationalized. The "external struggle," *la lucha en el exterior*, called for establishing links abroad with the media, humanitarian organizations, churches of all denominations, political parties, human rights organizations, labor federations, and sympathetic governments. Diplomacy and lobbying abroad became critical to the strategy of armed struggle.
- *"Alliances" in the United States.* The insurgents did not see either the society or the government of the United States as monolithic. Vietnam demonstrated to practitioners of revolutionary warfare that U.S. society includes an array of potential allies that could be courted if the cause was properly packaged. Moreover, the U.S. political system is accessible with the help of solidarity networks.
- *Maintenance of external support.* The guerrillas recognized that an external patron alone cannot initiate or win an insurgency. Nevertheless, external patrons can sustain an internal war by providing limited training, resources, and technology. Patrons must be cultivated constantly, however; otherwise they may prove unreliable. The Guatemalan insurgents had to work at convincing Cuba and the Sandinistas that they were worth the investment and risk. The insurgents also sought alternative sources of training, weapons, and ammunition.

During the formative years of the EGP there were few prospects for Cuban support. Although many of the leaders of the EGP had been trained in or traveled to Cuba and other Soviet bloc countries during the 1960s, Cuban interest in the revolutionary struggle in Guatemala was minimal, compared to Havana's support for insurgency in Nicaragua and El Salvador.

The death of Che Guevara in Bolivia in 1967, closer relations with the Soviets after the invasion of Czechoslovakia in 1968, the courting of military "progressives" in Peru and Panama in the early 1970s, support for the "peaceful road to socialism" (as exemplified by Chile), and the desire to improve diplomatic relations in Latin America all contributed to a lessening of Castro's commitment to revolutionary armed struggle. After a period of accommodation, Cuba focused attention on Africa beginning in 1975. Thus, the EGP evolved virtually independently of Cuba, the Soviet Union, and the international communist support network. The EGP had few prospects for significant and sustained Cuban assistance *until* the success of the Sandinista guerrilla insurrection in 1979.[6]

In addition to their own initiatives, the guerrillas ironically relied on the government's counterinsurgency tactics from 1978 to 1981 for legitimacy, popularity, and growth. Far from destroying the insurgency, the operations of military and paramilitary forces helped the guerrillas mobilize a small portion of the population and helped to fortify the image of government repression that was projected to the international community.

In the mid–1960s, the FAR, the MR–13, and the PGT had operated effectively only in the capital and five departments located in the lightly populated Petén and northeastern region. Never numbering more than five hundred armed guerrillas, seldom operating in a column of more than thirty and never taking a department capital, their most destructive attack against the military was the 1966 ambush and killing of twelve soldiers in Zacapa. In contrast, the EGP began with a cadre of twelve in 1972, but by early 1982, guerrilla strategy and government counterinsurgency tactics combined to increase guerrilla forces to more than five thousand fighters.[7]

In early 1982, guerrilla units operated in at least half the republic's twenty-two departments and maintained a deeply rooted infrastructure in the six-department region of the Indian highlands (see map). The guerrillas often operated in columns of two hundred and systematically attacked and often occupied and destroyed government municipalities, police stations, military outposts, and other symbols of public authority. From 1972 to 1982, the guerrillas killed several thousand national policemen, military, and paramilitary troops. (During the Zacapa insurgency, government forces had accounted for only a small fraction of the casualties.) By 1982 the guerrillas had become a formidable political and military force in Guatemala and, just as important, had extended their diplomatic reach into the United States, Western Europe, and Latin America.

The Evolution of Counterinsurgency Strategy

The counterinsurgency tactics employed by the government from 1978 to 1981, rather than reducing the threat, swelled guerrilla ranks.[8] Each presidential election became less and less convincing; each succeeding death of a popular rural or urban leader or paramilitary raid against a village in the highlands seemed to push more Guatemalans into the arms of the guerrillas.

In 1979, two internationally recognized opposition leaders were assassinated: Manuel Colom Argueta, former mayor of Guatemala City and leader of the United Revolutionary Front Party, and Alberto Fuentes Mohr, former minister of foreign relations and founder of the

Social Democratic Party. Their deaths indicated that opposition leaders—no matter how responsible, patriotic, or nonviolent—were considered a threat. Labor and peasant leaders, party officials, students, lawyers, doctors, and teachers were added to the list of the assassinated. Their numbers grew. In 1972, "political" deaths ranged from 30 to 50 a month; by 1980, deaths ranged from 80 to 100 a month; by 1981, the number of killings had reached 250 to 300 a month.

As the deaths mounted, so did opposition to the regime. Both Marxist and non-Marxist resistance to the government flourished. In April 1978, the *Comité de Unidad Campesina* (CUC) was formed to organize and mobilize the rural population. In February 1979, the *Frente Democratico Contra la Represión* (FDCR) was established, representing, at least on paper, several hundred professional, student, trade union, religious, and political organizations. In 1981, these organizations, along with others such as the *Frente Popular 31 de Enero*, formed the *Frente de Unidad Patriotica Nacional*. Most of these groups were either front organizations of the guerrillas or were strongly sympathetic to the guerrilla cause.

Guerrilla organizations also sought unity. By the late 1970s, several independent guerrilla fronts had emerged in Guatemala. While the Sandinistas consolidated their power in Nicaragua and the guerrilla war intensified in El Salvador, the four guerrilla groups participating in the Guatemalan insurgency signed an agreement in November 1980 forming the *Unidad Revolucionaria Nacional Guatemalteca* (URNG).[9] By mid-1981, the government faced a more unified opposition, one that had support links with the international community—in the East and West.

The growth of organized opposition made it apparent that Guatemala was a house divided against itself. Also, the insurgency was no longer the only threat facing the government of President Romeo Lucas Garcia (an army general and former minister of defense) in 1980. The government could no longer ignore the fact that it had a civil war on its hands. Moreover, the dimensions of the problem had begun to attract considerable international attention. While the assassinations of Colom Argueta and Fuentes Mohr shocked Guatemala, two other incidents drew international headlines: the May 1978 Panzos incident, where fifty to a hundred Indians were killed by military forces, and the January 1980 siege and accidental burning of the Spanish embassy when Guatemalan security forces attempted to remove protesters. After the latter incident, in which thirty-eight people were killed—including twenty-one Indians from Quiché who helped seize the embassy—Spain broke off diplomatic relations with Guatemala.

As Guatemala moved toward the 1982 presidential elections, the government's domestic and international support continued to deteriorate. In the two months preceding the March 1982 elections, the number of politically related deaths reached the unprecedented level of one thousand. Under the scrutiny of the international press, and despite the claims of electoral fraud, President Lucas's former minister of defense, Gen. Angel Anibal Guevara, was declared the winner.

With the election of General Guevara, the government appeared to face more of the same: corruption, inefficiency, violence, growing body counts on the rural battlefield and streets of the capital, stronger and larger guerrilla organizations, and further diplomatic isolation. Then, three weeks after the election, army units from the capital led by a group of junior military officers surrounded the National Palace. The young officers (most were lieutenants, captains, and a few majors) demanded the resignation of President Lucas and negotiated the establishment of a junta headed by Gen. Efrain Rios Montt. The junta invalidated Guevara's election and enacted a new government code in April, replacing the existing constitution.

The junta was dissolved in June 1982, leaving Rios Montt as president and minister of defense. On 1 July, the government declared a state of siege and established special judicial tribunals to handle cases of subversion. Military conscription increased, reservists were called to active duty, and civilians were mobilized and armed into units to defend their local communities. On 15 September 1982, the Council of State assumed its duties, among which were consulting with the president in formulating new codes for political parties and elections. For the first time in Guatemalan history, the Indian population was given a role in formulating national policy. Of the thirty-five council seats, ten *indigenas* represented distinct Indian ethnic groups.[10]

The Military Government of General Rios Montt

Although allegations of electoral fraud in the March 1982 election were the immediate cause, the coup of 23 March was aimed at corruption, violence, and the loss of national prestige. The junior officers who carried out the coup made the following statement in the first radio communiqué after ordering troops to surround the National Palace:

> [Given] the situation to which the country has been taken by means of the practice of fraudulent elections, accompanied by the deterioration of moral values, the splintering of democratic forces, as well as the disorder and corruption in the public administration, it has become impossible to resolve these problems within a constitutional framework.

All of which makes it imperative that the army assume the government of the republic.[11]

General Rios Montt, in one of his first public statements, noted that the coup was a political act that would lay the basis for *political* solutions for the nation. In a major address to the nation, Rios Montt provided further elaboration on his views regarding national security and the nature of the insurgency threat:

> If we close our eyes, increase the number of soldiers and policemen, and we attack the subversives, we can do it [defeat the guerrillas]. And in three months the guerrilla will return. . . . Security does not consist of arms, tanks and airplanes. This is not even five percent of the requirement for a national security policy. Security lies in the relationship between the state and the people. . . . Security lies in the sense of trust between state and people—that both will meet their respective obligations . . . today. But we have been corrupt. . . . We [the military] are here to complete a mission: institutionalize the state and channel resources and benefits to those in need.[12]

The military government under Rios Montt immediately sought to create a comprehensive strategy to deal with the military, political, and socioeconomic threats posed by the URNG insurgency. This approach required a much more discriminating counterinsurgency strategy, less dependent on pure military force. Just as important, the military government wanted to strengthen its political position in the region with a more positive, active diplomacy. Strengthening its position required establishing legitimacy and broader domestic and international support, which required controlling violence against the citizenry and minimizing public corruption. Finally, the Rios Montt regime began to establish a "public record" to make political dialogue with the United States possible, as a prelude to renewed military cooperation between the two countries.

Under Rios Montt the Guatemalan General Staff developed a counterinsurgency strategy with three core elements:

- The number of men under arms and the number of smaller units deployed within the "zones of conflict" increased significantly. Along with this mobilization effort, in July 1982 the government issued a military code of conduct to improve relations between the army and noncombatants. The chief of staff also attempted to improve command and control of planning, implementing, and monitoring of military operations.

- The efforts to establish civilian defense forces (CDFs) in the highlands were intensified and expanded throughout the region where guerrillas operated. The government made specific efforts to mobilize several thousand Indians into village CDFs in the "Ixil Triangle," a region of the northern Quiché department located in the geopolitical heart of the EGP.

- A socioeconomic assistance plan in the "zones of conflict" (a tactic reminiscent of the military's successful civic action programs during the 1960s insurgency) was initiated. The Committee for National Reconstruction (CRN) linked the provision of food and services to families and support for small community development projects to the formation of civil defense patrols. Formed after the 1976 earthquake to coordinate international assistance, the committee became a coordinating agency for civic action and social assistance to encourage the establishment of civil defense forces. The ultimate purpose of the strategy was to establish trust between the armed forces and the rural population.

The EGP, ORPA, and, to a lesser extent, the FAR and PGT, had anchored their political hopes in the nine-department region of the highlands. Shortage of land, low prospects of employment, minimal health services, inadequate educational opportunities, and severe malnutrition were endemic to the Indian highlands population. Thus, a political struggle began in mid-1982 between the URNG coalition of guerrillas and the Guatemalan government and armed forces over the allegiance of hundreds of thousands of men and women, many of whom were struggling to survive under conditions of abject poverty. Both sides believed that the loyalty of the highland population would ultimately determine the outcome of Guatemala's civil war. The potential pool of human resources for an insurgency was staggering; however, the highlands Indians did not turn en masse against the military and General Rios Montt.

In July 1982, the stage was set for the determining confrontation between the military and a Marxist-led, Indian-based insurgency in Guatemala's highlands. Under the leadership of General Rios Montt, the military had prepared for this battle by changing the political and counterinsurgency strategies. In some ways, these adjustments paralleled the *strategic* shift the guerrilla leadership had made in the early 1970s in the aftermath of the failures of the first-generation insurgents.

The Manwaring Paradigm and
the Case of Guatemala, 1982–1985

To examine the Guatemalan counterinsurgency case systematically and to permit further comparative analysis, I draw from Max G. Manwaring's six criteria for successful counterinsurgency.[13] The assessment of the Guatemalan counterinsurgency campaign during the 1982–1985 period will focus specifically on each of these factors.

Legitimacy

After nearly four years of governing, the presidency of General Romeo Lucas Garcia had lost the little legitimacy inherited from the 1978 national elections. Corruption, political violence, lackluster leadership, and a growing insurgency had undermined whatever legitimacy existed internationally and domestically— even within the armed forces. The 23 March 1982 coup by young officers reversed this situation sufficiently to allow the Rios Montt military government to take military, political, and diplomatic initiatives against the allied guerrilla forces of the URNG.

The average citizen in the streets had applauded the coup, and some even came to see the military institution as a liberator from the nightmarish years of 1978–1981. With the successful coup, an authoritarian but charismatic retired general took hold of the government as chief of state. Though his tenure lasted only sixteen months (from 23 March 1982 to 8 August 1983), his image, vision, speeches to the nation, sometimes outrageous statements, and dynamic leadership provided the government and the military the needed reorientation to deal with the insurgency. General Rios Montt facilitated a modest cleaning out of the senior ranks of the Guatemalan officer corps (only two generals were permitted to stay on active duty), eliminated the notorious Judicial Police detachment (known as the DIT) within the National Police, removed partisan party politics from national policy formulation and implementation (the Congress was disbanded and a corporate-style Council of State was established), and initiated an anticorruption campaign that drew substantial national support.

Despite being controversial, General Rios Montt provided the government and military with a real national leader for the first time in the war against the URNG guerrillas. Rios Montt, unlike previous political and military leaders, captivated the media as well as the nation. His Sunday "sermons" to the nation via television and radio carried messages of good citizenship, governmental accountability, national honor, and family values, as well as the need to defeat the guerrillas politically, socially, and militarily. His message was clear: the state as well as the citizenry had to be mobilized if the insurgency was to be defeated.

The March coup generated a new institutional mystique for the armed forces (not necessarily welcomed by most officers), and General Rios Montt provided a symbol of political leadership that for sixteen months created the respite needed to turn the army from the road of self-destruction and onto a road that would lead to a guerrilla defeat in three years.

Organization for Unity of Effort

Aside from Rios Montt's character, the most striking Guatemalan postcoup feature was that the government and armed forces reorganized to implement a distinctly different counterinsurgency strategy from that inherited from the Lucas Garcia era. Within weeks of the coup, a "special" General Staff was organized to develop a national counterinsurgency campaign plan. The Committee for National Reconstruction (CRN), along with the Civil Affairs Section of the General Staff, was ordered to inventory the needs of the population in the "areas of conflict" and to devise a plan to provide needed goods and services to these areas.

The military zones where the insurgency was being fought underwent changes in command structure and personnel. Coordinating bodies for all government agencies were established in the "areas of conflict." The senior coordinator in each area was the senior military commander of the zone. It was the responsibility of the military to ensure that the combined politico-military plans designed by the presidency, the Ministry of Defense, *and* the civilian ministries in the capital were actually carried out in isolated rural areas where the counterinsurgency war was being waged.[14]

The strategy to reorganize institutional relations had several objectives: (1) ensure that the military was joined by other governmental agencies in the war against the URNG guerrillas; (2) coordinate rural development efforts with military campaign plans and establish armed civil defense patrol units in those villages subject to guerrilla presence or attack; (3) provide an accountability process for the use of scarce government and international resources being directed at the "areas of conflict"; and (4) encourage the participation of the citizenry in counterinsurgency strategy programs at the community level.

External Support for the Government and Military

If the Guatemalan case diverges somewhat from the Manwaring model, it is on the issue of external support. Because of a combination of events of the past decade, the Guatemalan military found itself without a major external patron. Difficulties with the U.S. government in the mid–1970s, first over Belize and then over human rights, deprived the Guatemalan military of external military assistance from an ally that had supported their war against an insurgency in the 1960s.

As Guatemala's internal situation began to deteriorate in the mid–1970s, so did its foreign relations—especially with the United States. In 1975, after some twenty years of unquestioning and unfaltering military assistance to Guatemala, the United States found itself caught between two allies in a territorial dispute. Throughout the 1970s, Guatemala threatened a colony of Great Britain, neighboring Belize, which eventually gained its independence in September 1981. Guatemala had claimed Belize as part of its own sovereign territory.[15]

Under pressure from London, the United States decided not to deliver military equipment, purchased or on order, that the British believed Guatemala could use in an invasion of Belize. This U.S. effort failed to change Guatemala's stance on Belize or to prevent Guatemala from improving its military capabilities. Guatemala responded by purchasing arms, equipment, ammunition, and training in Europe, Asia, Israel, and the international black market.

The episode, however, marked a dramatic shift in relations between the United States and Guatemala. This breach was widened in 1977 by U.S. policies on human rights.[16] In March 1977, Guatemala reacted to the Carter administration's human rights policies by unilaterally renouncing military assistance agreements with the United States. The Guatemalan foreign minister explained that the annual human rights reports required by the U.S. Congress for countries receiving foreign assistance "constitutes an unacceptable intervention into the internal affairs of another state—something that is totally impermissible between two sovereign states."[17]

Although scaled-down training and spare parts purchases from the United States continued into the early 1980s, such military assistance was almost insignificant, given the magnitude of the war. The Guatemalans came to rely on equipment, weapons, and ammunition purchases (based on cash, barter, or loans) from such countries as Israel, Taiwan, Yugoslavia, Belgium, Argentina, perhaps South Africa, and numerous international arms dealers. The Guatemalans were also able to purchase civilian version, U.S.-manufactured, Bell helicopters that were later modified for combat operations. Thus, despite international isolation and U.S. government prohibition on the sale of lethal items and the training of Guatemalan military personnel, the Guatemalan armed forces (unlike the Nicaraguan National Guard in 1979) never exhausted their supplies of weapons or ammunition.

Nonetheless, the reluctance of most major arms exporting countries to provide military equipment, weapons, and ammunition to Guatemala did have a significant impact on the counterinsurgency strategy, especially after the March 1982 coup. Neither dependent upon nor vulnerable to a major external patron, Guatemalans turned to their own national resources for the war against the URNG. For example, unable to develop the necessary air mobility for troop transport, logistics, and medivac, the Guatemalan Air Force turned to the civilian Aero Club to provide aircraft, helicopters, and pilots. While the Guatemalan Air Force had to support army units in the field (numbering more than twenty thousand soldiers) with no more than four to six helicopters on any given day, the Aero Club could provide three to four times that many helicopters and small aircraft to fly most support missions, with the possible exception of combat operations.

The force-multiplier for Guatemalan troops in the field was not aircraft nor artillery, but the civil defense forces in the "areas of conflict." Static positions could be defended by the better armed civilians (especially their own villages and municipal town halls), and joint patrols increased the number of army troops by 50 percent to 200 percent on a given operation. This form of force-multiplier was more economical and occurred on the ground where the guerrillas were operating, not at a great distance from the battlefield when using aircraft and artillery.

The Committee for National Reconstruction was another example of the innovative techniques employed to obtain resources to fight the insurgency. The committee searched throughout the international community for humanitarian assistance to help those villages affected by the war. The CRN was able to gather millions of dollars' worth of medicine, clothing, basic food stuffs, cooking oil, tin roofing, and construction tools. Thus, despite Guatemala's pariah status in the early 1980s, the CRN was able to obtain and distribute valuable resources within the context of a national counterinsurgency strategy.

The refusal of the United States to sell specific aircraft and weapons in 1975 and the example of the Nicaraguan National Guard in 1979 contributed to the Guatemalan effort to be as self-sufficient in military supplies as possible. The Guatemalans also sought to diversify their supply sources. The dual strategies of self-sufficiency and diversification meant that the Guatemalan military was not dependent on a single patron of source for battlefield capabilities or institutional survival.

Intelligence

Good, not to say lucky, intelligence operations led to the destruction of twenty-eight URNG safe houses in Guatemala City from mid–1981 to early 1982. The amount of weapons recovered (mostly new and unpacked) was staggering. Explosives, ammunition, communication equipment, propaganda, and uniforms of Guatemalan army personnel and police were also found in these safe houses. Given the fact that a large URNG guerrilla front had established a strong presence, Vietcong-style, in the department of Chimaltenango (only a thirty-minute drive from the capital), the prospects for a "final offensive" directed at Guatemala City had to be taken seriously. Intelligence methods (including computer analyses of phone, gas, and electricity accounts) taught most recently by Chilean and Argentine intelligence agencies to Guatemalan military officers proved quite effective.[18]

The likelihood of linking the URNG's internal front in the capital to the guerrilla front operating in Chimaltenango for the purpose of carrying out a Sandinista-like popular insurrection had been destroyed by the Guatemalan intelligence service *prior* to the March 1982 coup. What remained in the aftermath of the coup, however, were the entire, multifront guerrilla armies of the URNG, stretching from Chimaltenango to the western and northern regions of Guatemala along the border with Mexico. The counterinsurgency strategy developed by the Rios Montt government required a more intense intelligence/psychological operations program at the grass-roots level of the insurgency.

The Rios Montt counterinsurgency strategy was based on public appeals to logic (the likelihood of which side would eventually win the war between government and guerrillas), national honor, and civic duty. The strategy also included coercive measures, such as withholding basic food commodities from villages not supporting the army, pressure on those who refused to join civil defense patrols "voluntarily," and threats if information on other villages or villagers was not forthcoming. For intelligence to work down to the grass-roots level of the insurgency, several factors had to be effectively and fairly implemented.

The intelligence needed to carry out the new counterinsurgency strategy relied on (1) senior military zone commanders willing and able to coordinate government ministries and mobilize the population to support government programs and military operations; (2) local military commanders willing to deal with all the facets of fighting the insurgency—not just the military aspect; (3) civil defense forces led by local and popular figures; (4) effective control over the often abusive military commissioners responsible for recruiting army conscripts and providing intelligence at the village level; and (5) an active and well-staffed civil affairs company responsible for carrying out civic action and psychological operations in the villages and, more importantly, collecting "social intelligence." The latter was critical to keeping the military zone commanders and the senior strategists in the capital aware of guerrilla activity and support at the village level, community socioeconomic needs, and the *performance* of government agencies and officials at the village and municipal levels. These "social intelligence" reports were presented by the military zone commander at monthly or bimonthly meetings in the capital to review the progress in the war against the URNG.

Discipline and Capabilities of the Military

One of the first measures adopted in May 1982 was to increase the battlefield capabilities of the Guatemalan armed forces. To improve the capabilities of the army to carry out the counterinsurgency strategy, the General Staff issued directives that (1) called up five thousand reservists (about twenty-five rifle companies); (2) assigned to active duty about a hundred recent graduates of the Adolfo V. Hall military high school system; (3) commissioned as lieutenants in the Guatemalan Air Force several dozen civilian pilots who owned or operated helicopters and small aircraft; (4) upgraded officer, NCO, and specialist professional performance through short courses on patrolling, psychological operations and civic action, intelligence, and advanced officer training presented at the Center for Military Studies (CEM); (5) increased the productivity of Guatemala's nascent military industrial complex (munitions, combat boots, uniforms, rations); and (6) organized and mobilized more than two hundred thousand peasants into hundreds of civil defense patrols (10 to 15 percent of these *patrulleros* were actually armed with rifles and shotguns).

The issue of "fixing" the discipline problem was more difficult and controversial. To blame senior military and political officials in the capital for the problems of the nation and the strength of the URNG insurgency was easy. For senior and midgrade officers to accept the blame for alleged abuses against noncombatants or alleged sympathizers of the guerrillas by their troops was not as easy—and quite often rejected. The General Staff had to move slowly on the related issues of discipline and the treatment of the civilian population.

Efforts were made, on paper, to explain to the officer corps and the soldiers in the field the importance of proper military discipline on the battlefield. Seminars were held with the commanders at the *Politecnica* (Guatemala's military academy) and the Center for Military Studies to discuss the importance of the new code of conduct and rules of engagement issued by the General Staff in mid–1982. Personnel from the Psychological Operations Division of the Military Public Relations Office and the Civil Affairs Directorate provided talks, posters, and General Staff directives on these two topics to officers and troops in the field.

The combination of the strength of the "old way of doing business" against guerrillas and suspected guerrillas, the hazy and isolated nature of fighting an insurgency, and the provocation tactics of the guerrillas meant that few guerrillas would be captured alive, that probable or suspected guerrilla sympathizers would be treated badly, and that abuses by military personnel (including military commissioners and civil patrolmen) would continue—ordered, condoned, or at least unpunished by officers at all grade levels.

Although the abuses continued, though at a lower level than prior to the March coup, the number of noncombatant deaths in fact declined. This decline was due largely to the military's strategy of separating the population from guerrilla strongholds: if the army could not stay and defend the area, the villagers had to leave and destroy their crops. If the army stayed, the villagers had to organize and arm themselves to defend their village and support military operations in the local area. Food and medicine were under the direct control of military authorities in the "areas of conflict."

Although these measures appear to be draconian, they in fact led to a more rational use of military force in populated areas. The operational strategy of the military under President Lucas Garcia had been simply to sweep an area repeatedly to establish contact with the guerrillas. There was little the villagers could do to protect themselves from either the guerrillas or the army. There was no way to define their allegiance to the government if the army never stayed or the government presented no programs of support. The postcoup strategy, despite its harsh measures, permitted the villagers to establish their loyalty, and the government and military demonstrated to the villagers that there was a general plan that could include a permanent military presence in the area.

The grayish haze of who supported the government and who supported the guerrillas quickly became distinctly black and white.

Thus, although battlefield deaths increased on both sides as the government took the initiative from mid–1982 through 1984, actual noncombatant deaths decreased significantly.

The social costs of the strategy were high: the displacement of hundreds of thousands of villagers from the combat areas; the often coerced involvement of thousands of villagers (aged fifteen to fifty-five) in the civil defense patrols; a virtual dependency on the army for food, health, and services in the strongest guerrilla areas; and the subjection of the rural population to the impunity of military authority.

Reducing External Assistance to the Guerrillas

The Guatemalan guerrillas were regarded as the "poor kids" on the Central American block. Throughout the 1970s and into the 1980s the guerrillas were provided the "leftovers" after the Sandinista and then the Salvadoran guerrillas had received their needed supplies. Each of the Guatemalan guerrilla factions (EGP, FAR, ORPA, and the PGT/N) sought its own resources abroad, including safe havens, training, weapons, funds, and access to a global transportation network provided by such countries as Cuba, Vietnam, Libya, several East European countries, and the Soviet Union. Because the patrons of "revolutionary armed struggle" had higher priorities, the Guatemalan guerrillas, much like their adversaries the Guatemalan armed forces, came to rely more on themselves for their own survival.

This is not to say that the guerrillas did not turn to the world outside Guatemala in search of assistance. They sought support from the Soviet Communist Party, the Vietnamese, the Cuban government, and after 1979 from the Sandinista government in Managua. Nevertheless, the respective guerrilla organizations recognized their vulnerabilities in the mid–1970s and implemented a strategy based, for the most part, on periodic but limited external assistance.

One factor that remained constant, and continues to be a principal asset of the Guatemalan guerrillas, is the porous Mexican border and permissive environment provided by the Mexican government and security officials. While limited assistance from Cuba, the Soviet Union, Vietnam, and Sandinista Nicaragua was helpful, the "open border" between Mexico and Guatemala was a necessary condition for the continued viability of the Guatemalan insurgency. In fact, it has been Mexico City—not Havana, Managua, Moscow, or Hanoi—that determined the survivability of the Guatemalan insurgency.

The Guatemalan military and government have been more successful in controlling material assistance from Marxist suppliers than in stopping material support from Mexican sources. For domestic political and symbolic reasons, Mexican authorities have been reluctant to seal off the border with Guatemala permanently or to make difficult or impossible the movement of guerrilla leaders in and out of Mexico City. They have also done little to prevent the purchase (on the open market) of equipment and materials that contribute to the guerrillas' lethal capabilities inside Guatemala. This situation constitutes the major *diplomatic* failure of the Guatemalan government in dealing with the URNG insurgency.

Guatemalan Lessons

The Guatemalan counterinsurgency campaign of 1982–1985 rates reasonably well when compared to the Manwaring model of indicators that are essential in defeating guerrillas. The four-year counterinsurgency effort, based on the six criteria, would be given the following marks: "Excellent" on legitimacy, organization, and intelligence; "Good" on external support for the government and the discipline/capabilities of the armed forces; and "Poor" on the ability to reduce outside aid to the guerrillas. It was political and diplomatic shortcomings that diluted a counterinsurgency strategy that produced quick, spectacular results against a guerrilla insurgency on the verge of possible victory in early 1982. By late 1984, the URNG had been badly beaten militarily and driven back to sparsely populated and isolated mountains of the Guatemalan highlands and to areas along the Mexican border.

There are two reasons why the URNG guerrilla organization still continues to survive as a military force in 1991. The first is the failure of Guatemalan diplomacy to remove the "Mexican factor" in URNG support. The second is the reluctance of Guatemalan political, military, and business leaders to offer a credible, institutionalized political opening (with a guarantee of security) to the guerrillas in the aftermath of their staggering military defeats during the 1982–1985 period.[19]

Are there lessons to learn from the Guatemalan case in counterinsurgency? Utilizing Manwaring's criteria for a successful government outcome in fighting an insurgency, the answer is an apparent "yes." There are, however, several qualifications that must be acknowledged on the "lessons" because of conditions unique to Guatemala.

Military government. The March 1982 coup brought about the establishment of a military government. Despite the fact that President Lucas Garcia was a retired army general and former minister of defense, the military was actually resource poor, and the civilian ministries played no part in supporting military operations against the guerrillas. Under Rios Montt, the military and government in general were mobilized, and military strategists had access to all public sector resources to carry out a national campaign plan against the URNG guerrillas. Unlike the Lucas Garcia regime, military leaders and strategists under Rios Montt had authority over civilian ministries, manpower, and equipment in carrying out the counterinsurgency strategy.

Nature of the insurgency. Most observers will argue that the URNG cannot be compared to the Sandinistas of Nicaragua or the Farabundo Martí guerrillas of El Salvador. The URNG did not have the resource levels, firepower, communication equipment, senior and midlevel leadership with professional military training abroad, or battlefield strategy attributed to the other Latin American guerrilla movements. The URNG was in fact a more vulnerable guerrilla force than those in El Salvador, Nicaragua, Colombia, or Peru. Thus, the Guatemalan government and armed forces were, comparatively speaking, dealing with the weakest insurgency in Latin America.

Terrorism and "genocide" as counterinsurgency. The Guatemalan military and paramilitary forces have long been accused of relying almost exclusively on terror (in the form of assassination, kidnapping and disappearance, torture, and systematic destruction of villages) to defeat both the FAR/PGT/MR–13 insurgency in the 1960s and the URNG insurgency of the 1980s. Guatemala, during the 1970s and 1980s, did rank high on the lists of human rights organizations for incidents of politically related deaths, kidnappings, claims of institutionalized torture, and even accusations of committing "genocide" against the highlands Indians. Do terrorism and violence serve as effective tools in counterinsurgency? If employed systematically as a tactic, at what point do terror and violence become counterproductive? Within what broader counterinsurgency national strategy can each be a productive tactic in defeating an insurgency?

In the case of Guatemala it is possible to document that the combination of military operations, paramilitary activities, and so-called death squads terrorism did little to suppress the insurgency. The URNG forces grew dramatically in manpower and territory during the worst period of government abuses from 1978 to 1981. Something more than "repression" must help explain the success of the military strategy *after* the March 1982 coup. Several of the Manwaring factors (such as legitimacy and unity of action by government and military) appear more significant in determining a successful outcome in counterinsurgency than the use of pure violence and coercion against the population.

"Independence" from the United States. Success in Guatemala and failure in El Salvador, according to many Guatemalans and some experts on counterinsurgency, are attributable to the "U.S. factor," that is, the overwhelming presence of the United States in El Salvador since 1981 and a virtual nonpresence in Guatemala since 1977. In Guatemala's case, there is no U.S. Congress to worry about, nor concern over human rights reports affecting conditional U.S. military, economic, and financial assistance. Did the lack of the U.S. presence and assistance permit the Guatemalan army, especially during the 1982–1984 period, to implement a successful counterinsurgency strategy that they may not have been able to do otherwise?

Again, one can turn to the dramatic difference in government and military behavior from 1978 to 1981 under President Lucas Garcia and the postcoup period under General Rios Montt. The U.S. absence (including the politics of conditioned foreign assistance) and a no-holds barred counterinsurgency strategy did not produce a guerrilla defeat; instead, the no-holds barred strategy nearly led to the self-destruction of the Guatemalan armed forces and victory for the URNG.

To some extent, the absence of the U.S. training and logistical link forced the Guatemalans, after the coup, to rely on their own creativity, on meager but diverse international resources, and required them to design a counterinsurgency strategy appropriate to the existing conditions. The military had to turn to the civilian bureaucracy and professionals of its own government, to a mobilized and armed rural population, and to political and psychological warfare programs and strategies (including a national election to bring about a democratic transition and civilian rule in 1986) as a means to defeat the guerrillas militarily and remove the URNG as a political option for Guatemalan society.

Notes

1. For an account of Central Intelligence Agency (CIA) operations to topple the government of Arbenz, see Stephen Schlesinger and Stephen Kinzer, *Bitter Fruit: The Untold Story of the American Coup in Guatemala* (New York: Doubleday and Co., Inc., 1982).

2. A multitude of factors, including luck, played a role in the military defeat of the guerrillas between 1966 and 1968. For an assessment of the counterinsurgency strategy, the guerrillas' organizational weaknesses, and the role of the United States, see Brian Jenkins, Caesar D. Sereseres, and Luigi Einaudi, *U.S. Military Aid and Guatemalan Politics* (Los Angeles: Arms Control and Foreign Policy Seminar, 1974).

3. Labeling the guerrilla strategy of the 1960s as nothing more than *acción improvisada*—improvised action—the founders of the EGP set out to learn

the lessons of the past before entering into politico-military warfare. A personal account of the origins of the guerrilla movement in Ixcan and its growth between 1972 and 1976 is found in Mario Payeras, *Los Dias de la Selva* (Mexico: Editorial Nuestro Tiempo, 1981).

4. The doctrine of the guerrilla *foco* was presented in its purest form by Ernesto Guevara, *Che Guevara on Guerrilla Warfare* (New York: Praeger Publishers, 1961). The foremost chronology of *foco* warfare is Regis Debray, *Revolution in the Revolution: Armed Struggle and Political Struggle in Latin America* (New York: Monthly Review, 1967). A challenge to orthodox Marxist theory, the *foquista* approach to revolution emphasized the military dimension of conflict, arguing that a small armed group could create the conditions for revolution without the urban mass base previously thought necessary. All the guerrilla movements following the *foco* strategy succumbed to military defeat during the 1960s.

5. For an elaboration of this strategy of provocation and mobilization by a guerrilla strategist, see "La Toma de Nebaj," *Polemica* (Costa Rica), no. 3 (January-February 1982).

6. In the early 1980s, the relationship between the EGP and other Guatemalan guerrilla organizations and Cuba was influenced by the Cuban experience in the Nicaraguan civil war. Sources that help develop this point include Edward Gonzalez, "Institutionalization, Political Elites and Foreign Policies," in Cole Blasier and Carmelo Mesa-Lago, eds., *Cuba in the World* (Pittsburgh: University of Pittsburgh Press, 1979); William M. LeoGrande, "Foreign Policy: The Limits of Success," in Jorge I. Dominguez, ed., *Cuba: Internal and International Affairs* (Beverly Hills: SAGE Publications, 1982); Edward Gonzalez, *Cuba Under Castro: The Limits of Charisma* (Boston: Houghton-Mifflin, 1974), pp. 113–145; U.S. Department of State, *Cuba's Renewed Support for Violence in Latin America*, Special Report No. 90 (Washington, D.C.: GPO, 1981); and John Maclean, "Cuba and Panama Giving Aid to Somoza's Foes," *Chicago Tribune*, 17 June 1979.

7. Deputy Assistant Secretary of State for Inter-American Affairs Stephen Bosworth stated that the guerrillas constituted a formidable threat to the Guatemalan government. He indicated that "full-time trained, armed guerrillas may number as many as 3,500 . . . supplemented by approximately 10,000 irregular 'local defense' guerrillas . . . and a support infrastructure of some 30,000-60,000 sympathizers." This information was provided to the House Banking Subcommittee on 5 August 1982. By comparison, a 1982 estimate by Guatemalan military intelligence placed the number of all armed guerrillas at 5,000 to 6,000, with at least five times that number in the *fuerzas irregulares locales* (FIL) and support infrastructure. It was also believed that the four guerrilla groups operated in approximately a dozen distinct military fronts throughout Guatemala.

8. This section draws heavily from previous publications of the author, particularly *Report on Guatemala: Findings of the Study Group on United States-Guatemalan Relations*, SAIS Papers in International Affairs 7

(Washington, D.C.: Foreign Policy Institute, SAIS, The Johns Hopkins University, 1985), pp. 17–49.

9. This agreement was signed in Managua by the *Ejercito Guerrillero de los Pobres* (EGP), the *Organización del Pueblo en Armas* (ORPA), the *Fuerzas Armadas Rebeldes* (FAR), and a dissident faction of the *Partido Guatemalteco del Trabajo* (PGT/Nucleo).

10. For a description of the functions and membership of the Council of State, see *Correo Politico* 3 (Guatemala City), no. 133, 23 September 1982. It was actually a thirty-one-member council with thirty-one alternate members, because the four political parties—National Liberation Movement (MLN), Christian Democratic Party (DCG), National Renewal Party (PNR), and Nationalist Authentic Central (CAN)—declined to name representatives.

11. Translated by the author from Military Communiqué No. 1 issued in late morning of 23 March.

12. Translated by the author from a transcript of a broadcast to the nation by Rios Montt on 5 April 1982.

13. See chap. 1 for a detailed description of the Manwaring paradigm.

14. For details of the military campaign plans and the link between counterinsurgency strategy and a democratic transition to civilian rule, see Alfonso Yurrita, "La transición del régimen militar al civil en Guatemala," in Louis Goodman, et al., *Los Militares y la Democracia* (Peitho: Montevideo, Uruguay, 1990), pp. 125–139.

15. For a more detailed discussion of the "cooling" of military relations in the mid–1970s, see David F. Ronfeldt and Caesar D. Sereseres, "U.S. Arms Transfers, Diplomacy and Security in Latin America," in Andrew J. Pierre, ed., *Arms Transfers and American Foreign Policy* (New York: New York University Press, 1979). The specifics of the dispute between Guatemala and Belize can be found in P. K. Menon, "The Anglo-Guatemalan Territorial Dispute over the Colony of Belize," *Journal of Latin American Studies* 11 (Fall 1979): 343–371.

16. This was not the first time the United States had sought to prevent Guatemala from purchasing arms. During the 1948–1954 period, the United States pursued an arms blockade because of Guatemala's "leftist" tendencies. The Guatemalan military eventually was forced to purchase weapons from the Eastern bloc—thus providing further evidence of communist penetration for those critics of the Arbenz government.

17. Diplomatic Note to U.S. Embassy, Guatemala, from the Guatemalan Foreign Ministry, dated 11 March 1977. The note went on to say that the government of Guatemala "declines in advance any military equipment that is conditioned on judgments that any foreign government may make on matters exclusively internal to Guatemala." President Kjell Laugerud, a retired army general and former minister of defense, made his feelings known on numerous occasions, stating that he "could not permit any country to sit in judgment of Guatemala."

18. Since the mid–1960s, Guatemala's various intelligence services, including the Intelligence Directorate (D–II) of the General Staff, the *Archivos* of the Presidential Staff, and the *judiciales* of the National Police,

have been accused of relying heavily on assassination, kidnapping, torture, intimidation, and complicity with "clandestine" anticommunist death squads. In this paper I focus primarily on those intelligence innovations introduced by the Rios Montt counterinsurgency strategy.

19. Perhaps, even with military defeat, the URNG would not have accepted a political dialogue and negotiation in 1985. The domestic and international conditions that finally led to such discussions in 1990–1991 did not exist in 1985, despite the military successes of the government. In 1985, the URNG guerrillas still numbered fifteen hundred; the Sandinistas were still in power; the El Salvadoran guerrillas were strong; the Guatemalan military, according to human rights organizations, still had one of the worst human rights records in Latin America; and the Guatemalan government was still treated cautiously by most foreign governments, including the United States.

ETHIOPIA*

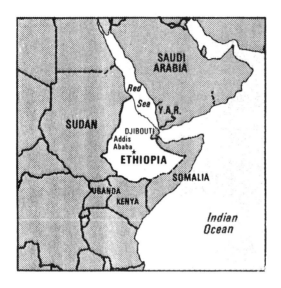

CHRONOLOGY

1970 Eritrean People's
Liberation Front (EPLF)
formed; Marxist-
Leninist platform; help
from USSR, Cuba,
China, Syria, Libya.
1974 Emperor Haile
Selassie overthrown.
1975 Tigrayan People's
Liberation Front
organized.
1977 Lt. Col. Mengistu
Haile Mariam emerges
as Ethiopian dictator;
massive USSR support,
20,000 Cuban advisors.
1984–1985 Catastrophic
famine.
1986 Mengistu all-out
offensive fails.
1988 EPLF and TPLF seek
help from West.
1989–1990 EPLF and
TPLF leaders travel to
United States and
Europe. USSR ends
declining military aid.
United States mediates
peace talks.
1991 Mengistu flees;
insurgents triumph.

COUNTRY DATA

Area 472,000 sq. miles (about the size of Texas,
Oklahoma, and New Mexico combined).
Capital Addis Ababa (population 1.5 million).
Population 46 million.
Per Capita Income $121.
Ethnic Groups Oromo 40%, Amhara 25%,
Tigrayan 12%, Sidama 9%.
Religions Muslim 40%–45%, Ethiopian
Orthodox Christian 35%–40%, indigenous
beliefs 15%–25%.
Literacy 60% of population.
Work Force Agriculture 79.8%, Industry and
commerce, 20.7%.
Infant Mortality Rate 145 per 1,000 live births.
Life Expectancy 44.5 years.
Government People's Democratic Republic .

UNIQUENESS OF CASE STUDY

Eritrean and Tigrayan Marxist insurgents
succeed after several decades against Haile
Selassie and then the Mengistu Marxist government by gaining legitimacy and by Mengistu's
loss of outside support.

Source: The map and some of the country data are from State Department "Background Notes."

7

Ethiopia: A Successful Insurgency

James Cheek

Introduction

The Eritrean and Tigrayan insurgents finally succeeded after several decades in winning their respective wars against the government of Ethiopia (initially that of Emperor Haile Selassie and later that of Mengistu Haile Mariam). It therefore is appropriate to apply the Manwaring paradigm from the perspective of the insurgents to describe and analyze how and why they succeeded. In doing so this chapter will also deal with how and why the government failed. Thus, the reader can draw conclusions and learn lessons from the experiences of both the winning and the losing sides.

The Eritrean (EPLF) and Tigrayan (TPLF, later EPRDF) insurgent groups had little contact with the outside world, or the outside world with them. Consequently, little research and published information on them are available other than news reports concerning their civil and military campaigns and operations. I have therefore relied heavily on the personal knowledge and insights gained from my active involvement with Ethiopia since 1985 and my extensive discussions with the insurgents since 1989. The views and opinions expressed in this chapter are solely mine and do not necessarily represent those of the Department of State or any other U.S. government agency.

Background to the Conflict

Armed conflict has plagued Ethiopia throughout its troubled history. Abyssinia, the precursor to modern-day Ethiopia, was a feudal, tributary empire. It expanded and contracted through the centuries depending on the military strength of its successive rulers, who had to hold together by force and manipulation disparate, lesser kingdoms and ethnic groups while fending off persistent external threats, especially from Arab states. The colonial era brought new conflicts to Ethiopia. Italy conquered and created the colony of Eritrea in 1890 and successfully invaded Ethiopia in 1935–36. Defeat of the Italians in 1941 restored the rule of Haile Selassie to Ethiopia and brought British rule to Eritrea. British rule of Eritrea ended in 1952 when it was federated with Ethiopia pursuant to a United Nations (UN) resolution.

The Eritrean Insurgency

Phase I of the Eritrean insurgency began in 1959 with emergence of the Eritrean Liberation Movement (ELM), a relatively small armed organization operating in urban areas. By 1964 the ELM had been eliminated as a military force by a rival organization, the Eritrean Liberation Front (ELF), formed in Cairo in 1961, which concentrated in rural areas on conducting small-scale guerrilla actions. A 1964 coup in Sudan, which brought to power a regime permissive of Eritrean insurgent operations from its territory, was a boon to the emerging ELF. The increasing alignment of the Addis Ababa government with Israel during the sixties also brought the insurgents valuable Arab support and assistance.

By the late sixties, the ELF had thousands of fighters, organized primarily along tribal lines, in five autonomous regions. A combination of power struggles among contending leaders, tribal differences, and tensions created by the inclusion of Christians into what had been an almost exclusively Muslim organization brought emergence of the breakaway Eritrean People's Liberation Front (EPLF) in 1970. The EPLF differed from the ELF in its emphasis on leadership in the field (rather than outside the country), unification of all fighters into a single army, and a more considerate and democratic approach to the civilian population. Armed clashes between the two rival guerrilla groups ensued from 1970 to 1974. There were periods of coexistence and cooperation, albeit fragile, between the two groups from 1975 to 1980. In 1981, the EPLF virtually eliminated ELF forces from the field and drove ELF leaders into exile abroad.

Reflecting the view of its dominant young leaders, the EPLF adopted an avowedly Marxist-Leninist platform and increasingly defined liberation for Eritrea in terms of full independence from Ethiopia. As a result, the EPLF received military assistance from the Soviet Union, Cuba, and China, which augmented support from various Arab states, especially Syria and Libya. The significance of this assistance is indicated by Paul Henze's assessment that "dissidence in Eritrea amounted to very little until the late 1960's when radical Arabs and communists began stoking the rebellion."[1]

EPLF Secretary General Isaias Afeworke, however, flatly denies that the EPLF ever received any "military aid from the Soviet Union, Cuba, and China." Isaias does acknowledge that Cuba trained "some fighters in the sixties, before the formation of the EPLF."[2]

The Ethiopian government's recognition of China in 1971 ended Chinese support for the Eritrean cause. The emergence of the Mengistu Marxist government in 1977, following the 1974 overthrow of Emperor Haile Selassie, brought an abrupt shift of Soviet and Cuban military aid on a massive scale to the new regime in Addis Ababa. Arab support for the Eritreans also declined during this period as a result of the demise of the Muslim-oriented ELF. Thus, by 1980, the EPLF was left to rely almost totally on itself and the financial support it received from large Eritrean exile communities abroad.

The Tigrayan Insurgency

As the insurgency in Eritrea took hold and grew, another blossomed in the neighboring region of Tigray. Once the rulers of Abyssinia during the long reign of the Axumite kings, the Tigrayans lost out to the ascending Amharas and their Shoan Dynasty kings in the latter part of the nineteenth century. Decades of Shoan domination and exploitation reduced once-powerful and wealthy Tigray to a backward, undeveloped agricultural region of subsistence farmers. Tigrayan resentment of this exploitation erupted in 1943 in the Weyane (popular) rebellion, which was quickly crushed by the imperial government in Addis Ababa. Although Emperor Haile Selassie managed to manipulate a succession of subordinate Tigrayan rulers and control the region, he did little to satisfy the real grievances of the Tigrayan people.

A military coup against the emperor in 1961, while he was abroad on a state visit to Brazil, failed. It did elicit from the aging emperor some modest steps toward "modernization" of the backward, feudal society that he ruled, however. As part of this process Haile Selassie established in 1961 Ethiopia's first national university in Addis Ababa, appropriately named Haile Selassie University (HSU).

Marxism-Leninism became a popular ideology on the HSU campus. Both students and professors embraced Marxism as a quick, revolutionary formula for moving their country from feudal backwardness to the modern era. In the early seventies Tigrayans left the HSU campus in large numbers and went to the isolated mountain regions of western Tigray; there in February 1975 they founded the

Tigrayan People's Liberation Front (TPLF). The longtime leader of the TPLF Meles Zenawi (now president of the Transitional Government of Ethiopia) was one of these students. Meles, like many others, abandoned his studies in 1974 to join the insurgents in the mountains of the Shire district of Tigray.

Enjoying the benefits of remote, difficult-to-reach areas of operations, sanctuary in Sudan, and support and sympathy from the local populace for their opposition to Amhara oppression and exploitation, the Tigrayan insurgents not only survived but prospered. The ranks of their fighters swelled, and they gradually mastered the tactics and techniques of hit-and-run guerrilla warfare. By the mid-seventies the TPLF was sufficiently threatening to cause the United States to withdraw all of its Peace Corps volunteers from Tigray for security reasons. Even then, though, TPLF forces numbered only in the several thousands, and they were unable to take and hold any towns outside of their base area in the far west of Tigray. They did, however, range increasingly farther from this area, striking throughout Tigray.

To this day TPLF leaders, including Meles Zenawi, deny that their movement ever received any outside military assistance. They do acknowledge help in later years from the EPLF, which they say was reciprocated at times, but downplay the significance of this help to their protracted struggle. The intelligence available, albeit very limited, supports TPLF claims of almost total self-reliance.

Causes of the Insurgencies

Both the Eritrean and Tigrayan insurgences were rebellions against the central government in Addis Ababa, and both were fueled by deep-seated ethnic resentment of domination by the ruling Amhara elite of the central Shoan region. This resentment, however, took somewhat different forms in the two regions. The Eritreans, by virtue of their long colonial experience with the Italians, unquestionably considered themselves *superior* to the Amharas. Indeed, they were more developed politically and economically. At the time of Ethiopian annexation in 1962, Eritrea had a rather well-developed infrastructure of roads, railroads, harbors, and communications; a growing industrial sector; schools; and even a functioning elected parliament. As Robert D. Kaplan has observed,

> Trade unions were established and political culture came to be more advanced in Eritrea than anywhere else on the continent outside of Egypt and South Africa. Whatever its sins, Italian capitalism proved to be a liberating social experience for the Eritreans.[3]

Ethiopia, still an economically backward state governed by a feudal tributary monarchy, had few or none of these attributes at the time of annexation in 1962. Haile Selassie's solution to this disequilibrium was to bring Eritrea down to a level with the rest of his empire. As Kaplan further notes,

> Selassie never respected the autonomy agreement. Eritrea's independent institutions were gradually subverted, political parties were banned and Tigrinia, Tigre and Arabic were suppressed as the languages of Eritrea and replaced by Amharic.[4]

The Eritreans came to perceive the Amharas as just another foreign power intent on subjugating and colonizing their land and its people. Although the Italian colonialists had done the same, they also brought material and other benefits to Eritrea. Thus, for Eritreans, liberation from this yoke became the focus of their struggle and independence their ultimate objective.

The Tigrayans had a different perspective. Once the rulers of Ethiopia, they considered themselves an integral part of it. The Amharas were not foreign colonizers but rather minority oppressors of their fellow Ethiopians, especially larger ethnic groups such as the Tigrayans and the majority Oromos in the southern and eastern regions. Paul Henze, the leading U.S. expert on Ethiopia, concluded in his 1985 analysis on rebels and separatists that:

> It seems unlikely that its Marxism is the prime reason for the TPLF's relative success in gaining the support of a sizable proportion of the Tigrayan populace. Past Tigrean history would lead to the conclusion that the momentum derives instead from the Tigreans' . . . perception of themselves as coequals with the Amhara (and on the scene well before them) in leading the Ethiopian empire.[5]

The TPLF, as its name indicates, initially set out to liberate the "Tigrayan people" from Amhara oppression and domination. They were convinced that this oppression had led to the exploitation of their region and to their being reduced to second-class status not only politically but economically, culturally, and socially as well. Their success in convincing the people produced the groundswell of popular support they began to enjoy throughout Tigray. This support not only gave the TPLF ample recruits but also motivated its adherents to sacrifice and to fight long and hard.

The TPLF presented its cause as that of all the people of Ethiopia, including even the Amharas, whom they portrayed as equally oppressed by the increasingly brutal and dictatorial Mengistu regime. In discussions with me during the last year of the war, TPLF chairman Meles Zenawi frequently articulated this broadening of the struggle to encompass all of Ethiopia. He actively sought to expand the movement and ally with other insurgent groups. TPLF alliance with one of these groups, the Ethiopian People's Democratic Movement (made up largely of Amharas), produced the expanded Ethiopian People's Revolutionary Democratic Front (EPRDF) in May 1989. Meles's efforts to woo other rebel groups, especially the OLF of the Oromos, failed, but the latter group did lessen its hostility to the EPRDF and pursue parallel military operations with it and the EPLF.[6]

Exit the Emperor, Enter the Dictator

The overthrow of Haile Selassie in a relatively benign and bloodless coup by younger officers in 1974 was to affect profoundly the Eritrean and emerging Tigrayan insurgencies. Initially the coup aroused hopes that it would bring to power a progressive, democratic regime that could unite Ethiopia and end the rebellions. As Henze observed, in the case of Eritrea,

> There was good reason to believe that a major portion of the leaders of the various Eritrean factions (who had never been united) could have been drawn into serious negotiations with the revolutionary government. There was some chance that these could have led to a settlement based on a revised formula for autonomy—going back perhaps to that which had been adopted in 1952.[7]

Such hopes were dashed in 1977 when Lt. Col. Mengistu Haile Mariam emerged victorious from a bloody internal power struggle as chairman of the revolution's Provisional Military Administrative Committee (popularly known as the Derge). Embracing Marxism-Leninism as his guiding political and economic ideology and allying himself totally with the Soviet Union, Mengistu set about to crush the insurgencies, especially in Eritrea. With massive Soviet military aid (approximately a billion dollars a year) Mengistu rapidly expanded the army into the largest in Africa (some 350,000) and equipped it with modern Soviet weaponry.

Viewing Leninism as the most effective system for imposing ironfisted, one-man dictatorial rule, Mengistu eventually created the full panoply of Marxist-Leninist organizations: a Workers' Party of Ethiopia complete with Politburo, Central Committee, and People's Congress and a network of party control organizations that extended to both rural village and urban neighborhood levels. With Soviet and East German assistance Mengistu also built up a large internal security apparatus that extended its tentacles throughout the military, the government, the party, and all of Ethiopian society. All other organizations, even religious, were brutally suppressed; and their leaders executed, thrown into prison, or exiled.

Because both the EPLF and the TPLF were avowedly Marxist-Leninist movements with similar Party/Central Committee/Politburo/Chairman organizational structures, the emergence in 1977–78 of an ostensibly "brother-socialist" regime in Addis Ababa was a particular challenge to them. Initially, it seemed as if the new regime in Addis Ababa might "steal the insurgents' flag," offering a better, more effective solution to the problems of the feudal economic and political backwardness of Ethiopia. Accordingly, an initial impact of the changes that took place in Ethiopia between 1974–77 was to slow the momentum of the insurgencies.

The Eritreans were initially intrigued by the prospect that they might at long last have a government in Addis Ababa with whom they could cooperate to solve the long-festering problem of Eritrea. The EPLF, itself long supported by the Soviet Union, also saw Soviet alliance with Mengistu as potentially promising, offering the prospect of Soviet influence being used on behalf of a just settlement of their conflict with Ethiopia.

According to Meles Zenawi, the TPLF, from the beginning, was much more skeptical of the revolutionary changes in Addis Ababa. The TPLF adopted a lower profile, wait-and-see attitude and kept their forces intact to see what would result for them. They did not have long to wait. It soon became apparent that the Mengistu regime was even more determined than its predecessors, and certainly more able, to crush the insurgencies in Eritrea and Tigray.

Instead of relieving the grievances of the Eritreans and Tigrayans, Mengistu only made them worse. His policies of collectivization, forced resettlement, and restrictions on internal movement had a decidedly negative impact on Tigray. According to Meles Zenawi, Mengistu's policies enhanced Tigrayan perceptions of oppression from the center and increased their poverty and hopelessness. The fact that an Amhara elite continued to dominate the new government fed long-standing Tigrayan resentment on this score. The net, longer-term effect was only to increase popular support for the TPLF and to escalate its armed resistance.

A similar impact was felt in Eritrea. Eritreans came to perceive Mengistu and the Derge regime as even more colonialist in their approach to Eritrea than their imperial predecessor. As the Soviets and Cubans abandoned their former Eritrean allies totally and threw themselves wholeheartedly behind Mengistu and the Derge, hopes of their exercising a salutary influence were dashed. Instead, they supported an all-out offensive in early 1977 by the much larger Derge army, now joined by a large air force and even a navy. Mengistu raised the war in Eritrea to new heights of terror, destruction, and suffering for the people. He became, as Paul Henze noted, "more deeply entangled in fighting in Eritrea than Haile Selassie had ever been."[8]

Although the EPLF and TPLF clung to standard Marxist-Leninist rhetoric and organizational structures almost to the end of their struggle in 1991, whatever meaning ideology had had gradually began to dissipate. A new political and economic realism emerged in the insurgent movements. The dismal failure of the Marxist economic system not only in Ethiopia but also in the Soviet Union and Eastern Europe also speeded up the process of ideological rethinking among the rebels.

Beginning in 1989, the EPLF and the TPLF also began to rethink their attitudes toward the United States and the West. During 1989–90 both Isaias Afeworke and Meles Zenawi traveled to Washington and several European capitals, and contacts were openly established with the U.S. government.[9]

This process evolved in 1990 into the United States' playing an active mediating role in the Eritrean conflict and culminated with the U.S. government convening the London All Parties Conference in the final days of the war.

Rarely has the U.S. government so quickly and effectively established such cooperative working relationships with rebels out of power before they came into power. That the Bush administration also managed to maintain its diplomatic relationships with the besieged government in Addis Ababa is particularly remarkable.

With this background on the insurgent movements, the causes of the insurgencies, and key historical events that affected them, we can now apply the Manwaring paradigm to the conflicts that lasted for more than thirty years in Ethiopia and eventually produced insurgent victories.

The Manwaring Paradigm

The following sections apply Manwaring's six principal components to the successful Eritrean and Tigrayan insurgencies.

Legitimacy

Manwaring maintains that "the thrust of a revolutionary program relies on grievances such as political, social, and economic discrimination as the means through which the government is attacked."[10] The governments of both Emperor Haile Selassie and dictator Mengistu Haile Mariam provided ample grievances on which the Eritrean and Tigrayan rebels could focus their revolutionary programs.

The Eritreans probably had the easier time in convincing their people that they were the victims of "foreign, colonial domination" from an uncaring, faraway regime in Addis Ababa. Although the government occasionally used both civilian and military officials of Eritrean descent, it never seriously attempted to present itself as other than what it was, a regime dominated by members of the Amhara ethnic group governing primarily for its own self-interest. Even the wiser and more adept Haile Selassie succumbed to outlawing manifestations of the Eritrean culture and language. Rather than trying to adapt the political, economic, and social institutions that it inherited in Eritrea to its own ends, the imperial government simply abolished them and tried to impose its own, different institutions.

This mistake was compounded by the Mengistu regime, which removed most prominent Eritreans from government, with certain token exceptions, and waged the war there almost exclusively with officers and men from the central and southern regions. This policy enabled the EPLF to portray Derge forces as a colonial army of occupation bent on the suppression and destruction of all that was indigenously Eritrean.

In the contest for legitimacy, the Eritrean insurgents also enjoyed other advantages. By embracing the cause of independence, later defined as "self-determination," the EPLF occupied undeniable moral high ground in the eyes of their people. Externally, though, this played to the disadvantage of the EPLF. Most foreign governments, bound to an unquestioning respect for the "sovereignty and territorial integrity" of a fellow member of the "family of nations," opposed per se secessionist or separatist movements. The enshrinement of this principle in a unanimous Organization of African Unity (OAU) resolution, adopted in Cairo in 1964, deprived the Eritreans of open, legal, and moral support from most of the continent. Until Mengistu's 1977 break with the West, this principle also ensured strong backing for Addis Ababa from the United States and West European governments.

Fortunately for the Eritreans, the Sudanese, following a 1964 coup in their country, chose to ignore the principle of respect for their neighbor's sovereignty and territorial integrity. Until they switched sides in 1977, the Soviets and other communist regimes did likewise and openly supported the Eritrean struggle. When the Muslim-dominated ELF waged the struggle, prior to 1961, many Arab states also supported the insurgents.

For all practical purposes, Mengistu ceded the battle for internal legitimacy to the Eritreans when he embarked in 1982 on his all-out "Red Star" campaign to crush them militarily. Thereafter, the Addis government waged war on the people, bombing indiscriminately and brutally suppressing them. It abandoned any pretense of waging war on political, economic, and social fronts in Eritrea. The regime, however, did continue to capitalize on Ethiopian nationalism to mobilize support against the Eritrean secessionists in the rest of the country, even to the end.

The contest for the crown of legitimacy was much closer in Tigray, especially during the reign of Haile Selassie. A skilled manipulator of men, the emperor, through guile and deception, played off various Tigrayan elements against one another and retained a modicum of Tigrayan acquiescence, if not support, for his rule. With a much smaller and poorly equipped army, his suppression of dissent in the region was less destructive as well. On economic and social fronts, however, the emperor failed to contest the opposition effectively. Little effort was made to develop Tigray economically or to give it essential infrastructure such as transport, communications, schools, and hospitals. This neglect of the needs of his people was not limited to Tigray, as the subsequent overthrow of Haile Selassie confirmed, but it was particularly costly in Tigray, where the emperor was contending for legitimacy with emerging opposition groups.

Mengistu, by pursuing misguided Marxist economic and social policies, saved the TPLF from itself. His application of forced resettlement almost exclusively to Tigray following the 1984–85 drought and famine cost him dearly in the eyes of the Tigrayan people. His restrictions on internal movement of Tigrayans, who traditionally had worked as seasonal migrant laborers throughout Ethiopia, was in the view of TPLF leader Meles a monumental blunder and great boon for the TPLF.

Nevertheless, the battle for legitimacy was not easily won by the TPLF. The open espousal of Albanian-style Marxism by Marxist-Leninist League adherence within the TPLF not only alienated most foreign (even communist) governments but also frightened many

Tigrayans. Despite the obvious advantages of doing so, the TPLF did not alter its rhetoric until very late in the conflict.

Fortunately for the TPLF it did not actually practice the Albanian Marxism that it preached. Following its occupation of Tigray in the late 1980s, the TPLF abstained from imposing doctrinaire Marxism-Leninism on the people. To the contrary, it began to return property seized by the Mengistu regime to private ownership, to free peasants from Mengistu's collectivization and villagization schemes, and to permit those forcibly resettled to return home if they wished.

TPLF administration of Tigray was also benign and permissive, especially when contrasted with that of the Derge. It permitted the establishment of local councils and encouraged people to decide for themselves local issues of governance and administration. Despite its extremely limited resources, the TPLF also encouraged private enterprise and local economic development, giving Tigrayans a freedom never theretofore experienced in such matters. The TPLF was especially adept in handling religion, not only permitting freedom of worship but also returning property that Mengistu and his Workers' Party had taken from Tigray's powerful religious communities. Such wise policies gave the TPLF a clear victory in the battle for the hearts and minds of the people. A consistent application of such policies to areas outside of Tigray that the TPLF overran in the latter months of the conflict undoubtedly paved the way for and facilitated its surprising military victories.

In sum, in both Eritrea and Tigray, the failure of the government and success of the insurgents in the area of legitimacy confirmed Manwaring's thesis that legitimacy is the most important single dimension that can determine the outcome of an insurgency.

Organization for Unity of Effort

Both the EPLF and the TPLF had good, close-knit organizational structures (see Figure 7.1). At the highest operational level, the Politburo, composed of nine or ten members, each with specific responsibilities (security, foreign relations, etc.), functioned very much as a cabinet under the leadership of the front's secretary general. Little is known about the inner workings of the EPLF and TPLF politburos. They reportedly engaged in extensive discussions, striving to reach a consensus on major issues and operational matters. Policies and long-range programs for the two groups were established by their respective congresses and central committees.

Both EPLF Chairman Isaias Afeworke and TPLF Chairman Meles Zenawi, in my extensive dealings with them, seemed to be very much in charge of their respective movements both militarily and

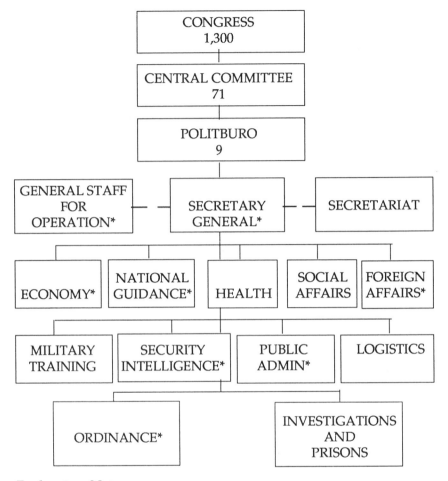

Explanatory Notes:
1. The numbers in the Congress, Central Committee, and Politburo boxes are the number of members of each of these bodies.
2. The asterisks indicate that the particular department or section was headed by a Politburo member (in the case of National Guidance, two Politburo members). The distribution of the more powerful Politburo members indicates the importance the EPLF attached to particular functions as well as the well-balanced nature of its organization among military, political, economic, and security areas.

Figure 7.1 Organization of the Eritrean People's Liberation Front (EPLF)

politically. They clearly were not a one-man band, however, and did appear to delegate authority to others for specific responsibilities.

Years of living together in the bush and sharing common hardships and dangers engendered a strong sense of comradeship among the insurgent leadership groups. Nevertheless, differences over both strategy and tactics undoubtedly existed. The EPLF was a diverse organization of Christians and Muslims, highlanders and lowlanders, and different tribal and linguistic groups. It was known to have internal debates over key issues such as the prosecution of the war, peace negotiations, and the independence question. Although more homogeneous, the TPLF was believed also to have internal dissension, particularly in later years, over the movement's commitment to Marxism and its relations with other rebel groups, especially the Oromos.[11] The TPLF also experienced a leadership battle, eventually resolved by the ascendency of Meles Zenawi and the departure of two high-ranking members of the TPLF leadership in 1987.

In the end though, a consensus prevailed in the EPLF and the TPLF throughout their respective long struggles. Remarkably, there were no significant defections to the government from either movement. Both movements pursued integrated military, political, economic, and social/psychological strategies. Their eventual success owed much to their effective organization for pursuing their respective campaigns against the government.

The Mengistu government had a similar Politburo organization at the top (nominally subordinate to a National Congress and Central Committee), but it functioned quite differently from those of the rebels. Almost from the beginning Mengistu Haile Mariam governed as an all-powerful dictator much in the manner of Josef Stalin or Adolf Hitler. Although Politburo members enjoyed some authority within their respective spheres of responsibility, all were clearly subordinate to Mengistu. Chairman Mengistu had pronounced (often uninformed) views on almost every subject from agriculture and education to military strategy and tactics. Politburo members seemed to be trying always to divine Mengistu's opinion and to tailor their own accordingly. Those who did not did not last for long.

In prosecuting the war Mengistu employed a triad organizational structure of separate military, party, and security components that extended from the top down to the field level. Military units from the high command down to brigade or battalion had not only a military commander but also a Workers' Party political officer and an Internal Security Agency officer. These officers operated independently of one another and reported through their own channels upward to their respective headquarters. Only at Mengistu's level were the three components, each reporting separately to him, brought together.

Although the military commander was nominally in charge of his unit, the political and security officers, especially the former, did not hesitate to dabble in unit affairs, including campaign strategy and military operations. At times, their views prevailed over those of the military commanders. Thus, at all levels authority was fragmented, and there was no consistent unity of effort to address counterinsurgency problems. This flawed government organization for pursuing the struggle was a significant factor in the government's failure to defeat the insurgents, as Manwaring's theory would suggest.

Military and Other Support to a Targeted Government

According to Manwaring, if a threatened government is provided unobtrusive material and/or nonmaterial support consistently over a long term, its chances of success in a counterinsurgency situation are considerably enhanced.[12] Because of the reversal of U.S. and Soviet fortunes that followed the exit of the emperor and emergence of the dictator Mengistu, Ethiopia provides a unique opportunity to compare and contrast U.S. and Soviet military and other support to the successive insurgent-targeted governments there.

Ethiopia emerged from World War II as a new strategic ally of the United States in the Horn of Africa. As a result, when the United Nations resolved the future of the former Italian colony of Eritrea in 1950 the United States supported its federation with Ethiopia. As Secretary of State John Foster Dulles explained when the federation was effected in 1952: "From the point of view of justice, the opinions of the Eritrean people must receive consideration. Nevertheless, the strategic interest of the United States . . . (makes) it necessary that the country has to be linked with our ally Ethiopia."[13]

Following the signing of base agreement and military assistance treaties in 1952–53, substantial economic and military assistance flowed steadily and consistently from the United States to Ethiopia. Assessing this assistance relationship Henze concluded,

A pattern was set that persisted through 1977; economic aid always exceeded military aid. American personnel in Ethiopia carrying out economic assistance programs always outnumbered military assistance personnel. Military aid was kept at a level that did not permit expansion of Ethiopia's armed manpower above 50,000 and discouraged acquisition of military equipment beyond Ethiopia's realistic needs or ability to maintain. From its very beginning the U.S. military assistance program was strictly geared to conservative estimates of Ethiopia's internal security requirements and ability to meet limited international security obligations.[14]

U.S. economic, military, and diplomatic support clearly seems to have met Manwaring's requirements for consistency and long-term duration. The support was also well balanced between economic and military and appropriately blended to include training, educational, and cultural components and even one of the United States' largest and most successful Peace Corps contingents. Why then, did the emperor's government not succeed against the Eritrean and Tigrayan insurgents? Two explanations can be offered.

First, it can be argued that, because U.S. military assistance was so conservatively programmed, it did not give Haile Selassie either the quantity or the quality of weapons, advice, and training needed for military victory over the insurgents. Although U.S. and other military support (mostly advisers from Britain, Sweden, and Israel) was sufficient for the Ethiopian government to contain the insurgencies, it fell short of what was required to defeat them, especially given the substantial support to Eritreans from the Soviets and Arabs during this period.

Second, U.S. support for the Ethiopian government was fatally flawed because it failed adequately to address the issue of "legitimacy." As noted in the examination of legitimacy, the emperor gave the insurgents ample means to attack him in this area because of his neglect of the genuine grievances and basic needs of the Eritrean and Tigrayan people. Although he made some halting concessions to modernization, Haile Selassie made none of the basic economic, political, and social reforms needed to remove his nation from feudal backwardness, where it essentially remained until his downfall in 1974.

Despite its close relationship with and substantial support for the emperor and his government, the United States apparently did not press them to make the structural reforms necessary not only for counterinsurgency success but also for their own survival. Admittedly, the essentiality of this component for a successful counterinsurgency effort was not so widely accepted in the fifties and sixties as it is today. The United States had yet to learn the lessons that later would emerge from its experiences in Southeast Asia and Central America. In addition, an insistence on respect for human rights and social justice had not yet emerged as key elements of U.S. policy in supporting friendly governments.

It was a tribute to the consistency of U.S. support for the Ethiopian government that it continued even after the overthrow of the emperor in 1974. In his comprehensive "Anatomy of a Revolution" article, Paul Henze noted,

> U.S. economic aid programs continued without interruption and U.S. military support for Ethiopia was sharply *increased* after 1974. One-third (in dollar value) of all military aid provided by the USA to Ethiopia over the 25-year period 1953–78 was delivered *after* the revolution. These deliveries included what was then one of the most advanced American aircraft, the F5–E.[15]

Surprisingly, the United States seemed undaunted by the dethronement of its longtime friend and ally Haile Selassie and was, apparently, initially somewhat hopeful for the future in Ethiopia. Even the bloody aftermath of the coup and the emergence of Mengistu did not deter the United States from continuing its support. The Carter administration did not suspend military aid until November 1977 (to both Ethiopia and Somalia), and U.S. economic aid was not terminated until 5 July 1979.[16]

It was left to Mengistu to make the break with the United States and shift to the USSR, a move he began secretly as early as 1976. When the switch to the Soviets emerged openly in 1977 it was both swift and massive. Large amounts of Soviet weaponry (tanks, artillery, and aircraft) were quickly dispatched by air and sea to Ethiopia along with thousands of Soviet and Cuban advisers. With Ethiopia bogged down in heavy fighting in Eritrea, which the rebels seemed to be winning, Somalia's Siad Barre, himself bolstered after years of large-scale Soviet military aid, revived a long-standing border dispute and invaded eastern Ethiopia. The result of this misguided move was to seal the emerging Soviet relationship with Mengistu and to bring about a sudden switch of sides by the Soviet Union from Somalia to Ethiopia. Henze noted in 1990 that,

> When the Somalis made use of the arms the Soviets had supplied to attack Ethiopia in the summer of 1977, the Soviets hesitated only briefly, then came to Ethiopia's "rescue" with 20,000 Cubans and a billion dollars worth of arms. This was only the beginning of a lavish program of military assistance for Ethiopia, amounting to perhaps as much as $12 billion and which has yet to come to an end.[17]

Employing U.S. military aid (the recently supplied F5–Es were particularly useful) and the new Soviet arms and Cuban fighters, the Derge quickly halted and drove back the Somali offensive. It then turned this firepower with a vengeance on the advancing Eritreans. Aided by Soviet naval bombardments on coastal areas, Ethiopian forces rolled back the Eritreans to a relatively small mountain enclave at Nakfa in northeast Eritrea from which it was unable to dislodge them, despite repeated massive and costly assaults.

The Eritreans were able to survive and eventually push back the Ethiopians and regain significant towns. Consistent massive Soviet military support enabled Mengistu to try again with another all-out offensive in 1986. Although the Eritreans were once again driven back into their northeastern enclave, victory continued to elude Mengistu, and he eventually had to break off the costly offensive at the gates of Nakfa. As Henze observed,

> The continued high level of arms supplied to Ethiopia shows the extent to which the Soviets underwrote Mengistu's repeated but unsuccessful Eritrean and other northern offensives. There can be no question of "superpower competition," for no one was competing with Moscow.[18]

Although Soviet support had not terminated, in reality it was rapidly coming to an end. Another major shift in Soviet policy in the Horn was about to occur. By 1990 internal developments in the Soviet Union (the emergence of *glasnost* and *perestroika* and mounting economic failure) had sapped both Soviet interest in and their capacity for "adventurism," not only in Africa but in Afghanistan as well.

In addition, Mengistu's own failures, not only militarily but politically, economically, and socially, had convinced the Soviets that he was a "loser," and an expensive one at that. As the last deliveries on its long-term military assistance agreement with Ethiopia were made during 1990, no new agreement was concluded with Mengistu (despite his repeated appeals), and the flow of Soviet arms gradually ceased. Lacking hard currency because of his destruction of the Ethiopian economy, Mengistu desperately turned to North Korea but to no avail. The North Koreans, despite Mengistu's admiration for them and his friendship with Kim Il-sung, apparently had also concluded that Mengistu was doomed.

The Manwaring model is therefore applicable as well in the area of military and other support of the targeted government. True to Manwaring's theory, when the support on which the Mengistu regime had become so totally dependent was withdrawn, "the possibilities for success against an insurgency were minimal."[19] In a subsequent section, we will turn to the insurgent side and examine the question of outside aid to them.

Some final points on outside support to the Mengistu government should be made, however. Although the Soviets were lavish in their military support for Mengistu, they were miserly in their economic assistance to his regime. Beyond substantial supplies of petroleum, little other than military assistance was forthcoming from the Soviet Union or its East European allies. The economic assistance that was given had little developmental impact. Mengistu's misguided Marxist economic policies, which he maintained until the end despite urgings for change from communist allies, ensured this. The Soviets, like the Americans with the emperor, also failed adequately to press Mengistu to address the real grievances of the insurgents in political, economic, and social areas.

Intelligence

Although the Mengistu regime had a large internal security apparatus, its effectiveness was limited largely to areas under government control, to keep them in line. The Derge was unable to penetrate EPLF or TPLF leadership and organizational structures either to neutralize or to destroy them. This failure was due primarily both to the strength of rebel discipline and to their hold over the people in their areas of control. There were simply few, if any, chinks in the rebel armor in intelligence and internal security areas.

There is little evidence that the Soviets did much to help correct this deficiency, possibly because of their own ineptitude in counterinsurgency intelligence. Although Derge military and security intelligence technology and dominance of the air gave them reasonably good tactical military intelligence, they knew little of rebel plans and intentions in the strategic area. In addition, Mengistu's own style of governing and his injection of party sycophants into military units discouraged subordinates from "telling it like it was."

Little is known of EPLF and insurgent intelligence operations and capabilities, but they apparently were fairly effective. The marginalization of Eritreans and Tigrayans in Ethiopian military, party, and governmental structures served to deprive the rebels of this potential source of intelligence, though some inside information undoubtedly was obtained by them. In the final months of the conflict the rebels seemed particularly adept at tracking and anticipating enemy force movements and dispositions.

On balance, however, neither government nor insurgents seem to have enjoyed any significant advantage in the area of intelligence. Accordingly, this aspect of the conflict was somewhat of a standoff between the government and insurgents.

Discipline and Capabilities of the Armed Forces

Discipline, determination, dedication, and motivation are critical in an insurgency; the rebels had a superabundance of all these. In many respects the EPLF and the TPLF can be said to have written the manual for successful insurgent performance in these areas.

Discipline of EPLF and TPLF fighters and political cadres was remarkable in both victory and defeat. Based on my personal knowledge of the rebels and extensive discussions with their leaders, I attribute this discipline to the following:

- Recruitment into both EPLF and TPLF ranks was strictly voluntary.[20] They never impressed or forcibly recruited. Moreover, adherents were free to depart at any time, though peer pressure on them to remain must undoubtedly have been great.
- Political indoctrination of fighters by the insurgents was most effective. They emphasized the positive goals of their respective insurgencies: ending "colonial" rule and independence for the EPLF and liberation from Amhara domination and a fairer share of national resources and power for the TPLF. Revenge and demonization of the enemy were discouraged.
- Both movements were strictly egalitarian. There were no privileged elites, and hardships and dangers were shared equally by all. Officers not only fought alongside their men but wore the same clothes, ate the same rations (often extremely sparse), and lived among them.
- Leadership concern for their troops was real and consistent. Fighters knew their movement would do its utmost to care for them, especially if wounded or disabled, and to provide for their material needs to the best of its abilities. As a result, the rebel fighters were extremely self-assured.
- The EPLF and TPLF also demanded that their forces always be considerate not only of the civilian population but of the enemy as well. The rebels were both fair and flexible in dealing with the people and actively sought to win them over by the example the rebels provided to them. Remarkably, throughout decades of brutal conflict, the rebels committed no atrocities or terrorist acts. Their conduct, both as combatants and occupiers, was exemplary.

During the conflict and in the victorious aftermath the rebels have been universally commended for their dedication, which made them fight, and for their discipline, which made them fight well. Observers, however, should not lose sight of the above attributes of the insurgent movements, which explain the rebels' uncommon dedication, determination, and discipline.

At this time the Ethiopian army for its part had a highly professional officer corps, which, when left alone, was capable of leading and motivating its troops in the field. During the Mengistu years, however, the officer corps was degraded professionally by periodic purges (even executions ordered personally by Mengistu) and by persistent interference from party ideologues and above all from Mengistu himself. The Soviets, perhaps suffering from the same deficiencies, did little to alleviate this interference.

The Ethiopian regular soldier was tough and capable of fighting well. As Mengistu greatly expanded his forces, however, he resorted increasingly to forced conscription, often seizing "cannon fodder" off the streets and from homes and schoolrooms. Although government forces were well equipped, thanks to ample Soviet arms and munitions, training of these recruits was poor, especially in the later years of the conflict when they were dispatched quickly to the front. The result was poor discipline, dedication, and motivation to fight. In the final years of the conflict, government troops surrendered en masse to advancing insurgent forces. The rebels, by treating these prisoners humanely and usually disarming and releasing them to return home, exploited this situation to the maximum. Eventually, the Ethiopian army simply collapsed and gave up, though a few regular units performed effectively to the very end of the war.

In sum, most of the strengths of the insurgents were the weaknesses of the government forces. The Mengistu regime proved incapable of correcting these weaknesses, though it did begin in the later years of the conflict to address them, with Israeli advice and assistance. Such advice and assistance, from Mengistu's point of view, were too little and too late. The regime's military failure was compounded by its poor performance on political, economic, psychological, and social fronts. As the Manwaring paradigm would suggest, the inevitable result was failure effectively to counter the insurgents and eventual defeat on the battlefield.

One intriguing question emerges from the outcome of the conflict in Ethiopia. Would Mengistu have failed in the areas of discipline and capabilities of his armed forces if he had maintained his support relationship with the United States? Could we, would we, have saved him?

Reduction of Outside Aid to the Insurgents

As noted earlier, EPLF leaders deny allegations that they received military assistance from the Soviet Union and communist countries or from Arab countries. TPLF leaders also deny having ever received any outside military aid, despite suspicions that they in fact did. In any event, the Soviets and communist governments switched support to the government after 1977. A waning of Arab interest in the insurgent EPLF as Muslim influence within them diminished eventually ended most of whatever support they were giving.

Ironically, though, the indiscriminate provision of massive amounts of Soviet arms and supplies to the Mengistu regime gave the insurgents a new source of outside aid. As Henze has concluded,

> During the 1980s the two large north Ethiopian insurgencies shed dependence on outside—largely Arab—help to maintain their momentum. They have acquired a major share of their weaponry and supplies from the Ethiopian military as a result of capture, abandonment or sale. Shipments of Soviet military aid which continued to arrive at Ethiopian ports through the first weeks of 1990 have been sustaining internal conflict on both sides.[21]

The only way the Ethiopian government could have reduced this aid to the insurgents would have been to defeat them on the battlefield, which increasingly it was unable to do. The government found itself in a vicious cycle. As the government lost matériel to the insurgents the rebels became even stronger through effective incorporation of this equipment into their order of battle and, consequently, captured or forced abandonment of even more arms and supplies. This process of attrition of government arms and supplies and accretion of those of the rebels accelerated greatly in the late eighties as the government suffered major defeats and losses of installations in both Eritrea and Tigray.

Particularly impressive was the ability of the rebels to master the use and deployment of heavy military equipment. The Eritreans took the lead when they overran the garrison and large supply depot at Afabet in March 1988, acquiring large numbers of tanks, artillery pieces, and mobile multiple rocket launchers. Within a matter of months the EPLF was operating and effectively deploying this equipment in the field. The TPLF followed suit in February 1989 when they took Inda Selassie and precipitated the nearly complete withdrawal of government forces from Tigray within a month, leaving substantial heavy arms and supplies in rebel hands. The TPLF wisely halted its offensive at this point and initiated a crash program to learn how to operate and use the heavy arms captured.

Fortunately for them success drew the TPLF and the EPLF closer, enabling the TPLF to obtain critical training and advice from the Eritreans. Interestingly, the rebels' own self-training proved more effective than that which the government forces had received from thousands of Soviet trainers and technicians. By the last year of the conflict, both the EPLF and the TPLF had transformed themselves from lightly armed, hit-and-run guerrilla forces into heavily armed regular units capable of successfully waging large-scale conventional warfare.

As noted previously, the insurgents, from the outset, enjoyed relatively unrestricted sanctuary and access to support facilities in Sudan following a coup there in 1964. As the conflict dragged on, the Sudanese commitment to the rebels only increased, driven by the emperor's close relations with Israel and especially by his permitting the Israelis to support southern Sudanese insurgents operating from Ethiopia. Mengistu's break with Israel might have improved relations but was offset by his establishment of a Marxist-Leninist system, which was an anathema to the anticommunist, Muslim Sudanese. When the southern Sudanese again rebelled in 1983 Mengistu retaliated by giving sanctuary and extensive military support to the Sudan People's Liberation Army (SPLA). Despite much talk from both sides about reciprocally ending support for the other's insurgent movements and improving relations, nothing changed. Until the very end in April 1991, the EPLF and the TPLF continued to enjoy full Sudanese support and uninhibited freedom of operations from and through Sudan, as did the SPLA in Ethiopia. Unrestricted use of Port Sudan was particularly important to the Eritreans and Tigrayans, as were their operations in Khartoum, which linked them with the outside world.

From 1988 both the TPLF and the EPLF actively sought outside political, moral, and diplomatic support. Their offices in Washington, London, and several other cities abroad mounted modest public relations and information campaigns. Although inhibited by their Marxist image, the Eritreans and Tigrayans won some sympathy and support from private individuals and organizations. Although no foreign government, except Sudan, openly backed the rebels, the United States and several European governments did begin to take them more seriously and to have a dialogue with them. The insurgents benefited in the public relations arena from the Mengistu regime's own very bad image, made worse by its handling of the massive famine in 1984–85.

On balance, neither side scored any significant victories in the battle for outside political, moral, and diplomatic support. The EPLF and the TPLF, however, did establish mutually beneficial relations with the U.S. government, which served the interests of both movements in the final year of the conflict and its immediate aftermath.

In sum, TPLF and EPLF self-reliance and ability to appropriate a large portion of the Soviet military aid to the government provided them ample means for waging war, and Sudan gave them the sanctuary needed. The government was simply unable to separate the insurgents from their internal and external sanctuaries and means of support. Government failure in this aspect of the conflict contributed greatly to its eventual defeat.

Lessons Learned

Legitimacy, as Manwaring maintained, was a crucial factor in determining the outcome of the Ethiopian insurgencies. The EPLF and the TPLF pursued widely popular, legitimate goals of self-determination and more just and equitable treatment for the people. Equally important, they both fought and governed in a manner that enhanced their legitimacy. Although the government's goals of preserving the nation were both popular and legitimate, the regime of Mengistu Haile Mariam eventually lost legitimacy in the eyes of even its own people. The result was victory for the insurgents and defeat for the government.

The EPLF and TPLF perfected highly effective political and military organizations for waging their struggles. The organization of the government, however, was fatally flawed and eventually proved incapable of effectively waging war, governing the country, or managing the economy.

Outside military support was also a critical factor in determining the outcome. The rebels enjoyed limited outside military support, primarily in the earlier years, but never became dependent on it.[22] The government, in contrast, became almost totally dependent on massive outside military support from a single source, the Soviet Union. When this support was withdrawn, in part because of the Mengistu regime's own ineptitude and failures (in political, economic, and social as well as military areas), the government could no longer sustain its troops in the field. The insurgents' ability not only to appropriate but also to employ effectively the outside military support of the government contributed greatly to their military successes. In the final analysis, the

Soviet Union, ironically, provided the insurgents the wherewithal to defeat the government.

The government concentrated almost exclusively on the military dimension of the insurgencies, generally ignoring their critical political, economic, social, psychological, and diplomatic dimensions. The government's principal outside supporters, first the United States and later the Soviet Union, failed to exert sufficient pressure on the government to make the basic structural reforms necessary to respond effectively in these critical areas of the conflict. The EPLF and the TPLF, on the other hand, pursued reasonably effective political, economic, social, and diplomatic strategies.

The discipline, dedication, determination, and motivation of the EPLF and TPLF forces were exceptionally high throughout the long war, regardless of whether they were winning or losing. Their programs of recruitment and political indoctrination, leadership style, and treatment of the people and their foe provide a model for successful insurgency.

The secure sanctuary, logistical facilities, and supply lines consistently provided to the insurgents by Sudan contributed greatly to their success. The government was unable to mount effective political and diplomatic strategies for depriving the rebels of this vital support.

Notes

1. Paul Henze, "Anatomy of a Revolution (I)," *Encounter,* June 1986, p. 7.

2. Letter of 9 November 1991 to the author from Isaias Afeworke, secretary general of the Provisional Government of Eritrea.

3. Robert D. Kaplan, "The Loneliest War," *Atlantic Monthly,* July 1988, p. 61.

4. Ibid., p. 61.

5. Paul Henze, *Rebels and Separatists in Ethiopia. Regional Resistance to a Marxist Regime,* Rand R-3347-USDP (Santa Monica, Calif., December 1985).

6. Oromo people constitute Ethiopia's largest ethnic group, numbering approximately a third of the population. Concentrated in western and southern Ethiopia, they have a long history of being subjugated by both the Amharas and the Tigrayans. Their largest insurgent group, the Oromo Liberation Front (OLF), was much smaller than either the EPLF or the TPLF.

7. Paul Henze, "Anatomy of a Revolution (II)," *Encounter,* July 1986, p. 18.

8. Ibid., p. 19.

9. When I went to Sudan as U.S. ambassador in November 1989, the

Department of State authorized my establishing liaison relationships with the insurgent organizations (EPLF, TPLF, and OLF) via Khartoum. These regular diplomatic contacts proved very fruitful, enabling us to acquire substantial information on these hitherto little-known groups and their leaders. My relations with EPLF leader Isaias and TPLF leader Meles became close and were especially intense and mutually beneficial during the final months of the conflict.

10. Max G. Manwaring, ed., *Uncomfortable Wars: Toward a New Paradigm of Low Intensity Conflict* (Boulder: Westview Press, 1991), p. 20.

11. Although the Oromo Liberation Front was much weaker militarily, the majority status of the Oromos and their presence in extensive southern and western areas where neither the Tigrayans nor the Eritreans were present made them politically significant. Sensitive to this, the TPLF and EPLF strove to accommodate the OLF and to forge alliances with it.

12. Manwaring, *Uncomfortable Wars*, p. 22.

13. Quoted in Kaplan, "The Loneliest War," p. 61.

14. Paul Henze, "The United States and the Horn of Africa: History and Current Prospects" (unpublished paper circulated at Conference on International Relations in the Horn of Africa, Cairo, 27-30 May 1990).

15. Henze, "Anatomy of a Revolution (II)," p. 16.

16. David Korn's *Ethiopia, The United States and The Soviet Union* (Carbondale: Southern Illinois University Press, 1989) exhaustively examines in chap. 3 Carter administration efforts to salvage the U.S. relationship with the Mengistu regime.

17. Henze, "United States and the Horn of Africa," p. 14.

18. Ibid., p. 16.

19. Manwaring, *Uncomfortable Wars*, p. 22.

20. The 1988 State Department *Country Report on Human Rights Practices* on Ethiopia cited "reports" of EPLF forcible recruitment of Afar tribesmen for military service. The EPLF has denied this allegation.

21. Henze, "United States and the Horn of Africa," p. 18.

22. TPLF Secretary General Meles Zenawi has stated to the author that "There was no external military support for the TPLF at any stage of the struggle." See note 2 above for a similar denial by EPLF Secretary General Isaias Afeworke

PERU*

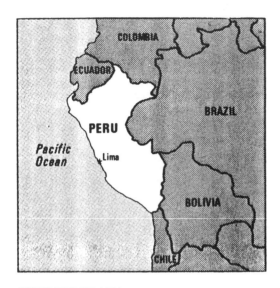

COUNTRY DATA

Area 496,222 sq. miles (three times larger than
California).

Capital Lima (population 6 million).

Ethnic Groups Indian 45%, mestizo 37%,
white 15%, black, Asian, and other 3%.

Religions Roman Catholic.

Literacy 79% of the population.

Work Force (5.2 million) Agriculture 38%,
Industry and mining 17%, Government and
other services 45%.

Infant Mortality Rate 91 per 1,000 live births.

Life Expectancy 60.8 years.

Government Constitutional republic.

UNIQUENESS OF CASE STUDY

The Shining Path's insurgency began in 1980 as
Peru was returning to civilian rule, which
included the largest legal Marxist left wing in
Latin America. It has grown steadily since, even
while eschewing outside assistance, but does
receive substantial income from "taxes" on
drug trafficking.

CHRONOLOGY

1970 Communist Party of
Peru-Shining Path (SL)
established.

1980 SL launches attacks
in Ayacucho.

1981 State of emergency
declared in Ayacucho.

Mar 1982 SL frees 247
from Ayacucho prison.

Dec 1982 First Emergency
Zone under Army
control.

1984 3,588 casualties in
Peru from political
violence.

Jun 1986 SL Lima prisons
riots; 256 inmates
killed.

May 1988 SL Labor Day
parade in Lima.

Jun 1988 SL no. 2 leader
captured.

Jul 1988 SL leader
Abimael Guzmán
Reynoso's interview in
El Diario (Lima).

Mar 1989 SL captures
police post in Upper
Huallaga Valley (UHV).

Nov 1989 Army restores
control over UHV.

Jun 1990 and **Mar 1991**
Raid on SL Lima safe
houses.

Jul 1990 45 Tupac Amaru
Revolutionary Move-
ment (MRTA) leaders
escape.

Jun 1991 SL declares
"strategic equilibrium."

Source: The map and some of the country data are from State Department "Background Notes."

8

The Shining Path in Peru: Insurgency and the Drug Problem

David Scott Palmer

The insurgent movement that calls itself the Communist Party of Peru (*Partido Comunista del Peru* or PCP) and is called by others Shining Path (*Sendero Luminoso*, the SL, or Sendero) is both a paradox and an anachronism. It is a paradox because SL began the armed struggle on 17 May 1980, the eve of Peru's first national elections in seventeen years, and has continued civil warfare in spite of three successive national democratic elections (and four municipal elections) and the largest legal Marxist left in Latin America. SL is an anachronism because it espouses in Peru a militantly orthodox, Maoist view of national and international revolution even as communism lurches from crisis to crisis and comes apart at the seams in the rest of the world.

Nevertheless, Shining Path has grown steadily by whatever indicator one uses to measure the movement: armed cadre, from less than 100 in 1980 to more than 6,000 in 1991; sympathizers, from a few thousand students and peasants in Ayacucho in the early 1970s to 50,000 to 60,000 nationwide in the early 1990s; insurgency-related incidents, from a few score in 1980–81, mostly in Ayacucho, to a few thousand in 1990–91, mostly in other parts of Peru; deaths from the political violence, from 12 in 1980 to 3,708 in 1990; property damage totaling some $20 billion through 1991, about half of Peru's gross national product.[1] It is little wonder, then, that a small industry of journalists and social scientists known as "senderologists" has sprung up over the past ten years to try to explain the Shining Path phenomenon.[2]

Shining Path had its origins in 1962 and 1963, in the provincial Ayacucho organization of Peru's then single-line (Moscow) Communist

Party.[3] The reopening in 1959 of Ayacucho's university, San Cristóbal de Huamanga, which had operated from 1674 to 1885, brought levels of activity unknown for decades to this sleepy isolated departmental capital. Unlike other Peruvian universities, San Cristóbal's educational mission at its refounding was designed specifically to respond to local needs—education, nursing, rural engineering, and anthropology, not law, medicine, or literature. This mission included a significant university extension service, also unique among national universities at the time.[4] Although most of the 550-odd students at San Cristóbal by 1963 were from Ayacucho or Apurímac and were often native Quechua speakers who had learned Spanish in public schools, almost the entire faculty of about forty came from outside the region, attracted by what were then the best paying university teaching positions in the country.

Among the faculty was Abimael Guzmán Reynoso, newly doctored from the University of San Agustín of Arequipa, who arrived in mid-1962 to teach in the education program at Huamanga.[5] Guzmán soon became the catalyst for the radicalization of the university as head of the teacher training school, director of personnel, and leader of the Maoist faction of the local Communist Party after the Moscow-Beijing split in December 1963.[6] His forces controlled the University of Huamanga between 1968 and 1975; during this period they proselytized actively among the students (whose numbers increased from 1,451 in 1968 to 4,467 in 1974), deepened their understanding of the ideological underpinnings through intensive study groups, and expanded their contacts with the more than 300 Indian communities of the Ayacucho countryside.

Guzmán and several of his key lieutenants made a number of extended trips to China, where they observed the Cultural Revolution (1966–1976) firsthand and were trained in guerrilla strategy and tactics. Guzmán's forces broke away from the national Maoist party between 1968 and 1970 and came to be known as Sendero Luminoso; by 1980 Guzmán's faction had become far and away the dominant Maoist group in Peru. When SL lost control of the university in 1975, they made no attempt to regain influence; in fact, that year Guzmán resigned his university position. While Guzmán taught at the national teachers' university, La Cantuta, just outside Lima in 1976 and 1977, much of the PCP's energies between 1975 and 1980 were devoted to building ties with the rural population of Ayacucho as part of its preparation for launching the People's War.[7]

At the same time, the negative effects of the military government's agrarian reform (1968–1980) were being widely felt in Ayacucho.[8] This ambitious project effectively eliminated large landowners from Peru and placed most of the affected lands (some 8.5 million hectares) in the hands of cooperatives. Those who gained most were the ex-landowners' tenants and the government employees who came to administer the new cooperatives. Although close to four hundred thousand families benefited from the reforms nationwide, in Ayacucho the figure was very small because of the abundance of communities and the dearth of large private estates.[9] Peru's agrarian reform model, in short, did not work in Ayacucho. It left people worse off than they had been a decade before, just as Sendero was expanding its activities in the area. The Ayacucho peasants' situation was exacerbated as well by a relative decline in central government budget expenditures in that department from 3 percent in the 1960s to 1 percent in the 1970s (only education expenditures expanded).[10] Ayacucho remained one of the departments least attended to by central authorities at a time when the state was expanding and the rhetoric of resource redistribution was pervasive. The 1981 census points up Ayacucho's continuing poverty and marginal status when compared to Peru as a whole.[11]

This is the context in which the Shining Path movement developed. The distinguishing characteristics include (1) strong, dominating leadership by a single individual; (2) a leader and a group of subordinates from a university milieu; (3) a provincial rather than a national capital university as the movement's incubator; (4) a setting in which a rigid, orthodox, Maoist ideology could be developed and inculcated for more than a decade; (5) a university setting with an explicit commitment to assist the local population and to educate predominantly local students in professionally relevant programs to benefit regional development; (6) a poor, rural, mostly Indian population living in or connected to communities rather than *haciendas*; (7) declining central government expenditures in Ayacucho in the 1970s after substantial expansion in the 1960s, except for education (a significant exception, given Sendero's proselytizing priorities); (8) central government application during the 1970s of an extensive agrarian reform that was quite inappropriate for Ayacucho and that actually made most *campesinos* worse off; (9) a continuous rhetoric of reform and of structural transformation by the military government that was not accompanied in Ayacucho, at least, by actions benefiting the local population.

The Shining Path's Ideology

Sendero's ideology reflects its origins.[12] The Maoist view of reality is based fundamentally on the central role of the peasantry and a rural-based revolution. At the same time, it recognizes the need to forge an alliance with the urban proletariat before the final strategic objective of encircling the cities to force the collapse of the state can be attained. It includes the conviction, most likely forged from being in China during the height of the Cultural Revolution, that a revolutionary communist movement can succeed only if it finds the correct line and pursues it faithfully by continuous internal debate and elimination of deviant views. Constant purging and continuous purification to ensure that the correct line prevails are essential components of the revolutionary ethos of the PCP. The leader ensures that deviations do not prosper and that their adherents are properly chastised.

Guzmán's unwavering commitment to the proper formulation and application of the principles of "Marx-Lenin-Mao, principally Mao" contributes to a cult of personality in the movement that replicates that of Stalin and Mao and that Guzmán sees as essential for the revolution's ultimate success. From the perspective of President Gonzalo, Guzmán's nom de guerre, international communism is in crisis because it did not follow basic principles of continuous internal revolution and cult of personality after winning power in a number of countries. The collapse of communist governments in the Soviet Union and Europe, the worldwide crisis of communist revolutionary movements, and the challenges now faced by continuing communist regimes such as China reflect, in Guzmán's view, their pursuit of incorrect and misinterpreted ideologies. The PCP, Shining Path, Guzmán holds, is following the correct communist line almost alone and will eventually be vindicated by revolutionary triumph in Peru. Peru will then become the center of a new, purer pursuit of a new worldwide communist revolution.

Such ideological commitment has become for Sendero and its followers a secular religion, a guide for all aspects of life, and a vow in which advancing the revolution through deeds is far more important than life itself.[13] This submission to the larger cause is manifest to outsiders who have viewed Shining Path militants' demonstrations in prisons or in the field and helps explain the remarkable capacity of a small number of militants to wreak havoc in the body social, politic, and economic of Peru. This same commitment redefines objective reality in ideological terms and then acts as if the ideological interpretation was reality itself.

Ideology, in effect, becomes a blinder that obscures reality in the name of the revolution. Selective and pinpointed acts of terror neutralize alternatives, especially local politicians, government development workers, church outreach, and non-PCP Marxist union or community organizers. The only acceptable alternative is Sendero's own "generated organisms," even when they do not reflect or respond to the real or perceived needs of the local peasant or worker population. Shining Path, in effect, pursues ideology at the expense of reality, convinced that its own "scientific interpretation of history" represents the real interests of the proletariat and will inevitably triumph.

In the final analysis, then, Sendero's projection of its ultimate victory is based not on gaining the support of the population but on defeating those who would protect that population—government, church, unions, peasant organizations, and foreign development agencies. Any assessment of the possibilities for Sendero's success depends, then, on an evaluation of the government's capacity and staying power.

The Manwaring Paradigm

The Manwaring framework is a useful device for making such an assessment.[14] The six elements outlined in chapter 1 provide an analytical tool for considering the insurgents' chances for success.

Legitimacy. Concerning the legitimacy factor, Peru has had successive elected civilian governments at both national and local levels since 1980, the longest period of continuous constitutional rule since the 1895–1914 period.[15] Some twenty parties or groupings across the political spectrum have competed for political office, and most have been successful at one level or another. The presidency has been won by three different party constellations: Fernando Belaúnde Terry and Popular Action (*Acción Popular* or AP) of the center right in 1980, Alan García Pérez and the American Popular Revolutionary Alliance (*Alianza Popular Revolucionaria Americana* or APRA) of the center left in 1985, and Alberto Fujimori and Change 90 (*Cambio 90*) of the center in 1990.[16] In Congress, AP representatives held the majority from 1980 to 1985; APRA, from 1985 to 1990; and an APRA plurality followed by *Cambio 90* and the largely Marxist left beginning in 1990. In municipal elections, AP delegates held the first plurality nationwide in 1980; the leftist coalition United Left (*Izquierda Unida* or IU), in 1983; APRA, in 1986; and a conservative coalition, Democratic Front (*Frente Democrático* or FREDEMO), in 1989.

Citizen participation in the electoral processes was high, ranging from 80 to 90 percent in presidential and congressional elections, and 60 to 80 percent in local voting. Although the Marxist parties did not succeed in winning the presidency during this period, they were the second most numerous group in Congress until divisions sapped their combined voting strength in 1990. Peruvian Marxists were the largest left party aggregation in electoral support in all of Latin America.

The level of popular support for incumbent elected heads of state, measured by periodic surveys, has ebbed and flowed from more than 70 percent to less than 10 percent (as of June 1991, Alberto Fujimori's approval rating was about 30 percent but by December it was more than 60 percent).[17] These same surveys indicate that respondents' commitment to democracy remains very high, however. More than 90 percent favor democratic rule over military or revolutionary alternatives, a figure that remains in that range despite Peru's economic crisis.[18]

If legitimacy or the moral right to govern is defined concretely as the presence of (a) national and local elections, (b) viable political alternatives, (c) high overall levels of participation, (d) access by the Marxist left, and (e) high commitment to democracy, then the government of Peru more than met the test between 1980 and 1992. However, President Fujimori surprised everyone on April 5, 1992, when he suspended congress and the judiciary and assumed emergency powers with the support of the armed forces in a self-coup (*autogolpe*). This undermined the legitimacy of the democratic process at the national level. Even so, 70 to 85 percent of the population supported these steps initially, local and regional governments were not affected, and Fujimori promptly announced a set of plebecites and elections to restore democracy fully by April 5, 1993.

Still, several significant qualifications must be made. One is that most surveys dramatically underrepresent Peru's human periphery— the urban slum dwellers, rural farm population, Indians, and citizens within highland and jungle Emergency Zones (EMZ) set up to deal with the insurgency. Therefore, it is unclear how this significant sector of the population views the government, but this component is the main target of Shining Path attentions.

Another qualification is that Sendero is not very interested in popularity but claims legitimacy through ideology and dogma. Its leadership believes it knows what the population needs based on its "scientific interpretation of history." SL is prepared to do whatever has to be done, including legitimating itself through selective violence and intimidation.[19]

A third factor affecting government legitimacy is that Shining Path views the country from the perspective of the periphery, to which the center (i.e., the national government and the formal economy) does not and never has responded very effectively.[20] Legitimacy, from the perspective of the center, is the extent to which the institutions of the *central* government have the moral right and authority to govern. The national government must establish its legitimacy with the periphery. This is precisely where Sendero Luminoso has been emphasizing its own definition of legitimacy.

Fourth, government forces of order, the police in particular but also the military, have been accused of substantial human rights abuses since 1983 in pursuing the insurgents, including as many as three thousand cases of "disappeared" persons. In addition, a weak and ineffective national court system has been unable to offer timely trials for two-thirds to three-quarters of the prison population accused of terrorist activities related to the insurgency.[21]

Fifth, the unexpected economic "shock" program of President Fujimori that began in August 1990 has exacerbated the economic hardship faced for the last several years by Peru's lower classes. As of 1991 fully two-thirds of the country's twenty-two million people were estimated to be below the poverty line; between two and three million in Lima alone were relying on neighborhood soup kitchens to sustain themselves.[22]

Sixth, a growing number of communities in the countryside were unable to hold valid elections or retain local officials because of insurgent harassment or fear of retaliation. At least 140 mayors and local government authorities were killed by the guerrillas, and hundreds more have resigned. Abstention rates in the 1989 municipal elections approached or exceeded 50 percent in several highland departments, and as many as 500 districts (of Peru's 2,106) did not have candidates.[23]

If the concept of legitimacy is expanded to include activities in and the perceptions of Peru's human and geographical periphery, as well as government abuses primarily within that periphery, then an alternative view much less favorable to the central government's moral right to govern emerges. The overall result is very clearly a mixed one—a set of factors favoring Peru's governing institutions and another set undermining their legitimacy. Sendero works primarily in the periphery and seeks to exploit the legitimacy crisis there, while the government relies on the center to maintain and extend its moral authority. The standoff favors the forces of order for now, but with no guarantee that it will continue to do so.

The role of foreign governments and international institutions is a significant factor related to the legitimacy of the Peruvian state that must be taken into account as well. The García administration pursued a set of nationalistic policies that included limiting repayments on Peru's $18 billion foreign debt to 10 percent of export earnings in 1986 and 1987, abandoning all such payments from 1988 through the end of his term, nationalization of a foreign oil company—Belco Petroleum— without speedy compensation, and a messy attempt at private bank nationalization. Such actions alienated significant foreign actors, including the U.S. government, the World Bank, the Inter-American

Development Bank, the International Monetary Fund, and private money center banks. As a result, international financial support for the Peruvian government virtually dried up during the last eighteen months of García's administration.

This left the incoming Fujimori regime, on top of all its other problems, financially bereft. Only in September 1991, after fourteen months of economic shock treatment domestically and multiple gestures of reconciliation internationally, was Peru's government able to restore its creditworthiness abroad and resume the flow of desperately needed foreign financing. The U.S. government played a significant role in this process out of concern for Peru's domestic crises, including the insurgency, and committed some $90 million in economic and military assistance as well. These actions by foreign governments and institutions provided crucial and timely support for the government of Peru and bolstered its legitimacy at a vital point in its struggle against the guerrilla forces. Fujimori's public approval levels rebounded, and he was able to turn his attention from the economy to the insurgency, even though the benefits of Peru's reinstatement into the international financial community were not yet visible within the country as of early 1992. The *autogolpe* will further delay Peru's economic regeneration because it provoked some bilateral aid suspension—including U.S. military assistance—and a holdup in international organization disbursements. This can only work against the government at this crucial juncture.

Organization for unity of effort. As for the second factor, organization, the government of Peru has had great difficulty in giving the insurgency the highest national priority and coordinating a response effectively, efficiently, and systematically from the top down. President Fernando Belaúnde delayed committing the military to confront the insurgency directly for more than two and a half years after the first Shining Path actions were carried out on the eve of the 18 May 1980 elections, when the guerrilla organization was small, poorly trained and equipped, and concentrated in the Ayacucho area. He misdiagnosed the group for some time as petty bandits, then insisted on linking Sendero to international guerrilla support networks, and finally was convinced that a military response alone would suffice. By the time he left office in July 1985, Shining Path was larger, more dispersed, and far better trained. Furthermore, military excesses in Ayacucho and surrounding areas had alienated a significant portion of the population that government forces were ostensibly there to protect.

President García redirected the counterinsurgency effort through purges of military and police personnel believed to have committed excesses or thought to be corrupt and combined military and economic responses in the most affected areas. He also pursued initiatives to decentralize government to a degree through establishing regional assemblies and to link central authorities and local populations in Peru's Indian heartland (which García called the Andean Trapezoid) through periodic direct discussions (known as *Rimanacuy*). These initiatives appeared to have some impact during the first two years of García's term, as agricultural output increased, human rights violations declined, and political violence casualties were reduced.

The coherence of this new government approach to the insurgency began to unravel in June 1986, however, when police and military put down a prison rebellion coordinated by Shining Path in which at least 256 militants were killed, scores after surrendering. The military and police had acted on what they thought were García's explicit instructions to "do whatever you have to do to stop it"; but in the ensuing controversy Peru's president did not back them up. Subsequently, the military and police increasingly were accused of not pursuing the counterinsurgency diligently enough, with the occasional exceptions of able officers taking individual initiatives.[24]

In 1988 and 1989, Shining Path gained almost complete control of the Upper Huallaga Valley (UHV), began a large-scale expansion and shift of tactics in Lima, harassed communications between the countryside and the capital, and on occasion virtually shut off food supplies to Lima from the highlands.[25] Military-police rivalry flared up, especially in the UHV, highlighted by the failure of the armed forces to rescue a besieged police post at Uchiza in March 1989.[26] Human rights violations increased sharply; new economic resources to affected areas all but ceased with the growing national economic crisis; and García's government was embarrassed by the mass prison escape of the leadership of Peru's other guerrilla movement, the Revolutionary Tupac Amaru Movement (*Movimiento Revolucionario Tupac Amaru* or MRTA).

Thus, promising beginnings under APRA to build a coordinated and coherent government approach to the insurgency foundered. Politically, the top leadership and its counterinsurgency programs were discredited. More than one-third (63) the country's 183 provinces were under military control as of July 1990, and insurgent violence and incidents continued to increase.[27] Organizationally, police-military rivalry overshadowed both reorganization of the police forces and the establishment, ostensibly for better coordination, of a single Ministry of Defense. Economically, inflation rose to more than four digits during García's last three years (1,600 percent in 1988, 2,700 percent in 1989, and 7,650 percent in 1990);[28] the government budget in real terms was cut in half, dramatically reducing the center's capacity to implement official policies against the insurgency. One of the few improvements was in the capacity of official intelligence services, now more closely coordinated, to track Shining Path and MRTA personnel, which led to a number of dramatic captures of important insurgent leaders and documents from 1988 onward.

President Fujimori declared on 28 July 1990 in the inaugural address of his five-year term that dealing with the insurgency would be a top priority of his administration. He organized a national coordinating body with himself as the head and announced that he would personally direct counterinsurgency efforts. During his first fifteen months in office, however, his attention was concentrated on Peru's dramatic economic crisis. Only in late 1991 did he declare the insurgency to be the country's number one problem, press for and receive from Congress temporary emergency powers to pass laws to deal with the problem, and begin to act. Some, particularly in Congress, criticize Fujimori for being too close to the military and for operating what amounts to a de facto military regime with a symbolic civilian head of state. Nonetheless, the prospect of new resources for the government, the military, and the economy may increase the effectiveness of government in responding to the insurgent challenge just as organizational coherence is being restored as well. The April 1992 *autogolpe* was a major steback to this process.

Over the life of Shining Path's people's war, the insurgent organization has been presented by various analysts as a model of coherent organization for unity of effort.[29] Among its central characteristics are a single unquestioned dominant leader with a penchant for organization and strategy; a small central committee for long-term planning and national coordination of specific initiatives; regional committees and organizations to plan and direct operations in their geographical areas; a five-tiered recruitment process, with advancement by demonstrations of discipline and successful actions from sympathizer to militant to cadre to coordinator to commander; and specialized annihilation squads.[30] Sendero's ability to execute precisely planned and targeted actions has long confounded and sometimes embarrassed government authorities. In addition, insistence on ideological orthodoxy, the "one correct line," lends coherence to its operations. "Taxes" levied on drug trafficking operations in the UHV have given it an independent financial base as well.

As it has expanded, however, the leadership has had more and more difficulty in keeping control of all aspects of the organization. The tension is particularly great between the central command structure and regional command autonomy, as well as over exclusive pursuit of the hard military line versus greater efforts to win support among peasants and workers. Expansion has also opened gaps in Shining Path's internal security defenses that the government has been able to exploit at times. Still, the continuing unquestioned dominance of Guzmán, President Gonzalo, has kept the organization sharply focused on its mission of undermining the authority of the state to be able at some point to overthrow it. As of early 1992, Shining Path still appears to be in a stronger position in organization for unity of effort than the government, although recent signs were pointing to some shift in favor of state authorities. The April *autogolpe* reversed this trend by diffusing security forces' attentions.

External support for the targeted government. The third factor focuses on the degree to which the government consistently receives assistance to pursue its efforts to end the insurgency. As the discussion above indicates, the policies of the García regime resulted in the cutoff of most outside credit and assistance and provoked Peru's worst domestic economic crisis since the War of the Pacific (1879–1883). The result was a dramatic weakening of state capacity both in dealing with the insurgency and in state services to the citizenry. This decline enabled Shining Path to expand much more rapidly than it had expected, to the point that organization spokesmen were beginning to predict a Sendero victory during the 1990s.[31]

U.S. economic assistance continued in the $75 million per year range, but restrictions because of security threats limited its effectiveness. Military assistance was for all intents and purposes prohibited under the provisions of the Brooke-Alexander amendment. War on drugs legislation did permit security assistance to stop drug production and trafficking; this was one area where U.S. aid to Peru increased during the García administration, but at modest levels (from $4 million in 1985 to about $12 million in 1990). Peru is the world's largest producer of coca for use in the manufacture of cocaine (about 65 percent). Only in September 1991, after extended negotiations with the Fujimori government, was a substantial economic and military assistance package approved (about $60 million in economic aid and $25 million in military aid).[32]

The U.S. Congress, deeply concerned abut continuing human rights abuses, conditioned the military assistance to demonstrated improvements in Peru's armed forces human rights record and remains worried that these resources might militarize the drug war.[33] As of mid-1992 it is not at all clear that the U.S. government will continue to provide substantial and continuing assistance to Peru for dealing with the insurgency. The new resources made available until their cutoff after the April 1992 Fujimori self-coup could only be used where the drug problem and the insurgency problem intersect, almost exclusively in the UHV. Because the conflict is virtually a nationwide one, however, the Peruvian government will have to rely on its own resources or find them from outside sources other than the United States to pursue the insurgency in other parts of the country. The *autogolpe* only increased this need.

Reduction of insurgents' external support. Reduction of outside assistance may be an important factor for most insurgencies, but in the case of Shining Path it takes on a distinctive if not unique dimension.[34] Sendero has eschewed all outside aid in the name of self-sufficiency and ability to control its own destiny. It is believed that the PCP of Guzmán has not received any such aid since the end of the Cultural Revolution in China (1976); before that some resources came from Chinese government authorities and possibly from Albania as well.[35] Although becoming isolated from the international communist movement as Sendero organized for the armed struggle was forced upon him, Guzmán made a virtue of necessity. For several years after 1980, when the insurgency began, Sendero relied exclusively on domestic sources of supply. These were primarily police arms caches taken in raids on ill-defended stations, weapons taken from individual police personnel targeted for assassination, and massive thefts of dynamite from the many mines that dot remote slopes of the Peruvian highlands.

Beginning with Shining Path's first incursions into the UHV in 1984–85, however, new possibilities for supporting an expanding guerrilla organization presented themselves. These involved tapping into the wealth generated by the growing of coca, the preparation of cocaine paste, and the transport of the paste on small planes to Colombia from the scores of airstrips hacked out of the forest throughout the UHV. The army confronted Sendero directly in 1985 and soon forced it out of the valley for the most part, but when the insurgents returned in force in 1988 they began to "tax" producers, manufacturers, and exporters in areas under their control. In this endeavor Shining Path was competing with MRTA and, on occasion, corrupt elements of the police, but by 1989 it had firmly established itself as the dominant force in the UHV. These drug production and trafficking "taxes" were variously estimated to produce between $30 million and $100 million per year for Sendero. It is not known with certainty how these funds are used; the most plausible explanation is that a significant portion covers expenses associated with running a national organization of five to six thousand armed cadre, four to six thousand support staff, and fifty to sixty thousand sympathizers in various organizations Shining Path calls "generated organisms."[36] Expenses may include some arms brought in by the mostly Colombian drug smuggling planes.

Shutting off this resource flow would be a complex undertaking at best and perhaps impossible until Americans and Europeans give up cocaine. U.S. and Peruvian government efforts to reduce coca production and increase interdiction have not proven successful. More coca has been grown in the UHV in almost every succeeding year since records have been kept.[37] Until some viable alternative crop can be grown to meet the financial needs and expectations of the eighty to a hundred thousand coca farmers in the UHV and their families, eradication and interdiction will continue to enrage the growers and drive them into the arms of Sendero for protection. When the Peruvian military has separated the drug issue from the insurgency issue in the UHV to fight Sendero and MRTA and let the coca growers alone, as it did in 1985 and in 1989, it has run afoul of its own government and that of the United States. This may be the only case of an ongoing insurgency being largely financed by the U.S. cocaine consuming public.[38] Therefore, cutting off outside aid to the Peruvian insurgents requires quite different measures from those for other insurgencies, past and present. The most manageable way is to get Shining Path out of the UHV, but to date that approach has had other consequences that neither the Peruvian leadership nor the U.S. government has found acceptable.

Intelligence. This element has posed an ongoing challenge for the Peruvian government. Until the separate information gathering agencies of the military, the police, and the presidency were joined in 1987–88, overlapping collection and coordination were major problems. So, too, was the difficulty of having good information but poor ability to persuade the responsible actors to act in accordance with the intelligence available. For example, it appears that rather good information was available on Shining Path in the early years indicating that it was about to begin the armed struggle and concerning specific military operations, but it was very difficult to get action agencies to take the information seriously. Shining Path's first major confrontation in Ayacucho, the March 1982 attack on the prison that freed Sendero prisoners and put the country on notice that this was a movement to take seriously, was predicted well in advance by police intelligence and even occasioned the dispatch of reinforcements from Lima. The officer-in-charge in Ayacucho refused to believe the reports, however, and kept the reinforcements in barracks at the other end of town from the prison. The minuscule guard at the jail was quickly overcome by a large Sendero detachment, while another kept the "reinforcements," along with the rest of the police, pinned down inside the barracks.[39] This pattern was repeated on other occasions.

Recent coordination has improved the collection and evaluation process, and greater appreciation of the threat by the units entrusted with response has increased the success rate of operations against Shining Path. Capture of the person widely believed to be Guzmán's second-in-command, Osmán Morote Barrionuevo, in Lima in 1988 was a major accomplishment, as were raids in 1990 and 1991 on Sendero safe houses in Lima and elsewhere, which netted of a number of second-level leadership figures and a large number of documents and files. The dramatic success in rounding up virtually the entire leadership of MRTA in 1988 and 1989 has been underemphasized in light of their escape in June 1990 but represents another major intelligence success.

The government has significant difficulties infiltrating Sendero for various reasons. One is the way in which Sendero recruits—choosing often very young secondary school students, women, and disillusioned local labor union officials or elected authorities. Another is the way in which it tests recruits for potential advancement—often by requiring them to form part of an assassination squad and to deliver the final shot to dispatch the targeted individual. A cell structure keeps a recruit from knowing the names of colleagues, all members have aliases, and the hierarchy of activity and responsibility insulates significant figures in the organization. This challenge means that much government information on Sendero comes from outside observation and defections, interrogation of captured militants, and analysis of intercepted documents.

Although a growing subversive organization poses more of a threat, it also provides greater opportunities for intelligence gathering. A small group of intelligence officers in the center of the government's apparatus has gained a reputation for particularly astute interpretation with a substantial computer analysis capability; such credibility means that the responsible agencies and officers are more likely to act appropriately on intelligence received.

Shining Path, on the other hand, fosters the impression that "the revolution has a thousand eyes and ears." Their designated militants do their homework to find out who the most respected figures in a community or organization are, where they live, and what they do. They are then approached to help; rejections may bring threats or reprisals. Individuals in organizations important for Sendero—unions, the telephone or the electric company, the Ministry of Justice, the police, or the military hospital—are approached, often through family members, to become informants or are militants trained for specific duties and hired by these companies or government entities.[40] Cases have turned up of psychiatric nurses who deliver to SL sensitive personal information on police or military officials, electrical engineers who provide maps of key towers or installations, justice ministry employees who lose or delay files of arrested Sendero activists, and the like.[41]

Although the impression of Shining Path intelligence capacity may be much greater than it actually is, just the perception adds to uncertainty and enhances the image that the organization wishes to project. The economic crisis and decline in government salaries over the past four years probably have made it easier for Sendero to recruit. It is not really known if SL, on balance, has a more effective intelligence apparatus than the government. It is probably a standoff, with the government gaining some ground in the last three or four years.

Discipline and capabilities of the armed forces. Regarding the final factor, the Peruvian military has long had the reputation of being one of the best trained and best prepared in Latin America.[42] The air force is second in size and capacity only to Brazil in South America; the navy third after Brazil and Argentina. The army is also one of the region's largest and best equipped. These improvements in the military's capacity are the result of an extensive modernization program begun in the early 1970s with substantial assistance (about $1.2 billion) from the Soviet Union for the army and air force and from Great Britain, Italy, and the Netherlands, among others, for the navy. Officer selection, training, and advancement are based primarily on merit. Technical noncommissioned officer specialists are highly trained and well compensated, while conscripts make up the bulk of the enlisted forces.[43]

With regard to the insurgency, however, the armed forces have several problems. One is that most of the modern equipment and training provided by the Soviet Union and others is designed for conventional defense concerns and is not at all suited for countering guerrilla warfare. Second, even with the expansion of the insurgency in the late 1980s, the military dedicates less than 20 percent of its forces to it. The armed forces continue to be focused on Peru's traditional defense concerns, the northern border with Ecuador and the southern border with Chile. Third, the command structure has been ponderously slow in responding to challenges posed by the insurgents and often ineffective as a result. Fourth, the army has been slow to adopt rapid reaction tactics on the ground and has been haphazard at times about a lack of proper equipment, particularly helicopters in working order. Fifth, commands normally rotate on an annual basis, so that continuity based on close knowledge of local situations is difficult to achieve.[44]

Sixth, it has been general military policy not to recruit personnel from the area in which they will serve or assign personnel to their home areas. Because of regional ethnic and linguistic differences, this policy has handicapped the armed forces in gathering accurate information and in making an appropriate response. It is possible that many human rights violations stemmed from the military's lack of knowledge and understanding of local situations. Seventh, tension between the police and the army has created severe problems in coordination of effort at times, particularly in the UHV, where police have been working with the U.S. government to fight the drug trafficking problem and the army has been working on its own to fight the insurgents.[45]

Finally, the economic crisis has had a dramatic effect on the armed forces. The 1991 budget was half of that for 1990. Salaries of top generals, as of mid-1991, were less than $200 a month; for enlisted personnel, army or police, about $15 a month. Funds for maintenance of personnel were so drastically cut back that some units had to furlough troops for part of every month so that they could live off the local economy. During 1991, early retirements and resignations of army and navy officers and technical specialists were exceeding 100 a month, so that voluntary early separation from the services had to be temporarily suspended.[46]

In spite of these problems the military did cope. Supplemental appropriations helped. The special counterinsurgency units increased. The six separate intelligence services combined into one unit, and the previously separate army, navy, and air force ministries formed a single Ministry of Defense. The army was contemplating ways to extend periods of service and was beginning to recruit personnel locally to serve locally. President Fujimori made the insurgency the country's first priority as of late 1991 and was given temporary extraordinary legislative powers to facilitate prosecution of the war. The April 1992 self-coup extended those powers for at least a year, but at the considerable cost of losing U.S. military and economic support and of eroding the legitimacy of central government by suspending democracy.

As Sendero now argues, the 1990s will be the decisive decade for the insurgency in Peru. The fight ebbs and flows but continues to wreak great hardship on the country and much of its population. Analysis of the struggle and the government's response using the factors of legitimacy, organization, external support to the government, reduction of outside aid to the insurgents, intelligence, and armed forces' discipline and capabilities leads to a mixed answer about the likely outcome. Shining Path is clearly superior only in organization now that the government of Peru has reinserted itself into the international financial and foreign assistance community. The government clearly had the edge in legitimacy until the April *autogolpe*. Both sides have had their successes concerning use of intelligence. Armed forces' capabilities may also show advantages for each side, given the problems the Peruvian military has had in providing appropriate forces and responses to the insurgent military challenge. The key factor that will likely tip the balance is the degree to which the government can regenerate economic growth and basic government services over the next three to five years to give a more tangible dimension to the somewhat abstract legitimacy it was able to maintain until April 1992. Early signs indicated that Fujimori's self-coup was a grave miscalculation which will reduce rather than increase the government's capacity in these critical areas. If this does indeed prove to be the case, the advantage in Peru's ongoing internal war shifts toward the insurgents of Shining Path.

Notes

1. Various sources have been keeping the grisly score. Among the most authoritative are DESCO (Centro de Estudios y Promoción del Desarrollo), *Resumen Semanal*, through November 1990, and DESCO, *Boletín Informativo*, since January 1991. DESCO information is drawn primarily from newspaper accounts. Another is the Peruvian Senate's Special Commission on Political Violence (Comisión Especial del Senado sobre Causes de la Violencia y Alternativas de Pacificación Nacional), headed by Sen. Enrique Bernales and often called the Bernales Commission. See *Violencia y Pacificación* (Lima: DESCO y Comisión Andina de Juristas, February 1989). Updates appear regularly. The main sources for the Bernales Commission are the Peruvian government's Ministry of Defense and Ministry of the Interior. Their estimates of casualties are consistently 10 percent to 15 percent higher than DESCO's. In English, Sandra Woy Hazelton has been keeping track annually since 1984 in "Peru," *Yearbook of International Communist Affairs* (Stanford: Hoover Institution Press, yearly); Cynthia McClintock also provides much information about Sendero as well as the larger political and economic context of Peru in her annual country analysis (since 1985) in *Latin America and Caribbean Contemporary Record* (New York: Holmes and Meier, yearly). A recent summary presentation and analysis is my own chapter on "National Security," in Rex Hudson, ed., *Peru: A Country Study*, Library of Congress Federal Research Division (Washington, D.C.: GPO, 1992), chap. 5.

2. Many are represented in the Spanish compilation of previously published articles, Heraclio Bonilla, ed., *Crisis, violencia, y conflicto étnico en los Andes* (Mexico: Consejo Nacional para la Cultura, 1992). Another edited collection, in most cases of studies not published before, is my own *Shining Path of Peru* (New York: St. Martin's Press, 1992).

3. For a comprehensive treatment of Shining Path from its beginnings through the first phase of the armed struggle (1980–1982), see Gustavo Gorriti, *Sendero: Historia de la Guerra Milenaria en el Perú, vol. I* (Lima: Editorial Apoyo, 1990).

4. The university's distinctive mission is eloquently presented by its first rector (president) Fernando Romero Pintado, in "New Design for an Old University," *Américas*, December 1961.

5. I arrived at about the same time as a Peace Corps volunteer (PCV) invited to teach English and social sciences, which I did with two PCV colleagues between September 1962 and November 1963. I recount my experiences in "Expulsion from a Peruvian University," in Robert E. Textor, ed., *Cultural Frontiers of the Peace Corps* (Cambridge: MIT Press, 1965), pp. 243–270, not learning until years later that the "unseen hand" behind the removal of the Peace Corps from the university was Guzmán himself, his first significant political victory.

6. For an insightful account in English of Guzmán's concerns and activities before, during, and after his University of Huamanga experience, see Gustavo Gorriti, "The War of the Philosopher-King," *New Republic*, 18 June 1990, pp. 15–22.

7. A comprehensive account of Shining Path's development at the university and in Ayacucho during the 1970s, much of it from direct observation, is Carlos Iván Degregori, *Ayacucho 1969-1979: El surgimiento de Sendero Luminoso* (Lima: Instituto de Estudios Peruanos, 1990). This important book is now being translated and will soon be published in English by the University of North Carolina Press.

8. For a discussion of the early years of agrarian reform in Ayacucho and its negative effects, see my *"Revolution from Above": Military Government and Popular Participation in Peru, 1968–1972*, Latin American Studies Program Dissertation Series no. 47 (Ithaca: Cornell University, 1973), pp. 203–227.

9. My estimates from data gathered at various government offices in Ayacucho and at the agrarian reform headquarters in Lima were that less than 20 percent of Ayacucho peasants who needed land would actually benefit from the redistribution there. Palmer, *"Revolution from Above"*, p. 194.

10. Government expenditures data from Cynthia McClintock, "Democracies and Guerrillas: The Peruvian Experience," *International Policy Report* (Washington, D.C.: Center for International Policy, September 1983), Table 3, p. 4. Education expenditures data are from Peru's 1981 census, Instituto Nacional de Estadística (INE), *Censos Nacionales: VIII e Población, III de Vivienda, 12 de junio de 1981: Departamento de Ayacucho*, vol. 1 (Lima: INE, 1983), pp. vii–xii.

11. Ayacucho and neighboring departments of Apurímac and Huancavelica were the three poorest in the country at this time. In Ayacucho, life expectancy was 44 years, only 7 percent of the residents had running water, and only 14 percent had electricity (INE, *Censos Nacionales*, pp. ix–xvi).

12. This ideology is presented in various SL publications. One of the most significant is the June 1988 interview of Guzmán by Luis Arce Borja and Janet Talavera Sánchez, "La entrevista del siglo," *El Diario* (Lima), 24 July 1988, pp. 2–47. Others include Partido Comunista del Perú (PCP), *Desarrollemos la guerra de guerrillas*, Lima (?): Ediciones Bandera Roja, 1981; and PCP, *Bases de discusión*, Lima (?): Ediciones Bandera Roja, 1987. For a summary analysis,

see Cynthia McClintock, "Theories of Revolution and the Case of Peru," in Palmer, *Shining Path*, 225–240.

13. See a parallel analysis in Carlos Iván Degregori, "A Dwarf Star," *NACLA Report on the Americas*, December 1990–January 1991, pp. 10–16.

14. Max G. Manwaring, "Toward an Understanding of Insurgency Wars: The Paradigm," in Max G. Manwaring, ed., *Uncomfortable Wars: Toward a New Paradigm of Low Intensity Conflict* (Boulder: Westview Press, 1991), pp. 19–28. A more methodologically oriented version of this research, entitled "Insurgency and Counterinsurgency: Toward a New Analytical Approach," has been accepted for publication in *The Journal of Small Wars*.

15. In 1990, regional assembly elections were held for the first time as well, thereby expanding procedural or formal democracy in Peru still further.

16. The location on the political spectrum specified here refers to how parties presented themselves in the electoral campaign and how they were perceived by the voter. AP and APRA retained their preinauguration orientation during their terms of office; Fujimori, however, is widely viewed as shifting to the right after taking office. His April 1992 self-coup (*autogolpe*) confirms this rightward shift.

17. As reported in DESCO, *Resumen Semanal*, vol. 14, no. 623 (7–13 June 1991): 1 and vol. 14, no. 651 (20 December 1991–2 January 1992): 1.

18. These surveys are carried out regularly by the Peruvian polling organization, Apoyo, S.A. They do show some deterioration in the enthusiasm for democracy, but as yet no significant shift to either a military or a revolutionary alternative.

19. This is a central theme of the analysis of Tom Marks, "Making Revolution with Shining Path," in Palmer, *Shining Path*, 191–205.

20. Government's failure to deal effectively with the periphery is one conclusion of David Scott Palmer, "Rebellion in Rural Peru: The Origins and Evolution of Sendero Luminoso," *Comparative Politics*, vol. 18, no. 2 (January 1986): 127–146.

21. Human rights abuses and judicial limitations in Peru have been detailed regularly by the State Department, Amnesty International, and Americas Watch, among others. For examples, see citations in notes 27 and 33. Also Amnesty International (AI), *Peru: Violations of Human Rights in the Emergency Zones* (New York: AI, August 1988).

22. See, for example, David P. Werlich, "Fujimori and the 'Disaster' in Peru," *Current History*, vol. 90, no. 553 (February 1991): 61–64, 81–83, esp. 82.

23. David Scott Palmer, "Peru's Persistent Problems," *Current History*, vol. 89, no. 543 (January 1990): 5–8, 31–34.

24. The best known case is that of General Alberto Arciniega in the Upper Huallaga Valley in 1989. One discussion is found in José Gonzales, "Guerrillas and Coca in the Upper Huallaga Valley," in Palmer, *Shining Path*, 105–125. Also see Arciniega interview by Raúl González, "La batalla por el Huallaga: Las armas de un general," *Quehacer* 62 (December 1989–January 1990): 38–43.

25. See discussion in Nelson Manrique, "La década de la violencia," *Márgenes*, vol. 3, no. 5–6 (December 1989): 137–180.

26. See Gonzales, "Guerrillas and Coca."

27. Department of State, "Peru," in *Country Reports on Human Rights Practices for 1990*, Report submitted to the Committee on Foreign Affairs, House of Representatives and the Committee on Foreign Relations, U.S. Senate, February 1991 (Washington, D.C.: GPO, 1991): 110–123. This has been an annual report since 1977 as required by 1976 legislation.

28. Official figures as compiled by INE and reported in DESCO, *Resumen Semanal*, January 1989, January 1990, and January 1991.

29. Most forcefully by Gordon A. McCormick, *The Shining Path and The Future of Peru* (Santa Monica: The Rand Corporation, 1990).

30. For details, see Gabriela Tarazona-Sevillano, "The Organization of Shining Path," in Palmer, *Shining Path*, 171–190.

31. For example, in statements attributed to Luis Arce Borja, editor of the Sendero-controlled *El Diario*, in Europe during 1991.

32. For a discussion of U.S.–Peruvian relations up to and including this approval, see David Scott Palmer, "United States–Peru Relations in the 1990s: Asymmetry and Its Consequences," in Eduardo Gamarra and James Malloy, eds., *Latin America and Caribbean Contemporary Record, 1989–90*, vol. IX (New York: Holmes and Meier, 1992).

33. See the detailed critique by Americas Watch, *Into the Quagmire: Human Rights and U.S. Policy in Peru*, An Americas Watch Report (New York, September 1991).

34. The Khmer Rouge in Cambodia/Kampuchea and the Revolutionary Armed Forces of Colombia (Fuerzas Armadas Revolucionarias Colombianas —FARC) in Colombia seem to have had experiences during some stages of their insurgencies that are similar to that of Shining Path. They took advantage of resources provided through drug production and trafficking within their countries to become virtually self-sufficient movements.

35. Degregori, *Ayacucho 1969–1979*.

36. This conclusion is Cynthia McClintock's, based on interviews in Peru.

37. Department of State, Bureau of International Narcotics Matters, *International Narcotics Control Strategy Report* (Washington, D.C.: Department of State Publication, March 1991).

38. As noted above, FARC is another, but presents much less of a threat to Colombia at this point than Shining Path does to Peru.

39. Gorriti, *Sendero*, 253–286.

40. See, for example, Michael L. Smith, "Shining Path's Urban Strategy: Ate Vitarte," in Palmer, *Shining Path*, 127–147.

41. Tarazona-Sevillano, "Organization of Shining Path."

42. John Keegan, "Peru," *World Armies* (Detroit: Gale Research Co., 1983), 469–474.

43. Palmer, "National Security."

44. Ibid.

45. Ibid.

46. Ibid.

IRAN*

COUNTRY DATA

Area 636,294 sq. miles (slightly larger than Alaska).

Capital Tehran (population 7–10 million).

Population 49.8 million 1986 est. (includes 1.5 to 2 million Afghan refugees).

Per Capita Income $1,667.

Ethnic Groups Persians, Azeri Turks, Arabs, Turkomans and Baluchis and Lur, Bakhtiari, and Qashqai tribes.

Religions Shi^ci Muslim 93%, Sunni Muslim 5%, small minorities of Jews, Christians (including Armenians and Assyrians), Baha^cis, Zoroastrians.

Literacy 48% of the population.

Work Force Agriculture 40%, Industry and commerce 33%, services, 27%.

Infant Mortality Rate 10 per 1,000 live births.

Life Expectancy 54 years.

Government Islamic Republic (constitution ratified December 1979).

UNIQUENESS OF CASE STUDY

Iran's state-sponsored terrorism and support of insurgencies finds its ideological base in Islamic fundamentalism and Iran's role as vanguard in a pan-Islamic revolutionary movement.

CHRONOLOGY

1979 Revolutionaries over-throw shah. Students seize U.S. embassy.

1981 Khomeini creates "Islamic Liberation Movements Office" to export revolution. Iranian Islamic Revolutionary Guard Corps sent to Lebanon. Iranian-sponsored coup against Bahrain quashed.

1983 Bombing of U.S. embassy in Beirut.

1984 "Independent Brigade" formed for covert operations abroad.

1985 Assassination attempt on Kuwaiti emir.

1988 U.S.S. *Vincennes* downs Iranian airbus by mistake, killing 290 people. Bombing of Pan Am Flight 103 over Lockerbie, Scotland.

1985–1991 Campaign of taking hostages in Lebanon.

Source: The map and some of the country data are from State Department "Background Notes."

9

Iran: Terrorism and Islamic Fundamentalism

Sean K. Anderson

Unfamiliar Threats in the Middle East

Since 1979 the Islamic Republic of Iran has carried out hostilities against the United States, other Western nations, and pro-Western Middle Eastern nations. Such actions range from belligerent propaganda campaigns, to state-sponsored terrorism and insurgencies, to conventional combat with its neighbors and U.S. forces. The ongoing hostilities have usually fallen short of conventional war, however, and consequently can be considered as a low-intensity conflict (LIC).

Iran's attempts to export its revolution to other Muslim nations present unusual challenges to U.S. national security analysts, policymakers, and administrators. Unlike in most other revolutionary insurgencies against pro-Western governments, the ideological mainspring for Iran has been Islamic fundamentalism rather than Marxism-Leninism. The ideology of Islamic resurgence has captivated large segments of the populations in various Muslim countries. Like the radicalized leftists of the Americas, most Islamic fundamentalists view the United States as the source of their societies' woes and their main enemy. Iran's leaders have undertaken the role of vanguard in this pan-Islamic revolutionary movement.

Iran's revolution and sponsorship of other Islamic fundamentalist insurgencies test the applicability of models of regional conflict to the Middle East. Most regional conflicts and insurgencies elsewhere in the Third World have involved Marxist-Leninist insurgencies backed by Soviet, Cuban, or Chinese aid. Because Marxist thought stems from the same European Enlightenment background as classical liberal democracy, analysts dealing with Marxist insurgencies ordinarily can grasp the insurgents' doctrine and program readily. Because Islamic fundamentalism differs so much in background from the Western political tradition, it is harder for analysts both to read correctly the fundamentalists' intentions and to suggest the means to counter them.

Another important difference about fundamentalist insurgencies is that they were not directly related to cold war hostility between the United States and Soviet Union. Islamic insurgencies will continue in the post–cold war period. Moreover, even before seizing power Iran's Islamic revolutionaries had resolved to resist any attempt by the West to co-opt their revolutionary agenda. Iran's fundamentalists aim rather to restore a powerful pan-Islamic state by unifying other Muslim nations under their own standard of Islamic revolution.

Insurgencies and regional conflicts outside the Middle East usually have involved jungle warfare, where forest cover has allowed guerrillas to achieve control over large areas, thus undermining the government's claims of effectiveness and legitimacy. By contrast most Middle Eastern countries consist largely of desert terrain with most of their populations concentrated in cities or adjoining oases, factors not conducive to such guerrilla warfare, as the Palestine Liberation Organization (PLO) and Iranian leftist guerrillas discovered in the 1970s.[1]

Despite such objections the regional conflict model developed by Max G. Manwaring does apply to the current Middle East.[2] In explaining Iran's attempts to foster Islamic revolutions outside its borders the Manwaring model can help develop appropriate U.S. proactive policy and responses.

The Regional Threat in the 1990s

Iran undertook major support of terrorism and insurgencies during the past decade, as others have sufficiently documented.[3] Three major developments suggest Iran will continue, or even increase, this role in the next decade: the consolidation of Iran's revolutionary regime, Iraq's defeat in the Persian Gulf War, and changing Soviet policy toward the Middle East.

The Consolidation of the Islamic Republic

By 1983 the Islamic regime had sufficiently established its legitimacy to perpetuate itself following Ayatullah Ruhollah Khomeini's demise. The post-Khomeini regime has avoided the scenarios of civil war between competing factions or rival successors. Moreover, the Islamic Republic has never renounced its right to sponsor terrorism or insurgencies against its enemies. Hopes that Iran would normalize relations with the West were further hindered by Khomeini's decree authorizing the assassination of Salman Rushdie, whose *Satanic Verses* had outraged Islamic sensibilities worldwide.[4]

Khomeini's reluctance to renounce using force to spread the Islamic revolution leaves his successors locked into his overall revolutionary ground plan. This strategic vision consists of five stages.[5] The first stage was to lay the revolution's groundwork; the second, to overthrow the shah's regime; and the third, to establish an Islamic state within Iran. Those first three stages were achieved by the time the shah's regime had collapsed. The fourth stage of exporting Iran's revolution to the rest of the Islamic world began after the revolution, when Iran started to sponsor insurgencies in the Persian Gulf region and Lebanon as well as terrorist activities abroad. The final fifth stage would be to reunite all Muslim countries into a revived Islamic empire. These last two stages remain unfulfilled but were explicitly sanctioned by Khomeini and his hard-line successors. Targets for subversion include Saudi Arabia, Iraq, and the conservative Arab emirates in the Persian Gulf. Lebanon quickly became a target of opportunity, while Egypt, Turkey, and Israel have witnessed attacks by groups allied with Iran.

Although official statements of the Iranian Foreign Ministry have lately softened their anti-Western rhetoric, this apparent moderation has been belied by actual increased Iranian involvement in covert operations abroad. In April 1990, for example, the U.S. Department of State's annual report on state-sponsored terrorism noted that Iran alone had shown a marked increase in its reliance on terrorism.[6]

Khomeini's institutional arrangements to safeguard the Islamic Republic make it nearly impossible for any Iranian government to renounce exporting the revolution or pursuing pan-Islamism for the foreseeable future. Upon seizing power Khomeini established several "revolutionary foundations," parallel to existing governmental institutions, to prevent them from departing from the "line of the imam." One example is the Islamic Revolutionary Guards Corps (IRGC), which quickly was set to watch over the regular military to prevent coups against the regime and now is effectively assimilating the regular forces through a program to integrate the Iranian military. Moreover, the government structure often delegated identical missions to different government offices, causing duplication of efforts, quarreling among officials, and intragovernmental turf-battles. Nonetheless, this duplication ensured that efforts to fulfill the mission would not languish because of official complacency or quiet obstructionism.

Factional alignments among the clergymen now ruling Iran block any quick departure from the imam's line. At least three clerical factions contend for power within Iran. Shifting alignments and the obscurity of their intramural differences defy efforts to sort these clergymen into clear-cut categories of "moderates" or "radicals," but one can make some distinctions according to how individuals and factions rank their priorities for the regime.[7] One side believes that building institutions, public order, and social and economic stability should take precedence over pursuing an external revolutionary agenda. An opposing side believes that achieving unfulfilled revolutionary priorities, namely, fighting "Zionism and imperialism," aiding the "oppressed," and opposing "dependent, reactionary regimes" in the region, are more important than domestic development and prosperity. Among these "revolutionists" are the former Interior Minister ᶜAli Akbar Muhtashami and former Prosecutor General Khoiniha, who was once the "spiritual adviser" of the students holding the U.S. embassy hostages. A third category is made up mainly of politicos among the Islamic fundamentalist politicians who switch support from one side to the other as politically expedient. Among such "politicos" is Iran's current president, ᶜAli Akbar Hashemi-Rafsanjani.[8]

None of these factions, however, actually disavows pursuing the export of the revolution or pan-Islamism as strategic objectives of the Islamic Republic, nor do any factions question the propriety of using terrorism or supporting insurgencies against other governments as means to achieve these objectives.

Following Khomeini's death the duplication of official and unofficial organs overseeing the export of the revolution left no single power broker in a position to rein in all the subversive enterprises undertaken to export the revolution. Factional competition for Khomeini's mantle of revolutionary leadership gives the revolutionist faction incentives to use its resources to step up active measures abroad to counter steps by institutionalists to normalize relations with Western and regional countries.[9]

The Defeat of Pan-Arabism

Iraq's defeat during Operation Desert Storm increases the likelihood that Iran will intensify its own low-level warfare. First, as Manwaring has emphasized, the real struggle in such regional conflict is over the legitimacy of the governments under attack, as opposed to that of the insurgents and their backers. Second, the failure of the Iraqis' high-intensity conventional efforts to achieve their strategic objectives vindicates the approach that Iran has generally preferred in its own ongoing hostilities with the West and other regional nations. Finally, the destruction of Iraq's regional mini-superpower status and the humiliation of its leadership leave Iran as the leading local contender for regional policeman status.

The two main indigenous ideological forces hostile to Western interests in the Middle East have been pan-Arab nationalism and Islamic fundamentalism. Both movements deny the legitimacy of the existing nation-state system in the Middle East, viewing current states and borders as artifacts of European colonialism.[10] Both movements are also mutually antagonistic, however. Pan-Arab nationalism has a secular, antitraditionalist orientation and is based on a chauvinistic view of the Arabs' superiority over other nations. More important, Islamic fundamentalism calls for a return to strict observance of traditional Islamic law and therefore abominates the secularism of the pan-Arabists. Therefore, the recent Iraq-Iran war was not merely a border war or clash between two strong-willed leaders, but rather an ideological holy war between pan-Arabism and Islamic fundamentalism.

Since Khomeini's death Iran has lacked any charismatic figure capable of inspiring a comparable following among Muslims outside of Iran, particularly among the Arab Muslims. The Iraqi victories in the final days of the Iraq-Iran war also helped to promote the prestige of Saddam Hussein and his Ba'thist brand of pan-Arabism within the Arab world. Moreover, Saddam Hussein's defiance of the United States and the Western coalition's demand to withdraw from Kuwait briefly made him seem heroic even to many non-Arab Muslims.

Saddam Hussein's subsequent failure to fight the coalition, or to turn the war into a pan-Arab campaign against Israel, has tarnished his own image as a pan-Arab leader. It has also damaged pan-Arab nationalism's claims to legitimacy, which depend on military success in time of war.[11] Islamic fundamentalism not only fills the void left by deflated pan-Arabist hopes but also explains theologically why the Iraqi regime failed to defeat the West. Unfortunately the recent successes of Operation Desert Storm have ill prepared the U.S. public and Congress for dealing with the alternative long-term threat of Iranian-sponsored regional insurgencies in the Persian Gulf or elsewhere. Saddam greatly obliged his enemies by blatantly defying the international community in a manner impossible to let pass, and by amassing his infantry and armor in concentrations and positions that facilitated their destruction by the coalition's technologically superior conventional arms. Pan-Islamic insurgencies, by contrast, will involve regional insurgencies permitting no technological quick fixes such as surgical strikes and quick withdrawal, and requiring much commitment of resources over a greatly extended time span.

Pan-Arabism's failure makes Islamic fundamentalism and low-intensity warfare more credible to Arab Muslims. Meanwhile, Iran still remains the only Islamic fundamentalist regime committed to supporting Islamic insurgencies beyond its own borders.

The Exit of the Soviet Union

Mikhail Gorbachev's program of restructuring led the Soviets to cut their losses in Afghanistan and Eastern Europe and also to revamp their Middle Eastern policy. Despite long-standing alliances with radical Arab states, Moscow proceeded to establish full diplomatic relations with conservative Arab states, such as Oman and the United Arab Emirates, while also wooing Saudi Arabia. The single boldest departure from the Soviet Union's position since 1967, however, was its growing rapprochement with Israel. Shortly after becoming general secretary, Gorbachev elaborated his "new approach" to foreign policy by announcing that "Israel has the right to exist, to its sovereignty, and we understand its security concerns."[12] On 4 August 1986, the Soviet Union announced its intention to seek normal diplomatic relations with Israel. These fundamental changes proceeded from realistic reassessments of Soviet foreign policy objectives and performance. The implicit renunciation of support for "national liberation movements," the withholding of all but moral support for its erstwhile Arab ally Iraq in the Gulf War, the collapse of the hard-line cliques within the Soviet Union who might have reversed this trend, and the dismantling of the former Soviet state together indicate that the governments succeeding the Soviet state will no longer seek to confront the United States in the Middle East.

These are bitter blows to hard-line Arab regimes and to pan-Arabists throughout the Middle East. Moscow will no longer offset U.S. support for Israel. The hard-line regimes' dependence on Soviet arms and credits constrains their ability to sponsor low-level warfare or insurgencies against Western interests or conservative regimes in the region. For Arab Muslims whose faith in pan-Arabism and Soviet support has been dashed by the recent Persian Gulf War, the Islamic resurgence now offers the best promise for continuing the struggle against Israel and Western influence in the Middle East. Iran's own sponsorship of insurgencies does not similarly depend on the goodwill and backing of one major external actor.

In summary all these developments portend increasing incentives and opportunities for Iran to sponsor insurgencies and low-intensity warfare against U.S. security interests in the Middle East in the name of Islamic fundamentalism.

Islamic Resurgence and the Iranian Revolution

Understanding the contest between fundamentalist insurgents and targeted national governments requires understanding the nature of the fundamentalist cause. The expression "Islamic fundamentalism" misleadingly suggests an analogy with Christian fundamentalism. Judeo-Christian tradition posits a radical distinction between the "kingdom of God" and the kingdom(s) of this world. So-called fundamentalist Islam radically rejects such a separation of life into secular and religious domains, or any separation of politics and religion. The closest analogy in Western Christianity would be the prorevolutionary "liberation theology" of Latin America rather than the private pietism of Protestant fundamentalism.

What Westerners have called "Islamic fundamentalism" Muslims prefer to call "al nih*dh*at al Islami," meaning "the Islamic movement," or better, "the Islamic resurgence." Central to the Islamic resurgence is its insistence on reviving and comprehensively applying a unitary system of Islamic law covering all private and public affairs. This closed and comprehensive legal system stems from the Quran, an even larger body of traditions, authoritative commentaries, historic consensus, and judicial precedents. The various Islamic resurgent movements hold in common certain beliefs:

- that the Islamic laws have comprehensive solutions for all economic, social, diplomatic, criminal, and civil problems;
- that Islamic law is itself perfect, immutable, and organic, not to be abrogated in part or amended;
- that the current Islamic world, with its mixture of traditional Muslim and contemporary Western laws and institutions, and its division of the historic Islamic empire into several nation-states, represents a deviation from true Islam; and
- that the religious duties of *jihad*, holy war, or of "enjoining the good and forbidding the evil," permit violence to rid Muslim lands of un-Islamic laws, institutions, rulers, foreign powers, and agents when other means fail.

Despite Muslim fundamentalists' claims to exclusive possession of the "true Islam," not all Muslims or Islamic institutions necessarily endorse such pretensions or agree with the aims or methods of Islamic fundamentalists, particularly on issues concerning when violence becomes religiously permissible and what kinds of violence may be lawfully used. Not all Islamic fundamentalists are linked to Iran or approve of Iran's vision and methods; nor does the Iranian regime give its blessings and support to all bona fide Islamic fundamentalists.

Interpretations of Islamic law vary between nations, depending on which school of Islamic jurisprudence is dominant in a given region. For instance because Iran's Islamic movement has the unique twist that in Shiᶜi Islam only the clergymen have the prerogative of interpreting the Islamic laws, the Islamic revolution there entailed the rule of government and society by the Shiᶜi clergy. Most Sunni schools of jurisprudence, however, reject the very idea of a distinction between clergy and laity among the believers so that many Sunni Muslim fundamentalists find the clericalism in Iran's model a severe stumbling block.

Three ideological characteristics of the Iranian model of Islamic resurgence stand out: (1) the goal of revitalization of Islam in the public realm, particularly the application of the *Shariᶜah*—the canon of sacred law in Islam—through the rule of the Shiᶜi clergy; (2) Iranian nationalism, not as a secular faith or national program, but rather as an assertion of traditional, national values as opposed to foreign, Western values; and (3) "revolutionism"—the faith that the existing order is fundamentally corrupt and incorrigible and that only revolutionary violence will magically transform the society and achieve social justice.

These three components are not fully congruent with each other but coexist in tension: Chauvinistic nationalism, whether Arab or Iranian, is in direct contradiction with the universalistic spirit of Islam. Even though Iran's Islamic rulers have worked to promote the status of the Arabic language and literature within Iran, Arabs continue to suspect the Iranians of *shuᶜubiyya*, a covert and insidious anti-Arab sentiment. Likewise although the seizure of the U.S. embassy and hostage-taking in Tehran could be rationalized on the basis of revolutionist appeals or claims of national grievances, those actions violated explicit and well-known provisions of Islamic law guaranteeing the immunity and safe passage of diplomats, even of enemy nations.

Structural Components of the Revolution

Three structural characteristics were essential for creating an effective Islamic revolutionary mass movement in Iran and for setting up Khomeini's authoritarian-bureaucratic Islamic state. These included: (1) an overseer class of Islamic clergymen, in the "line of the imam," who have the central role in leading the revolution and ruling society, performing judicial, legislative, and executive functions; (2) a class of educated, skilled Muslim laymen who could manage the state bureaucracy or who would form the future officers' corps in the revamped military of the Islamic Republic; and (3) the unskilled, uneducated, and poor lay mass following who were capable of being mobilized to carry out the tasks set by the other two classes and were known as the "Hizbullah," literally the "Party of God."[13] These followers were mobilized and supervised on behalf of Khomeini by the Friday Prayers leaders, the clerics attached to local mosques, or by the trustees in charge of the religious bequests that ordinarily served as charity and society welfare organizations. The clergymen's work also involved material efforts among these poor to alleviate their misery combined with a heady indoctrination into the revolutionary version of Islam being promoted by the imam.

These three structural components are essential to operationalizing the first three stages of Khomeini's strategic vision. The clergymen are the brains and nerves of the revolution, and the greatest time and patience had to be devoted to building up this infrastructure. The Hizbullahi mobs are needed for the actual revolutionary violence to bring down the targeted regime and to provide proregime vigilantes to help protect the new Islamic order. The educated Muslim middle classes are needed to run the bureaucratic administration of the Islamic state once it is established. Iran's own experience has become the pattern for its attempts to export its revolution.

Exporting the Revolution

Whenever Iran has sought to export its revolution, its first task was to bring together in a target country a nucleus of revolutionary Islamic clergymen dedicated to Khomeini's vision of Islam. These clerics, in turn, would begin recruiting their more educated and talented lay followers into nascent revolutionary organizations. Finally this network, extending through mosques and their associated teaching institutions, would mobilize the Muslim poor at large in the targeted area.

An important consequence of the foregoing was that the Iranian regime found its most promising terrain for the export of its revolution in those Muslim lands having those rudiments with which to build a mass movement. Lebanon had a large number of Shiꞌis, who also followed the Twelve Imam school dominant in Iran and who had their own clerical leaders, as well as a small cadre of well-educated and ambitious laymen. Lebanon also had large numbers of poor, unskilled, and uneducated Shiꞌi commoners who had their own peculiar litany of grievances. The confessional political system in pre-1975 Lebanon had denied the Shiꞌa full representation and participation while the Palestinian guerrillas occupying southern Lebanon often abused the native Shiꞌis' rights.

Iran has had more success in replicating its own revolutionary pattern in Lebanon than elsewhere, but the experience there reveals some of the difficulties in exporting Iran's revolution at all. The longest phase of Khomeini's strategic plan involved the preparation for revolution through the creation of a network of disciplined Shi'i clergymen committed to an Islamic revolution, lasting at least fourteen years. In Lebanon a similar preparation took place through the missionary activities of the Iranian clergyman Imam Musa Sadr, who began to organize the Shi'a of Lebanon as early as 1968.[14] In 1975 he helped create the Amal militia to enable the Shi'a to defend themselves. If the capture of West Beirut by Amal in 1983 signaled the debut of Lebanon's Islamic insurgency as an equal player in Lebanon's civil war then the preparation phase there lasted roughly fifteen years. The lead time was roughly the same in both cases, but in those two cases most of their preparations benefited from the fundamentalists' obscurity and the targeted regimes' inattention to their potential danger. Developing fundamentalist cadres in other countries may still require lengthy preparation, but post–1979 Middle Eastern regimes are now keenly alert to these dangers and more apt to take active measures to counter the development of revolutionary infrastructures.

Even the Lebanese Islamic movement is not an unqualified success: The Shi'a of Lebanon are split between the pro-Iranian Hizbullah and the more indigenous Amal movement, a division that stems from a split among the Shi'i clergy between the followers of Musa Sadr and those of Muhammad Hussein Fadlullah.[15] Amal has become alienated from Iran in part because Tehran does not share Amal's understanding of the problems of the Shi'a in Lebanon's politics while Amal has been unwilling to subordinate itself wholly to Tehran's geopolitical calculus.[16] Moreover, the rift that opened between Syria and Iran after Operation Desert Storm led Syria to restrict greatly Tehran's ability to support its clients in Lebanon.

Applying the Manwaring Model

The Manwaring model helps explain why the Iranian revolution of 1979 was possible and Iran's aims in exporting its revolution. Because Iran's own experience guides its understanding of other insurgencies, the 1979 revolution explains much of current Iranian strategy.

Legitimacy

First, regime legitimacy is the primary target of insurgents. In the Middle East legitimacy is primarily related to the Islamic and nationalistic credentials of the government rulers. Prerevolutionary Iran's unresponsive, corrupt political system and social stagnation were at best necessary, but not sufficient, conditions for the shah's loss of authority. His regime was ultimately undone by the Shiᶜi clergy's destroying his credibility as an Islamic and nationalistic leader. They attacked his de facto alliance with Israel, his "subservience" to the United States, and particularly those elements of his development program that conflicted with Islamic tradition and the sentiments of Iranian Muslims.

Since the revolution, the "centers of gravity" on which Iran has focused in the "legitimacy war" against targeted states likewise include the Islamic and nationalist credentials of their leaders, governments, laws, and institutions. Attacks on Saudi Arabia and the Persian Gulf emirates focus on the supposed illegitimacy of monarchy in Islam and the alleged unworthy moral character of the rulers. In the case of republics friendly to the United States the attacks often focus on their alliance with a supporter of Israel. In Iraq's case attacks have focused on the secularist and un-Islamic nature of the Baᶜthist pan-Arab ideology as well as portraying Saddam Hussein's regime as covertly pro-American and even pro-Israeli.[17]

More insidious attempts to delegitimize regional governments use agents-provocateurs in "armed propaganda." Because legitimacy is "first the purview of the governed" a government can forfeit its moral claim to govern if it allows itself to be provoked into violating the norms of the society.[18] Through bombings in Kuwait and Saudi Arabia, including an attempt to assassinate the emir of Kuwait on 26 May 1985, and the rioting provoked by Iranian agents during the Hajj in Mecca, Iran has been seeking to provoke the targeted regimes to reactions that might destroy their Islamic and national credentials before their own citizens.[19]

Organization for Unity of Effort

Second, victory belongs to those who best organize a unified effort in political, economic, diplomatic, military, and psychological/propaganda efforts. The shah encouraged factionalism and backbiting among his courtiers and military officers to forestall coup conspiracies. Such a regime systematically divided against itself proved ill prepared to withstand the challenge that arose in 1978.[20] Incapable of lateral cooperation without the shah's personal oversight and direction, the Iranian military was not prepared to deal with any major operation, much less policing a civilian insurrection. Once the shah left the country at U.S. prompting, his military crumbled within ten days. By contrast Khomeini created institutions to perpetuate his revolutionary agenda upon their own momentum even after his death.

Just as Iran has safeguarded its revolution through creating multiple, redundant, and competing government agencies and revolutionary foundations, it has tried similarly to institutionalize the export of the revolution. The "Islamic Liberation Movements Office," decreed by Khomeini in February 1981, provided a command structure for operations abroad put under the operational aegis of the Islamic Revolutionary Guards Corps. This office became the chief source of military assistance to Islamic insurgents supported by Tehran, such as the Hizbullah militia in Lebanon and the al Daʿwa Party in Iraq.[21] On 26 May 1984, in response to Khomeini's complaint that the exporting of the revolution was not being pursued actively enough, the Islamic Guidance Ministry also sponsored the creation of "an independent brigade for carrying out irregular warfare in enemy territory" by coordinating efforts by Iranian special forces units and the IRGC.[22]

Various "revolutionary foundations," such as the Foundation for the Oppressed, served to support insurgent activities. Even the Office of Hajj and Ziyarat responsible for organizing Iran's contingent of pilgrims to Mecca and Medina was co-opted into service for revolutionary agitation of other Muslim pilgrims and Saudi nationals. Since 1981 Iran has also been organizing annual international conferences of Friday Prayers imams, other Muslim clerics, and religious scholars to build support networks throughout the Muslim world. Iran also created the Supreme Assembly of the Islamic Revolution in Iraq located in Tehran to direct Muslim revolutionaries against the Iraqi regime.

The externalizing of Iran's revolution by multiplying the same revolutionary infrastructures developed within Iran beyond its borders suffered from a major conceptual flaw, however. When conflicts between competing institutions or personalities within Iran got out of hand Imam Khomeini often intervened directly, and the Iranian state used its legal authority to force a resolution of the conflict. Today Khomeini's successors lack the stature needed to intervene effectively when such events occur. Furthermore, without systematic centralized control over external operations, revolutionists inside Iran's government and military have used operations outside Iran to exert domestic coercion in pursuing their own domestic political agenda.[23] This factionalized control undercuts the unity of effort needed to ensure Iran success in its support of Islamic insurgencies elsewhere.

External Support

Third, victory belongs to those having the best, most consistent external support. In Iran's revolution this maxim applies not so much to support the Islamic revolutionaries received but rather to the lack of consistent U.S. moral and material support for the shah's regime, a lack that aided its downfall. Although Khomeini and his followers got support from Syria, Libya, Iraq, the PLO, and the Popular Front for the Liberation of Palestine (PFLP), such ties were of short duration and contributed only marginally to the success of the revolution. Although anti-shah Iranians did receive guerrilla training in Palestinian-run training camps in Lebanon and South Yemen, the main weapons used by the clergy against the shah's army were anti-regime sermons, mass demonstrations, and orchestrated civil disobedience rather than armed struggle as such. The lack of consistent external support was most evident in the Carter administration's wavering support for the shah. This inconsistent support was due to the lack of a common strategic vision and unified effort on the part of the U.S. administration at that time. The National Security Council (NSC) under Zbigniew Brzezinski viewed the Iranian situation primarily as a threat to U.S. security while the State Department under Cyrus Vance was more concerned with human rights abuses under the shah.[24]

Although Iran's revolutionaries relied then on largely self-generated resources and momentum, today they do not export their revolution merely by moral exhortations to other Muslims to imitate their example. Although Tehran has often disclaimed financing or arming subversives, evidence to the contrary abounds. One Hizbullah leader in Lebanon, Shaykh ᶜAbbas al Musawi, confessed very frankly that funding for Hizbullah "comes mainly from Tehran."[25] Iranian technical assistance to vehicle-bombers in Lebanon and in smuggling arms and explosives into Bahrain, Kuwait, Saudi Arabia, and other Persian Gulf emirates has been substantially documented.[26]

On the other hand the Iranian regime maintains that conservative, pro-U.S. Muslim governments can continue in power only through the consistent support of the United States. Therefore, U.S. diplomatic and military personnel and facilities in targeted countries have become the "center of gravity" for attacks by Iranian-backed insurgents. Because Iran and its client insurgents view all U.S. citizens residing and working in the Middle East as spies or agents promoting Western influences, future insurgent actions will no doubt continue to target U.S. diplomatic and military officials as well as private institutions and citizens.

Intelligence

Fourth, victory belongs to those having the best intelligence and correct understanding of the nature of the conflict. Four systemic flaws in U.S. intelligence compromised the ability of the United States to foresee and possibly forestall the Iranian revolution. Two of these flaws were peculiar to the case of Iran but conceivably could be repeated elsewhere, namely, a lack of independent control over field intelligence gathering and the "ring around the embassy" syndrome. The other two flaws are more general, namely, a poor use of area specialists or specialized knowledge in the policy-making process, and culturally bound perceptions and analyses.

Independent control over intelligence. Although the Central Intelligence Agency (CIA) helped create SAVAK, the shah's security and intelligence organization, after 1972 the CIA came to depend on SAVAK for all in-country reporting.[27] The CIA maintained most training and outfitting contacts with SAVAK's Seventh Directorate, which concerned international counterintelligence, rather than SAVAK's Second Directorate, which dealt with domestic political opposition.[28] The shah had his own reasons to prevent his Western allies from learning about any viable noncommunist opposition within his realm. SAVAK accordingly withheld information from the CIA concerning the right-wing religious fundamentalist opposition.

The "ring around the embassy" syndrome. The U.S. embassy in Tehran was isolated by SAVAK plainclothesmen preventing contact between the local opposition and embassy staff.[29] The embassy was further isolated from within by what staffers called "the Armenian Mafia." Although Armenian Christians represented only 0.5 percent of Iran's population, they made up about 50 percent of native contract employees at the embassy. Often they behaved arrogantly toward Iranian Muslims having business with embassy offices and discriminated in favor of Armenians when hiring other contract workers.[30] This factor compounded greatly U.S. ignorance of cultural currents shaping the Iranian revolution.

Poor use of area specialists. Despite having personnel in the diplomatic and intelligence communities with background knowledge, field experience, and area expertise valuable for policymakers on the brink of Iran's revolution, the U.S. intelligence system failed to identify and make timely use of these human resources. As Manwaring points out, in the "war against subversion" a knowledge of the insurgent leadership is vital because the leadership nucleus and its trained cadre are the vital centers of any insurgency.[31] The United States knew virtually nothing about the Shiʿi clergy or Khomeini.

Prior to the revolution, when a senior CIA Iranian affairs analyst proposed studying the Shiᶜi religious leadership in Iran and their politics, his superiors dismissed the proposal as trivial. Another analyst learned that an Iranian informant had already compiled an extensive study on the Iranian clergy lost somewhere among the embassy files in Tehran. Unable to get case officers in Tehran to help locate and forward that document, the analyst eventually had to go to Tehran personally to retrieve it.[32] Former State Department Iran Country Director Henry Precht summarized the situation so: "We spent very little time with [Iranian area specialists] relative to their value."[33]

Cultural blindness. Our expectations often limit what we can perceive, especially when dealing with intangibles such as culture, values, tastes, and ideas. One NSC staffer recalled that "there were no relevant models in Western political tradition to explain what we were seeing in Iran during the revolution."[34] Most U.S. development programs operated on the assumption that societies develop linearly from a traditional to a transitional and finally to a "modern" state. Until 1978 the shah's Iran seemed the most dramatic example confirming this view. This preconception of what development and revolution should look like vitiated U.S. efforts to derail the revolution, for it prevented U.S. observers from coming to grips with the fundamentally theocratic nature of Khomeini's movement.

Following the revolution direct information regarding Iranian direction of special operations and insurgencies has remained scant because of lack of human intelligence resources. Clearly policy administrators need both to develop human intelligence resources and to make better use of Middle Eastern and Islamic specialists.[35] Developing civilian and military advisers who are "culturally aware, politically knowledgeable" as well as technically prepared will increase the human intelligence resources needed for tracking the ever-changing regional conflict environment, especially in the Middle East.

Discipline and Capabilities of the Armed Forces

The fifth requirement for victory under the Manwaring model is flexible use of the best disciplined armed forces and police. As noted earlier, the antiriot capabilities of the shah's security forces were severely limited. Khomeini's strategy in the streets was to create cycles of demonstrations of increasing popular participation and confrontational severity. According to Shiᶜi custom a forty-day mourning period followed each "martyrdom" of anti-shah protestors killed in police confrontations. Forty days later memorial demonstrations were held with heightened emotions concluding this official mourning period. During these commemorations agitators would provoke more confrontations, causing more deaths and another, more severe forty-day cycle.

Blame for the shah's inability to contain such a predictable pattern of demonstrations must be shared by Congress for canceling the Agency for International Development's Public Safety Program in the early 1970s. U.S. aid in anti-insurgency training for Iran's armed forces had paid off in the successful use of Iranian forces against leftist insurgents in the Siahkhal affair in 1975 and also in fighting the communist-backed Dhofari insurgents in Oman in the same period. Had Iranian gendarmes and municipal police been given comparable training in crowd and riot control perhaps they might have avoided unnecessary violence and killings that provided Khomeini with the "martyrs" needed to fuel the cycle of demonstrations.

Once exporting the revolution began in earnest, Iranian authorities have sought to create civil disturbances in neighboring countries to foster similar popular movements. Among the Shiᶜa of Persian Gulf emirates the mourning observances held on each anniversary of Imam Hussein's martyrdom became occasions for such demonstrations leading to riots. During the 1979 Hajj Iranian agitators began organizing demonstrations among their own pilgrims to provoke crackdowns by Saudi officials. By inciting Saudi police and troops to violate the religious sanctuary of Mecca during the Hajj, Iranian agitators sought to discredit the Islamic credentials of the Saudi regime before the thousands of pilgrims from throughout the Muslim world. Each year the intensity of these demonstrations grew worse until 1987, when rioting killed four hundred people. Just prior to the 1988 Hajj the Saudi government severed relations with Iran and so suspended the yearly influx of Iranian pilgrim-agitators.

Although Middle Eastern deserts do not favor guerrilla war, indigenous insurgent tactics focus instead on creating mass demonstrations in cities. One example is the Palestinian *intifadeh*, which has outdistanced previous attempts to bring pressure on Israel through guerrilla warfare or terrorist attacks. The center of gravity in this form of violence is the civilian police force's inadequate crowd and riot control capabilities. Substituting military force to suppress rioting usually leads to violence and feeds the dynamism of such demonstrations. Such crackdowns not only highlight the police's lack of control but also portray the regime as antipopular before its own citizens, making it harder for that government to maintain internal unity of effort. These also delegitimize such regimes before U.S. public opinion, so undercutting consistent moral and material support from the United States.

Reduction of Outside Aid

Finally, victory belongs to the side better able to deny outside aid to its enemy. During the Iranian revolution support for the shah was undercut in two ways. First, the domestic turmoil, oil field strikes, and campaign of intimidation directed at foreigners working in Iran drove foreign investment away from Iran and brought the economy to a standstill. Second, Khomeini's liberal-nationalist followers conducted a shrewd public relations campaign with the Western media both to play upon Western ambivalence over Iran's human rights record and to disguise the true nature of Khomeini's envisioned Islamic Republic.[36] This strategy combined a public opinion war with the war against outside support for the shah.

After the U.S. embassy seizure in 1979 the liberal-nationalist elements lost out to fundamentalists in intramural power struggles. Those who replaced them had such antipathy toward the West and ignorance of Western political systems that they largely dropped efforts to cultivate a favorable press and influence opinion in the West. The war against U.S. support for targeted regimes was stepped up, with violent attacks upon the U.S. diplomatic, military, and commercial presence throughout the Middle East. This policy has actually backfired, however. With each new terrorist act committed against U.S. citizens, beginning with the takeover of the U.S. embassy in Tehran, U.S. public opinion has increasingly favored confronting Iran.

Following Khomeini's death Tehran has been backing away from its self-imposed diplomatic isolation and has softened the tone of its official statements meant for external consumption. It has not, however, dropped its anti-Western stance in its public discussions at home and has actually increased its external operations. If Tehran deliberately resumes the double-edged approach followed before the seizure of the U.S. embassy it would eventually organize efforts to lobby Congress or to influence the U.S. public. Although this possibility may seem farfetched one need only recall how often in the course of the hostage crisis in Lebanon U.S. officials expressed hopes that Iran would use its "influence" on its Lebanese client militias to secure the release of the U.S. citizens they held hostage and how often President Rafsanjani offered to "mediate" this problem in exchange for material concessions from the United States. By using such tactics in the future Tehran could continue to undermine targeted regimes through client insurgencies while also seeking to undermine consistent

U.S. support for those governments through manipulation of Western public opinion or offers to use its "good offices" to remedy a given crisis to its own advantage.

The other side of the support equation is that Iran's regime realizes that open high-intensity confrontation with the United States would be futile and that to maintain itself it needs Western trade and credits that the United States is able to withhold. Maintaining the linkage of diplomatic/economic isolation of Iran with Iran's support of regional conflict will remain a necessary, though not sufficient, condition to force Tehran to desist from exporting its revolution.

Conclusion

Reacting to Iranian-backed LIC merely as a military problem is insufficient. A proactive strategy must go beyond countering the military tactics of Islamic fundamentalist movements to bolstering the legitimacy of governments targeted by insurgencies. The most pressing concern of Middle Eastern regimes is not the Arab-Israeli question or relations with the superpowers but rather regime security and stability. Such security means protection from attacks by neighboring regimes and from subversion from within.[37] External security can be provided readily enough through the conventional military protection of allied nations while astute diplomacy can help defuse conflict between states. Internal stability, however, depends on a regime's ability to maintain its own legitimacy. A necessary condition for effective U.S. support is the commitment of the target regime to maintain a unified effort to protect its authority to govern in the eyes of its own people. In this respect there are unique aspects of the Islamic resurgence that should be considered in applying the Manwaring model to the Middle East and developing a proactive strategy. The following problems should be addressed by policymakers who are responsible for dealing with the continued instability in the region.

The first potential problem area is that of the relation of a targeted regime to its people. Among the indicators of government legitimacy that Prisk lists are the approval of social institutions and openness of political participation to the public.[38] The key institution of legitimization in the Middle East is the Islamic religion. Most of the Islamic clergy and many laity are very conservative traditionalists who feel religiously obligated to fight any social innovations perceived as threatening Islamic values. Thus, they often suspect that modernization measures are really covert means for a Western cultural assimilation of Muslim society. Therefore, U.S.-sponsored developmental programs will require subtlety and sensitivity to help allay such suspicions. Fortunately conservative Muslims are also suspicious of insurgent movements claiming the sanction of Islam, as these are also social innovations that depart from traditional orthodoxy. The center of gravity in Iran's plan for exporting its revolution, on which all things depend, is the Islamic clergy of targeted countries. Without their support no amount of external agitation can delegitimize a targeted regime. Tehran has made great efforts to attract both the Sunni and Shiᶜi clergy in any given country, but as a basic minimum it needs the active support of the local Shiᶜi clergy before it can hope to build a revolution there. Therefore, the Persian Gulf emirates may find it expedient to give their native Shiᶜi clergymen more of a material and moral stake in the status quo.

Prior to the Persian Gulf War Iraq had convinced Kuwait, Saudi Arabia, and the other emirates to follow its own policy of suppressing their native Shiᶜis. With Saddam Hussein's defeat by the coalition and his continuing persecution of Shiᶜis in southern Iraq, including the Shiᶜi holy cities of Najaf and Karbala, it is timely and prudent for the emirates to seek some degree of reconciliation with their Shiᶜi subjects, and particularly with the Shiᶜi clergy.

With regard to the openness of the political process, the participation of reform-oriented Islamic groups in elections in Egypt, Tunisia, Turkey, and elsewhere holds the possibility that such groups may eventually develop more support for democratic processes and thus become less inclined to support fundamentalist insurgency movements. The 1992 events in Algeria cast a shadow on the prospects for such democratic accommodation, however, when the Algerian government scuttled the electoral process in the face of a fundamentalist ascendency in the polls. Although the Persian Gulf emirates have not chosen to adopt electoral democratic processes they still have more informal modes of participation and consultation by which their reformist fundamentalist groups could be co-opted into greater support of their governments. Such measures to strengthen the legitimacy of their governments must originate within each of these regimes. Without such measures it will be difficult to create or maintain unity of effort from within.

The second problem area is the U.S. relationship with such targeted regimes. Without more visible signs of increasing political participation within these societies it will be difficult for the United States to maintain consistent support for these regimes. The problem is, how can support for regimes whose governmental forms and social norms may be accepted by their own peoples but are regarded by our own as alien or even abhorrent be justified before Congress and the U.S. public? Any signs that the citizens of those countries are dissatisfied over their lack of political participation could spur U.S. critics of such regimes to demand reducing or ending U.S. support.

Two sober considerations militate for continued U.S. support for those conservative pro-Western regimes despite their failure to satisfy some ideal norms of democratic perfection. First, the alternatives to such regimes in reality are not likely to be any more democratic or pro-Western, especially if Iran succeeds in exporting its revolution to them. Second, their geopolitical importance to U.S. security interests is such that we cannot afford to allow the same fate to befall them as befell Iran.

A third, more prosaic, reason should also be noted. These regimes have been our friends and allies in the past, and it would be unjust for us to forsake them in the future. To do so because such regimes are nondemocratic and patriarchal would be to mistake a specious moralism for morality in foreign policy. Whatever else "democratization" may mean it cannot be equated with nondemocratically coercing conservative Middle Eastern states to adopt values and policies that we have democratically chosen as being suitable for ourselves. In judging issues of political participation or social justice in such countries the perceptions of those who live in the societies under question should carry more weight than the judgments of outsiders relying solely on liberal democratic abstractions.

Finally even with widespread adoption of more democratic norms and open electoral competition, Islamic fundamentalist parties that are hostile to the United States may come to power democratically. Such trends seem to have been appearing in some Islamic societies. Nonetheless, there is a vast difference between a reformist Islamic party, which will respect legal norms, coming to power democratically and a Hizbullahi insurgent group, which is committed to hostility with the United States, seizing power. Even with a growing Islamic resurgence the United States need not accept a foreign policy that presupposes some necessary opposition between Islam as such and U.S. interests. Rather, U.S. foreign policy needs only to regard whether each Muslim nation chooses to pursue friendship or enmity with the United States.

Notes

1. The failure of the Fedayeen-i Khalq assault on the Siahkhal barracks in 1975 and the Iranian communists' attack on the city of Amol on 8 November 1981 was not due to lack of forest cover because the guerrillas in each case had chosen areas that were heavily forested along the Caspian Sea coast.

Rather, the guerrillas failed because they had not won the loyalty of the people of Gilan Province, who helped the government forces flush out the leftists, and had not won legitimacy among the people of Amol or the rest of Mazandaran Province, who also helped the government forces crush the communists' "spontaneous uprising." These examples confirm Manwaring's emphasis on the war for legitimacy as the key to regional insurgency.

2. See Max G. Manwaring, ed., *Uncomfortable Wars: Toward A New Paradigm of Low Intensity Conflict* (Boulder: Westview Press, 1991), especially chap. 2, "Toward An Understanding of Insurgency Wars: The Paradigm," by Max G. Manwaring, and chap. 6, "The Umbrella of Legitimacy," by Courtney E. Prisk.

3. Bruce Hoffman, *Recent Trends and Future Prospects of Iranian-Sponsored International Terrorism*, R-3783-USDP (Santa Monica: The Rand Corporation, March 1990) reviews some of the major official and unofficial organizational channels connecting the Islamic Republic of Iran with terrorist and insurgent groups outside of Iran.

4. The imam's successor as supreme religious leader of Iran, Ayatullah ᶜAli Khamenehi, has renewed this death sentence on each anniversary of its promulgation despite Rushdie's open recantation, a fact underscoring the essential continuity of the regime's policies into the post-Khomeini period.

5. See Joseph Alpher's "The Khomeini International," in *Washington Quarterly* 3, no. 4 (Autumn 1980): 55–57, for a discussion of Khomeini's political theory and plan of action.

6. Department of State, *Patterns of Global Terrorism: 1989*, Publication 9743, (Washington, D.C.: GPO, April 1990), pp. 46–47.

7. The existence of more than two major factions within the Iranian Majlis (Islamic Consultative Assembly) was referred to in passing by President Hashemi-Rafsanjani in an interview with the Persian daily *Jumhuri-yi Islami* on 17 July 1989 (FBIS-NES-89-147, 2 August 1989, pp. 50–52). Shireen T. Hunter has elucidated the difficulties in using the terms "moderate" and "radical" to characterize Iranian factions in her article, "Post-Khomeini Iran," *Foreign Affairs* 68, no. 5 (Winter 1989–1990): 134, 139–140.

8. Nikola B. Schahgaldian, *The Clerical Establishment in Iran*, R-3788-USDP (Santa Monica: The Rand Corporation, June 1989) has a more thorough, updated discussion of the leading personalities and factional alignments within the Iranian Shiᶜi clergymen. See especially pp. 35–82.

9. See also Amir Taheri, *Holy Terror: Inside the World of Islamic Terrorism* (Bethesda, Maryland: Adler & Adler: 1986), pp. 110–111.

10. G. Hossein Razi, "Legitimacy, Religion, and Nationalism in the Middle East," *American Political Science Review* 84, no. 1 (March 1990): 69–91.

11. Fouad Ajami, *The Arab Predicament: Arab Political Thought and Practice since 1967* (Cambridge: Cambridge University Press, 1982), pp. 32–33.

12. "Excerpts from Remarks of Gorbachev and Mitterrand to the Press in Paris," *New York Times*, 5 October 1985, p. 4.

13. The name "Hizbullah" is taken from the Quran (Surat al Mujadilah,

verse 22) to describe the true Muslim believers. It was used in this more political manner in Iran from 1980 onward and became the name of the new Shiꞌi militia created in Lebanon in opposition to the older Amal militia.

14. In 1968 Musa Sadr created the *Harakat al Mahrumin*, the "Movement of the Deprived," as a means of politically organizing the disenfranchised Shiꞌa.

15. Shimon Shapira, "The Origins of Hizballah," *Jerusalem Quarterly* 46 (Spring 1988): 117–118.

16. The activities of Tehran-backed insurgents in Lebanon have come to reflect more the internal dynamics of the power struggles between rival factions within Lebanon with ever less reference to Iran's own sense of priorities in that region. This was most dramatically shown in the tragic cases of the U.S.S. *Vincennes'* downing of the Iran Air airbus and the murder of U.S. Marine Corps Lt. Col. William Higgins in Lebanon: When the *Vincennes* incident occurred on 3 July 1988, the captors of the U.S. hostages in Lebanon did no more than issue some threats against the hostages' lives. When a Hizbullah leader, Shaykh Abdul Karim Ubaid, was captured by Israeli agents on 29 July 1989, however, the captors murdered Higgins in reprisal. Had the captors been fully dependent on and responsive to Iranian wishes, it seems unlikely that they would have left the hostages unharmed following the *Vincennes* incident, in which more than two hundred Iranian civilians were killed, only to take revenge later for the abduction of one Lebanese Shiꞌi religious leader.

17. The Iraqi war against Iran was referred to in the official Iranian press as *jang-e tahmil*, "the imposed war," that is, the war supposedly imposed on Iraq and Iran by the "pro-American" Saddam Hussein. Following the Israeli air raid on the Osirak nuclear reactor outside Baghdad on 9 June 1981, Khomeini and the official Iranian news media even accused Saddam Hussein of complicity with the Israelis in the destruction of the Osirak plant.

18. Prisk, "Umbrella of Legitimacy," pp. 70–71.

19. On 26 May 1984 the Islamic guidance minister of Iran presented the top officers of the IRGC and Iranian armed forces with a special plan to coordinate terrorist activities abroad with the direct participation of the Iranian military. An essential ingredient of the agitational-propaganda part of the plan was to create disturbances in Mecca during the Hajj with a view to discrediting the Saudi dynasty and as a prelude to overthrowing it. The severity of clashes in the Hajj began to increase afterwards until, in the Hajj of 1987, riots led to the deaths of more than four hundred people. See Senate Subcommittee on Security and Terrorism, *Report On State Sponsored Terrorism*, (Washington, D.C.: GPO, 1985), pp. 130–134.

20. James A. Bill notes, "The failure of the Pahlavi system to build political institutions and its promotion of social cynicism and factionalism provided a legacy that ensured chaos and violence." "The Politics of Extremism in Iran," *Current History* 81, no. 471 (January 1982): 9.

21. Alvin H. Bernstein, "Iran's Low-Intensity War Against the United States," *Orbis* 30, no. 1 (Spring 1986): 149–150.

22. Senate Subcommittee on Security and Terrorism, *Report on State Sponsored Terrorism.*

23. Hoffman, *Recent Trends and Future Prospects,* p. 22.

24. Objections over human rights led to a year-long restriction on sales of tear gas and riot gear for Iran's civilian police, a ban lifted only after a disastrous incident on 8 September 1978 when soldiers untrained in riot control opened fire on demonstrators in Tehran's Zhaleh Square.

25. "Hezbollah Leader Interviewed on Ties to Iran," NC101527 Paris AFP in English 1514 GMT 10 July 1985 (FBIS-MEA-85-133, 11 July 1985, p. G3).

26. "Saboteurs' Cache of Arms, Ammunition Discovered," GF171913 Manama WAKH in Arabic 1805 GMT, 17 December 1981 (FBIS-MEA-81-243, 18 December 1981, p. C1); "Iranian Envoy to Syria Linked to Suicide Attacks," TA061241 Tel Aviv, *Ma°ariv* Hebrew report by Shefi Gabay, 6 November 1983, p. 3, (FBIS-MEA-83-218, 9 November 1983, p. I3); "Four Iranians Arrested With Bomb Materials," LD070942 Kuwait KUNA in Arabic 0850 GMT, 7 June 1984 (FBIS-MEA-84-111, 7 June 1984, p. C20).

27. Michael Ledeen and William Lewis, *Debacle: The American Failure in Iran* (Alfred Knopf: New York, 1981), pp. 39, 118.

28. Barry Rubin, *Paved with Good Intentions: The American Experience and Iran* (Middlesex: Oxford University Press, 1980), p. 181.

29. Ibid., p. 179.

30. James A. Bill, *The Eagle and the Lion: The Tragedy of American-Iranian Relations* (New Haven: Yale University Press, 1988), pp. 389–390.

31. Manwaring, "Toward an Understanding of Insurgency Wars," p. 26.

32. Bill, *Eagle and the Lion,* pp. 417, 419–420.

33. Henry Precht, Foreign Service Institute Conference, "Revolution in Iran," 12 November 1985.

34. Gary Sick, *All Fall Down: America's Tragic Encounter with Iran* (New York: Random House, 1989), p. 164.

35. For example, the U.S. Army ran a foreign area specialist program in Iran during the 1950s and early 1960s. By stationing talented language officers throughout Iran's countryside this program also helped overcome the isolation of U.S. officials from currents in the country at large. See Bill, *Eagle and the Lion,* pp. 421–422.

36. Alpher, "Khomeini International," p. 66.

37. Shahram Chubin, "Gains for Soviet Policy in the Middle East," *International Security* 6, no. 4 (Spring 1982): 125.

38. Prisk, "Umbrella of Legitimacy," p. 73.

AFGHANISTAN*

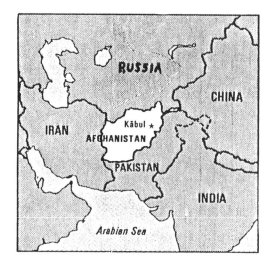

COUNTRY DATA

Area 260,000 sq. miles (about the size of Texas).

Capital Kabul (population 2+ million).

Population 11 million (plus about 2.7–3.5 million refugees in Pakistan and 1+ million refugees in Iran and the West (1985 est.)).

Density 42.31 per sq. mile.

Per Capita GNP $273.

Ethnic Groups Pukhtun/Pushtun (Pathan), Tadjik, Uzbek, Turkmen, Hazara, Baluch, Nuristani.

Religions Sunni Muslim 80%, Shiᶜi Muslim 20%, (pre-war).

Literacy less than 10% of the population.

Infant Mortality Rate (pre-war) 181.6 per 1,000 live births. (U.S. 13.8 per 1,000).

Life Expectancy 36.6 years males, 37.3 years females.

Government Afghanistan call itself a nation since 1747.

UNIQUENESS OF CASE STUDY

Superpower support could not overcome the imposed central government's lack of legitimacy, nor could external support compensate for *mujahideen* insurgents' lack of unity and legitimacy that prevented a rapid rebel victory after the Soviet army withdrew.

CHRONOLOGY

17 Jul 1973 Daoud overthrows Afghan monarchy.

27 Apr 1978 Communists seize power, Daoud killed.

21 Mar 1979 Herat uprisings.

27 Dec 1979 Soviet invasion.

May 1986 Najibullah replaces Babrak Karmal.

Jun 1986 Gorbachev announces limited withdrawal.

14 Apr 1988 Geneva accords.

14 Feb 1989 Soviet withdrawal completed.

Mar 1989 Massive Soviet aid flow while aid to resistance cut.

Sept 1991 U.S.-USSR agreement to suspend arms aid by 1 January 1992.

Nov 1991 Moscow talks with resistance and withdraws military advisers.

Dec 1991 Soviet Union ends flow of arms and aid cut off.

Source: The map and some of the country data are from State Department "Background Notes."

10

Afghanistan: Low-Intensity Conflict with Major Power Intervention

David C. Isby

"The Soviets invaded Afghanistan. They took away our home. They called themselves our friends, and made themselves our masters. For that, we give them war, unceasing war, and we will not be the ones who tire first." Resistance commander *Maulavi* Shafiullah was killed in action in March 1985 a few weeks after he explained why he and his fellow Afghans resisted what seemed overwhelming odds.[1] The Soviet military was fighting against the divided people of one of the world's twenty poorest nations. Still, Shafiullah was right. The Afghans were willing to fight against foreign domination, regardless of cost. The Soviets did tire first.

Afghanistan was the high watermark of the Soviet empire. The Soviet military went into Afghanistan in 1978–79 following policies and worldviews that then seemed compelling in Moscow.[2] At that time, the global "correlation of forces" appeared to have changed in Moscow's favor.[3] In the late 1970s Soviet policy—in Afghanistan and elsewhere—emphasized armed force, both in resource allocation and as a tool of statecraft.[4] Subsequent Soviet writers have identified the policies of "the era of stagnation" with the view that armed force was the key determinant of national strength and will, and the most effective tool to accomplish policy goals, as exemplified by deploying the SS–20 intermediate-range ballistic missile (IRBM) force against Europe.[5]

When the Soviets left Afghanistan in 1989, it was a new world, where the use of Soviet armed force was seen not as invincible, but as counterproductive.[6] The SS–20 missiles were being transformed, following the 1987 treaty with the United States, from a key policy tool into expensive scrap metal. Afghanistan was hardly the sole cause, but its role in starting more than one Soviet "paradigm shift" is unmistakable.[7] The crisis of Soviet governance had superseded the motivations that brought the troops into Afghanistan, though the war did not end in 1989 with the Soviet withdrawal.

Great power intervention has been present throughout the Afghanistan war, both before and after the 1979–1989 occupation. In 1989–1991, however, Gorbachev presided over a limited liability commitment in Afghanistan, with diplomatic support, military advisers, a limited combat role, and extensive military and economic aid for their clients in Kabul.[8] Because of the strong elements of continuity in Soviet policy the war in Afghanistan was not truly a civil war until the end of the Soviet Union in 1991.

Applying the Manwaring Paradigm to Afghanistan

The six factors of the Manwaring low-intensity conflict (LIC) paradigm are valid and effective for understanding the war in Afghanistan and can be applied to all the participants. As has been suggested for other low-intensity conflicts, the basic shape of the Afghanistan war is pentagonal. The five parties have been the Afghan people, the pro-Soviet Kabul regime, the Afghan resistance (the regime to a lesser and the resistance to a greater extent coinciding with the people), the Soviets, and the Afghan resistance's outside supporters. Moreover, these five participants were and are deeply divided (except the Soviets in their 1978–1989 heyday). Each is an individual mosaic of competing allied groups and interests rather than a concrete slab.

Legitimacy

In many ways, LIC in general, and that in Afghanistan in particular, is about legitimacy.[9] Weak legitimacy is endemic in Third World governments, and warfare normally indicates a crisis of legitimacy. The key question of an insurgency is usually how legitimate is the government. From 1978 to 1989, the answer to that question in Afghanistan was: marginally.[10] The experience of the war in Afghanistan suggests that legitimacy is the major factor that will determine the outcome of that conflict. Without it, improvements and successes in the other five factors of the paradigm may be possible but will matter little.

The war did not emerge over a long period of time but was widespread within a year of the 1978 communist seizure of power in Kabul.[11] The war in Afghanistan was not caused by long-term problems of political, economic, and social injustice or underdevelopment in Afghanistan.[12] The cause was the actions of the Kabul regime (and their Soviet supporters) after the 1978 coup that cost it the (limited) claim on legitimate power that had accrued to Afghan governments since the first one in 1747. The Kabul regime of 1979–1989—installed and maintained by infidel foreign invaders who killed the previous head of state and then turned their massive firepower on the population—had little chance to improve legitimacy while the Soviets were still there.[13] The Manwaring paradigm stresses that a foreign military presence can damage the legitimacy of the target government, but seldom has it done so as dramatically.[14]

Lack of legitimacy crippled Soviet political war-fighting. The Afghans did not fight for lack of land reform, development, or educational opportunities; they fought to have the Soviets removed. The Soviet presence failed to have legitimacy with most Afghans, with most other nations (as shown by the widespread international condemnation), and with most Soviets as well after 1985.[15] The Soviets' actions in Afghanistan demonstrated their realization of the importance of legitimacy: their search for it became more intense after the rise of Gorbachev in 1985. Still, they lost what the Manwaring paradigm rightly sees as this single most important battle of a LIC.[16]

Afghanistan showed the importance of meeting expectations and demonstrating competence to establish legitimacy. Failure to meet widely held expectations undercut claims to legitimacy. The communist Kabul regime delegitimated itself after the 1978 coup (in the eyes of most Afghans) by failing to meet expectations of how an Afghan government should act. The regime itself saw the coup as a revolutionary act, aimed at destroying previous governmental, religious, and societal practices (and those practitioners) it despised as backwards and replacing them with itself—a centralized, avowedly non-Islamic, secular force, committed to modernization. The regime's communist opposition to traditional religious and societal practices, especially those yielding governmental legitimacy, and the increasing link with the Soviets in 1978–79 made the Kabul government ab initio illegitimate—hence not subject to subsequent improvement—to most Afghans.

The Kabul experience in 1978–79 contrasts with the seizure of power by Mohammed Daoud, the "red prince," in 1973. Daoud's coup ended the Afghan monarchy but stressed continuity. He sought to be perceived as consistent with the traditional sources of Afghan religious and societal legitimacy.[17] Thus, only a few Afghans took up arms against Daoud (though this group included Gulbuddin Hekmatyar, who would become the most skilled and most revolutionary member of the resistance's Pakistan-based political leadership, and Ahmad Shah Massoud and Abdul Haq, who would prove the most effective field commanders of the 1979–1989 war). In contrast to Daoud's skillful moves to gain legitimacy, in 1978 the regime's actions led to war.[18]

Kabul's cheapjack Stalinism was limited to 1978-79, and the Soviets tried to undo its lasting effects.[19] The Soviet-installed chief of state, Babrak Karmal, opened his first radio broadcast from the Soviet Union the day after the 1979 invasion with the traditional Islamic benediction.[20] Islam—diverse and divided Afghanistan's great unifying, self-defining force and common belief—is interwoven with the totality of life, culture, and society, with the exception of that of modernized elites in Kabul and other large cities. As defined in Afghan terms, Islam was the central legitimating factor in the conflict and the prime motivating and ideological factor for the Afghan resistance. Afghans not siding with the Soviets termed the war a *jihad* (holy war), and those who fought it *mujahideen* (holy warriors). The implicit threat to Islam inherent in communism limited Afghanistan's divided Communist Party, and the attempts by the Soviets and Kabul to increase their legitimacy after the 1979 invasion were predominantly defined in Islamic terms.

The grounds for legitimacy in Afghanistan were greatly influenced by the combination of superpower involvement and limited modernization. Islam's great importance was enhanced because nontraditional institutions—such as bureaucracy and trade unions—were weak. Legitimacy of the central government at any time in Afghanistan was limited. Kabul's pre-1978 centralized but limited authority over rural Afghanistan was shattered by the regime's brutal campaign to consolidate power in 1978–79.

Conversely, there was a strong tradition of legitimate Afghan resistance to central authority.[21] This had historically meant limited resistance, just as Kabul's authority had itself been limited. The only times when Afghan resistance to central authority became nationwide and the fighting no longer limited was when the government in Kabul was perceived as a foreign creation, either British or, in 1979–1989, Soviet. Autonomy is a prerequisite for any Afghan institution to be perceived as legitimate; control by foreigners, even Islamic ones but especially infidels, is seen as un-Afghan.

Afghanistan's experience points out that judging legitimacy is relative rather than absolute, and that anticipated performance rather than actual capabilities is the common yardstick. The initial world condemnation of the invasion did not fade in part because the powerful Soviet military was unable to meet expectations that it would soon defeat the Afghans. The Soviets—and much of the world—expected that the experience of Hungary in 1956 and Czechoslovakia in 1968 would be repeated in Afghanistan in 1979 and that the use of Soviet troops to replace one Soviet-backed regime with another would be accepted eventually.[22]

In December 1979, the Soviets believed that judicious use of military force would soon solve their Afghan problem.[23] Within six months, it was apparent it would not, and the Soviets evolved a broad range of tactics—diplomatic, political, and military—along with their attempt to increase legitimacy as part of their war-fighting in 1980–1989. They insisted on downplaying communist ideology and saw the Kabul regime as a state in the "national democratic" stage of development. The Soviets attempted to use Islam as a legitimating agent, as in their consolidation of power in central Asia.[24] They created a National Fatherland Front as used in the consolidation of power in central and eastern Europe.[25] They reached back to traditional Russian counterinsurgency and attempted—more successfully than with other tactics—to embrace and co-opt traditional authority, exploiting ethnic divisions and using tribal militias to "divide and conquer."[26]

These tactics failed. Prior to 1989, neither the Kabul regime nor the Soviets could legitimate themselves in terms of Islam or of preexisting Afghan patterns.[27] Those who did accept the regime tended to come from groups with special interests in its preservation. Some were ideologically committed to the regime (the members of Afghanistan's two Communist Parties, their supporters, and those on the Soviet payroll) or opportunists (such as the illiterates who became army officers). Others were economically or politically dependent on the Kabul regime (a group increasing with the internal refugee populations in the cities, and greater cross-border trade with the Soviets). Other supporters were committed to modernization or susceptible to nontraditional appeals (such as some army officers and state school teachers) or looking for an outside counterbalance to preexisting tensions (such as Uzbeks resenting Pathan domination). In addition, the Soviets, after 1980, made efforts to draw those threatened by the resistance into this ragged coalition.[28] Success remained limited, however, even when Kabul continued this policy after the Soviet withdrawal.

The Soviets certainly did not identify legitimacy with democracy, unlike many involved in Western LIC. Neither has much of the resistance. Nonetheless, the parties in Afghanistan have looked to elections as legitimating actions. Other acts of local and national self-determination with strong Afghan traditions have been used by all sides in attempts to bolster legitimacy. Two examples are the *jirga* or *shura*, both of which represent collective decision-making and consensus-building.[29] Several *loya jirgas* (the calling of a national gathering) were held in Kabul. Kabul, acting as executive agent for the Soviets, also called tribal *jirgas*—cross-border gatherings of the leadership of Pathan tribes from both Afghanistan and Pakistan.

The 1989 removal of Soviet combat troops allowed Kabul's chief of state, Dr. Najibullah, to make himself appear as the rational Afghan alternative both internationally and to a (numerically relatively small) receptive internal audience. His ability to improve regime legitimacy remained limited in 1989–92, however, despite his extensive efforts and undoubted political skills. After the Soviet withdrawal, the Kabul regime did not so much increase its legitimacy—although it was increased—as the Afghan resistance undercut their own.

The resistance and legitimacy. The Afghan resistance had a "free ride" on legitimacy from 1979 to 1989 because they were opposing the Soviets. The legitimacy of anticolonial and antisuperpower resistance in the Third World, established over previous decades, had been underlined by resurgent Islam. In 1989, once the Soviets withdrew their combat forces, the calculus of the Afghanistan conflict changed, and the balance between apparent Afghan alternatives changed.[30] Legitimacy had to be reevaluated.

The legitimacy of the Afghan political leadership based in Pakistan was undercut by their actions in 1989.[31] The leadership appeared eager to put in an early claim for their right to exert strong centralized power in a way that no Afghan government ever had, with the notable exception of the communist Kabul regime of 1978–79. The leadership appeared anxious to exclude the Afghan Shiᶜa, most of the field commanders, and Afghans opposed to the leadership's Pakistani military and Arab supporters. At the same time that the leadership (pressured by these foreign supporters) tried to secure its potential power by cutting out allies, it further undercut its position by awarding its sinecure "governmental" positions according to political and personal loyalties rather than competence or participation in the war.

A resistance movement that draws so much of both its legitimacy and its motivation from such transcendent goals as religion and independence finds leaders dominated by foreigners, even Islamic ones, hard to accept. The hands-on role of supporters in the 1989 formation of the Afghan Interim Government at Hadjibad, near Rawalpindi, showed that these Afghans lacked autonomy. The Pakistan-based leadership was, in the absence of a strong base of legitimacy among the fighting men inside Afghanistan, subjected to foreign direction.

The perception of foreign control was perhaps inevitable, given the political leadership's location in exile and dependence on outside aid, but the absence of effective Afghan institutions led the Pakistanis to perceive there was no alternative to imposing their own agenda.

This perception of lack of autonomy exacerbated long-standing resentment among many Afghans at the leadership's corruption and failure to demonstrate competence or capability in governmental functions (a failure the leadership ascribed to Pakistani interference).

This broad spectrum of limitations, some self-inflicted, others imposed by allies, became increasingly important as the resistance inherited the onus of rising expectations with the Soviet military's departure. Fierce fighting by the Kabul regime backed by a massive Soviet aid flow blocked resistance military victory in 1989, but the resistance's crisis of legitimacy helped ensure that it was met by desperate defense rather than government units changing sides (a key to victory in 1992) or a popular rising in Kabul.

The resistance's crisis of legitimacy was brought about by their failure not only to appear autonomous and competent, but to secure diplomatic recognition, political unity (or at least coherence), independence from outside control, and military success, all of which were widely expected after the Soviet withdrawal in 1989. The resistance, united against the Soviet invaders, could not agree on any positive program. Political platforms ranged from decentralized representative democracy to centralized Islamic revolution. The inability to present an effective alternative government for Afghanistan undercut resistance claims to legitimacy until Najibullah's power base collapsed in 1992.

In 1989, lack of anticipated success was the main reason for the failure to achieve diplomatic recognition. This lack of success came, in turn, from a combination of war-weariness, lack of motivation coming from an absence of confidence in the leadership, and an unwillingness to take risks in what was widely seen as the last stages of the war. Overconfidence and poor planning by the Pakistan-based political leadership and their Pakistani supporters led them to put their weight behind a coup de main. This led to the hastily planned failed resistance attack on Jalalabad.

In 1989, the effect of collateral damage from inaccurate resistance rocket attacks on Kabul, atrocities, and acts of violence by revolutionary Afghans and foreign volunteers, many directed at Afghans in Pakistan or in resistance-occupied areas of Afghanistan, undercut legitimacy. This effect was felt not only among the population of Kabul but among many resistance supporters both in Pakistan and Afghanistan and was compounded when it became apparent that the resistance leadership was unable or unwilling to curb such abuses.[32]

Organization for Unity of Effort

Organization for unity of effort was a potential Soviet strength undercut by failures of legitimacy. Leninist models of political organization and development provided an emphasis on unity of effort and a concrete link between political and military action, which are absent in some Western practitioners.[33] It also provided the Soviets with institutions to implement policy. Although Western nations have no "Department of Democracy" for political war-fighting, the international departments of the Communist Party of the Soviet Union and the republic parties were important participants in the Soviet war in Afghanistan.

Unlike other low-intensity conflicts (most notably that in South Vietnam) where unity of command was not achieved, the Kabul regime's dependence on the Soviets resulted in a unified war-fighting effort (at considerable cost to Kabul's perceived legitimacy) in 1979-1989.[34] Soviet advisers throughout Kabul's government and military made the real decisions.[35] The Soviets had relied on the adviser system for control in the Polish civil war. It allowed the reality of Soviet control while training indigenous officers and maintaining the appearance of sovereignty. The reliance on advisers also reflected the small number of Afghans who were both technically competent and loyal to Kabul. After Soviet withdrawal, the advisers remained, until 1992, in reduced numbers.[36]

Unity of command does not necessarily mean effectiveness. The war in 1979-1989 was apparently fought largely from Moscow and Tashkent, leaving few decisions to local commanders. There is evidence of continued Soviet high-level involvement—those on the scene may have considered it meddling—in the details of war-fighting in Afghanistan.[37] This contrasts with the Soviet war against the Basmachi in central Asia and with most successful Western counterinsurgency experiences such as in Malaya and the Philippines.[38]

There was never a single Soviet "viceroy" in Kabul. In Kabul there was division between the leadership of the Limited Contingent Soviet Forces Afghanistan (LCSFA), those officers based at the Soviet embassy, and those advisers running the Kabul regime and its military. The Communist Party and Soviet intelligence (KGB) also had substantial roles in directing the war in Afghanistan. Even in 1989-1991, when the Kabul regime took over the unitary war-fighting effort, the deep divisions within the leadership proved a burden.

The resistance. Lack of organization for unity of effort crippled the Afghan resistance but was inherent in their nature as a people in arms and thus inherently decentralized. This decentralization—in other words, the fact the resistance was an integral part of Afghanistan—helped the resistance achieve its greatest success, the negative one of not being defeated by the Soviet military. The resistance acted in ways that might not have represented proven guerrilla tactics but were consistent with Afghan life and society. It is significant that the Westerners who best understood the resistance were not specialists in guerrilla warfare, but anthropologists who thoroughly knew Afghanistan, such as Olivier Roy and the late Louis Dupree.

Resistance weakness of organization for unity of effort flowed from limitations in perceived legitimacy, the lack of a shared political vision, the divisive effect of outside supporters' policies, and the ethnic division of the Afghans; all stronger after 1989. The ultimate resistance victory was not due to addressing these fundamental issues but from overcoming them temporarily to topple a weakened Najibullah, which Soviet aid and foreign interference had prevented in 1989. Pakistan and Saudi Arabia (previously concerned about opposing Iranian influence) cut back their strong support for Hekmatyar after 1990; he no longer was their chosen unifying policy instrument in Afghanistan. Ethnic politics brought together the pro-Kabul Uzbek and Turkmen militias with Ahmad Shah Massoud's predominantly Tajik resistance organization, its legitimacy buttressed by perceptions of competence and autonomy. The war ended not through a united Afghan effort, but rather a series of regional agreements, using ethnic and tribal loyalties as their basis.

Traditional Afghan divisions and distrusts were compounded by the war. To the tensions between ethnic groups and between Sunni and Shiᶜa were added those divisions between traditionalists and two divergent streams of Afghan Islamist politics, fundamentalist and revolutionary. The gap between those Afghans resisting in Afghanistan and those in Pakistan was often deeper than that between political parties. Suspicion of both modernization and educated Afghans by those whose roots were in rural society was widespread and led to many educated Afghans splitting off from the resistance.

Despite many field commanders' extensive efforts in 1989–91 to overcome Pakistan's controlling military influence, their focus remained local, not national. Thus, the 1992 government in Kabul was dominated not by field commanders but the once-discredited

Peshawar-based Pathan leadership. Ethnic loyalties and the perception that only a Pathan could rule Afghanistan—not battlefield strength—proved enduring.

Type and Consistency of Support from Outside Participants

Outside support for the Kabul regime meant Soviet support, which depended on resource allocation decisions in Moscow. In 1979–1989 the Soviet military could provide support that was almost unlimited, but this did not yield success. The Soviet military presence was seen as a mistake and counterproductive by the mainstream of Soviet politics in 1991.[39] Soviet military and economic aid allowed the Kabul regime to fight in 1989–91.[40] Its cessation led to Najibullah's fall.

Aid could not have substituted for troops in 1979, however. The Soviet assessment in 1979, that without a major military intervention the Kabul regime would fall to its own people, was probably correct. The Soviet occupation, though destructive of legitimacy, allowed the rebuilding of Kabul's military and intelligence assets after their 1979–80 collapse. The Kabul regime forces of 1989–1991 were created while Soviet troops carried the weight of the conflict.

Soviet support in the 1979-1989 period was not limited to truck convoys and airlifts. The Soviets' support included diplomatic support, which had considerable cost. The war became a major stumbling block in their foreign relations until the signing of the Geneva accords in 1988. Aside from India's anti-Pakistan orientation, what international legitimacy the Kabul regime enjoyed before 1989 came from the Soviets' mobilizing their clients and supporters.

Type and consistency of support for the resistance. The resistance depended on the substantial flow of aid through Pakistan, which was largely the result of international support from the United States, Saudi Arabia, China, and a number of other Islamic and Western nations. The aid that trickled through Iran largely originated there. Although the allocation processes (used by both Pakistan and Iran to further their policy goals) were the source of much bitterness among the Afghans, by the mid-1980s the resistance enjoyed aid that greatly exceeded that of other, more efficient, guerrilla forces. The U.S. covert program alone reportedly provided more than four hundred thousand Kalashnikov rifles by mid–1991.

Because of this level of support, however, breaks in the aid flow such as the 1989 hiatus, even if temporary, represented a blow to rising expectations and had a great impact. The aid hiatus in 1989 was the result not of Soviet action, but of U.S. and Pakistani decisions. U.S. policy was based on estimates that the conflict would end in eight to ten months. Pakistan did not want weapons in the hands of field commanders, who were likely to be opposed to the Pakistan-sponsored, Peshawar-based political leaders and unlikely to yield power to them. These decisions were compounded by unrest in China, source of many of the weapons, resulting in missed weapons shipments.

The result of the aid hiatus was that many field commanders (who had been waging war a decade before with a handful of bolt-action rifles) suspended offensive operations in 1989–90 because they received few artillery rockets or mortar shells. More to the point, they failed to receive the motivation and direction that would have led them to continue fighting.

Reliance on foreign aid also decreased resistance legitimacy, but, like the Soviet military presence for the regime, it was needed for survival. Foreign aid programs were good at arming Afghans, less so at making them effective. Helping Afghans to evolve the effective structures of guerrilla war—such as alternative national and local government or military training—was difficult and would have encountered Pakistani interference. By 1990, foreign developmental and humanitarian aid going inside resistance-controlled Afghanistan had in some areas created a culture of dependency. In other ways, aid also proved counterproductive. For example, rather than improving battlefield tactics, Afghans operating south of the Hindu Kush tended to minimize their casualties and take advantage of longer-ranged weapons such as 82mm mortars and 107mm rockets by relying on often ineffective stand-off barrages at the expense of taking ground or defeating enemy units. Relying exclusively on firepower or materiél does not yield results for either guerrillas or counterguerrilla forces.

In other areas of outside support, the resistance had less clear-cut success. Diplomatic aid was limited by the resistance's inability to evolve institutions that could take part in international affairs. Afghan adaptation to the demands of war was undercut by the movement of educated Afghans away from the conflict to become refugees.

General observations. Afghanistan confirms that although foreign military involvement can be a lifesaver, it often comes with a high cost in legitimacy. This caveat applies whether the foreign connection is as large and firepower-intensive as the Soviets in 1979–1989 or as limited and covert as the Pakistani and Arab involvement with the resistance in 1989.

Afghanistan also confirms the importance of consistent and effective military and economic aid. Pakistan funnelled aid to allow the resistance to keep fighting from 1979 to 1989. The Soviets effectively waged their limited liability war in 1989–1991; without

Soviet aid the war would have ended in 1989. Training and advisory efforts can also be vitally important but come with a higher political cost as they come to resemble foreign involvement. In 1989–1991, Soviet aid allowed Najibullah to glue his regime together. It could not prevent the increasing ethnic divisions within it that finally destroyed it. When Moscow's gold stopped flowing, so did many non-Pathans' willingness to support Najibullah's regime.

For many parties, without diplomatic assistance, their cause will lack international impact; and Afghanistan shows the importance of this form of aid in both multinational forums and bilateral relations. The willingness of foreign supporters to make Afghanistan an issue in the world's relations with Moscow was a critical element in outside support.

Intelligence

Intelligence proved to be, like organization, an area where potential Soviet advantages could not be parlayed into larger successes. The Soviets had extensive intelligence assets but less ability to act on intelligence in a timely and effective manner. The Soviets were aware of the importance of intelligence, as demonstrated by their willingness to allocate resources to this area, but there is little evidence of lasting Soviet success because they did not use intelligence information effectively.[41]

The Soviets in 1979–1989 created and controlled the Kabul regime's intelligence and secret police apparatus.[42] Because Kabul had used previous secret police organizations primarily in intercommunist warfare in 1978–1979, the Soviets created a new organization: KHAD (later WAD), the *Kheddamat-e-Etela^cat-e-Dawlati* or State Information Agency, a KGB clone and surrogate with a shared role as both secret police and intelligence organization. KHAD/WAD's first leader, Dr. Najibullah, was handpicked for loyalty not to the Afghan Communist Party, but to Moscow. His effectiveness with KHAD helped lead the Soviets to install Najibullah as chief of state.

KHAD's local successes, though greatly feared by the Afghans, did not yield strategic advantage. KHAD was extensive, running large nets of agents and informers. The resistance was thoroughly infiltrated. KHAD also fielded military units, on the model of the KGB. It worked alongside the KGB in Afghanistan and acted as a surrogate for activities such as terrorism in Pakistan.[43] Yet, the Soviets did not use this intelligence effectively. Although some important resistance leaders were targeted and eliminated there was no sustained campaign against the resistance leadership. Despite extensive intelligence information on resistance logistics and operations, there were few surprise defeats.

Soviet war-fighting was less dependent on intelligence than were Western-style counterinsurgency tactics, relying less on small unit patrolling and targeted strikes and more on massive firepower and area strikes.[44] Soviet target acquisition lacked responsiveness, as demonstrated by limited counterbattery fire against Afghan weapons despite the use of a wide range of Soviet sensor systems. It was hard for the Soviet military to target mobile groups of Afghan guerrillas, which is one reason why the more static civil population was usually the Soviets' target.

Intelligence capabilities in the resistance. The resistance had a technically unsophisticated but effective intelligence capability, largely in the area of human intelligence (HUMINT). The resistance had sympathizers throughout the Kabul regime (many high-ranking) and in the Soviet Army who would pass along intelligence, often at great personal risk. The Soviets had to assume that anything the Kabul regime knew was also known by the resistance.

Resistance "eyes and ears" throughout the country in best guerrilla warfare style became adept at recognizing tactical intelligence indicators: Soviets frantically working in the vehicle park suggested an impending offensive. Afghan couriers on motorcycles move faster than Soviet combined arms columns; only heliborne or special operations forces could use the element of surprise.

Discipline and Capabilities

Most of the forces in the Afghanistan conflict fell short in discipline and capabilities, enhancing the value of the effective few on each side. Najibullah's regime fell after Ahmad Shah Massoud's forces allied with formerly pro-Kabul Uzbek and Turkmen militia, the two most capable and (in Massoud's case) disciplined forces in Afghanistan. Despite the political impact of the Soviet commitment, Moscow never provided the numbers (only six of over two hundred divisions), capabilities (too few skillful infantry) or discipline (too many atrocities) required for military victory.

As all sides fell short on the battlefield in Afghanistan, this favored the side that only had to survive: the resistance in 1979–1989 and Kabul in 1989–1991 (the end of the Soviet Union precluded any longer-term viability); both held the upper hand militarily despite their inability to take and hold large areas.

The Soviets and the Kabul regime. The Soviets lacked both the discipline and the tactical skills the paradigm considers necessary for success. How the Soviets fought affected both their own domestic attitudes toward the war and the military and the Afghan attitudes toward the Soviets.

Soviet tactical shortcomings were, in many cases, inherent in their attempt to try to fight a long-term, inexpensive, "cheap and nasty" low-intensity war emphasizing the (ultimately unsuccessful) political elements of consolidation. There was also an obvious desire to minimize the number and the rate of their own casualties, reflected in the relatively slow tempo of most combined arms operations.

The Soviet military did not lose on the battlefield, but neither did it successfully adapt. Widespread atrocities and more widespread firepower undercut the successes of other elements in Soviet war-fighting.[45] It was hard to talk of economic development and women's rights when Soviet bombs were falling throughout the country. Soviet atrocities were so widespread that they were unlikely to have been accidents or simply the inevitable result of counterinsurgency conflict.

Discipline (or its absence) and lack of battlefield success both affect legitimacy. Kabul's initial atrocities (some done under Soviet direction, such as the Kerala massacre in 1979) were instrumental in spreading the war. This cycle of atrocity and reprisal came home to the Soviet military. The 1980s saw increased internal violence, much of it interethnic, in the Soviet military; more Soviet soldiers were beaten to death in those years than were killed by weapons' fire in Afghanistan.[46]

The failure of the Soviet military to maintain internal discipline and to gain battlefield success in Afghanistan destroyed the Soviet military's claim—intact since 1941—to have first priority on state resources and to be the only Soviet institution that was effective, even if inefficient.[47] The Soviet perception that their expensive military, despite all the capital and human resources that had been invested in it, "could not even beat the Afghans" made it hard to accept that this force could be the "one sure shield" of the homeland that Yuri Andropov had once claimed it was.[48]

Some adaptation to counterinsurgency tactics was seen in Afghanistan but was apparently not a major Soviet goal.[49] The Soviets only made limited adaptation to what two U.S. experts termed "the first principle of counterguerrilla tactics . . . to take the guerrilla as the model and fight him in his own style."[50] Adaptation included using different operational approaches during the war, the widespread use of helicopters, and, most notably, the use of special operations forces in 1984–1987.[51] The Soviets did not lose the war militarily but discovered the limits of military force for achieving great power political goals in Third World insurgencies.[52]

Military incapacity undercuts legitimacy, as followed the collapse of Kabul's military in 1979–1980. Kabul's battlefield success in 1989—without direct Soviet involvement—redeemed some legitimacy. Conversely, military success can also provide legitimacy as long as it does not undercut other Afghan requirements for legitimacy. The Peshawar-based political leadership went to Kabul in 1992 partly re-legitimated by the backing of Massoud's capable troops.

The resistance. The Afghan resistance's shortcomings in military capability and discipline, which had been overshadowed by their strengths in 1978–1989, were highlighted by their 1989–1991 failures. There was no single, central authority to allocate resources, impose discipline, and initiate training. The nature of the resistance as a people in arms also imposed largely valid societal guidelines on how to deal with other Afghans. For example, in 1978–1988 there were relatively few resistance killings of noncombatants or of captured Kabul regime enlisted personnel. (Soviets, officers, regime activists, Communist Party members, and KHAD agents were another matter.)

Because of this expectation of resistance conduct, failures became more important after the Soviets left. Before then, any crimes were largely overshadowed by the enormity of Soviet devastation; after the withdrawal, they were skillfully exploited by the Kabul regime with psychological warfare aimed at the urban population. Resistance atrocities also increased divisions among the resistance itself.

Similarly, the increased level of interresistance conflict in 1989–90, especially that between Ahmad Shah Massoud and Gulbuddin Hekmatyar's forces north of the Hindu Kush, further highlighted divisions in the resistance and undercut claims of competence to govern Afghanistan and, hence, legitimacy.

In 1979–1989, the Afghan resistance was unable to field a significant number of general purpose, highly capable military forces. Neither training above what would be considered individual or squad level in the West nor effective tactical organization has been general or institutionalized. There was no Afghan equivalent of the North Vietnamese Army, able to move from province to province.

Despite this shortcoming, many Afghan leaders are excellent. Ahmad Shah Massoud emphasized discipline and his trained units were decisive in holding Kabul in April, 1992. As guerrillas, some Afghan commanders, such as Abdul Haq at the height of his operations around Kabul, mounted sophisticated and well-planned actions. Other groups throughout the country were also distinguished by battlefield success.

Ability to Reduce Outside Aid

Soviet aid was vital for Kabul. Soviet fuel, food, and hard currency limited inflation and bought loyalties; weapons helped hold the resistance at bay and were bartered for temporary alliances. Its cessation led to the fall of Najibullah.

While maintaining their own aid flow, the Soviets sought to reduce that to the resistance. Soviet diplomatic pressure—especially the implicit threat of escalation against Pakistan—limited the donors' willingness to provide aid to the resistance, especially in the first years of the war. It helped prevent the supply of Stinger surface-to-air missiles (SAMs) prior to 1986.

Soviet pressure on Pakistan to reduce outside support for the resistance was not limited to diplomacy. In the mid to late 1980s, the Soviets waged the world's most extensive campaign of state-supported terrorism in Pakistan, using the Kabul regime's intelligence service as executive agents. Dissident tribes, religious groups, and other opponents of the central authority in Pakistan received arms and funding, resulting in a number of clashes with the Pakistani authorities. The Soviets mounted a series of cross-border airstrikes. This campaign did not cut off the flow of aid to the resistance, however. Pakistan, backed by the major aid donors, held firm.

In the case of Iran, however, the Soviets' diplomacy helped limit the scope of aid provided to the resistance. Iran, preoccupied with the war with Iraq, feared Soviet hostility. Iran's limited aid went to strengthen the internal position of current or potentially pro-Iran groups within the resistance.

Cutting supplies from foreign sanctuaries to areas of operations has been a major element of sustained efforts in many low-intensity conflicts, especially that of the United States in South Vietnam and the French in Algeria. The Soviets were unwilling to invest resources on the scale of these two examples to cut the resistance's main supply routes from Pakistan, even though these were the target of both special operations and major offensives. Interdiction was also carried out by the extensive bombing of the countryside, especially south of the Hindu Kush. The resulting depopulation made moving supplies difficult for the resistance. It also encouraged the formation of pro-Kabul militias by local inhabitants who had become economically dependent on the regime.[53]

The dependence of the Peshawar-based resistance's political leadership on aid donors hurt their legitimacy, especially inside Afghanistan, where the fighting men had little respect for those who did not share their hardships. The flow of aid was used, especially south of the Hindu Kush, for Pakistani political goals. The allocation of aid by Pakistani Inter-Service Intelligence (ISI), especially their support of the revolutionary Hezb-e-Islami party of Gulbuddin Hekmatyar, was a highly divisive issue among the Afghans. Both reliance on outside aid and ISI hostility to the emergence of institutions they did not control hurt Afghan attempts to build effective political and military organizations.

In the global village, effective aid also must include access to the information media. The West was willing to provide aid—diplomatic as well as covert and humanitarian—because its citizens knew about the brutal war the Soviets were waging and saw the human cost. The West's journalists brought out the news of Afghanistan, and private groups spread this information and mobilized support.

Soviet aid could not substitute for Najibullah's flawed legitimacy; it could only fund armed forces to postpone the reckoning. Similarly, the aid funnelled to Hekmatyar by ISI and Saudi Arabia could not compensate for his lack of broad-based support inside Afghanistan nor for his image as a foreign tool; he was greatly weakened by the reduction of this support in 1990–1991—he had backed Iraq in the Gulf War. Massoud received comparatively little aid from ISI, but was able to use the internal resources of non-Pathan Afghanistan to oust Najibullah. Once Kabul fell, Hekmatyar's forces, despite the strength resulting from the years of aid, could not overturn Massoud's willingness to use his forces to support Hekmatyar's rival politicians from Peshawar.

Conclusions

The Afghan resistance's flaws were deep and substantial, but what mattered more than all the times when it fell short were its strengths inherent in Afghan life and society and, above all, its great commitment to the struggle that Shafiullah so eloquently expressed in 1985. The Manwaring paradigm suggests that both the failure of the Soviets to defeat the resistance in 1979–1989 and the failure of the resistance to defeat the Kabul regime in 1989–1991 were not flukes but rather the logical outcomes of limitations, primarily in legitimacy, that undercut the effective elements of their war-fighting. The no-win, no-peace situation of 1989–1991 was the result of this broad spectrum of both regime and resistance strengths and weaknesses. In 1992, the Peshawar leadership could take power in Kabul because, despite all their failings, they were much closer to what the Afghan people saw as legitimate than Najibullah had been.

The war is hard to present as a model for future conflicts because of the direct Soviet military involvement. The influence of Afghan people and society on the conflict was also unique. Nonetheless, though the dynamics of the conflict are predominantly Afghanistan-specific rather than reflecting a general model of low-intensity or counterinsurgency conflict, the Manwaring paradigm is still applicable, with some modification to reflect Afghan realities.

The first such modification is a small one. It is intended that the paradigm cut all ways. This requires slight redefinition of the factors. It also requires taking the divisions within each party into account and not overgeneralizing the actions and goals of participants who have deep and fundamental antipathies despite being on the same side.

The second point is that legitimacy is more than the first and most important of the factors; it is a necessary precondition for improvement in other areas. This has not always been the case in other counterinsurgency conflicts, especially prior to 1945, when there was often less of an emphasis on legitimacy. The powers of communications and popular consciousness have underlined the importance of perceived legitimacy, both internationally and internally. The Soviets in Afghanistan failed to legitimate either their presence or their client's regime. They never had legitimacy, and the resistance political leadship squandered much of its own.

The third point is that a major change in the international or internal conditions of the conflict can lead to the reexamination of the relationship of all the factors. In 1989 the Afghan resistance, widely seen in the West and even in the Soviet Union as victorious, failed militarily, politically, and diplomatically against the Kabul regime. Changing the Soviets' intervention from one of direct participation to limited liability made Afghanistan a different war, but their involvement continued up to the end of the Soviet Union.

The fourth point is to look at which elements of the paradigm implicitly assume the use of Western-style rather than Soviet-style counterinsurgency. Soviet goals and methods in Afghanistan were different—especially on the battlefield—from those the West has normally associated with effective counterinsurgency warfare, perhaps best epitomized in the decisive stages of the insurgencies in Malaya and the Philippines. The Soviets have taken pains to point out that they were not engaging in counterinsurgency, which they see as an imperialist form of warfare.[54]

This may be a distinction without a difference. The Soviets were unwilling to embrace many of the elements the paradigm sees as essential to effective counterinsurgency. This helped ensure that the

Soviet approach, with its emphasis on military action and the imposition of Moscow-oriented institutions, really resulted not in consolidation and integration into Moscow's control, but in temporary pacification. The Soviets could not offer the people of Afghanistan a convincing and desirable future after the war, and all the rhetoric directed to that end had little effect. The Kabul regime, in 1989–1991, was able to present the Afghans living in the cities it occupied an alternative future, but one defined in negative terms: not to be ruled by revolutionary elements of resistance. The Kabul leaders were able to do this despite their continued use of many of the elements of Soviet-style war-fighting in Afghanistan, such as Scud missiles and airstrikes against the countryside, because they could point to the benefits of Soviet aid.

The Soviets came to many of the same tactical conclusions (despite broad philosophical differences) that have characterized Western counterinsurgency campaigns. Some of these included the perception of the war as basically a political action, the importance of helicopters for both firepower and mobility in countries with difficult terrain, and the importance of effective intelligence and target acquisition (it was not lack of firepower the Soviets suffered, but inability to apply it against the guerrillas). They also recognized the need for effective indigenous forces to carry as much of the fighting as possible, and the need for specialized counterinsurgency light infantry.

Although their overall approach to war-fighting in Afghanistan proved ineffective, the Soviets showed themselves capable of some effective tactics as a part of this effort, especially their attempts to divide and conquer, their willingness to write off the hinterland, and their corresponding lack of emphasis in winning the proverbial "hearts and minds." They concentrated instead on important areas and people and applying massive firepower to every other area and everybody else. These could not offset the larger failures of the Soviet approach. Even this unsophisticated approach requires the carrot as well as the stick. The Soviets offered much stick and few carrots.

The Soviet approach to war-fighting in Afghanistan was consistent not only with Leninist models of political consolidation, but also with the Soviet military's then-current operational thinking for general wars and the historical Russian and Soviet approach to counterinsurgency conflicts. The lessons of the war in central Asia in the 1920s, the Polish civil war of 1944–1949, and the suppression of resistance in the Baltic states and the Ukraine in 1944–1954 were available to guide Soviet actions in Afghanistan, as was the study of Western counterinsurgency.[55] Few things are as perishable as institutional memory and military capability, however, and counterinsurgency warfare had not been a priority for the Soviet military for many years.[56]

The Soviets never linked stability with justice, but with the imposition of pro-Moscow rule. The rapidity with which Soviet-installed regimes disintegrated in central and eastern Europe during the revolutions of 1989 suggested, among many other lessons, that Soviet-style political consolidation, the great unattainable goal of the 1979–1989 war effort in Afghanistan, simply does not last unless backed up by armed force. The revolutions of 1989 also showed how corrosive to claims of legitimacy was the perception that a regime owed its inception and maintenance to the Soviets and their tanks (or their surrogates and their tanks). The Soviet approach, with its underlying reliance on force, did not lead to consolidation after all. This flaw in the Soviets' biggest paradigm—the one on which they had built so much of their control both externally and internally—first became apparent in the unforgiving mountains of Afghanistan.

Notes

1. Interview with Shafiullah, February 1985. A *maulavi* is a graduate of a *madrassa* or a religious teacher.

2. Bill Keller, "Secret Soviet Party Documents Said to Admit Afghan Errors," *New York Times*, 17 June 1988, p. A1, A7. Richard Beeston, "Soviet Journal Blames U.S.S.R. for late-1970s Confrontation," *Washington Times*, 20 May 1988, p. A8. Philip Taubman, "Soviet Afghan Drive Called Decision of a Few," *New York Times*, 30 March 1988, p. A11. Aaron Trehub, "Boglomov Reveals Opposition to Afghan Invasion," *Radio Liberty Research*, RL 116/88, 17 March 1988. Elizabeth Engue, "Soviet Author Repudiates 'Brezhnev Doctrine,'" *Radio Liberty Research*, RL4/88, 20 December 1985.

3. A. Bogmolov, "But Who Was Mistaken?" *Literaturnaya Gazeta*, 15 March 1988, p. 10, translated in FBIS-SOV-88-050, *FBIS Soviet Union Daily Report*, 16 March 1988, p. 19. Ikuda, "Academician Says Troops in Afghanistan 'Mistake,'" *Ashai Shimbun* (Tokyo), 12 March 1988, p. 6, translated in FBIS-SOV-88-050, *FBIS Soviet Union Daily Report*, 15 March 1988, p. 2.

4. Criticisms of the Soviet decision to invade, including with it a reduced assessment of the utility of military force in international relations, include Professor Vyacheslav Dashichev, "East-West: Quest for New Relations. On the Priorities of the Soviet State's Foreign Policy," *Literaturnaya Gazeta*, 18 May 1988, p. 14, translated in *FBIS Soviet Union Daily Report*, 20 May 1988, pp. 4–8; Aleksandr Prohankov, "Defense Consciousness and New Thinking," *Literaturnaya Gazeta*, 6 May 1988, pp. 4–5, translated in *FBIS Soviet Union Daily Report*, 9 June 1988, p. 74; and Aaron Trehub, "Soviet Press Coverage of

the War in Afghanistan: From Cheerleading to Disenchantment," *Report on the USSR* 1, no. 10 (10 March 1989): 1–4.

5. An example of the discussion of the costs and benefits of Afghanistan can be seen in Lyudmila Shchipakina, "Motherland Is Welcoming Its Sons," *Krasnaya Zvezda*, 22 May 1988, p. 2, translated in FBIS-SOV-88-100, *FBIS Soviet Union Daily Report*, 24 May 1988, pp. 33–34.

6. Ye. Primakov, "Novaya fil°sofiya vneshney politiki" (New philosophy of external policy), *Pravda*, 10 July 1987, p. 4.

7. Bernard E. Trainor, "Afghans and the Soviet Psyche: Military Myths Fade as Troops Pull Out," *New York Times*, 15 February 1989, p. A12. Bernard E. Trainor, "For Soviets in Kabul, One Last Road," *New York Times*, 28 January 1989, pp. 1,5. Additional information supplied by Lt. Gen. Trainor.

8. Sayid Naim Majrooh, "Soviet Strategy in the Wake of the Geneva Agreement," *Afghan Information Centre Monthly Bulletin*, no. 85 (April 1988): 10–20.

9. Douglas S. Blaufarb and Dr. George K. Tanham, *Fourteen Points: A Framework for the Analysis of Counterinsurgency*, report BDM/W-84-0175-TR (McLean, VA: The BDM Corporation, 31 July 1984), p. II–9.

10. See Amin Saikal and William Maley, *Regime Change in Afghanistan. Foreign Intervention and the Politics of Legitimacy* (Boulder: Westview Press, 1991), especially chap. 3.

11. Ralph H. Magnus, "The PDPA Regime in Afghanistan," in Peter J. Chelkowski and Robert J. Pranger, eds., *Ideology and Power in the Middle East* (Durham: Duke University Press, 1988), pp. 274–296; Anthony Arnold, *Afghanistan's Two-Party Communism* (Stanford: Hoover Institution Press, 1983); and Anthony Arnold and Rosanne Klass, "Afghanistan's Divided Communist Party," in Rosanne Klass, ed., *Afghanistan. The Great Game Revisited* (New York: Freedom House, 1987).

12. See Olivier Roy, *Islam and Resistance in Afghanistan* (Cambridge: Cambridge University Press, 1986), especially chaps. 5 and 6.

13. This point is widely documented, graphically in John Gunston, "SU–24s, TU–16s Support Soviet Armed Forces," *Aviation Week and Space Technology*, 29 October 1984, pp. 40–44.

14. Blaufarb and Tanham, *Fourteen Points*, p. I–4, IV–6–9.

15. Nicholas Daniloff, "Afghan War Finally Hits Soviet Home Front," *U.S. News & World Report*, 16 December 1985, pp. 41–42; John F. Burns, "Soviets Are Glum about Kabul's Future," *New York Times*, 10 February 1989, p. A8; Christopher Walker, "Poll Reveals Most Russians Want Afghanistan Pull-Out," *Times* (London), 2 November 1987, p. 8; and Sallie Wise, *The Soviet Public and the War in Afghanistan: A Trend towards Polarization*, (paper of Soviet Area Audience and Opinion Research, Radio Liberty-Radio Free Europe, March 1987).

16. Col. L. Shershenev, "The Afghan Counterrevolution," *Zarubezhnoye Voyennoye Obozreniye*, no. 3 (1985): 7–14, translated in JPRS-UMA-85-043, 26 July 1985, pp. 33–42, certainly displays an awareness of the complexity of the Soviets' opponents.

17. See Saikal and Maley, *Regime Change*, chap. 2.

18. Louis Dupree, *Afghanistan* (Princeton: Princeton University Press, 1980), pp. 762–763.

19. Roy, *Islam and Resistance*, chap. 7.

20. Quoted in Thomas T. Hammond, *Red Flag over Afghanistan* (Boulder: Westview Press, 1984), p. 148.

21. Dupree, *Afghanistan*, pp. 118–121.

22. Jiri Valenta, "Soviet Decisionmaking on Afghanistan," in Jiri Valenta and William Potter, eds., *Soviet Decisionmaking for National Security* (London: George Allen & Unwin, 1984), pp. 218–236.

23. "International Situation—Questions and Answers," Program, 10 February 1989, translated in *FBIS Soviet Union Daily Report*, 13 February 1988, pp. 35–36. "Soviet General Talks of Failure in Afghanistan," *New York Times*, 23 January 1989, p. A5. "General in Kabul Says Red Army Falls Short," *Washington Post*, 23 January 1989, p. A12.

24. Alexandre Bennigsen, *The Soviet Union and Muslim Guerrilla Wars, 1920–1981*, N-1707/1 (Santa Monica: The Rand Corporation, August 1981).

25. The elements of the tactics applied in Poland politically and militarily are detailed in Lucja Swiatokowski, "The Imported Communist Revolution and the Civil War in Poland 1944–49" (Ph.D. thesis, Columbia University, 1982), University Microforms DEO82-11136. See also Frederic Smith, "The War in Lithuania and the Ukraine against Soviet Power," in Charles Moser, ed., *Combat on Communist Territory* (Chicago: Regenery, 1985).

26. Dr. S. B. Majrooh, "Afghan Militia Force: A New Failure of Kabul-Soviet Authorities," *Afghan Information Centre Monthly Bulletin*, no. 42 (September 1984): 2–3.

27. Eden Naby, "The Changing Role of Islam as a Unifying Force in Afghanistan," in Ali Banuazizi and Myron Weiner, eds., *The State, Religion, and Ethnic Politics* (Syracuse: Syracuse University Press, 1986), pp. 124–154.

28. Olivier Roy, *The Lessons of the Soviet-Afghan War*, Adelphi Paper 259 (London: International Institute of Strategic Studies, Summer 1991), pp. 25–26.

29. Dupree, *Afghanistan*, pp. 248–251 and Roy, *Islam and Resistance*, pp. 20–27.

30. Roy, *Lessons*, p. 17.

31. Roy, *Lessons*, pp. 56–64.

32. "Eight Soviet Planes Destroyed in Kabul Fire," *Washington Post*, 27 June 1988, p. A13. Gary Lee, "Guerrilla Missile Barrage Kills 11 in Kabul, Tass Says," *Washington Post*, 10 May 1988, p. A15.

33. Mark Storella, "The Central Asia Analogy and the Soviet Union's War in Afghanistan" (Paper presented at the Afghanistan Forum, New York, 1984).

34. Mark Urban, *War in Afghanistan*, 2d ed. (London: Macmillan, 1990) pp. 148, 314–316.

35. For example, see Dr. S.B. Majrooh, "Situation in Kabul. Interview with a Chief Justice," *Afghan Information Centre Monthly Bulletin*, no. 38 (May 1984): 10–11.

36. David C. Isby, "Soviet Advisers in Afghanistan—The Involvement

Continues," *Jane's Intelligence Review* 3, no. 6 (June 1991): 244–248.

37. One example at an operational level is described in David C. Isby, "Panjsher VII," *Soldier of Fortune* 10, no. 2 (February 1985): 34. See also David C. Isby, *Weapons and Tactics of the Soviet Army* (London: Jane's, 1988), pp. 397–399.

38. Blaufarb and Tanham, *Fourteen Points*. Alexandre Bennigsen, "The Soviet Union and Muslim Guerrilla Wars, 1920–81: Lessons for Afghanistan," *Conflict* 4, no. 2–4 (1983): 301–323.

39. For example, see Marshal of the Soviet Union Sergey F. Akhromeyev's views in Aleksandr Borisovich Pumpyanskiy, Yevgeniy Rusakov, and Sergey Rogov, "Is Everything Reasonably Sufficient?" *Novoe Vremya*, no. 14 (April 1991): 14–19, translated in FBIS-SOV-91-091, *FBIS Soviet Union Daily Report*, 10 May 1991, pp. 33–40, especially p. 36.

40. David C. Isby, "Soviet Arms Deliveries and Aid to Afghanistan 1989–91," *Jane's Intelligence Review* 3, no. 8 (August 1991): 348–354.

41. On Soviet reconnaissance in Afghanistan, see Isby, *Weapons*, pp. 369–372.

42. On the Soviet control of KHAD/WAD, see Joseph Collins, "Afghanistan: The Empire Strikes Out," *Parameters* 12, no. 1 (1982): 32–34.

43. "Zia Says Afghans Train Subversives," *Washington Times*, 28 June 1988, p. A7. Anthony Arnold, "The Soviet Threat to Pakistan," and Richard P. Cronin, "Pakistani Capabilities to Meet the Soviet Threat from Afghanistan," in Theodore L. Eliot, Jr., and Robert L. Pfaltzgraff, Jr., eds., *The Red Army on Pakistan's Border* (Washington, Pergamon-Brassey's, 1986).

44. Col. Ali Ahmad Jalali, Ph.D, psc, "The Soviet Military Operation in Afghanistan and the Role of Light and Heavy Forces at Tactical and Operational Level," *Report of Proceedings, Boeing Light Infantry Conference*, Seattle, 1985, pp. 161–181.

45. This has been widely documented, most thoroughly in Alexander Alexiev, *Inside the Soviet Army in Afghanistan*, R-3627-A (Santa Monica: The Rand Corporation, May 1988); "Soviet Youth Newspaper Reveals Traitors, Torture, in Afghanistan," *Washington Times*, 10 February 1989, p. A11; Gennadiy Bocharov, "International Life: Afghanistan," *Literaturnaya Gazeta*, 15 February 1989, pp. 13–14, translated in *FBIS Soviet Union Daily Report*, 17 February 1989, pp. 16–20; "Sakharov Hears of Soviet Firing on Own Troops," *Los Angeles Times*, 1 March 1989, p. 5.

46. Peter Pringle, "Death without Glory," *Independent Magazine*, 19 October 1991, pp. 26–30, p. 27.

47. Ralph Boulton, "Military Brass Tarnished by Defeats in Soviet Elections," *Washington Times*, 31 March 1989, p. A7.

48. John F. Burns, "An Army with Its Spirit in Disarray," *New York Times*, 7 February 1989, p. A10. John F. Burns, "Soviets Are Glum about Kabul's Future," *New York Times*, 10 February 1989, p. A8.

49. Douglas Hart, "Low Intensity Conflict in Afghanistan, the Soviet View," *Survival*, March-April 1982, pp. 61–67.

50. Blaufarb and Tanham, *Fourteen Points*, p. II–9.

51. David C. Isby, "Soviet Special Operations Forces in Afghanistan, 1979–85," *Report of Proceedings, Boeing Light Infantry Conference*, Seattle, 1985, pp. 182–197. David C. Isby, "Soviet Airmobile and Air Assault Brigades," *Jane's Defense Week* 14, no. 11 (14 September 1985). David C. Isby, "The Vertical Threat: Air Assault and Airmobile Brigades of the Soviet Army," *Amphibious Warfare Review* 3, no. 1 (August 1985): 52.

52. Aleksandr Prohankov, "Afghan Questions," *Literaturnaya Gazeta*, 17 February 1988, pp. 1,9, translated in *FBIS Soviet Union Daily Report*, 18 February 1988, pp. 32–34. Lt. Col. A. Oliynik, "We Believe in a Peaceful Life," *Krasnaya Zvezda*, 16 April 1988, translated in *FBIS Soviet Union Daily Report*, 22 April 1988, p. 22. A. Rubin, "Afghanistan and After," *Sovetskaya Russiya*, 23 March 1989, p. 3, translated in *FBIS Soviet Union Daily Report*, 23 March 1989, pp. 16–17.

53. Henry S. Bradsher, *Afghanistan and the Soviet Union* (Durham: Duke University Press, 1985), pp. 113, 117, 149–153. Anthony Arnold, *The Soviet Invasion of Afghanistan*, 2d ed. (Stanford: Hoover Institute, 1985), pp. 96–111.

54. Scott R. McMichael, "Soviet Counter-Insurgency Doctrine—An Ideological Blind Spot," *Jane's Soviet Intelligence Review* 2, no. 10 (October 1990): 465–467.

55. Captain Keith D. Dickson, "The Basmachi and the Mujahidin: Soviet Responses to Insurgency Movements," *Military Review* 65, no. 2 (February 1985): 29–44 and Colonel L. Shershnev, "Under a Party Assignment," *Kommunist Vooruzhennykh Sil*, no. 23 (December 1985): 32–37, translated in JPRS-UMA-86-020, 28 March 1986, pp. 69–77. Evidence of the systematic study of military lessons of Western counterinsurgency conflicts can be seen in the series of articles in *Voyenno-Istorischeskiy Zhurnal* from 1982 to 1984, dealing with different military elements of counterinsurgency.

56. Scott R. McMichael, "Soviet Counter-Insurgency Doctrine—An Ideological Blind Spot—Part Two," *Jane's Soviet Intelligence Review* 2, no. 11 (November 1990): 482–485.

EL SALVADOR*

COUNTRY DATA

Area 8,260 sq. miles (about the size of Massachusetts).
Capital San Salvador (population 1,400,000).
Population 5.1 million (mid-1985 est.).
Density 595 per sq. mile.
Per Capita Income $700.
Ethnic Groups Mestizo 89%, Indian 10%, Caucasian 1%.
Religion Predominantly Roman Catholic, with active Protestant groups throughout the country.
Literacy Urban areas 62%, rural areas 40%.
Work Force (2.49 million) Agriculture 50%, Industry 22%, Services 27%.
Infant Mortality Rate 71 per 1,000 live births.
Life Expectancy males 62.6 years, females 66.3 years.
Government Republic (Constitution 20 December 1983).

UNIQUENESS OF CASE STUDY

Salvadoran democratic leaders, with substantial U.S. support, moved toward transforming their society as part of a successful effort to defeat and/or reincorporate dissidents into the constitutional political process.

CHRONOLOGY

1972 Military robs José Duarte of presidential elections; guerrilla bands grow in 1970s.
1979 Coup d'etat. Officers announce reforms and intent to establish democracy.
1980 Junta government under Duarte implements agrarian and other reforms.
1981 Farabundo Martí National Liberation Front (FMLN) "final offensive" fails.
1982 Election of constituent assembly. Alvaro Magaña elected provisional president. Constitution drafted.
1984 Duarte elected president. Begins negotiations with FMLN. National elections 1985 and 1988. Earthquake 1986.
1989 Alfredo Cristiani elected president. FMLN November offensive fails. Jesuits murdered.
1990 United Nations mediates negotiations.
1992 Peace accord. FMLN integrated into political process.

Source: The map and some of the country data are from State Department "Background Notes."

11

El Salvador: Transforming Society to Win the Peace

Edwin G. Corr and Courtney E. Prisk

Introduction

The Government of El Salvador and the Farabundo Martí National Liberation Front declare that they have reached definitive accords that . . . culminate with the negotiation of all the substantive issues. . . . Its execution will put a definitive end to the Salvadoran armed conflict.[1]

On 31 December 1991 the government of El Salvador (GOES) and the Farabundo Martí National Liberation Front (FMLN), negotiating under the mediation of the United Nations' secretary general, agreed to end the armed conflict that had claimed as many as seventy-five thousand lives and wreaked destruction on the economy of that small country over the previous twelve years.[2] The El Salvador of the 1990s is markedly different from the violent, chaotic days of 1980. Isolated political killings still occur, but the space for political action is much greater and enjoyed by all groups of the political spectrum. The society is more open, there is greater freedom, the institutions are improving, and the peace for which Salvadorans have yearned so long appears to have been achieved.

El Salvador's internal transformation during the war seems to distinguish this country's low-intensity experience from others. Several countries have repeatedly proclaimed victories over revolutionaries (e.g., the Philippines, Guatemala, and Colombia), only to see within a few years the resurgence of violence and insurrectional activity. Victories were won, but the serious underlying social, economic, and political problems that spawned revolutions had been little changed.

Each party to the Salvadoran conflict is able to claim some success. On 16 January 1992, the GOES and the FMLN signed the peace accord, both claiming victory. Joaquín Villalobos stated it was the first revolution won through negotiations.[3] For the government's part, constitutional order has been maintained, all major power contenders are now incorporated into the political process, and institutions are in place for a viable democracy.

There is still much to be done. The FMLN must influence radical elements to accept the progress being made and must work within the constitutional system. The GOES must create an effective judicial system and, as the economy grows, find means to distribute the wealth to correct the root social and economic problems. Only if progress toward these goals is maintained will the threat of low-intensity conflict (LIC) be removed. Without such progress, the country is likely to return to violence and conflict, as have the other countries mentioned above.

The events leading to the 16 January accord and the end to armed conflict are significant. The FMLN began in January 1981 as a Cuban-supported, loose confederation of insurgent factions whose goal was to create an insurrection in El Salvador similar to that which occurred in Nicaragua in July 1979. Supported by Cuba and the Soviet Union, the FMLN planned to defeat the armed forces of the country, rally the people to support a new order the FMLN would impose, and install a Marxist-Leninist government along the lines of the Sandinistas and the Cubans. The failure of the insurrection, the subsequent moves of the FMLN to establish a classical insurgency, and the ability of the government of El Salvador to build a new order based on democracy, which finally became strong enough (with the help of a changed international situation) to discredit and to conclude successful peace negotiations with the FMLN, are the subjects of this case study.

Background

El Salvador has a violent history of oligarchic rule and, since the 1930s, of domination by the armed forces. By the end of the 1960s there was significant opposition to the existing system. The Christian Democratic Party (PDC) under José Napoleón Duarte became the principal political opponent of the military-dominated governments and was supported by the small, traditional Communist Party. Slow progress in ending military government and restructuring society caused many young leftists to look for other means to create change. After a decade of growing radicalization of a "new left," increasing violence, and repressive responses by successive military governments, a group of young Salvadoran armed forces officers carried out a military coup on 15 October 1979. Their announced purpose was to end the violent, chaotic situation in their country, to restructure the society and economy, to ensure justice, and to create a viable democracy.

Attempting to take advantage of the situation, the radical left, which aspired to "total insurrectionist revolution" à la Castro's Cuba and the Sandinistas' Nicaragua, immediately and violently opposed the armed forces. Subsequently, other political groups actively opposed the new junta government, especially the violent radical right, which had operated death squads against reformists during the seventies and which sought to protect its privileged position.

Joined by the PDC under the leadership of Duarte, the civilian-military junta began an extensive agrarian reform program, as well as other reforms. Even while beginning to implement successfully the reforms, the junta was threatened by a growing insurgency. The armed forces in January 1981 barely defeated the so-called final offensive of the Castro-forged FMLN coalition of radicals. It failed because the people did not rise up as FMLN leaders had erroneously expected. A prolonged, debilitating insurgency began. Because of the offensive, President Jimmy Carter announced resumption of military aid to El Salvador just before leaving office. He also suspended the large aid program to Nicaragua because of Sandinista support for the FMLN.

The Salvadorans held free elections in 1982 to select a constitutional assembly, named Alvaro Magaña provisional president from 1982 to 1984, wrote a constitution, and held presidential elections in 1984. Duarte won. He opened the first of what was to be many attempts at negotiation with the FMLN, but the guerrillas spurned his invitation to negotiate peace and to reincorporate themselves into Salvadoran society to work for a more just and democratic country.

Municipal and congressional elections were held in 1985, when the PDC won a majority of the National Assembly, and in 1988, when the PDC recognized the victory of the center-right National Republican Alliance (ARENA) for the assembly. More than one million Salvadorans participated in elections on 19 March 1989 and elected the ARENA candidate, Alfredo Cristiani, as president.

The three major issues in the 1989 election were the insurgency, government corruption, and the faltering economy. There had been a 22 percent drop in gross national product from 1979 to 1982, an earthquake in 1986, two years of drought, one year of floods, seven years of deteriorating prices for El Salvador's exports, and continuous enormous destruction from FMLN sabotage. Notwithstanding these problems, by 1984, with the United States' help, the Salvadoran government had stabilized the economy. By 1987 the country had achieved a 2.6

percent growth rate. To critics of the government, however, it seemed by 1989 that the war and democratic reforms had reached an impasse and that the economy was deteriorating.

In the face of a nationwide guerrilla terrorist campaign to intimidate and disrupt the elections, a majority of the Salvadoran electorate participated in the 1989 elections, which were conducted over 90 percent of the country. The FMLN claimed that the turnout, lower than in previous elections, proved that the elections were not legitimate. Their logic and their terrorist tactics were rejected by all, however, including the Revolutionary Democratic Front (FDR), the political allies of the FMLN, who ran Guillermo Manuel Hugo Ungo for the presidency. The participation of the FDR in the 1989 presidential elections as part of the Democratic Convergence (CD) was significant, even though the CD finished a distant fourth. No longer could it be argued that all groups along the spectrum of Salvadoran politics were not represented in elections.

The 1989 elections were an important event in changing the imprisoning Salvadoran political cycle that political scientists had described as (1) an ever-increasing consolidation of power by a small elite, (2) increasing economic deprivation of the masses, (3) growing intolerance of dissent, and (4) increasing repression and coups.[4] When the PDC and José Napoleón Duarte relinquished control of the government to ARENA, Duarte's focus was on complying with the constitution. Duarte's insistence on honest elections regardless of the outcome and on the autonomy of the government's Central Electoral Council were important deviations from previous regimes' actions. For the first time in El Salvador's history, on 1 June 1989, one elected government peacefully transferred power to a government formed by the political opposition. Moreover, during its first six months in office, until the FMLN's November 1989 offensive, the new ARENA government did not cause the polarization of the country nor unleash the bloodbath of death squad activity that had been forecast.

The FDR's ability to campaign with relative freedom and security apparently wrought changes in the FMLN's intransigent negotiating position. The FMLN peace proposal of 23 January 1989 was structured to win international sympathy and included demands to violate the constitution (which the FMLN knew would make the proposal unacceptable and divisive among Salvadoran political groups), but it dropped FMLN insistence on power-sharing in the government and acknowledged elections as a legitimate means for selecting governments. This seemed to put the FMLN a step closer to reconciliation into society. The FMLN's sincerity was put into doubt, however, by its November 1989 (second) final offensive, for which the FMLN was preparing even while proposing its peace plan.

Since 1987, the FMLN's Marxist leaders had become intellectual prisoners of their own planning for a final offensive that they thought would spark a popular uprising and enable them to seize power. After thorough resupply of arms and munitions by Nicaragua and Cuba that qualitatively upgraded guerrilla capabilities, the FMLN launched a military offensive on 11 November 1989. The action was motivated by FMLN leaders' fears that their political base was narrowing both externally and internally and by their desire to strengthen the FMLN negotiation position vis-à-vis the government. The FMLN initiative failed militarily because they could not inspire popular support, but the final political outcome of the offensive was not initially clear. The lack of popular support for the November 1989 offensive, in addition to the poor electoral showing of the CD in the March elections, revealed the narrowness of the internal political base of the FMLN-FDR, as long as it endorsed violence.

The murder of six Jesuit priests and two women by a Salvadoran armed forces unit on 16 November 1989 during the FMLN offensive undermined the ARENA government and placed in jeopardy its assistance from the U.S. government. The effect of the atrocity on the government's position was offset somewhat by irrefutable evidence of Nicaraguan arms support by air to the FMLN during the November offensive. The Salvadoran government was also bolstered by the five Central American presidents' signing a communiqué during a 10–12 December 1989 meeting that condemned the FMLN offensive, recognized the legitimacy of the Cristiani government, and called for the FMLN to renounce violence that directly or indirectly affected the public. The presidents called for resumption of negotiations that would incorporate the FMLN into the political life of the country and requested demobilization of the FMLN forces by the United Nations (UN).[5]

Negotiations to incorporate FMLN guerrillas into elections and the political process were proposed unsuccessfully by the military juntas under Duarte and by the Magaña provisional government. After his election in 1984, President Duarte began a series of formal and informal talks with the FMLN-FDR. From then until the beginning of negotiations under UN auspices in 1990, the FMLN refused to negotiate except on terms that would dissolve the Constitution, permit the FMLN to share power and occupy territory, make no commitments to an election schedule, and place the FMLN in a position to take over as the government.

In addition to increasing consolidation and legitimization of the democratic system by the electoral process, there were other external and internal events that affected El Salvador. The notable changes in the Soviet Union under Mikhail Gorbachev and the rejection of communism by the countries in Eastern Europe altered the political complexion of the world and made Cuba, the Sandinistas, and the FMLN out of step and anachronistic. Then, on 25 February 1990 the electoral victory of Violeta Chamorro over the Sandinistas in Nicaragua further isolated the FMLN.

On 4 April 1990 in Geneva, under the auspices of the UN secretary general, the two sides signed an accord to resume negotiations in May 1990. The initial objective of the 4 April accord was "to terminate the armed conflict by political means in the shortest time, to promote democratization of the country, to guarantee the unrestricted respect of human rights, and to reunify Salvadoran society."[6] The government of El Salvador and the FMLN signed an agreement on 26 July 1990 on human rights that included establishment of a UN verification mission that began to function in the summer of 1991.[7]

After the July 1990 meeting the FMLN stalled progress in negotiations as they awaited the outcome of debate in the U.S. Congress on military assistance to El Salvador still hoping that the U.S. Congress would halt aid and enhance the FMLN's chances for a military victory. FMLN leaders met in New York with the UN secretary general in September 1990. While there, FMLN guerrilla leaders Shafik Handal, Salvador Samayoa, Mercedes de Carmen Letona, and Miguel Saenz spoke with a group of U.S. supporters whom they reportedly told:

> The negotiation . . . we have to view it as a very important political instrument for the change of the correlation of forces in the country. Everything they offer; we say it is not enough; we want more. So now we have reached an impasse. It has been very important for us that it be projected as an impasse. . . . We devised a scheme of failure and deadlock and we were able to avoid the deadline that we had for the middle of September.[8]

The deadline referred to was for accord on the conditions for a cease-fire, as the FMLN and Salvadoran government had agreed on in May 1990.

The Salvadoran government and the FMLN met in Mexico City in April 1991 and agreed on constitutional reforms concerning the armed forces, the judicial system and human rights, and the electoral system. These were to perfect further many reforms and changes that had already been adopted over the years by the Salvadoran governments.

The old Legislative Assembly, whose mandate expired on 30 April, voted positively on the negotiated reforms as the first step in adopting them as constitutional amendments.[9] Entry into force would require further affirmative votes by the new Legislative Assembly, whose members initially awaited negotiation of a cease-fire agreement before acting.

President George Bush released military aid to the El Salvadoran government in June on the basis of a determination in January that the FMLN did not seem sincere in seeking peace, was continuing to abuse citizens' rights, and was exacerbating the war through upgraded weapons. On 11 September 1991, at the urging of the presidents of Colombia, Mexico, Spain, and Venezuela, the Salvadoran Congress took the necessary and final votes to ratify all the constitutional amendments for implementation of the governmental restructuring except those affecting the armed forces. These were to be enacted as soon as there was agreement on a cease-fire.[10] In turn the FMLN agreed not to continue adding negotiating demands, as it constantly had.

An agreement was signed on 25 September 1991 to permit FMLN guerrillas to incorporate into a new police unit under the civilian Ministry of Interior rather than the Ministry of Defense, a promise that guerrillas demanded as a means of guaranteeing their personal safety. The prospects for a total agreement seemed near, but three rounds of follow-up talks in Mexico City ended with the FMLN continuing to increase demands and the two sides still sharply divided.[11]

In December, at the request of outgoing UN Secretary General Javier Perez de Cuellar, President Cristiani flew to New York to head the government's delegation after it became clear there was a chance to resolve the differences. The governments of the United States, Mexico, Spain, Venezuela, and Colombia all pressured the two parties to reach an accord, and the United States promised economic aid to ensure the success of an agreement.

Agreement on technical-military aspects of a cease-fire were reached, including the end of the military structure of the FMLN and the reincorporation of its members into the civilian, political, and institutional life of the country. Left unresolved was the demobilization schedule for the FMLN. The end of armed confrontation was to begin on 1 February 1992 and to end by 31 October 1992. Any outstanding differences about the formal agreement not negotiated by the two parties by 14 January 1992 were to be referred to the United Nations secretary general, who would arbitrarily resolve them, but the two parties themselves resolved the remaining issues. The final peace accord was signed in Mexico City on 16 January 1992.[12]

Salvadorans made progress internally during 1990 and 1991 in a number of areas. The openness of the Salvadoran political system was furthered by the 1991 municipal and National Assembly elections. The ARENA government agreed beforehand to expand the Assembly from sixty to eighty-four seats to enhance the participation and chances for success of smaller political parties. It was an act that strengthened democracy. The CD, composed of elements from the FDR, a political ally of the FMLN, won eight seats. The National Democratic Union (UDN), the Communist Party, won one seat. ARENA lost its majority in the Assembly. It was the sixth national election held since 1982, and all have been judged fair and honest by international observers. With liberalizing economic reforms, the economy grew in 1990 at 3.4 percent and at 3.5 percent in 1991.[13] There were further reforms of the judiciary and slow but inconclusive progress on specific human rights cases. Most important was the successful prosecution of an Army colonel and lieutenant on the Jesuit case.

Our look at El Salvador draws upon the paradigm developed by Max G. Manwaring as presented in chapter 1. The postulated six dimensions or subwars of this paradigm must all be addressed and fought simultaneously to have a lasting and peaceful solution to the insurgent conflict.[14] We use the paradigm to frame our comments on El Salvador, to draw up a scorecard for that country in each of the subwars, and to make conclusions about the overall prospects for achieving democracy and maintaining peace in that nation.

The Scorecard

Organization for Unity of Effort

Effective high-level direction and coordination of civilian and military programs have been big problems dating back to the 1980 junta governments. A major effort was made in 1983 and 1984 to carry out extensive civic action and development programs under armed forces' protection in the provinces of Usulutan and San Vicente to win the loyalty of the populace and to gain legitimacy for the government. The strength of the guerrillas at that time (twelve thousand) and the relatively small armed forces did not allow sufficient military security. There also was a problem with intra-armed forces politics, in which zone and detachment commanders and civilian politicians outside the targeted area demanded that similar projects be implemented in their areas, even though this demand did not conform to the national strategy and exceeded available natural resources. The first major effort at coordinating civilian and military programs failed.

With the election of President Duarte in 1984, an expanding armed forces, and improved Salvadoran military planning capacity, coordination began to improve. The Salvadoran armed forces developed a rudimentary national military plan by 1984, and it was rewritten and improved for each subsequent year. By 1985 the military was well out in front of the civilians. Seeing the need for integration of civilian and military agencies, the armed forces incorporated into their national military plan their own program for civilian agencies. This move was resented by civilian bureaucratic chiefs, but they did begin to develop their own parts of an integral civilian and military national plan.

When the armed forces retook the strategic Guazapa region in 1986, which they held through 1988, civilian agencies followed with their own programs, but they soon lagged. There was marked improvement in 1986 when the Municipalities in Action program was implemented, causing civilian agencies and the military at the regional and local level to begin working together, especially in conflict zones.[15] In 1988 the Duarte government's national plan included the Chalatenango Province campaign. Civilian and military leaders coordinated their actions and programs for Chalatenango beforehand, but implementation continued to be a problem.

With the arrival of the ARENA government there was initial slippage, soon to be overcome. The Cristiani government capitalized on planning done by the Duarte government to organize to fight the various wars. After fitful starts some improvement appeared in organization for unity of effort and toward development of a comprehensive national campaign plan. A key factor was the degree to which Cristiani maintained unity within his own political party and promoted his more moderate political agendas, as well as his ability to work with other institutions and political parties. This factor was very evident in the negotiating process with the FMLN. PDC cooperation as a "loyal opposition" and FDR cooperation with other political parties in negotiations were critical to national unity.

Under the 16 January 1992 peace accord, resolution of the issues dealing with the armed forces, the purging of military officers, the demobilization of the FMLN, and staffing of the new civilian police will be critical factors in maintaining governmental unity of effort. Equally important will be coordination of government entities in economic developmental efforts. Finally, there will have to be collaboration among the various democratic forces of the country to prevent resurgence of radical activity from both the extreme right and the left.

Type and Consistency of External Support to Targeted Government

From fiscal year 1979 through fiscal year 1991, the U.S. government provided more than $4 billion in assistance to El Salvador. Of this, about $3.35 billion was economic aid and about $1.03 billion was military assistance.[16] Total aid to El Salvador in fiscal year 1979 was about $9.5 million and included no military assistance. U.S. aid to El Salvador fluctuated from year to year and peaked in fiscal year 1985 at $565 million. By fiscal year 1990 it had dropped to about $315 million. By 1988, military aid began averaging around $85 million annually.[17]

Because of the focus of the U.S. government on assistance to East European nations, the level of aid to Central America was cut for fiscal year 1990, and economic aid to El Salvador dropped. The Congress in fiscal year 1991 withheld from the $85 million appropriated for the military $42.5 million to pressure the Salvadoran government on the Jesuit case and to pressure the FMLN and government of El Salvador to negotiate peace. President George Bush restored the amount in January 1991 because of FMLN aggression and their murder of two downed U.S. helicopter pilots.[18] For fiscal year 1992 the Congress through a congressional resolution again withheld $42.5 million of the $85 million for facilitation of the negotiating process and for use in integrating FMLN and armed forces personnel into society after a peace agreement.

A high percentage of U.S. economic assistance has been in support of the private sector, including a large development foundation called FUSADES. The United States has also assisted Salvadoran government programs concerned with the reconstruction of FMLN-damaged infrastructure, earthquake restoration, health, education, labor, land reform, the judiciary and election reforms, and human rights.

FMLN strategy since early 1983 was to "take the war to the U.S. Congress."[19] The Congress, however, has not been greatly divided over support to El Salvador, only on the levels and kinds of assistance and the conditions for disbursement. This relative unity contrasts greatly to the on-again-off-again situation of U.S. aid to the Nicaraguan Democratic Resistance (the contras). Nevertheless, lack of certainty, erratic funding levels, and long delays in delivery of funds and equipment by the Agency for International Development (AID) and the Defense Security Assistance Agency (DSAA) of the Defense Department caused Salvadorans serious problems in operational planning and rational acquisition. Ammunition and parts for which there might not be future funds were hoarded, and there was reluctance to risk helicopters because of long delays and doubts about replacements. Micromanagement of projects by individual congressmen and staffers held up agrarian reform, health projects, and the delivery of helicopters. From a strictly war-fighting or developmental planning perspective, slightly lower levels of aid with constancy and certainty would have been greatly preferable to higher amounts of aid erratically delivered.

The continuance of an adequate U.S. assistance program is an unknown in the future of El Salvador. The executive has made known its intention to provide economic assistance to El Salvador to help in a transition to normalcy and consolidated democracy in the post–civil war period. With the current budget cuts, the historical impatience of the U.S. body politic, the end of the cold war, and the attendant lessened security threat, it is possible that Congress will seek deep cuts in the aid to El Salvador, however. Analysis of the insurgent wars since 1945 tells us that a deep reduction in aid could create conditions conducive to resurgence of violence and destruction in the country. The cost of recovery from the personal and physical destruction of a prolonged war is great, and the ability to influence the creation of an economically and socially just society is directly related to U.S. willingness to provide consistent support now that the guns have stopped.

Ability to Reduce Outside Aid to the Insurgents

External support levels to the FMLN from Nicaragua, Cuba, and (indirectly) the USSR varied but were constant and substantial from at least 1980. Soviet assistance indirectly routed through Cuba specifically for the FMLN probably halted in 1989, when the Soviets announced publicly that they would stop shipments of war materials to Central America at least until the 25 February 1990 Nicaraguan elections. It seems likely, however, that Soviet deliveries scheduled prior to the announcement enabled the FMLN to prepare for the November 1989 offensive by replacing its U.S. manufactured arms and completely reequipping FMLN forces with AK-48 automatic rifles, Dragonov rifles, and ground-to-air missiles.

Central America was the last regional conflict on which the Soviets were disposed to cooperate with the United States to reduce conflicts. After 1989, however, the USSR was quite forthcoming on Central America, including joint statements urging the FMLN to reach a peace agreement and reincorporate themselves into Salvadoran society.[20]

Nicaraguan and Cuban help to the FMLN guerrillas involved brokering among factions to achieve and maintain unity, military training and political indoctrination, communications, propaganda and diplomatic support, finances, and arms and munitions. Robert Pastor, President Carter's national security adviser for Latin America, acknowledged Sandinista support for the FMLN during the Carter administration in his book, *Condemned to Repetition*.[21] From 1980 until 1991 there was ample evidence of Sandinista support for the FMLN, including interdictions of weapons. Crashes of two planes transporting equipment from Nicaragua to the FMLN during the November 1989 final offensive showed continued Sandinista support up to that point. The cargo of one plane included twenty-four Soviet-designed SA–7 anti-aircraft missiles.[22]

Observers expected Sandinista support for the FMLN to cease with the ascension of Violeta Chamorro to the Nicaraguan presidency in April 1990. Reports of shipments of materiél continued, however. President Chamorro acknowledged to Secretary of State James Baker the continued shipment of arms by the Sandinista Popular Army (EPS) to the FMLN while she was in the United States on 18 June 1990.[23] Further interdictions of weapons from Nicaragua destined for the FMLN occurred in July and August 1990. The SA–14 surface-to-air missiles used by the FMLN to shoot down Salvadoran aircraft in November 1990 were confirmed by the USSR as those supplied by the Soviets to the Sandinistas in 1986. On 2 January 1991, the EPS announced that Nicaraguan military personnel and Salvadorans had been detained for selling missiles to FMLN leader Joaquin Villalobos in Managua.[24] The Honduran Army captured yet another shipment of weapons being sent from the EPS to the FMLN on 22 February 1991, and interdictions continued as late as December in that year.[25]

With the bankruptcy of the communist system in the Soviet Union and worldwide, the inward orientation of East European countries, and the electoral defeat of the Sandinistas in Nicaragua, the FMLN's prospects for outside aid diminished greatly. They rested primarily on Castro's Cuba and the EPS. The pressure on the Soviet Union to decrease or stop aid to Cuba, the collapse of the Cuban economy, and the USSR's announcement in August 1991 that it intended to withdraw Soviet troops from Cuba gave hope that aid from Cuba to the FMLN would also decrease or stop. There were also renewed efforts by the Chamorro government to control the Sandinistas. During 1990–91, the ability of the Salvadoran government to reduce outside aid to the insurgents was significant.

Another component to reducing external aid to the FMLN was to diminish the significant amount of resources sent to, or diverted to, the FMLN from private groups of the United States and Western Europe. With the electoral defeat of the Sandinistas in Nicaragua many of these groups redoubled their efforts on behalf of the FMLN. The U.S. ability to reduce this source of support was impossible because of the desirable civic guarantees that protect U.S. citizens and because of the political sensitivities and costs to the U.S. and West European governments as a result of any efforts to repress such support.[26]

Intelligence

The Salvadoran government's success in finding, eliminating, and discrediting subversive organizations and revolutionary leaders was mixed. Although installed intelligence capacity grew tremendously and was extremely effective in specific instances, for example during the FMLN's kidnapping of Duarte's daughter and after the FMLN murder of unarmed Marine security guards, this dimension of the war was negative as an indicator for potential government success or failure. Timely processing and distribution of intelligence and sharing it among the various agencies of the government (or even between units within the military) and acting upon it still needed improvement. The problem apparently was caused primarily by government agencies and individuals maintaining autonomy by guarding information or placing the sharing of information in the too-hard-to-coordinate file.

The problem of proper utilization and control of intelligence agencies was addressed by removing the National Directorate of Intelligence (DNI) from the Ministry of Defense and placing it directly under the president. The reforms negotiated between the FMLN and the Salvadoran government in 1991 calling for disbanding the DNI are a sign that this indicator was moving from negative to positive as the armed conflict was ending. Still, the government will need to keep aware of FMLN and radical right activities and attitudes during the transition and demobilization period, and even afterward, to be sure that the FMLN leadership and the radical right continue to play by democratic rules.

Discipline and Capabilities of a Government's Armed Forces

The evaluation is also mixed but tends to the neutral to positive. The Salvadorans now possess a relatively formidable Central American military establishment, following the reduction of the previously much larger EPS. Salvadorans successfully expanded what was essentially a twelve-thousand-strong "praetorian guard," made up of police, firefighters, and soldiers, who were accustomed to abusing their authority, into a sixty-thousand-strong fighting force that increasingly acknowledges subordination to the civilian government, treats the citizenry better, and has considerable war-fighting capabilities.[27] An important reason that the Salvadoran military, despite its capabilities, did not do better militarily against the insurgent enemy was the insistence on maintaining a conventional war attitude at the expense of a greater counterinsurgency capacity.

It became popular among critics of the Salvadoran armed forces to denigrate their dedication and tactics and to characterize the war as having reached a "stalemate." Among those critics were some former U.S. military advisers who were frustrated by what they considered lack of tactical aggressiveness by Salvadoran officers and who were understandably impatient about ending the war. A number of these critics spent only short tours in the country, did not have fully developed language and cross-cultural skills, and were lacking in their understanding of LIC with its sociopolitical content and prolonged nature. The Salvadoran soldiers had shortcomings, but they were tough, experienced, and, by the mid-eighties, proficient. Their war was not that of a U.S. trainer who was proscribed from battlefield and from firing his weapon except in self-defense, and whose tour was for only a year or two. The Salvadoran military was at war for well over a decade.

Coming from far behind in 1981, the Salvadoran armed forces by 1984 had reduced the FMLN, which had reached a total of twelve thousand full-time combatants and deployed in battalion-size units, to six thousand full-time combatants and caused the FMLN to return to guerrilla and terrorist tactics. These very tactics steadily undermined guerrilla popular support. The withdrawal of foreign support for the FMLN because of changes in the international arena further jeopardized FMLN strength and in time would have further weakened the guerrillas vis-à-vis the Salvadoran armed forces.

It was not a permanent stalemate. In time the Salvadoran armed forces would have won through guerrilla attrition. It took the British fourteen years to put down the Malayan insurgency, with a first-class army of an industrialized power and during a time of few restraints about human rights in the conduct of war. The Salvadoran armed forces fought only twelve years to gain an acceptable peace. Had the FMLN not negotiated an end to hostilities, the guerrillas possibly could have lasted three to five years or more, but given the continuing successes in other aspects of the war, in the end the "stalemate" would have been resolved militarily in favor of the armed forces.

The discipline component of this dimension as it applies to El Salvador, notwithstanding the unconscionable murder of six Jesuit priests and two women in November 1989, improved over time. The ability to constrain soldiers from human rights abuses and to punish offenders vigorously is a fundamental measure of military discipline in a low-intensity conflict. President Carter suspended military assistance to El Salvador in 1977 because of the unacceptable human rights situation. The abuses became even more scandalous at the end of the seventies and the early eighties.[28]

El Salvador has come a long way since 1980, when U.S. embassy statistics on civilian deaths outside of combat recorded more than eight hundred deaths per month. Progress was notable after resumption of U.S. military assistance in 1981 and again after President Duarte's election in 1984. Rules of engagement were established to minimize indiscriminate warfare, especially by the air force. Training and standard operating procedures stressed human rights. By 1987 the monthly average for noncombat political deaths had fallen to twenty-three and by 1988 to nineteen a month. Public understanding about the perpetrators of the violence also began to change slowly during the second half of the decade. The FMLN was also acknowledged to be an atrocious violator of human rights. They murdered candidates, mayors, and others they charged with collaborating with the government's "counterinsurgency" program.[29] Added to these figures are the thousands of civilians who were wounded by guerrillas' mines, by machine-gunnings of vehicles during guerrilla transportation stoppages, or by guerrilla attacks in urban areas.

After ARENA won the presidential elections in March 1989, there was a highly publicized increase in assassinations of prominent persons. This increase projected an impression of a rapidly worsening situation. The Jesuit case during the FMLN offensive seemed to justify FMLN claims that the Cristiani government was returning to the atrocious human rights situation and oligarchical rule that prevailed a decade before. This was not the case, however, and in 1990 the number of killings clearly attributable to political motives continued to decline, reaching a low average of five per month. The number of suspicious or unexplained killings also declined.[30]

These numbers were still too high. If a lasting peace is to be realized, the Salvadoran government must control the military and hold it responsible for human rights abuses. The prosecution and sentencing in the Jesuit case of Colonel Guillermo Alfredo Benavides and an army lieutenant are positive indicators, but only time will tell if this event signals permanent change or is merely an exception to the immunity to prosecution that military officers have enjoyed. There are violent radicals of the right and left who may feel compelled to try through political killings to derail the peace process.

Government discipline over the armed forces and police is essential, both to prevent military and police abuses and to control and to prosecute extremists. The government and FMLN agreed in the 16

January 1992 Peace Accord to reduce the armed forces and to move the police, who have been part of the Ministry of Defense, to the Ministry of Interior. Both are good signs, but the desired results will only be realized if discipline is maintained.

Legitimacy

The final and most important dimension is legitimacy—the moral right to govern. Because the primary objective of an insurgent is to destroy the legitimacy of the incumbent government, the primary objective of that government must be to maintain and enhance its moral right to govern. The goal of the insurgent is to gain a legitimate right to govern. The strategic center of gravity in this key struggle is the relative rectitude of the contending organizations. Legitimacy also becomes the primary concern for external powers supporting the targeted government.

Indicators of Legitimacy

Governments have achieved legitimacy from a variety of sources, ranging from the divine right of kings to elite group acceptance to ideology to democracy. At the current stage of Latin American history it appears that democracy is the sole source for legitimization in this geographical area. What, then, are the conditions that Latin American governments must create to establish democracy and thereby gain legitimacy? Samuel Huntington defines a political system as democratic "to the extent that its most powerful collective decision makers are selected through fair, honest and periodic elections in which candidates freely compete for votes and in which virtually all the adult population is eligible to vote."[31] In doing this he draws on Robert Dahl, the foremost modern writer on democracy, which Dahl terms "polyarchy."

Dahl says a democratic system of government must satisfy three essential criteria:

> meaningful and extensive *competition* among individuals and organized groups (especially political parties) for all effective positions of government power, at regular intervals and excluding the use of force; a "highly inclusive" level of *political participation* in the selection of leaders and policies, at least through regular and fair elections, such that no major (adult) social group is excluded; and a level of *civil and political liberties*—freedom of expression, freedom of the press, freedom to form and join organizations—sufficient to ensure the integrity of political competition and participation.[32]

Though Huntington's and Dahl's definitions are suitable for the developed world they are not sufficient to satisfy most citizens and thinkers of the developing world. They attach a broader and deeper meaning to the concept of democracy. They see it as a means not only to freedom but also to improved economic well-being and justice. This goal requires relatively honest and effective government that can directly or indirectly enlist human efforts, extract resources, and ensure a fairly equitable distribution of expanding wealth. Equally important is the government's capacity to protect human rights and to curb excessive bureaucratic corruption. The creation and maintenance of these additional conditions mean there must be a continuing acceptance of the government by the major societal institutions of the country, not merely support by a majority of the voters on election day.

We will evaluate the Salvadoran political system by these key indicators of legitimacy in Latin America.

Political competition through free, fair, and frequent elections. Free elections require a basic degree of honesty in an open electoral process, the existence of accepted contending political parties that can campaign freely in the preelection period, and an environment in which a high percentage of the populace can vote without feeling coerced or endangered. Fostering increased pluralism, a viable opposition, and truly free elections means opening the door to the increased short-term inefficiency of democratic governance. It requires incumbent rulers to loosen control and centralized power.

This task is difficult in the midst of an insurgency, when governments are striving to gain sufficient power and capacity to get things done. Democratization means that the regime must move away from the traditional Latin American societal desire for apparent unanimity toward allowing greater personal freedom and open criticism of the government. It is a fundamental shift for many Latin Americans; and it is not an obvious, intuitively desired shift for leaders of many powerful institutions within the societies of this region. Nevertheless, free, fair, and periodic elections have become an essential requirement for legitimacy for the peoples of Latin America.

In El Salvador the successful implementation and consequent institutionalization of free and fair elections (1982, 1984, 1985, 1988, 1989, and 1991) have been heralded correctly as significant historical developments. The willingness and desire of the people to "turn out" to vote in six national elections, despite attempts by the FMLN to obstruct voting by interrupting public transportation, attacking polling booths, and waging a campaign of terror, are positive signs. The willingness of the FDR to participate in the 1989 and 1991 campaigns and the FMLN's reluctant acknowledgement since 1989 of elections as a legitimate means to power are significant. The FMLN's implicit recognition of El Salvador's 1983 constitution and of the legitimacy of the elected government is reflected in the FMLN positions in the UN-conducted peace talks.

Provisional President Alvaro Magaña, at the age of 55, voted for the first time in 1982, not because there were not previous elections, but because up to that time, he had seen no point in voting.[33] The 1988 and 1989 votes against PDC corruption and the first successful transfer of power from one civilian regime to another indicate that the institutionalization of the democratic process through fair and frequent elections has occurred in El Salvador.

Highly inclusive political participation. There are limits on the extent to which individuals can actually participate in making all political decisions affecting them; and these limits are established not only by constitutions and the nature of institutions, but also by history and culture. The constitutions of many Latin American countries, especially those of Central America, were written in the early and late nineteenth century to conform closely with the U.S. Constitution of 1787. In application, however, the powers of the chief executives in the Latin America countries became far greater; and the abilities of the legislative and judicial branches to act independently were limited.[34] Interest group formation was limited, and the majority of the people had little access to national decision makers. Military dictatorships were often the norm, and in civilian governments the leaders often were undisputed *caciques* (bosses).

The degree of legitimacy granted to a political system by the people of a society is related to the degree that they believe that the government "belongs to them," that it is responsive to them, and that they can influence its actions. Especially since World War II, Latin American society has become increasingly diversified, differentiated, and specialized in institutions and organizations. Over the past fifteen years there has been great liberalization of the political processes in Latin American countries. Fair and open elections seem increasingly to be the norm, and concomitantly there has evolved much greater civil participation.[35] More and more, lower class citizens are gaining a voice and a sense of belonging through their own organizations and the way in which political parties are forced to appeal to them.

Although growing freedom and political participation in El Salvador can be said to have begun in the 1960s, a giant step forward was taken with the democratic orientation of the juntas and subsequently the Duarte government. Even the FMLN has been strongly represented in the internal political process and debate, at first by its "front groups" in labor, refugee, displaced person, political prisoner, student, co-madres, and human rights organizations. These groups were given the ability to assemble, stage demonstrations, print their propaganda and political positions in newspapers, and appear extensively on television to defend and to advocate opposing political views. The campaigning and election of political party candidates allied with the FMLN made a major contribution to national reconciliation. The active participation of these parties' leaders in the National Assembly, the negotiating process, and the national debate belied the claims of the FMLN that the existing political system did not permit representation of all political persuasions.

That minimal degree of dialogue and consensus required for democracy to function is also expanding. As late as 1985 it was uncommon for politicians of widely differing ideologies to share ideas and seek compromise solutions for national problems. By 1988, this was no longer so. Witnesses at many social gatherings observed ARENA right-wing leader Colonel Sigfredo Ochoa in serious, cordial, and prolonged dialogue with returned FDR leader Ruben Zamora. Roberto d'Aubuisson in 1991 nominated Ruben Zamora for vice president of the National Assembly.[36]

The ARENA government remains on trial with respect to its commitment to an open society and constitutional democracy. The growing attention the ARENA government exhibits toward programs that address the desires and expectations of the general populace indicates that ARENA is influenced by the pressure exerted by popular involvement and participation. This influence is particularly evident in the ARENA government's (albeit reluctant) continuance, improvement, and gradual extension of the agrarian reform program, which many justifiably feared ARENA would try to quash.

Civic and political liberties. Dahl suggests that there must be sufficient civic and political liberty to ensure the integrity of political competition and participation. Under President Duarte an environment of freedom of dissent, expression, and assembly was created that would seem very difficult to reverse except by the reversion of the FMLN leadership to dictatorial goals, or by the ARENA government's turning back the clock to the pre-1979 period. Though there are still dangers from the FMLN and the extreme right, freedom of expression, freedom of the news media, and freedom to form and join organizations are a reality. These liberties are adequate to ensure the integrity of political competition and participation.

Bureaucratic capacity to promote economic growth and to extract and distribute resources. A government must have the capacity to accomplish the realistic expectations and demands of the citizenry.

This ability requires the existence of a reasonably effective and honest bureaucracy. Lord Acton's adage that "power corrupts and absolute power corrupts absolutely" is an underlying principle that should apply to any discussion of legitimacy. Indeed, corruption is one of the most pervasive factors in the loss of regime legitimacy.[37] Certainly this was the case in the demise of the Marcos regime in the Philippines and of the Somoza regime in Nicaragua.[38]

In addition to a relatively effective and honest bureaucracy, a government's legitimacy is enhanced by policies that foster economic growth in the private sector. Whether successful democratization is dependent on the growing prosperity of a market economy is still an open question theoretically, but history shows a high correlation between successful democratization and an open and expanding economy.

Underlying a government's capacity to implement economic and social policies and to ensure services is its ability to extract and distribute resources within society. There are three traditional areas where government extraction of resources is important: treasure, time, and blood. Important indicators of a regime's legitimacy are its ability to administer tax programs, to gain citizen loyalty and voluntary services, and to fill the ranks of its armed forces with disciplined soldiers.

The extent to which a government can extract and distribute resources is critical to its survival and to demonstrating legitimacy required to maintain external support. In the Western democratic view, the ability to extract sufficient resources through a sense of citizen responsibility and cooperation without resorting to coercion is a sign that the people support the government. For the people of the country, a key measure of legitimacy becomes how well the government is able to use those resources to provide basic services and protection for the people.[39]

The FMLN systematically attempted to immobilize the government and society by destroying power lines, transportation means, and other basic services. The FMLN did more than two billion dollars of damage to the Salvadoran economic structure over the past decade. These losses have been compounded by an earthquake causing more than one billion dollars in damages, and by droughts, flood, capital flight, and deteriorating prices for El Salvador's principal exports during much of the period. Maintaining competence in the delivery of services while attempting to fight insurgents is difficult.

The Salvadoran government is generally judged negatively in this area by large sectors of the population, at least in their public and political statements. The perception of corruption inside the PDC, from whom the populace had expected a higher standard of conduct, was a major factor in the party's defeats in 1988 and 1989.

In spite of citizen unhappiness with living conditions, El Salvador is today a different country with respect to economic structure and the distribution of political power from what it was twenty years ago, and the lower classes know this. The old oligarchy no longer has a stranglehold on the economy, and there are new middle and lower class political and economic forces that must be heeded. Wealthy businessmen remark that in their stores one must exercise care in treating people who enter. A decade ago farmers from the "lower classes" were sometimes asked to leave, the proprietors knowing they had no funds. Today that apparently poor farmer might very well pull out cash from a bank loan to purchase agricultural equipment and supplies he could not have afforded before. Some wealthy people lament that a decade ago when they went to better restaurants to eat they knew most people present—today, there is no telling what kinds of people might be there!

Because of the crisis of the early eighties Salvadorans had first to stabilize the economy and attend to immediate needs, which the Duarte government did. At the same time, with U.S. and Salvadoran armed forces' support, the government was implementing structural reforms to create possibilities for long-term development and self-sustaining economic growth. The Cristiani government embarked on programs to liberalize the economy by reducing government controls and monopolies and to encourage greater reliance on market forces and the private sector.

Despite the slightly positive economic growth of the last seven years, the economy has only held its own and not recovered from the tremendous decline of 1979 to 1982. In 1987 the gross national product grew at 2.6 percent, but per capita income in 1987 was still only $899, 27 percent lower than the 1978 level. Just over one of ten Salvadoran peasants had access to safe drinking water whereas four years earlier the figures were three in ten.[40] The infant mortality rate was the highest in Central America. Economic growth dropped again in 1988 to 1.6 percent and in 1989 to 1.1 percent, largely because of renewed violence by the FMLN.

Political conditions and the economic structure have, nevertheless, now been sufficiently changed to permit greater focus on development. In 1990 the Salvadoran gross domestic product (GDP) grew at a rate of 3.4 percent. Total exports recorded an increase, with nontraditional exports to areas outside of Central America growing at 34 percent. The fiscal deficit was cut, monetary discipline restored, and inflation controlled. GDP growth in 1991 was 3.5 percent and is projected at 4.3

percent for 1992.[41] Clearly, there is still much to be done. Governmental capacity and effectiveness still need improvement. Such improvements will be easier with peace and the cessation of destruction.

Fair and just judicial system. Regime corruption is nowhere more evident than in the administration of justice.[42] A judicial system that can be manipulated or bought is a fatal impediment to consolidating and maintaining a democratic society. For a government to be considered morally legitimate in Latin America today, persons and institutions within the nation must be subordinate to the rule of law.[43] The concept of majority rule and minority rights demands a milieu in which individuals and institutions can be held accountable on the premise that no one is above the law.[44]

This is a very weak area in El Salvador's fight for legitimacy, and a major negative factor. Recognizing the importance of an impartial and responsive justice system, the Duarte government instituted a judicial reform program in 1984 to improve the administrative, technical, and legal performance of its justice system. This program established a Revisory Commission of distinguished Salvadoran jurists who coordinated and drafted reforms and submitted legislation to the Congress. To change the Salvadoran mentality about justice, the commission also conducted public forums and training for law school faculties and political and civic groups. The Revisory Commission had by the beginning of 1991 drafted thirteen legislative bills that were enacted by the National Assembly. The Supreme Court and Attorney General's Office also have implemented a number of administrative reforms.

The government of El Salvador and the FMLN agreed during April 1991 on constitutional amendments on reorganizing the Supreme Court; selecting justices; providing the judicial branch with not less than 6 percent of the national budget; establishing a National Council for the Defense of Human Rights; and electing the attorney general and the director of the Defense of Human Rights Council. The constitutional amendments to implement these reforms were adopted by the National Assembly on 11 September 1991.

Despite these reforms and progress, the judicial system still has much to correct before it can be considered fair or just. The overall judiciary remains corrupt and subject to outside influence. Judges are paid low salaries, lack adequate staff, and can be fired at will. There is general reluctance to try or to adjudicate controversial cases. Despite progress, a backlog of cases exists, and there are numerous cases where known murderers and alleged human rights offenders have been set free. The law is not applied equally and impartially. Military officers and wealthy persons, despite improvements and the Jesuit case, are still somewhat above the law. People with resources find ways to influence the outcome of cases and to stay out of prison.

The reluctance and inability to prosecute human rights cases and corruption cases involving high-ranking civilian or military officials and the wealthy underscore "the absence of an effective system of justice in a society that traditionally suffers from a lack of accountability."[45] The Salvadoran Supreme Court's decision to close the case on the murder of Archbishop Romero (because the witness presented the evidence seven years after the killing) is a case in point. Under Salvadoran laws there is no legal time limit for presenting evidence. The witness, who implicated members of the extreme right, including Major Roberto d'Aubuisson, was deemed credible by both the Duarte government and the U.S. embassy.[46]

During 1991, after two years in office, there have been increasing allegations of and scandals related to ARENA Party members. In the tense and confusing times of a civil war, for a government to function and hold people accountable is difficult. Without a free and independent judiciary to adjudicate and try officials or persons of the elite societal levels, however, accountability is impossible, and corruption is widespread. This was and remains the situation facing El Salvador and portends poorly for the fight for legitimacy.

Active or tacit approval of social institutions. As difficult as extraction or distribution of resources is during an insurgency, the gaining and maintaining of tacit or active support from major societal institutions prove equally vexing. The basic problems of a society in transition cannot be solved by the central government acting alone. The effort requires the cooperation of the business sector, peasant and workers' unions, educational institutions, local governments, and, particularly in Latin America, the church and the military.

The score on active or tacit support of the societal institutions has moved from neutral to positive and shows sign of stronger positive growth. An essential and successful attitudinal change has been taking place within the armed forces over the past decade. The country's military leadership has made "upholding the Constitution and the Law the foremost objective of the military institution." [47]

The church has moved from a position at the beginning of the eighties in which a large part of the clergy was antigovernment and favorable to the guerrillas. Today there is still a small, radicalized part of the clergy that sympathizes with the FMLN, but most of the church supports the constitutional democratic system.

The breach between the business sector and the Christian Democratic government under Duarte was so great that it could not be bridged easily, and private sector resentment and distrust impeded a return of Salvadoran capital to El Salvador. With the Cristiani government, relations with the private sector are good. There still exists some private sector resentment because the government is continuing to support the agrarian reforms initiated under Duarte, but the moves by Cristiani to return coffee and other state monopolies to private control have marshalled support from this sector for the government.

The major group of societal institutions withholding support for the Cristiani government is labor. There have been serious problems with peasant unions because of right-wing ARENA efforts to impose leaders favorable to them in the cooperatives and ARENA's preference for individual landholdings versus production cooperatives. Although the ARENA government has to overcome serious objections of labor and peasants, the principal labor leaders are strongly committed to the current system of constitutional democracy. They see it as their only true hope for a better future and do not want a return to the past.

Prospects for El Salvador: The Total Scorecard

The 16 January 1992 peace accord ends low-intensity conflict in El Salvador only if one regards low-intensity conflict as primarily a situation of military confrontation. A broader understanding of low-intensity conflict, however, in which social, political, and economic "fronts" are also parts of the conflict, applies the principles of coping with such situations during the revolutionary environment prior to the outbreak of guerrilla warfare, during armed hostilities, and during the volatile transition period back to normalcy. The six indicators of the Manwaring paradigm are applicable for analysis and policy guidance during periods of violence and the potentially explosive periods before and after the armed hostilities.

In terms of the unity of effort, the Salvadoran government made great progress since 1979. It did so in the paradoxical situation of creating better coordination and effort against the guerrillas by those committed to the constitutional democratic system while at the same time permitting greater diversity, autonomy, decentralization, and peaceful competition among those groups. This was no mean feat. The remaining challenge to incorporate FMLN leaders into an overall unified effort to remove the underlying causes that permit revolution is a formidable one.

U.S. assistance to the governments of El Salvador was a great plus in the Salvadorans' successful efforts to establish a democratic system, carry out reforms, and achieve peace in their country. Such aid was perhaps the critical factor in the Salvadorans' success, especially during the early years of the insurgency. The policy and programs represent a success for U.S. foreign policy. There is little doubt, however, that the consistency and efficiency of the U.S. aid effort could have been improved. With the arrival of peace, foreign assistance to El Salvador will continue to be a vital element in helping Salvadorans make the difficult transition to a society working democratically to solve the problems of development.

A third positive dimension in helping the Salvadorans reach peace and maintain a consolidating democracy was the armed forces' increasing capability and discipline. Again, this dimension presents a paradox—in fact, several of them. The armed forces were necessary to prevent the strong, foreign-supported FMLN guerrillas from seizing power and imposing a Sandinista/Cuban style government. At the same time, taming the armed forces, reducing their political power, redefining their functions, and persuading and forcing them to submit to civilian authority and to cease from human rights abuses were essential to establishing the democratic system that the armed forces risk their lives to protect. The Salvadoran armed forces prevented an FMLN victory, helped force the guerrillas to the negotiating table, and acquiesced to a peace agreement that required the armed forces to reduce their numbers and budget, divest themselves of the police, and purge their officer ranks of comrades considered unworthy.

Perhaps no other institution was asked to give up as much for El Salvador to prevent the takeover of yet another authoritarian group and to begin creating a democracy—the consolidation and survival of which are still somewhat uncertain. The transition period for the armed forces is difficult. They must remain vigilant against a resurgence of FMLN efforts to dominate society by unconstitutional means while dismembering their own institution. The military must continue to subordinate itself to civilian rule and to cooperate with and encourage prosecutions of officers and soldiers who violate human rights and break the law.

The Salvadoran governments were fortunate in their ability to reduce outside aid to the FMLN, which was important in bringing the FMLN under control and forcing it to negotiate sincerely to reach a peace accord. This was linked to U.S. support over the years, the changing face of Nicaraguan politics, the bankruptcy of the communist system in the Soviet Union, the outbreak of independent governments in Eastern Europe, the disintegration of the USSR, and Cuba's decreased ability to provide aid to the insurgents.

The Salvadoran scorecard in the intelligence area and actions against subversion is mixed. Salvadorans were slow in establishing good counterintelligence capabilities and never became very effective in this area. Compared to other Third World countries, the Salvadorans created a rather sophisticated and functional intelligence apparatus to describe and act against the guerrillas. Nonetheless, they continued to be lacking in their procedures to fuse and distribute intelligence, to find and eliminate insurgent organizational structures, and to utilize intelligence to capture FMLN leaders. With peace the need remains for information about former FMLN members' and radical rightists' activities as they are incorporated into society. There is a possibility that the FMLN may seek to emulate their Sandinista comrades by trying "to govern from below" and eventually attain power through extralegal actions. The dissolution of the National Intelligence Directorate (DNI) and the distancing of the intelligence function from the armed forces, though necessary and correct, may cause a decrease in intelligence capacity when there is still a need.

In terms of the legitimacy of the constitutional political system that has emerged, El Salvador is not yet the democracy most people would like it to be. In our discussion of the indicators of legitimacy we noted that in terms of free, fair, and frequent elections, participation by the populace, the functioning of political rights, and active or tacit approval of the societal institutions, the governments of El Salvador have made significant positive gains. In the ability to extract and distribute resources equitably, although some gains have been made, the scorecard is discouraging. With peace, real success may now be made here, especially if the government continues to receive consistent outside support.

A fair and just judicial system for El Salvador is the weakest among the indicators of legitimacy. If efficacious actions continue to create a workable, independent, and fair system of justice, the prospects for consolidating a constitutional democracy, attaining lasting peace, and beginning to correct the root social and economic problems in El Salvador are enhanced.

Over the twelve years of war, Salvadoran governments' actions caused the FMLN to lose its ability to capture and securely hold territory, defeat other than small military units, and overrun and hold military garrisons. They could still ambush vehicles and stage stand-off rocket and mortar attacks against military garrisons, but in most instances damage was done to civilians, not to the military. The FMLN could still destroy transmission lines, bomb and sabotage, and turn off the lights temporarily in San Salvador.

The guerrillas in November of 1989 were able, at great cost, to invade populated San Salvador neighborhoods and hold them for a couple of weeks—a remarkable display of raw, brutal power and daring. The FMLN was defeated by greater military power and restraint, however. This FMLN "show of force" caused increased pressure from outside supporters for a negotiated settlement, but there is little evidence that such violent events served the FMLN in gaining greater popular support in El Salvador. The offensive may have helped to maintain cohesion among the FMLN militants.

The political base of the FMLN-FDR declined from the early eighties. Less and less could the FMLN command the loyalty of a significant percent of Salvadorans, whom they increasingly alienated by their tactics. The essence of revolutionary war is to gain legitimacy, to gain popular support, and to obtain political leverage from military activity. The FMLN lost its ability to achieve either popular support or political leverage among a sufficient percentage of the Salvadoran populace. Father Ignacio Ellacuria, who was murdered by an armed forces' unit during the November 1989 FMLN offensive, repeatedly and publicly declared from 1987 onward that even in Marxist revolutionary terms the FMLN's continued violence and terrorism had become senseless.

On the positive side, El Salvador today is different in many ways from the El Salvador of 1979. The country has changed significantly in terms of its political, economic, and social structures. Change in the world reduced, if not eliminated, foreign governments' support of the insurgents. A peace accord was signed, and the FMLN guerrillas are reincorporating themselves into the life of the nation. Still, there is much in El Salvador that has not changed, both good and bad. On the negative side, the country is poor, small, lacking in natural resources, and overpopulated. The distribution of wealth is badly skewed. The democratic process and fledgling political institutions are fragile. The justice system remains unjust. Implementation of additional bureaucratic restructuring, creation of a civilian police force, demobilization of the FMLN, and reduction of the armed forces present a great challenge. Finally, controlling recalcitrant radicals of the left and right who want to upset the existing political process requires exceptional leadership, decisiveness, understanding, and tolerance.

The chances for democracy and peace appear good for El Salvador, although external events, such as a worldwide depression, could dash prospects. Conditions improved markedly in El Salvador from 1981. Tremendous improvements were made after Duarte's 1984 election until 1987, when the effects of the catastrophic October 1986 earthquake and other factors stymied progress toward democracy and peace. The ARENA government under President Cristiani's leadership disappointed many of its critics by avoiding actions to polarize further the populace, worked to strengthen the democratic process, pressed the

FMLN to negotiate a solution to the war, and took measures to invigorate the economy.

The UN-mediated negotiations led to a peace in which all actors can claim success. The Salvadoran governments prevented the takeover by the FMLN, whose leadership was initially avowedly Marxist-Leninist; and the governments established a functioning democracy, carried out basic structural reforms, attained peace, and did so within the framework of the constitution. The FMLN can claim that its earlier insurrectional activity offset the radical violent right and prevented a return to the military-oligarchical governments of the past, and that, later, their military strength enabled FMLN leaders to negotiate for greater societal reforms and governmental structural changes than would have otherwise been attainable. The U.S. support, persistence, and faith in Salvadoran democrats of all sectors and from all political parties helped to contain the spread of Sandinista-type authoritarian governments in the early eighties and contributed to the creation of governments in Central America that are moving toward democracy and toward peaceful, better lives for their citizens.

Mistakes were made, but the big one—abandoning the democratic cause and the creation of legitimate government—was not.

Notes

1. From the Preamble of the 1 January 1992 Agreement, as quoted in "Pact on Strife in El Salvador," *The New York Times International*, 2 January 1992, p. A7. This chapter draws heavily on a paper prepared by the authors and presented by Prisk on a panel at the International Studies Association meeting in Washington, D.C. on 10–14 April 1990.

2. Minister of Defense General Rene Emilio Ponce on 24 July 1991 released the ministry's official statistics on deaths caused by the war since January 1981 as 30,907. See "Todo lo que ha hecho el FMLN en 11 anos fue enumerado por Ponce," *El Mundo* (San Salvador), 24 July 1991, p.3. The seventy-five thousand figure is that currently employed by human rights organizations and journalists. In the opinion of the authors, it is high.

3. *Miami Herald* (Panama edition), 17 January 1992.

4. Tommie Sue Montgomery, *Revolution in El Salvador: Origins and Evolution* (Boulder: Westview Press, 1982), p. 55. Also see pp. 34–40 for a discussion of this pattern. Additionally, for similar descriptions of this pattern see David Browning, *El Salvador: Landscape and Society* (London: Oxford University Press, 1971); and E. Bradford Burns, "The Modernization of Underdevelopment: El Salvador, 1858–1931," *The Journal of Developing Areas*, 16 (April 1984): 293–316.

5. United States Department of State, "Report on the Situation in El

Salvador," 1 April 1990, p. 3. See also "Dialogo sera directo entre las partes," *La Noticia Nacional* (San Salvador), 18 January 1990, p. 6.

6. "The Peace Process in El Salvador and the United Nations," Fact Sheet No. 1 of the United Nations Observer Mission in El Salvador (ONUSAL), published by the United Nations Department of Public Information, DPI/1149A-40697-July 1991-1M, p. 1. See also "Salvador and Rebels Agree to New Talks," *New York Times International*, 5 April 1990, p. A3.

7. Ibid.

8. United States Department of State, "Report on El Salvador Required under the Foreign Assistance Appropriations Act of 1991," January 1991, p. 1.

9. "Mexico Agreements," Fact Sheet No. 4 of the United Nations Observer Mission in El Salvador (ONUSAL), published by the United Nations Department of Public Information, DPI/1149D-40697-July 1991-1M, pp. 1–12.

10. "Complace a Estados Unidos reformas a Constitucion," *El Mundo* (San Salvador), 24 September 1991, p. 12.

11. Tim Golden, "Salvadorans Sharply at Odds as Parley Recesses" *New York Times International*, 23 October 1991, p. A3.

12. "Pact on Strife in El Salvador," p. A7.

13. Roberto H. Murray Meza, "El Salvador: The State of the Economy" (Paper presented at the 25 April 1991 Conference on "Transition to Democracy in El Salvador" at the Woodrow Wilson Center in Washington, D.C.), p. 15, and "El Salvador," *North-South Focus* (A North-South Center Publication, The University of Miami, March 1992), p. 4.

14. Max G. Manwaring, ed., *Uncomfortable Wars: Toward a New Paradigm of Low Intensity Conflict* (Boulder: Westview Press, 1991).

15. The Municipalities in Action program was introduced by Ambassador Corr after overcoming Agency for International Development resistance. From its inception by the Salvadorans it was very successful.

16. "AID aclara editorial sobre la ayuda a El Salvador" *Latino* (San Salvador), 23 September 1991, p. 17.

17. "USIS San Salvador Press Kit," Embassy of the United States of America, San Salvador, 1 November 1990, p. 9.

18. "Presidential Determination on Military Assistance to El Salvador," embodied in a memorandum for the secretary of state from President George Bush, Presidential Determination No. 91–15, the White House, 15 January 1991.

19. Courtney E. Prisk, ed., *The Comandante Speaks* (Boulder: Westview Press, 1991), pp. 3, 61, 65, 80 and 92. See also interview with Miguel Castellanos, former FMLN commander, by Max G. Manwaring, in San Salvador, September 1987.

20. Robert S. Leiken, "Gorbachev's 'Gift' to Bush in Nicaragua," *New York Times*, 18 May 1989. There were several joint U.S.-USSR statements afterward encouraging the FMLN to cease hostilities and incorporate into Salvadoran society, for instance, at a U.S.-Soviet ministerial in Moscow, 7–9 February 1990 (see "State Department Report on El Salvador, April 1990," p. 4, and "State Department Report on El Salvador, January 1991," p. 4).

21. Robert A. Pastor, *Condemned to Repetition* (Princeton, N.J.: Princeton University Press, 1987), pp. 217–221 and 223–228.

22. United States Department of State, "Report on the Situation in El Salvador," 1 April 1990, p. 4.

23. Clifford Krauss, "Nicaraguan Says Arms Still Flow," *New York Times International*, 20 June 1990, p. A3. Interdictions of shipments continued to be reported in the press, e.g., "19 viajes de trasiego de armas de sandinistas destinadas para FMLN," *La Prensa Grafica* (San Salvador), 16 April 1990, p. 25.

24. United States Department of State, "Report on El Salvador Required under the Foreign Assistance Appropriations Act of 1991," January 1991, pp. 3–4.

25. United States Department of State, "Report on El Salvador Required under the Foreign Assistance Appropriations Act of 1991," July 1991, pp. 5–6.

26. J. Michael Waller's *Third Current of Revolution* (Lanham, MD: University Press, 1991) treats this subject with respect to El Salvador.

27. Interview with Dr. Alvaro Magaña, provisional president of the Republic of El Salvador, by Max G. Manwaring, in San Salvador, El Salvador, 21 November 1987.

28. Joan Didion, *Salvador* (New York: Simon and Schuster, 1983). This book graphically depicts how each night victims' bodies were dumped in several areas of San Salvador.

29. United States Department of State, "Report on the Situation in El Salvador," 30 September 1989.

30. Corr interview with El Salvador desk officer of U.S. Department of State, 19 September 1991.

31. Samuel P. Huntington, *The Third Wave: Democratization in the Late Twentieth Century* (Norman, OK: University of Oklahoma Press, 1991), p. 7.

32. Robert A. Dahl and Edward Tufte, *Size and Democracy* (Stanford, CA: Stanford University Press, 1973), as cited in Larry Diamond, Juan Linz, and Seymour Martin Lipset in *Politics in Developing Countries: Comparing Experiences with Democracy* (Boulder: Lynne Rienner Publishers, 1990), pp. 6–7.

33. Alvaro Magaña, oral interview conducted by Dr. Max G. Manwaring and translated by A. E. Letzer for the Small Wars Operations Research Directorate, U.S. Southern Command, El Salvador, February, 1987.

34. Ralph Lee Woodward, "The Rise (and Fall) of Liberalism in El Salvador and Nicaragua," *Authoritarian Regimes in Transition*, ed. Hans Binnendijk, (Washington, D.C.: Foreign Service Institute, Department of State, June 1987), p. 116.

35. Paul G. Buchanan in his article "From Military Rule in Argentina and Brazil" proposes a very useful distinction between liberalization and democratization. Liberalization refers to a process of relaxation and an opening up of decision-making spheres. It involves a broadening dialogue between the outgoing authoritarian regime and various political actors over the future course of society. This dialogue is marked by a piecemeal granting of procedural concessions. It is largely an internal dynamic. Democratization

refers to the expansion of political participation through competitive elections and the rebirth of civil society—most evident in the reestablishment of collective identities and in the voicing of interests and demands on the part of social groups represented by organized agents. Democratization is very much an external dynamic that is often a response to liberalization.

36. United States Department of State, "Report on El Salvador Required under the Foreign Assistance Appropriations Act of 1991," July 1991, p.2.

37. Manwaring, *Uncomfortable Wars*, p. 18.

38. Theodore Friend, "Marcos and the Philippines," *Orbis* 32, no. 4 (Fall 1988): 575; and Jeffery W. Barrett, "Avoiding More Nicaraguas," *Washington Quarterly* 2, no. 4 (Autumn 1988): 174.

39. Charles de Secondet Baron de Montesquieu, *The Spirit of Laws*, vol. 37 of *Great Books of the Western World* (Chicago: Encyclopedia Britannica, 1952), p. 146.

40. Sam Dillon, "Dateline El Salvador: Crisis Renewed," *Foreign Policy*, no. 73 (Winter 1988–89): 157–158.

41. Murray Meza, "El Salvador: The State of the Economy," pp. 14, 15; see also "El Salvador," *North-South Focus*, p. 4.

42. Manwaring interview with Dr. Guillermo M. Ungo, in Panama City, R.P., 11 December 1987.

43. Thomas Hobbs, *The Leviathan*, vol. 23 of *Great Books of the Western World* (Chicago: Encyclopedia Britannica, 1952), p. 157.

44. Montesquieu, *Spirit of Laws*, p. 68.

45. Freedom House report, *Mission to El Salvador* (New York: Freedom Press, May 1989), p. 24.

46. Ibid.

47. Minister of Defense Eugenio Vides Casanova was fond of noting a dozen or more events that in previous decades would have caused a military coup but in response to which the armed forces remained obedient to civil authority and the Constitution. Members of the High Command described to Ambassador Corr, for example, how after the 22 January 1987 "strike" by the private sector, businessmen approached them to sound out the possibility of the military's staging a coup. The armed forces continue to be reluctant to deal publicly and rapidly with officers who may have been involved in human rights abuses or have covered up such abuses, but they are being pushed by key officers and by domestic and foreign pressures to take actions against officers, as demonstrated by the 1989 Jesuit case. The unity of the officer corps in the face of a civil war still takes precedence.

PART THREE

Implications and Conclusions

12

Government, Politics, and Low-Intensity Conflict

Thomas A. Grant

All political choices require trade-offs. Institutions that are proficient at some tasks are maladroit at others. Democracy, according to de Tocqueville, creates a society that gains decency and stability by sacrificing drama and nobility.[1] So, too, the U.S. political system is good at waging some kinds of wars and poor at handling others. The U.S. government can make war on the scale of World War II (high-intensity) and the Gulf War (mid-intensity) with a great deal of efficiency and potency; it cannot wage war at the lower end of the conflict scale with the same degree of skill. It is merely the nature of the beast: the political and bureaucratic character of the U.S. government renders it constitutionally unsuited for low-intensity conflict.

That statement does not mean that people within that government fail to recognize the requirements of low-intensity conflict (LIC), or that the United States is always doomed to fail when fighting "small wars." The defeat of the Huks in the Philippines, the gains made against the Vietcong after the Tet Offensive and the reorganization of the counterinsurgency effort in South Vietnam, the peace accord in El Salvador, the successes of the Marines in the "banana wars" of the first half of the century, and many other examples indicate that the U.S. government can prevail in some small wars despite whatever shortcomings exist. In cases when success was less than spectacular, or when it was completely elusive, a more tragic scenario played itself out: U.S. military and civilian representatives often knew what needed to be done but found it impossible to fulfill these strategies.

The genius of generalship is not merely knowing the principles of strategy, but also understanding how to apply them. Mao Zedong recognized that the principles of revolutionary warfare were easy to grasp, but that the trick was in knowing how to make them work in reality.[2] This trick is as much a question of mastering the bureaucratic machinery of war as it is of understanding the circumstances of the war itself.

The same is true of U.S. LIC efforts in counterinsurgency, proinsurgency, counterterrorism, rescue missions, peacekeeping missions, drug interdiction, and contingency operations (the last being a grab-bag term for limited, short uses of force, such as the raid on Libya).[3] Manwaring's principles of strategy for little wars are familiar truths, almost to the point of being truisms.[4] The key to victory in LIC lies less in grasping these fundamental points and more in winning the two-front war of implementing them. One front is, obviously, the international system, where the U.S. government plays out its efforts at LIC, and where officials must work within the limits of U.S. power and influence. The other, less obvious front is the domestic political system, which erects its own political and bureaucratic obstacles.

The Omnipresence of LIC

The difficulty the U.S. government has in handling LIC is bad news because LIC has become the norm in international conflict. There was a quiet revolution in strategy over the last half-century, moving with the same speed but much less visibility than the breakthroughs in military technology. This revolution is in the theory and practice of low-intensity warfare, as the rise and perfection of various forms of revolutionary warfare demonstrate. If there is anything distinctively new about the post-World War II strategic environment, it can be found at the extreme ends of the conflict spectrum, in nuclear strategy as well as LIC. Unfortunately, as adept as U.S. war planners are at nuclear strategy, U.S. skill at LIC has lagged. Again, this is less an intellectual failure on the part of many in the government than it is the slowness of institutions and doctrines to adapt.

Of the approximately thirty ongoing conflicts in the world, all of them can be classified as low-intensity wars. If you add the wars most likely to start in the near future one can see the omnipresence of LIC in the world atlas of warfare. Following the pattern of disintegration in Yugoslavia there could be similar civil wars in India, interethnic violence in the remains of the USSR, another try at Kurdish independence, an explosion of ethnic political tensions in many African nations, as well as further international terrorism, and the renewed, violent expression of economic and political resentments in Latin

America. There has been a general rise in the preponderance of LIC in the last century, a trend that will not change.

With the end of the cold war, the number of potential conventional wars has decreased slightly. There is now, however, less reason to fear conventional war because the risk of escalation to strategic nuclear levels is practically nonexistent in most regional conflicts. The Gulf War would not have happened during the cold war simply because of the anxieties inspired by fighting Iraq, a Soviet ally, in a major mid-intensity war on the doorstep of the southern USSR. On the other hand, there are also fewer conventional wars the United States will feel compelled to fight because the intense fear of any shifts in the "correlation of forces" between the United States and the USSR no longer exists. (In fact, as of this writing, there is no USSR.) Only a few potential adversaries in a conventional war—North Korea, Cuba, Syria, and Libya—present themselves in a post–cold war, post–Gulf War world.

Even during the cold war, LIC was the norm of actual conflict. Although the United States fought only two moderate-sized wars, in Korea and Vietnam, during the cold war it extended military assistance to scores of nations. Much of that assistance went to helping regimes or insurgents fight low-intensity wars in places such as El Salvador, Afghanistan, Angola, and the Philippines. Most of these regimes used this aid to fight internal wars: the majority of wars fought in the last century have been internal wars, while interstate wars have become much less common.[5] The United States has also used limited applications of force numerous times, in hostage rescues, peacekeeping missions, and contingency operations. With the addition of drug interdiction to the definition of LIC, the number of low-intensity wars waged by the United States has risen even higher.

Nonetheless, other kinds of warfare, nuclear and mid- to high-intensity conventional warfare, have dominated the attention and resources of the U.S. military. The consequences of a nuclear war of any scale, or of a war between the former Warsaw Pact and the North Atlantic Treaty Organization (NATO), made this preoccupation understandable. Low-intensity warfare may be more prevalent, but the stakes are much smaller than those of preventing World War III.[6] Additionally, as we shall see, there have been institutional prejudices against the kind of work required for LIC that have further hampered U.S. skill in fighting small wars. The cold war always provided an excuse for this prejudice: though the United States could afford to "lose" a minor ally to a guerrilla army or fail to make significant progress against terrorism, it could not afford to fail at maintaining nuclear deterrence or at ensuring that NATO was prepared to defend West Germany.

Without the cold war distraction, one might expect the United States to attend more to low-intensity warfare. To a limited extent, this explanation is true, but there remain many reasons why the United States still is politically, bureaucratically, and culturally unequipped for LIC. Part of the answer is that our institutions are poorly designed for handling LIC, and the other part is that LIC is inherently distasteful to Americans.

Low-Intensity Conflict and U.S. Politics

There is a multitude of reasons why the U.S. political system finds LIC indigestible. Many of these obstacles are institutional and subject to bureaucratic or legislative repair; others are rooted in U.S. political culture and the burden of history and are therefore less easily changed, if changing them is desirable at all.

Secrecy. The work of LIC demands secrecy, something that Americans distrust. For example, counterterrorism demands that nothing about the number, training, techniques, and deployment of elite counterterrorist units be made public. After the Church Committee hearings, the Iran-contra scandal, and revelations about corruption within a Delta Force unit, however, there is a great deal of discomfort with "secret warriors."

Unfortunately, the demands for accountability and secrecy are irreconcilable. One can only hope that training, discipline, and oversight will prevent most abuses of the privilege of secrecy, but no net, no matter how well woven, will ever catch all transgressions. Because LIC work requires extreme secrecy, often about whether a project even exists, LIC will always seem a little suspect to a large segment of U.S. society.

Political ambiguities. No war is ever free of moral and political ambivalence—even World War II, the "good war," had its troubling features. LIC, however, invites a great deal of ambiguity, something for which Americans have little tolerance.

Counterterrorism often leads to the assassination of known terrorists. Israel's assassination of Palestine Liberation Organization leaders in Tunis may have been effective in the shadow war against terrorism, but it was inherently distasteful to Western sensibilities. Counterinsurgency, renamed by the U.S. military as internal defense and development (IDAD) to remove the stigma of Vietnam, often requires a choice between evils. For example, it was not altogether clear to Americans who was worse, the Salvadoran military or the guerrillas. Counterinsurgency usually entails U.S. aid and pressure to shore up and reform an inefficient, corrupt, and abusive government; it is rare to have a morally splendid ally in counterinsurgency work, simply because morally pristine, administratively effective governments do not provide the inspiration or excuse for a guerrilla war.[7] Proinsurgency, or support for insurgent movements, frequently wades in the same political swamp: once the Soviets left Afghanistan, Washington became nervous about a *mujahideen* victory, which might install another militant Islamic theocracy in the Near East.

It is hard, then, for the U.S. political culture to stomach many low-intensity wars. The anti-Sandinista guerrillas, the contras, had a harder time finding supporters in the United States than they did inside Nicaragua. U.S. officials in Vietnam who served in the controversial Phoenix Program, which struck at key targets within the Vietcong political apparatus, are still defending the concept behind it while arguing that, in practice, they had little control over their South Vietnamese allies, who often used Phoenix to justify an indiscriminate assassination program.[8] The proposal to eradicate the drug problem in South America by radically altering the peasant economy of that region to give incentives to grow produce and flowers instead of coca plants inspires in many a mixture of skepticism about the potential success of such a program and doubts about the wisdom of transforming another society's economy this profoundly. Efforts to rig the political system of another society with techniques ranging from aid to opposition parties to black propaganda, as the United States did in the Philippines to defeat the Huks, are offensive to Americans, who believe in national self-determination and the sanctity of democracy.[9] It is confusing and troubling for most Americans to subvert institutions in a society in order to save it for democracy.

Conventional war is not without its moral ambiguities, as the aftermaths of the Korean War and the Gulf War demonstrate. The moral and political difficulties of waging conventional wars are, nonetheless, much smaller than those of low-intensity conflicts, which often require the deliberate targeting of the civilian population for coercion and recruitment, tinkering with the economic and political structures of sovereign states, and supporting clients whose beliefs and behaviors are often repugnant to us. LIC, then, is never likely to inspire much public support, except in rare cases such as the "drug war," when a clear public consensus exists about the nature and immediacy of a national security problem. In the post-Vietnam period, such consensus was rare, and it probably will be even more difficult to find or construct with the end of the Soviet threat.

Americans do believe in using force abroad. A majority of those polled in a 1991 survey published in *Foreign Policy* said that the United States should defend Western Europe or Saudi Arabia if those countries were invaded. On the other hand, only 28 percent were willing to support a U.S. military defense of the Salvadoran regime if it looked close to toppling, and, strangely, even fewer, only 22 percent, expressed support for U.S. military action to save the Aquino government in the Philippines.[10] U.S. citizens generally believe in allowing their government to use force when important interests are clearly threatened and are resistant to military deployments done in the name of more indirect and uncertain concerns. Low-intensity wars rarely threaten interests as significant as the Persian Gulf oil fields or the independence of Europe; the U.S. public, then, will always have doubts about the government involving itself, even only partway, in small, distant, and seemingly insignificant wars. If this were not true, then the Reagan administration would never have suffered the grief it did for "drawing a line" in Central America in the name of containment.

Duration. Low-intensity warfare is unlikely to inspire public or bureaucratic support because it normally takes a great deal of time to produce tangible, undeniable results. The Huk rebellion lasted for eight to ten years, depending on how one dates its conclusion, and even the clear-cut victory of the Magsaysay government did not end Marxist-inspired guerrilla warfare in the Philippines for all time. After a decade of conflict, the contra war ended, but what was resolved by its conclusion remains unclear. Fears of Vietnam-like quagmires aside, the U.S. political system is not founded on patience.

Part of the reason for this impatience is the global scope of U.S. interests and commitments. The U.S. government has only a limited amount of attention, resources, and energy to bring to bear on its foreign policy problems. It must make choices, as any organization does, about the problems to which it will immediately attend. No organization can normally afford to handle everything; hence, it must make strategic choices about which issues receive attention, and which are neglected.[11] When faced with regular crises, shifts in public and presidential foreign policy priorities, and the normal Brownian motion of international politics, it is difficult for the government to attend to any problem for very long.[12]

Unfortunately, even the smallest success in LIC normally takes years. It took an entire decade for airline hijackings to decrease significantly from the peak years in the seventies. The Angolan guerrillas reached the negotiation table only after sixteen years of civil war in Angola. The British government has endured "the troubles" in Northern Ireland for decades.

Yet, the U.S. government cannot hold any issue at the top of the agenda for very long, making it nearly impossible to deal with problems with distant or uncertain conclusions. Elected officials must justify their policies to the electorate every two, four, or six years, and often more frequently than that, if they want to maintain the clout that public support gives a politician. Foreign Service officers want to demonstrate that they had a positive effect during their posting abroad, as do Pentagon officials, in or out of uniform. The speed and profundity of results matter in U.S. politics, but gains appear slowly and imperfectly in LIC.

Perceived stakes. LIC is even more politically distasteful because the U.S. government rarely gives it high priority. When the Reagan administration "drew the line" in Central America and thus pushed the region to the top of the foreign policy agenda, the U.S. army in the early eighties had to ask five officers to command the MILGROUP in El Salvador before it found someone willing to accept the job.[13] The services have traditionally given few rewards for work in LIC, and the situation with civilian agencies is not much better. During the cold war, Europe was the place for ambitious careerists to go, not the developing world, where the majority of low-intensity wars occur. This situation has somewhat improved over the last several years, with the reorganization of the command structure for special operations, the creation of special offices in the Defense Department for special operations and low-intensity conflict, the expansion of the Army-Air Force program for the study of LIC, and the growth of a special LIC curriculum within many service schools. The Gulf War may have reversed some of these intellectual and structural improvements, however.

Low-intensity conflicts are low priority and are likely to stay that way. Terrorism, no matter how dramatic, still only menaces a handful of Americans every year. Drug interdiction has limited effectiveness, and it is but one tool among many in the drug war. Guerrilla wars often take place in countries where the United States seeks bases, listening posts, access to scarce raw materials, or other geopolitical benefits; but rarely are these interests vital. Where there are guerrilla wars, there will be horrible abuses of dignity and life that will engage our humanitarian impulses, but humanitarianism alone does not always move the United States to action.[14] None of what might happen if the United States fails at LIC can match the damage done by an Iraqi conquest of Saudi Arabia, a new Arab-Israeli war, civil war in the Soviet Union, or economic frictions with Europe or Japan. For the insurgents, however, victory and defeat are absolute.[15] To make matters worse, in spite of the Gulf War, we are still living with the strange belief, voiced by many opinion-makers and average citizens alike, that the end of the cold war erased war from the international map. After the cold war, and even after the Gulf War, many still see war as aberrant, a phenomenon that died along with the threat of a surprise Soviet nuclear attack.[16]

This is a shortsighted view of the emerging world and the U.S. role in it. Success at LIC can be the ounce of prevention that vitiates the need to fight a larger war in the future. War may be less likely between the nations of Europe or between the superpowers, but war in the developing world, shows of force, and the kind of warfare in the shadows common to LIC will continue and possibly increase.

Soft power. Not only do low-intensity wars seem less important, but they always seem less manageable than other forms of conflict. When we fight conventional wars, we are playing to our strong suit, massive military power supported by a large population, a huge industrial base, and a significant edge in military technology. In LIC, what matters more is "soft power,"[17] or what might be better called *leverage.*[18] In the universe of political influence, capability is only partly created by strength. Military or economic power is useful in some circumstances, but not all.

In LIC, many things matter more than strength. Finesse, for example, in separating the population from insurgents is more useful than military power when fighting a counterinsurgency war. Ham-handed measures like strategic hamlets or attrition-based search and destroy strategies are less effective than a knowledge of the local political circumstances and an understanding of the indigenous culture.[19] These intellectual achievements make it possible to build an effective program of incentives and disincentives that is sensitive to local and cultural peculiarities and will convince the local population to stop supporting or accommodating the guerrillas. As the history of successes and failures in counterinsurgency shows, military power used in ignorance of its effects in a foreign political setting is doomed to fail.[20]

If we were to take Max Manwaring's list of strategic priorities in LIC—legitimacy, constant and adequate support to the besieged government, organization, intelligence, discipline and capabilities of the armed forces, and reduction of outside aid to the insurgents—it is obvious that military strength clearly applies to only one of these components of LIC. The U.S. way of making war, relying heavily on massed firepower and maneuver, therefore little applies to low-intensity wars.[21]

LIC presents an uncomfortable situation for a superpower: it cannot use its considerable economic and military power to full effect in small wars. Certainly, the United States has more to invest in small wars in equipment, economic assistance, and numbers of available personnel, but the amount of foreign assistance the United States gives is perhaps slightly less important than its quality and certainty. On occasion, the quality of that aid has been quite good; in other circumstances, however, it has not.

The discomfort with LIC can lead to two neurotic institutional responses: one can deny that LIC is important, and therefore excuse oneself from dealing with a vexing problem; or one can claim that capability in one kind of warfare automatically translates into capability in all forms of warfare. Both are incorrect, as painful experience has shown. Little wars pull us in, no matter how uncomfortable they may be, and conventional war doctrines simply do not apply to counterterrorism, counterinsurgency, proinsurgency, and, arguably, drug interdiction. Peacekeeping and contingency missions require conventional war expertise, but they are only two among many kinds of LIC tasks.

Clearly, a full evaluation of our ability to use soft power in small wars is beyond the scope of this essay. One simple fact about our ability to use leverage to influence the behavior and policies of other states, however, is undeniable: when exerting leverage, we are trying to use influence on another sovereign country, giving us much less control over the situation "on the ground" than we might desire. The governments of El Salvador, Israel, and the Philippines can choose to listen to U.S. advice, or they can ignore us. Varieties of pressure are available to us, but this is only an indirect form of control over what military doctrines, economic reforms, and political changes these sovereign states will choose. We can try to persuade, cajole, or pressure the Salvadoran regime into prosecuting officers involved in death squads, but we cannot order them to do so. Unlike invading the coasts of Normandy, we cannot wield our gargantuan national power directly. If the Salvadoran regime is willing to lose millions of dollars in U.S. aid to protect the officer implicated in the killing of two labor leaders, we cannot be sanguine about the degree of leverage we have in low-intensity wars.

Institutional arrangements. One must make war with organizations as much as with weapons and personnel, and LIC is no exception. LIC demands specific institutional arrangements, however, for which the U.S. government is poorly suited.

Clausewitz said that in all wars, both interstate and "people's wars" (i.e., internal wars), unity of command is vital. Within the U.S. military services, there are frequent cases of disunity of command, especially in LIC situations. One can remember the Desert One debacle, the problems faced in Lebanon and Grenada, and the interservice rivalries in Vietnam as worst cases of this problem.[22] Certainly, there are success stories as well as failures, but the services have a historical aversion to interservice cooperation.

To make matters worse, LIC is rarely a military problem alone. LIC demands not only interservice cooperation, but harmony and collaboration between military and civilian arms of the U.S. government. On the civilian side, agencies as disparate as the State Department, the Defense Department, the Central Intelligence Agency, the National Security Agency, the National Security Council, the Treasury Department, the Labor Department, the Justice Department, and the Agency for International Development (AID) may have parts to play. Often they do not share the same understanding of the problem, nor do they agree upon solutions. Additionally, agencies may have strong disincentives to cooperate. AID, implicated in training police forces in Latin America in torture techniques and unhappy with involvement in the counterinsurgency portion of the Vietnam War, is wary of contributing to future counterinsurgency campaigns in the developing world. During interagency meetings on Central America, no clear hierarchy was established, often because no one wanted the responsibilities of "point man" in Central American policy.[23]

Doctrinal resistance. Gen. John Galvin's opening piece in *Uncomfortable Wars* is cause for both celebration and alarm.[24] For LIC advocates, it is good news that someone as highly placed as General Galvin and with such significant background in conventional war would recognize the importance of LIC. General Galvin's arguments for a doctrinal reorientation of the U.S. military to handle LIC better are reminiscent of similar positions taken by academics, policymakers, and military men in the late seventies and early eighties, when the current enthusiasm for "little wars" first began. They also echo the aborted counterinsurgency revolution of the sixties.[25] It is hard to be hopeful about the future of LIC as a significant part of U.S. military doctrine when every ten or twenty years, the wheel is reinvented, recognized as a significant breakthrough, and then left behind.

Part of the answer lies in simple hostility to LIC among some in the armed forces. During the Kennedy administration, the Joint Chiefs of Staff resisted efforts to retool the military in ways the president believed necessary for counterinsurgency, and in the eighties, similar resistance occurred when LIC advocates within the government tried to add LIC to the military's doctrinal repertoire. Many skeptics about LIC do not see it as different enough from conventional war to merit specialized techniques.[26] Others worry that there is too much for the armed forces to handle already and that LIC is not important enough to merit the strain to train, organize, and equip for it. Still others, unsure about the military's involvement in the antidrug campaign, feel that LIC will drag them into areas where it is inappropriate for the military to tread. Another set of critics see the work of many in LIC, such as the special operations forces, as oddities not worth supporting beyond the level of resources they already receive.[27]

Perhaps General Galvin has the correct answer: militaries, like any other organization, are inherently loath to change. His evocative phrase, the "fortress-cloister," may have a great deal of truth in it. If indeed the insularity of the U.S. military is difficult to pierce, then it will take a great deal of time, patience, and energy to make many in the fortress-cloister see the real landscape of modern warfare, in which LIC plays an increasingly large part. Setbacks should be expected because a wealth of patience and attention is unusual for the U.S. government to expend on any but the most dire problems, and many in the military (and elsewhere in the government, to be fair) are still not convinced by the LIC advocates.

The involvement of the military in drug interdiction is likely to accelerate the armed forces' discomfort with LIC. Many media commentators mistakenly assumed that, with the end of the cold war and the popularity of the so-called drug war, the services would rush into drug interdiction to preserve their funding and personnel levels. The enthusiasm for the drug war has not materialized as much as many expected because of the skepticism many in the military feel about that struggle. Many officers do not believe that the drug war is a *war*, in the sense of the national clash of arms for which they have been trained and prepared. The absorption of the dynamics and techniques of a new form of armed struggle, counterterrorism or counterinsurgency, is not the same as involvement in something smacking of a police matter. Many in the military have voiced concerns that too much participation in the drug war will reduce their readiness for a real war by straining their already dwindling resources.

Imbalances in will, organization, and interest. Because LIC is often a conflict between wielders of soft power, there are many reasons why the United States will always be at a disadvantage in low-intensity wars. Our opponents are patient; our political system is not. The organizations with which terrorists and guerrillas wage war are small, disciplined, and motivated; the institutions through which we manage LIC are large, unwieldy, and less single-minded. The insurgents often have a single objective; we normally have several competing goals, demanding trade-offs among them.

This is a bureaucratic, political, and diplomatic fact of life. We are victims of our success and our size, which makes us adept at some tasks, but not all. Superpowers have global reach, but they must balance competing priorities, forcing trade-offs between gains made in a country, in a region, in relations with other major powers, and in domestic politics. In El Salvador, we are not merely interested in that country's fate; we must also worry about how our actions in El Salvador affect the terms and tone of our diplomacy with neighboring Central American nations, all the rest of Latin America, Cuba, the Soviet Union, the Organization of American States, the United Nations, and the voters at home. The Farabundo Martí Front for National Liberation (FMLN), on the other hand, had fewer audiences it had to placate. For the FMLN, victory was everything; for the United States, defeat would have been merely an embarrassment.

Similarly, the institutions of the U.S. government experience the fragmentation and ensuing lack of coordination natural to an entity as large as they are. Although factionalism often does injure insurgent groups, on the average they face nothing like the coordination problems of the U.S. government. To make concerted progress on gaining battlefield supremacy, reforming political and economic institutions in a foreign country, and constructing a diplomatic shield behind which all this activity will occur, many agencies of the U.S. government not interested in or in the habit of cooperating must do so. The same is true of other forms of LIC, which equally demand orchestration of military, diplomatic, political, and economic action.

For these reasons, we must always be modest about our chances for success at LIC. Culturally, politically, bureaucratically, and doctrinally, the United States is hampered in dealing with the political ambiguities, complexities, and peculiarities of LIC. This is not to say that we are doomed when fighting small wars, only that we are not as capable at fighting them as we are at waging mid- to high-intensity conventional war or maintaining nuclear deterrence. This is not a call for the United States to abandon the very characteristics that hinder us in LIC—for example, a suspicion of secrecy or a sense of moral mission in world affairs. What we lose in fighting low-intensity wars, we gain elsewhere through our national character and political institutions. We must, however, understand what limits and obstacles we will encounter in fighting wars at the lower end of the conflict spectrum.

The Philippines, Vietnam, and El Salvador

One can see the importance of these bureaucratic limits in three different U.S. counterinsurgency campaigns, in the Philippines, South Vietnam, and El Salvador. Though bureaucratic and political arrangements were only one reason among many for the widely varying degrees of success in these three cases, they do show that the institutional characteristics of U.S. counterinsurgency efforts matter greatly.

The U.S. effort to help defeat the Huk rebels in the Philippines was one of the first successful counterinsurgency efforts after World War II, and it became a paradigm for future efforts for the United States in the same way that the Malayan Emergency became a touchstone for counterinsurgency in British military circles. The lack of bureaucratic problems in the U.S. aid mission during this counterinsurgency campaign was the classic dog that did not bark: the absence in this case of otherwise common political and organizational defects itself speaks volumes.

The U.S. military structure in the postwar Philippines was uniquely well suited to handle a counterinsurgency war against the Huks. The Joint U.S. Military Advisory Group-Philippines (JUSMAG) recruited a large number of Office of Strategic Studies (OSS) veterans and experts in unconventional and psychological warfare, including Edward Lansdale and Paul Linebarger. Their background in partisan warfare against the Japanese and Germans gave them the operational experience in fighting small wars they needed to understand and defeat the Huks' techniques.[28] U.S. advisers took great pains to understand the Filipinos and to tailor their advice to fit this society. The U.S. mission in the Philippines showed a great deal of patience and coordination of effort, creating an effective partnership among the embassy, JUSMAG, the Philippine government, and the Armed Forces of the Philippines (AFP). A real team spirit energized the work of JUSMAG, though this esprit de corps was not always shared with U.S. officials outside the Philippines.[29]

Many of the same elements existed in South Vietnam, but the chemistry was far less successful. Experts in the operational requirements of counterinsurgency warfare felt muzzled by both the South Vietnamese government and the Military Assistance Command, Vietnam (MACV). Frictions between agencies and services, and between different branches of the same service, were frequent. MACV valued expertise in conventional warfare more than a cultural and political knowledge of a country in the midst of a politico-military war.[30] The result was a strategy with a disproportionate emphasis on the military aspect of counterinsurgency, which was then bureaucratically compartmentalized and fragmented in application.[31]

El Salvador is a more mixed case. Again, many U.S. military advisers were experienced in the strategy of small wars (many were Vietnam veterans), but they often had to fight a military bureaucracy that neither understood nor recognized the importance of LIC. The Salvadoran government was extremely slow in producing a unified, coherent strategy for defeating the FMLN guerrillas; instead, the strategy emerged piecemeal. The Woerner Commission Report, which outlined military alternatives, was published in 1981; the National Campaign ⁻ˡⁱⁿ, which linked military operations with political and economic reforms, did not emerge until 1983.

Significant bureaucratic cleavages existed, both within the U.S. government and between the Salvadoran and U.S. governments.[32] Though both the MILGROUP and the embassy struggled to bring the disparate elements of policy and strategy together, their efforts were frequently undercut by legal restrictions, the scale and form of U.S. government assistance, and the constant and frequently damaging intervention by less-than-knowledgeable officials from Congress and the administration. (To be fair, these interventions were often helpful, especially when the Salvadoran government needed to be reminded of the seriousness with which the U.S. government took the war and the place of human rights issues in it.) The U.S. and Salvadoran governments (particularly the military components) frequently disagreed. While the Salvadoran military preferred to focus on the battlefield, U.S. advisers and diplomats (and Salvadoran civilian officials) urged greater attention to the political front. Salvadoran officers found it difficult to take advice from civilians, both Salvadoran and U.S., though civilians often had the missing piece of counterinsurgency that the Salvadoran army had missed. Additionally, threats to cut off aid and efforts to stabilize the battlefield worked at cross-purposes: though U.S. advisers were struggling to get the Salvadorans to think in the long term, the uncertain flow of aid from Washington compelled them to concentrate on short-term actions.

Though the process appeared messy and confusing to many observers, the Salvadoran and U.S. governments made much progress in the war, especially in wresting control of the battlefield from the insurgents, lowering the number of human rights abuses committed by the army and security services, and restructuring the government and the economy. Military progress, domestic reforms, and loss of foreign support convinced the FMLN to come to the bargaining table. The ability of the regime to survive militarily and politically thwarted the FMLN's hopes for either a Maoist-style final offensive or a mass uprising like the turmoil in 1979 that deposed Anastasio Somoza in Nicaragua. It remains to be seen if the accords agreed to in January 1992 will be sufficiently implemented and peace will endure.

Why this variation in success? What made the U.S. mission in the Philippines different? In large part, the answer lies in the expertise of the JUSMAG advisers. The possession of skill and the ability to use it are often very different things, however. In the Philippines, U.S. advisers were given the chance to do their work relatively unimpeded by theater commanders, service chiefs, and officials in Washington. Lansdale and his associates enjoyed a great deal of local control over their counterinsurgency work, largely because the services, the administration, the Congress, and the U.S. public never saw that great a threat emerging from the Philippines. A consensus over containment had formed in the United States, but the Philippines seemed a less important battlefield of the cold war than Central Europe or Korea. This allowed Lansdale, Philippine President Ramon Magsaysay, and their colleagues to work with a single-mindedness matching that of the Huks, but without the involvement of the entire U.S. national security apparatus.

JUSMAG also benefited from the lack of controversy surrounding its work. The wars in South Vietnam and El Salvador, on the other hand, became very controversial, exciting the U.S. political system to pull policy and strategy for these wars in several different directions. Congress wanted to assert its role; the military services and civilian agencies wanted to protect themselves from whatever fallout occurred; and, in a heated political atmosphere, at certain junctures there were policy differences between key actors (such as the MILGROUP commander in El Salvador and the commander of U.S. Southern Command in Panama).

The absence of controversy created a unique situation for the U.S. advisers working in the Philippines. Without the intense controversy like that surrounding the wars in South Vietnam and El Salvador, the U.S. political system did not intrude on the advisers' work on a yearly or even monthly basis. It was possible, then, to conceive of and apply a long-term strategy instead of a series of piecemeal, short-term actions designed as much to stave off congressional or public anger as to win the war. Without controversy, the demand for immediate results was also absent.

It was fortunate that, by unintended controversy or intentional rhetoric used by top policymakers, the Huk rebellion never became too important. By not drawing a line against communism in the Philippines the same way that John Kennedy and Lyndon Johnson did in South Vietnam, the U.S. government did not tie its fate to any particular Philippine government. Unlike their South Vietnamese counterparts, Philippine military and political leaders (with the exception of the agreeable Magsaysay) were never able to claim they were indispensable to U.S. interests. This helped U.S. advisers to avoid the problem of what one might call "reverse leverage," used against the United States by target governments to avoid reforms. In contrast, South Vietnamese corps commanders were often able politely to ignore advice and pressure from U.S. officials, as did many Salvadoran officers.

Perhaps more important, but in a very subtle way, the lack of controversy over the Philippines ensured that many elements of U.S. political culture would not constrain U.S. policy. If there had been more attention paid in the United States to the Huk rebellion, many more people might have grown anxious about a U.S. commitment to an indefinite conflict fought in unusual, often unpalatable ways (e.g., covert aid to Magsaysay's campaign to ensure his electoral victory in the 1953 presidential race). The distorting prejudices of U.S. political culture played little or no role in the Philippines, unlike El Salvador or Vietnam.

Size also worked in JUSMAG's favor. JUSMAG was a very small advisory group, numbering between twenty-five and sixty people, a manageable size for the coordination of a complex political and military effort. MACV, on the other hand, had a staff of 3,164 in 1961, and 23,310 in 1964. The natural bureaucratic fragmentation and inertia this created aggravated already fissiparous and hidebound tendencies in the creation and administration of U.S. policy for South Vietnam. For counterinsurgency, one important component of LIC, small is indeed beautiful, as compared to economies of scale. In El Salvador the number of military trainers was limited to fifty-five. The modest scale of JUSMAG in the Philippines and the MILGRP in El Salvador aided the partnership between itself and the U.S. embassy. Rather than suffering the bureaucratic separation of MACV and the U.S. embassy in South Vietnam, the diplomats and military advisers in the Philippines and El Salvador constituted real country teams.

Finally, JUSMAG was born in the infancy of the new U.S. national security bureaucracy. Many jurisdictional boundaries, procedural requirements, and doctrinal differences had not yet formed. The organizational environment in the late forties and early fifties allowed greater flexibility in approaching the Huk rebellion than U.S. advisers would experience only a decade or two later, when the national security bureaucracy had settled into a firmer shape.

One can see from this discussion how unusual the U.S. counterinsurgency effort in the Philippines was. Because of a combination of skill among key U.S. officials working in the field and some accidents of history, a unique opportunity existed to avoid the common problems experienced when the United States fights low-intensity wars. By virtue of the political and bureaucratic context, U.S. advisers in the Philippines were able to develop an effective long-term strategy for a war outside the norm of U.S. military engagements.

Conclusion

Most forms of LIC require surgically precise tools, not blunt instruments. The examples of the Philippines, Vietnam, and El Salvador discussed above, and other country studies in this book, show, unfortunately, that the U.S. government is not constituted for precision. One might believe that, after the cold war and the Gulf War, we might see the impetus for a radical restructuring of the U.S. military establishment, rendering it better suited for the subtleties and complexities of LIC. This period of transition in which our security interests are being reassessed and our defense establishment restructured is extremely important to our nation's future. Who will win the argument about the future role of LIC within U.S. strategy—a recognition of the nature, ubiquity, and importance of LIC or a familiar U.S. neo-isolationism, aggravated by severe budget restraints—remains to be seen.

Notes

1. Alexis de Tocqueville, *Democracy in America* (New York: Doubleday/Anchor, 1966), pp. 244–245.

2. Mao Tse-Tung, *Selected Works of Mao Tse Tung* (London: Oxford University Press, 1968). For an excellent analysis of Mao's thinking, see John Shy and Thomas W. Collier, "Revolutionary Warfare," in Peter Paret, ed., *Makers of Modern Strategy* (Princeton: Princeton University Press, 1986), pp. 822, 838–845.

3. See chap. 1, p. 8 for the definition of LIC given in the current U.S. Army manual for low-intensity conflict, FM 100–20. It is clear from this definition that LIC is far more complicated by virtue of the range of issues and tasks it encompasses than most military problems.

4. See Max Manwaring, ed., *Uncomfortable Wars: Toward a New Paradigm of Low-Intensity Conflict* (Boulder: Westview Press, 1991).

5. For a catalog of these wars, see Melvin Small and J. David Singer, *Resort to Arms: International and Civil Wars, 1816–1980* (Beverly Hills: SAGE Publications, 1982).

6. A good explanation for the reasons behind this can be found in Eliot Cohen, "Constraints on America's Conduct of Small Wars," *International Security* 9, no. 4 (Fall 1984): 151–181, and 165–177 especially.

7. Douglas Blaufarb, *The Counterinsurgency Era* (New York: The Free Press, 1977), pp. 1–21.

8. Dale Andrade, *Ashes to Ashes: The Phoenix Program and the Vietnam War* (Lexington: Lexington Books, 1990); see also Blaufarb on the moral ambiguities of counterinsurgency.

9. Cecil Curry, *Edward Lansdale: The Unquiet American* (Boston: Houghton Mifflin, 1988), pp. 204–206.

10. John E. Rielly, "Public Opinion: The Pulse of the '90s," *Foreign Policy,* no. 82 (Spring 1991): 79–96.

11. James March and Herbert Simon, *Organizations* (New York: Wiley Press, 1958); James March, *Handbook of Organizations* (Chicago: Rand McNally, 1965); Morton Halperin, *Bureaucratic Politics and Foreign Policy* (Washington: The Brookings Institution, 1974).

12. John E. Mueller, *War, Presidents, and Public Opinion* (New York: John Wiley and Sons, 1973).

13. A. J. Bacevich, James D. Hallums, Richard H. White, and Thomas F. Young, *American Military Policy in Small Wars: The Case of El Salvador* (Washington: Pergamon-Brassey's, 1988), p. 18.

14. A belated discussion of the national interest after the cold war is at last beginning, but it is taking strongly isolationist tones in many respects. A new kind of "America first" philosophy, deliberately exclusive of human rights considerations, is pervading the debate. For an example of this, see Alan Tonelson, "What Is the National Interest?" *Atlantic Monthly,* June 1991, pp. 35–53.

15. Edward Rice, *Wars of the Third Kind: Conflict in Underdeveloped Countries* (Berkeley: University of California Press, 1988), pp. 60–78.

16. John Mearsheimer's argument against this raised eyebrows; see "Back to the Future: Instability in Europe after the Cold War," *International Security* 15, no. 1 (Summer 1990): 5–56.

17. Joseph Nye, "Soft Power," *Foreign Policy,* no. 83 (Winter 1990–1991): 153–171.

18. A phenomenon best explained by Richard Cottam, in *Competitive Interference* (Pittsburgh: University of Pittsburgh Press, 1967).

19. Richard A. Hunt, "Strategies At War: Pacification and Attrition in Vietnam," in Richard A. Hunt and Richard H. Shultz, eds., *Lessons from an Unconventional War: Reassessing US Strategies for Future Conflicts* (Washington: Pergamon-Brassey's, 1982), pp. 48–117.

20. An opinion shared by many students of the Vietnam War, including Blaufarb, Richard Shultz, Robert Karnow, Andrew Krepinevich, Sir Robert Thompson, and many others.

21. Edward N. Luttwak, *Strategy: The Logic of War and Peace* (Cambridge: Belknap Press, 1987), pp. 96–99.

22. For excellent descriptions of disunity of command in Vietnam, see

Robert Komer, *Bureaucracy Does Its Thing*, R-967-ARPA (Santa Monica: The RAND Corporation, 1982); on the Iran hostage rescue attempt, the Grenada invasion, and the Lebanon peacekeeping mission, see James Adams, *Secret Armies* (New York: Atlantic Monthly Press, 1987), pp. 110–133, 222–255, 256–260; on Lebanon, see the Long Commission Report; on Iran, see the Holloway Report. On the deep historical reasons for divisions among the services, see C. Kenneth Allard, *Command, Control, and the Common Defense* (New Haven: Yale University Press, 1990).

23. For the difficulties faced by the "Core Group" making policy on Central America, see Roy Gutman, *Banana Diplomacy: The Making of American Policy on Nicaragua, 1981–1987* (New York: Touchstone Books, 1989).

24. General John C. Galvin, "Toward a New Paradigm," in Manwaring, *Uncomfortable Wars*.

25. The original wave of interest in counterinsurgency, one part of LIC, is exemplified by a famous reader from the early sixties on the subject; see Franklin Mark Osanka, *Modern Guerrilla Warfare* (New York: Free Press of Glencoe, 1963). For the most famous academic proponent of LIC as a distinct strategy in the eighties, see Sam Sarkesian, *The New Battlefield: The United States and Unconventional Conflicts* (New York: Greenwood Press, 1986).

26. Adams, *Secret Armies*, pp. 256–288.

27. Adams, *Secret Armies*, pp. 206–208, 265–267.

28. Larry Cable, *Conflict of Myths: The Development of American Counterinsurgency Doctrine* (New York: New York University Press, 1986), pp. 41–58; Lawrence M. Greenberg, *The Hukbalahap Insurrection: A Case Study of a Successful Anti-Insurgency Operation in the Philippines, 1946–1955* (Washington: United States Army Center of Military History, 1986), pp. 95–111.

29. An opinion shared by both Lansdale and his best (and by no means uncritical) biographer. See Curry, *The Unquiet American* and Edward Lansdale, *In the Midst of Wars: An American's Mission to Southeast Asia* (New York: Harper and Row, 1972).

30. Andrew Krepinevich, *The Army and Vietnam* (Baltimore: The Johns Hopkins Press, 1986), pp. 56–130.

31. Komer, *Bureaucracy Does Its Thing*, pp. 111–130.

32. For an excellent discussion of the problems encountered in formulating strategy for El Salvador, see John D. Waghelstein, *El Salvador: Observations and Experiences in Counterinsurgency* (Carlisle Barracks: U.S. Army War College, 1985); see also Bacevich et al., *American Military Policy*, pp. 8–18.

13

Low-Intensity Conflict and the International Legal System

John Norton Moore

Introduction

The message presented in this chapter is that widely held models about the origins and control of violent conflict between nations, including the low-intensity conflict or LIC spectrum, are themselves part of the problem in the continuation of such violent conflict. These models are a part of the problem insofar as they lead to a focus on policies that in the real world fail to add to deterrence of the aggressive use of force and conversely lead to an avoidance of policies that can make a more substantial contribution to peace.

The central symptom of this problem in the international legal system, as it is now applied, is the system's all-too-frequent failure to condemn systematically and strongly the aggressive use of force, particularly in the LIC spectrum, while simultaneously and perversely condemning and constraining the use of defensive force in response to such aggression. The net effect is that the international legal system's contribution to the deterrence of aggression, particularly in the LIC spectrum, is negligible. Thus, as widely applied, the legal system needlessly becomes largely irrelevant in dealing with a central challenge of our age.

Indeed, in some settings, conventional wisdom, with the best of intentions and the worst of consequences, on balance has actually aided aggression, thus turning the legal system upside down. It is as though the international legal system itself were suffering from a severe autoimmune disorder that has turned its own immune system, intended to zap the virus of aggression, against its defensive response to aggression.

Fortunately, the cure for the autoimmune response, if not wholly to the virus of aggression itself, is relatively simple. The remedy requires clear thinking about the nature of aggression and defense in the international system, coupled with a variety of policies intended to deter more effectively the entire spectrum of aggression. Such policies would include enhancing the international systemic response against aggression and in support of defense, particularly regarding the LIC portion of the spectrum. It must be understood that a legal system that treats the defensive response to overt or covert aggression the same as or more severely than it treats the aggression itself either is irrelevant in the real world of conflict avoidance or, worse, assists the aggressive attack. Unfortunately, although the cure is simple, it will nonetheless be difficult to reeducate against powerful conventional myths that seemingly promote peace and restraint but actually are the functional equivalent of a belief that the night air causes disease. In the real world they add nothing to—or even undermine—the deterrence of aggression.

Low-Intensity Conflict in Context:
Competing Models of Aggression and Deterrence

Each generation has a favorite panacea for creating and maintaining peace. From the turn of the century until World War I, it was the creation of third-party dispute settlement machinery for the rational handling of disputes between nations. From the aftermath of World War I until the present, there has been a major interest in creating effective international organizations for managing the peace. From the mid-1960s until the recent revolution in the Soviet Union and its subsequent disintegration, the principal focus of efforts to bring peace in our time has been on nuclear arms control at the central strategic front. Although all of these traditional techniques for war avoidance have an important role, third-party dispute settlement and arms control, at least as panaceas, seem to be rooted in a misleading concept of major wars arising because of disputes between nations, accidents, or spiraling arms races; and we have underestimated serious theoretical and real-world difficulties in building effective international organizations to manage the peace.

Within this intellectual tradition, the role of the international lawyer has been seen as seeking to reduce the lawful uses of force, thus progressively constraining the defensive response and increasingly treating both the aggressive attack and the defensive response as equivalent offenses against rational opportunities for diplomacy and third-party legal settlement. This mind-set is principally responsible for a majority opinion in the *Nicaragua* case before the International

Court of Justice (ICJ) that ignores the evidence of the "secret" or low-intensity Sandinista attack against El Salvador and the apparent perjury of Nicaragua's agent before the court about Nicaragua's involvement in this attack and, instead, condemns the lesser U.S. assistance to the contras in response.

There is today, however, a powerful body of evidence that the principal international wars of the twentieth century—World Wars I and II, the Korean War, the Indochina War, the Falklands War, the Iran-Iraq War, the war in Afghanistan, the conflict in Central America, and the recent Gulf conflict, among others—did not arise principally because of unresolved disputes (although they were a factor), accidents, or "arms races," but rather because of a synergy between two critical and necessary sets of conditions. The first set of conditions involves a typically totalitarian or, at least, nondemocratic regime bent on the use of aggressive force to alter the contemporary value map in fundamental violation of the United Nations Charter. The second set of conditions is a system-wide failure of deterrence in its broadest sense of the effect of international organizations against aggression, balances of power, military capabilities, defensive alliances, clarity or lack thereof about intentions to respond, the effectiveness of the international legal system, and economic interdependencies or lack thereof.

Where an aggressor is absent, as in United States–Canadian and Swiss-French relations, there is no risk of major war, even in the absence of deterrence. Where deterrence is present at effective levels, as it was in the North Atlantic Treaty Organization (NATO) against Soviet power, war can be avoided even if there may be aggressive intent. We should also note that the overwhelming majority of aggressive regimes in this century have been totalitarian, or at least nondemocratic, and they tend to exhibit what I have elsewhere called "the radical regime syndrome" of a one-party political system with a repressive internal security system.[1] One of the most interesting connections in this respect is that these regimes not only are aggressors in initiating major wars, but also are engaged in slaughtering their own people. One current researcher believes that these regimes may have killed about four times the total number of people killed in all of the major wars of the twentieth century combined.[2] Hitler's Third Reich, Stalin's Soviet Union, Ho Chi Minh's Vietnam, and Pol Pot's Kampuchea are examples. In contrast, democratic nations almost never attack other democratic nations or commit democide against their own people.

If this model of a synergy between an aggressive regime (typically a radical regime that is also engaged in democide or other massive human rights violations against its own people) and a system-wide deterrence failure is the principal model of major international conflict in our time, then the policies most useful in seriously working for peace are quite different from those that flow from the "conventional" legal, arms control, and peace studies models. The most useful policies include overall political engagement strategies (such as the Commission on Security and Cooperation in Europe or CSCE process) to promote more democratic regimes around the world—as a major component of the foreign policy of democratic nations—and a variety of means to strengthen system-wide deterrence against aggressive threats from radical regimes. It is of critical importance that we retain the military power effectively to deter such regimes (the Korean War partly resulted from a deterrence collapse driven by a precipitate U.S. demobilization after World War II). We must also send clear deterrence signals (here see World Wars I and II; the Korean War; the Indochina conflict—French and U.S. phases, particularly the U.S. phase after the Paris accords; the Falklands War; and, most recently and dramatically, the Gulf conflict). Finally, we must strengthen the overall international legal system to sanction aggression severely and, just as importantly, to support defense strongly against aggression.

It is largely the differential between the treatment of aggression and the treatment of defense that measures the effectiveness of the legal system in deterring aggression—*not* the degree to which the use of force is outlawed. If an aggressor knows that a potential victim state or its allies will be condemned as much as the aggressor, if not more, for a defensive response against an aggressive attack, then the real-world legal system that sends that signal is simply irrelevant as a factor in war avoidance; or even worse, it may encourage conflict. This point is so important, and so pervasively misunderstood in much of the legal literature, that I will repeat it with emphasis: *It is largely the differential between the treatment of aggression and the treatment of defense that measures the effectiveness of the legal system in contributing to the deterrence of aggression—not the degree to which the use of force is outlawed.* Moreover, this effect may be magnified when—as the model posits—the nondemocratic aggressor is little affected by internal criticism of "legal violations," but the responding democratic nation, precisely because it is democratic, may be substantially inhibited or deterred by such a charge of illegality.

Low-intensity conflict, it should be noted, seems also to fit the "new thinking" conflict model of an aggressive regime/deterrence failure synergy. In major part, although not exclusively, LIC is simply a range of actions—from sporadic terrorism through sustained insurgency—

pursued by insurgent groups or repressive regimes to attain their aggressive aims. Perhaps the major difference between LIC and conventional warfare is that the ambiguity and low visibility of low-intensity attack escalates the effect in the "conventional" model of ignoring the attack and largely focusing the systemic response against the defensive response to the aggressive attack.

Only when the aggression is as flagrant as the cross-border panzer attack of Iraq against Kuwait in August 1990—the first effort ever made to swallow a member state of the United Nations—does the system clearly condemn the attack and support the defense, and even then the action is opposed by many. Suppose that Iraq had sought the same result through support of an insurgency within Kuwait; would the world community have responded as it did? Would it have responded at all? In this connection it might be noted that one of the "lessons" Libyan leader Mu^cammar Qadhafi seems to have learned from the Gulf conflict is that Iraq should have pursued its objective by an indirect warfare or guerrilla strategy. In a recent address to the Benghazi Military Academy, Qadhafi told the graduates: "Had it [Iraq] sent guerrillas there, they would have occupied the whole region. . . ."[3]

The Role of Law in Aggression and Deterrence: A Case of Autoimmune Disease as Applied to the Spectrum of Low-Intensity Aggression

This chapter should not mistakenly be read as an attack against international law. I believe that, as intended under the United Nations Charter, a system of law that vigorously condemns aggressive attack—whether overt or covert—and mobilizes in important ways (and ways that may be predicted in advance) to support the defensive response against aggression—again, whether overt or covert—is of the utmost importance in promoting a more peaceful world. Indeed, I would assert that we greatly underestimate the important role a revitalized legal system could play. That legal system, however, must get back to basics. Aggression, whether overt or covert, must be clearly condemned. Defense, whether overt or covert, must be clearly supported and assisted. It also must be understood that it is the *differential* between the systemic treatment of aggression and defense that will largely determine whether the legal system will play a significant role in war avoidance.

Sadly, however, there are many reasons to believe that the present international legal system suffers from a severe autoimmune disease under which it treats the defensive response more harshly than the aggressive attack, particularly when confronted with LIC. Typically, international lawyers will respond to U.S. assistance and efforts toward collective defense against low-intensity aggression, such as assistance to the contras or the raid on Libya, by ignoring the aggressive attack that precipitated the U.S. response and by focusing their objections on the U.S. defensive response. By ignoring the long-term pattern of aggressive low- and mid-intensity attack, international lawyers characterize the response as an illegal "reprisal" to a single incident, or they overly narrowly condemn the action as nonproportional, even if, in reality, the action is insufficient to end the continuing low-intensity aggressive attack.

There are ample examples from the legal literature of declarations, statements, and judgments condemning defensive responses to low-intensity attack, with little focus on the precipitating aggression. Recurrent examples of this autoimmune disease occur in the historical record of Vietnam, the Cambodian *Mayaguez* raid, the Libya bombing raid, and Central America.[4] Most recently it was evident in statements of former U.S. Attorney General Ramsey Clark when he promoted the concept of war crimes trials against the United States in relation to clear Iraqi aggression in the Gulf conflict.[5]

In contrast to this typical thinking among many international lawyers, I believe that in the face of an ongoing pattern of low-intensity aggressive attack, it is certainly within the right of individual and collective defense to take necessary and proportional actions to end the attack, whether those actions are overt or covert.[6] This right of defense *is* classic international law, not the fashionable contemporary inversion of this principle. Indeed, if we are serious about peace in our time, it is as incumbent upon the international system as a whole to ensure effective deterrence against the low-intensity spectrum, and, for example, against Libyan terrorism worldwide and a continuing pattern of Iranian-encouraged hostage seizure, as it is to deter the panzer attacks of the Korean War or the Gulf conflict.

Recommendations for Strengthening the International Legal System to Deal More Effectively with Low-Intensity Aggression

Recommendations for strengthening the international legal system to deal with low-intensity aggression follow clearly if we have an accurate model of the most serious international conflicts. Thus, all of the following suggestions should be useful, as opposed to approaches that may make us feel virtuous but in the real world have little effect on promoting peace. These recommendations construct, in many respects, a prescription for promoting peace in our time—insofar as we can—and as such, may be thought of as helpful in promoting a "new world order."

First, though seemingly "weak," one of the most powerful foreign policy initiatives for the democracies is to "engage" totalitarian regimes systematically with the fundamental principles of the rule of law and democratic principles. The recent "rule of law" charter of the Copenhagen round of the CSCE process points the way.[7] This observer, for one, believes that the recent democratic revolution in the Soviet Union probably resulted considerably more from influences stemming from the Helsinki human rights process than from the entire history of U.S.-USSR arms control efforts. Rule of law engagement seeking to influence governments to move toward democratic principles will *not* be an overnight process. In this respect, a shift is already under way in U.S. foreign policy to encompass rule of law engagement, but it should receive even greater emphasis.[8]

Second, the United States, in coordination with other democratic nations, must seek to reinvigorate greatly international condemnation of aggressive attack, whether overt or covert, and simultaneously work to reinvigorate greatly the right of and support for defense against such aggression. These principles, if we make them twin core principles of democratic nations' foreign policy, have considerable ability to add to deterrence against aggression.

Next, in connection with strengthening the international system against aggression and in support of defense against aggression, we must apply these principles clearly to the low- and mid-intensity conflict spectrum. We must redouble efforts to condemn terrorism, hostage-taking, and aggressive indirect warfare and to support the full range of proportional defensive responses, overt and covert, against low-intensity and indirect aggression.

A few illustrative initiatives that might be taken internationally in support of the above goals include the following:

- The United States should consider creating a rule of law caucusing group within the United Nations (UN) system, gathering together nations from all regional groups that are prepared to support the above objectives. This group would serve as a focal point within the UN system to move the system, and the whole world, toward recognizing the importance of the rule of law nationally and internationally.
- The United States should seek to coordinate common democratic nation "white papers" exposing radical regime campaigns of LIC,

including attempted governmental takeovers, hostage seizures, and terrorism directed against civil aviation and other targets.

- The United States should initiate a serious international effort to explore ways to encourage deterrence applied at a personal level to regime elites engaged in international aggression, whether low-intensity or high-intensity. An effort at holding war crimes trials for Saddam Hussein is one example of seeking to apply personal-level deterrence. Deterrence of aggression must include deterrence of regime elites, particularly in radical regime settings. We have for too long focused on deterrence against a nation as an undifferentiated totality. To the extent that the radical regime syndrome is a major component of the problem, however, it may even be that radical regime elites should be the primary focus of democratic nations' deterrence strategies.
- Consistent efforts should be made internationally to foster understanding that the LIC spectrum, like the high-intensity spectrum, requires policies that will ensure effective deterrence. Without strategies of effective deterrence, it can be expected that low-intensity, state-sponsored violence will continue and possibly accelerate. I believe that the generally weak response of democratic nations to such low-intensity attack over the last three decades is a major part of the synergy contributing to the continuation of such attacks.

Finally, there is a series of actions that the United States and all democratic nations must undertake when responding to low-intensity aggression if their actions are to foster broad international understanding. First, *before* any defensive response is undertaken to an ongoing pattern of low-intensity attack, the United States should present evidence of the aggressive attack before the UN Security Council and notify the council that if the aggression continues, the United States will take appropriate action in response under Article 51 of the UN Charter. (Note that, consistent with protecting intelligence sources and methods, notification need not include *all* of the evidence of the attack.) This notification requirement is a legal obligation for a defensive response, and if it is neglected, the U.S. action will be politically harmed. Whether the action to be undertaken in response to aggression is overt or covert, it is not necessary to identify precisely what it will be or when it will take place. The occasion of Security Council notification should be used as a critical opportunity for generating public awareness of the nature of the continuing aggressive attack. If necessary, the evidence should be repeatedly presented before the Security Council.

Next, in cases of defensive response against low-intensity attack, it is particularly important to indicate that the response is in defense against *an ongoing and sustained pattern of attack, not* merely a response to what may have been the latest bombing or other terrorist attack in a series.

Moreover, it is very important that U.S. spokesmen clearly and consistently root responsive defensive actions in Article 51 of the UN Charter. Such an action should *not* be called a reprisal or anything other than a defensive response against ongoing armed aggression.

Finally, defensive actions should be carefully planned to be consistent with the laws of war and should be proportional, while employing adequate levels of force to prevail quickly and deter for the future. Too little force does not deter and simply discredits the defensive response. The Gulf defensive effort generally provides a good example of an appropriate response. Similarly, it is essential that governmental spokesmen fully respond in detail to the usual disinformation efforts suggesting that such responses are nonproportional or illegal. The defensive effort, if it is to prevail effectively, must also win the associated political struggle.

Conclusion

Secret aggression in the low- and mid-intensity conflict spectrum is one of the most serious world order threats of our age. Because of a drumbeat of propaganda concerning political objectives of the attack, coupled with obscure public perceptions of the origins of the attack and a pervasive mirror-imaging of aggression simply as a "dispute" requiring third-party resolution, the international system tends to ignore the aggressive attack while condemning the more visible defensive response. If, however, we are to discourage the low-intensity portion of the aggressive attack spectrum, then, as with overt aggression, it is essential that we understand the need for effective defense and deterrence against such attack. The international legal system can contribute to such deterrence in a substantial manner if, but only if, we make a strong differentiation between the treatment of aggression and defense, whether overt or covert. We must strengthen the international legal system to condemn aggressive attack strongly, whether such an attack is in the form of low-intensity terrorism, or hostage-taking, or armies on the march. Just as importantly, the system must be strengthened strongly to support the defensive response against such aggression, whether such a response is overt or covert.

Notes

1. In J. N. Moore, *The Secret War in Central America* (Frederick, MD: University Publications of America, Inc., 1987), p. 153 n. 2, I pointed out that radical regimes do not in all cases subscribe to a common ideology. Some, such as Cuba, are motivated by Marxism-Leninism; others, such as Iran under the Ayatullah Khomeini, by a religious vision; and still others, such as Libya under Mucammar Qadhafi, by a unique blending of nationalism with a charismatic leader. Despite substantial differences, in large measure they share the symptoms of what I have called the "radical regime syndrome." These symptoms include (1) a single-party political process, usually totalitarian, in which there are no free elections and in which the party is merged with the state in key respects; (2) massive denial of human rights and political freedoms at home, coupled with a pervasive and repressive internal security apparatus, a large number of political prisoners, and frequently even a denial of the right to emigrate; (3) a judicial system that in key respects is subordinate to the party and ruling elites; (4) hostility to collective organization and bargaining by labor; (5) national chauvinism, prejudice against minority religious or national groups, and frequently anti-Semitism; (6) a "cult of personality" surrounding current national leaders; (7) a high degree of militarization of society; (8) pervasive political indoctrination at home through state control of schools, youth and other organizations, and the media; (9) a belief in system expansion through force and a willingness to subsidize and promote terrorism and indirect attack; (10) hostility to pluralist democracy; (11) an effort to establish thoroughgoing state centrist economic management and a disdain for the private sector or private property as part of human freedom; and, (12) a failed economy, with economic development lagging behind that of comparable regional states that have relatively free markets.

2. See R. Rummel, *Lethal Politics: Soviet Genocides and Mass Murders since 1917* (New Brunswick: Transaction Publishers, 1990).

3. Y. Bodansky and V. Forrest, "Libyan Terrorism," Report for Task Force on Terrorism and Unconventional Warfare, House Republican Research Committee, 7 January 1992, p. 5.

4. On Vietnam, see, e.g., R. Falk, "The Cambodian Operation and International Law," in R. Falk, ed., *The Vietnam War and International Law*, vol. 3, *The Widening Context* (Princeton: Princeton University Press, 1972), pp. 33 and 49–50. (Even officially sanctioned terrorist attacks do not "constitute such a violation of rights as to validate a claim of self-defense.") See also E. Firmage, "Law and the Indochina War: A Retrospective View," in R. Falk, ed., *The Vietnam War and International Law*, vol. 4, *The Concluding Phase* (Princeton: Princeton University Press, 1976), pp. 25, 41. On the *Mayaguez* raid, see, e.g., J. Paust, "The Seizure and Recovery of the Mayaguez," *Yale Law Journal* 85 (1976): 774. On the Libya raid, see L. Henkin, "Use of Force: Law and U.S. Policy," in *Right v. Might: International Law and the Use of Force* (New York: Council on Foreign Relations Press, 1989), p. 37. "Extravagant

claims of right to act in self-defense have been the principal threat to the law of the Charter." Ibid., p. 50. Examples given include U.S. actions in Grenada, Libya, and Nicaragua; claims of self-defense in these cases are called "untenable in law." Ibid., p. 56. Also, see T. Yoxall, "Iraq and Article 51: A Correct Use of Limited Authority," *International Lawyer* 25 (1991): 967, 980.

5. See "After the War: Ramsey Clark Plans Inquiry," *New York Times,* 29 March 1991, p. A7.

6. See the authorities collected in Moore, *The Secret War in Central America* and see the dissenting opinion of Judge Schwebel in the *Nicaragua* case, 1986 *Reports of Judgments, Advisory Opinions and Orders* (The Netherlands: The International Court of Justice, 1986), pp. 14, 259, 334, par. 167. See also, for one of the best general treatments of this subject, M. McDougal and F. Feliciano, *Law and Minimum World Public Order* (New Haven: Yale University Press, 1961). Also see R. J. Erickson, *Legitimate Use of Military Force Against State-Sponsored International Terrorism* (Washington, D.C.: Air University Press, July 1989).

7. See U.S. Commission on Security and Cooperation in Europe, "Document of the Copenhagen Meeting of the Conference on the Human Dimension of the CSCE, June 1990" (Washington, D.C.: GPO, 1990).

8. For the breadth of the concept of "rule of law" here, see J. N. Moore, "The Rule of Law: An Overview," paper presented to the Seminar on the Rule of Law, Moscow and Leningrad, USSR, 19–23 March 1990 (USIA translation to Russian for conference proceedings publication, USSR, Progress Press, forthcoming). I presented this paper while serving as cochairman, with the U.S. deputy attorney general, of the U.S. Delegation to the Moscow-Leningrad Seminar on the Rule of Law.

The "rule of law" as intended here explicitly does not mean observing the legal niceties on the way to the gulag. Rather, the fundamentals of the rule of law are:

- government of the people, by the people, and for the people;
- separation of powers and checks and balances;
- representative democracy and procedural and substantive limits on governmental action against the individual (the protection of human freedom and dignity);
- limited government and federalism; and
- review by an independent judiciary as a central mechanism for constitutional enforcement.

For an example of rule of law engagement incorporated into contemporary U.S. foreign policy, see the president's August 1991 *National Security Strategy* report (The White House, Washington, D.C.: GPO, 1991, art. 14, col. 1), which states the following:

Recent history has shown how much ideas count. The Cold War was, in its decisive aspect, a war of ideas. But ideas count only when knowledge spreads. In today's evolving political environment, and in the face of the global explosion of information, we must make clear to our friends and potential adversaries what we stand for.

The need for international understanding among different peoples, cultures, religions, and forms of government will only grow. In a world without the clear-cut East-West divisions of the past, the flow of ideas and information will take on larger significance as once-isolated countries seek their way toward the international mainstream. Indeed, information access has already achieved global proportions. A truly global community is being formed, vindicating our democratic values.

Through broadcasts, academic and cultural exchanges, press briefings, publications, speakers and conferences, we engage those abroad in a dialogue about who and what we are—to inform foreign audiences about our policies, democratic traditions, pluralistic society and rich academic and cultural diversity. We will increase our efforts to clarify what America has to contribute to the solution of global problems—and to drive home democracy's place in this process.

14

Implications of Low-Intensity Conflict for United States Policy and Strategy

William J. Crowe

The foregoing chapters have examined low-intensity conflict (LIC) from a number of perspectives, leaving us with what I would consider a comprehensive treatment of the problems and challenges. The editors have asked that I take a broader look at the subject from the viewpoint of a U.S. policymaker.

I believe a few general observations are in order:

- There seems to be considerable handwringing in the politico-military community about the lack of an agreed definition of LIC. I hope that this series of commentaries puts this debate at rest. I come away with the distinct impression that this deficiency is much overdone. In a sense, it is like the term "civilian control of the military." For more than two hundred years this principle has guided our security structure and has yet to be defined specifically. We are, nevertheless, very much wedded to and governed by the concept.
- LIC has entered our strategic vocabulary only recently and to some suggests that something unique has been added. The fact is, however, that we have been grappling with these types of problems throughout the postwar era, as this book amply illustrates. We have considerable experience to draw on in addressing LIC's many facets, and we should take full advantage of this history.
- Like so many situations in today's complex world it is easier to describe the problems presented than to prescribe (or implement) effective solutions. Although our intellectual grasp of the subject is steadily improving, we have yet to solve the riddle of effectively organizing our republic to wage LIC.

In the foregoing chapters, three themes recur. First, the strategic climate we have lived in during the postwar decades is changing dramatically. Second, the shape of the emerging politico-military profile is in flux, will often involve LIC in one or more of its many forms, and will require thoughtful and multifaceted approaches by those governments directly affected, primarily Third World countries. Third, the United States will likewise have to reconfigure its thinking and machinery if it is to protect its interests successfully and assist friends in their search for stability. Now let me attempt to distill what our commentators say about these three challenges.

Throughout Part One there is strong agreement that the demise of the Soviet Union is transforming the globe from a bipolar to a multipolar environment. The threat of major nuclear war that loomed over every confrontation for so many years has now receded and promises to continue its retreat. Similarly, the people of the defunct USSR are consumed by internal concerns and have essentially stepped back from the world stage. These developments have unleashed a host of political and economic forces previously held in check by the superpower competition.

In other words, as one challenge has faded, others are emerging that will pose serious threats and in some respects will be more difficult to counter. The conventional wisdom of the past has lost much of its applicability. There is a consensus among our writers that the problems of population growth, ethnic and religious differences, the environment, the inequities between "have" and "have not" nations, the drug plague, and so on will pose increasingly serious stability challenges to the free world.

In a multipolar world, power (economic, religious, nationalism, ideological) is diffused and interdependence mushrooms. In the cold war the main contest centered on military strength—the ability of one player to influence the other through force or to deter the opponent from using physical means. In the new strategic climate the parameters of conflict will gradually alter as dissident movements (previously restrained) gather momentum but strive to avoid direct conflict and search for indirect methods to shape, manipulate, or influence events. The very fact that the stakes of confrontation are decreasing will make it more difficult for large powers to decide when and where to resist and, in turn, encourage those who are dedicated to change. Manwaring concludes that a multipolar world "could conceivably be a more volatile and dangerous one" than the clearly defined, bipolar world we have come to know so well. Moreover, these tendencies are reinforced by the growing interdependence that will characterize the new order.

Although there is, of course, room for further thinking and education on the subject, I believe there is little quarrel among outside strategists (as we see in this book) and within the policy councils of the government about the fundamental impact of the changes that are taking place.

Recognizing a strategic shift in the international community is only a first step, however. We must then analyze the nature of the anticipated individual struggles for control and legitimacy that threaten stability within an individual country or region. This analysis is a much more complex exercise.

Again, however, there is remarkable agreement that the emphasis will shift more toward social, political, and psychological factors than military. This does not mean violence will be discarded, but that it will be complementary rather than controlling. These groups— extreme nationalists, irredentists, and demagogues who lack sophisticated weaponry—must resort "to a more indirect conflict—one form or another of insurgency war." Inevitably, these pressures greatly broaden such contests into the realm of governance, economic security, ethnic complaints, and religious and ideological differences. The first aim is to create and nourish instability, thereby bringing the legitimacy of the ruling group into question. Violence will only be useful if it can contribute to that goal.

It is this conclusion that leads Manwaring to stress first and foremost the need for a government to establish its legitimacy. As he points out, corruption and incompetent governmental leadership have brought more than half the countries of the world to the point of economic and political collapse. "The gravity of the problem is hard to exaggerate." In turn, he proposes what he calls a people-oriented model to explain how LIC crises must be confronted if the opposition groups are to be defeated. He argues persuasively that countering efforts must include an organized mixture of political, economic, and public affairs programs—all of which will enhance a government's claim to power.

I personally witnessed the U.S. failure in Vietnam to establish a foundation of legitimacy and subscribe strongly to this imperative. The challenge is to move away from cold war concepts and toward a strategy designed to wage "social conflict," the focus of which is legitimacy. Legitimacy, of course, is not necessarily related to democracy as we know it or some rigid dogmatic formula. It can take many forms; it may be different in various societies. Determining what is legitimate in varying contexts will be a high-order challenge requiring a sensitive feel for the culture and accompanying circumstances. The fact is, however, a campaign that does not play to the "legitimate aspirations of people" as they see those aspirations is doomed to failure, no matter how strong the government is militarily. This is the prime lesson for threatened regions and elites in the coming decades.

Building on this principle, Manwaring constructs a basic architecture for dissecting and overcoming LIC crises. He isolates what he considers the relevant variables in controlling any conflict situation. Key to the whole sequence is the acknowledgment that to be successful the management of violence is only one element of a larger whole. In his construct success depends on:

- the degree of legitimacy,
- the organization for unity of effort,
- military and other support to a targeted government,
- the level of competence and discipline of a political actor's security forces,
- the effectiveness of intelligence, and
- the ability to reduce outside support to an illegal operation.

He considers these factors an interlocking set of actions within the overall effort. They should be pursued simultaneously and in some balanced fashion. None can be ignored, although the emphasis on each element may vary with the context.

Clearly one could argue with their completeness, wording, or nuances, but I find the paradigm both helpful and adequate. It takes into account the major dimensions of the total situation that must, in some fashion, be addressed. Though one could introduce other considerations, if a beleaguered government could meet these requirements the prospects of ultimate success will be good.

The paradigm says nothing about a government's ability to tailor its organization to these demands or to carry out the various tasks. It is only an intellectual or conceptual underpinning. The tough part is carrying out the strategy while under pressure from the insurgents.

In other words, the skill a regime exhibits in recruiting support, changing public attitudes, stamping out corruption, reorienting its bureaucracy, setting priorities, and mustering its resources is crucial. Translating strategy into action, dedication, statesmanship, and leadership will make the difference between victory and defeat.

This, of course, leads me to the third subject—what are the implications of these developments for Washington? Undoubtedly the U.S. government will on occasion be involved in LIC—as a friend, as an adviser, as a banker, as a participant. What are the barriers to an effective response, and can they be overcome? The Corr-Miller and the Grant chapters in particular address these questions, which in my view constitute the most perplexing aspect of LIC. As the case studies in this book illustrate, the intellectual analysis of regimes under pressures from dissident movements, insurgencies, and terrorist activity is quite advanced. The U.S. government's track record in dealing with such real-world crises is rather dismal, however; and if our country is going to participate effectively in the new international milieu, we will have to alter our ways.

For me the most important observation in the book was made early in Dr.Grant's chapter. "The genius of generalship is not merely knowing the principles of strategy, but also understanding how to apply them." This comment is never truer than in waging LIC, as the foregoing case studies make painfully clear.

Despite Washington's preoccupation with high- and mid-level conflict for the past forty years, the fact remains that the bulk of the wars waged were low-intensity fights (insurgencies, revolutions, terrorism, etc.). Either directly or indirectly the United States participated in many of these contingency operations. We have had considerable experience with LIC operations that we should draw on as we move away from the cold war.

This caution is particularly apt right now with Operation Desert Storm so fresh in our memory. The writers are unanimous in their advice not to be mesmerized with the recent war in Iraq as the premier model for future threats. We should study that conflict with care. It may offer useful lessons under certain conditions, but it bears little relationship to the LIC threats this book foresees and addresses.

I turn now to the specific challenges for the U.S. government. We are already seeing superficial signs that the bureaucracy is turning its attention now to LIC. Unfortunately there are built-in barriers to such a transformation. They are discussed at length throughout the book. Grant sums up his frustration when he opines, "Low-intensity conflicts are low priority and are likely to stay that way." I am not sure I agree altogether, but certainly it will take some fundamental changes in attitudes and bureaucratic organization (on both civilian and military sides of the house) before Washington can participate in the LIC arena with confidence.

Policy

Conventional wisdom argues that as the superpower contest recedes Washington will have more latitude for selecting the regions where it will concentrate and the LIC crises with which it will deal. Nonetheless, I saw very little discussion of criteria for determining when and where important U.S. interests are at stake. The very nature of LIC keeps the overall stakes low, camouflages the emergence of problems, and gives politicians lots of reasons to procrastinate before taking action. This problem is serious in the world of major conflict, but it is amplified many times in LIC situations, which are ill defined and represent only modest threats to countries outside of the local area. In fact the danger to U.S. vital interests may come from an accumulation of crises rather than from a single contest, and by the time this peril becomes apparent, the opportune time to react may have passed. Undoubtedly, this is both a serious and, in a sense, a new challenge that further muddies the distinction between peace and war.

It is probably premature to grapple definitively with the problem of determining exactly when and where U.S. interests are involved. Until some of the other more basic obstacles are overcome, expending too much energy on it may distract from more immediate tasks. Once the decision makers and the public are more sensitized to the character of the LIC challenge and more basic organizational adjustments are put in place, the government's ability to respond mechanically should improve. With this step, the task of addressing priorities should be an easier one. If our whole society is disrupted every time we decide to intervene or assist a Third World friend, then prioritizing LIC efforts will be impossible.

The responsibility for determining when our actual interests are at stake has always been with us. Now that the threat of major war is reduced and, in turn, concern for our survival attenuated, however, I would hope that these decisions would move away from the ideological pole more toward very practical concerns. Does an outbreak of LIC jeopardize U.S. economic interests (raw materials, markets, transportation modes and/or trade routes)? Will a change of government in a particular area limit U.S. ability to project military and/or diplomatic influence? Are traditional political commitments at stake that would reflect on the U.S. image or constancy?

If the predictions in this book about the future security environment are correct, Washington cannot interfere in every LIC crisis, nor should it want to. It will be imperative for the decision makers to develop some tough criteria for determining when the stakes are sufficient to justify U.S. involvement. It will not be easy or simple.

Bureaucracy

From a governmental perspective the preeminent lesson of this book is that the United States is "politically, bureaucratically, and culturally unequipped" for waging LIC. Given U.S. attitudes toward the conduct of war and given the traditional structure of the U.S. bureaucracy, in particular the military establishment, these are not simple barriers to overcome.

There is little quarrel among the commentators that LIC operations put especially heavy demands on the United States. Several chapters address in detail the reasons that our culture and institutions are poorly suited to wage LIC. As a people, Americans distrust secrecy, are intolerant of political ambiguity, have little patience for drawn-out efforts, and prefer commitments where the stakes are high and which lend themselves to technical solutions.

Because dealing successfully with LIC situations requires more than physical strength, our institutions find themselves quickly at a disadvantage. U.S. officialdom has historically treated peace and war as distinct and separate challenges and is simply not structured to cope with situations where social, political, and military considerations interact simultaneously. From the outset the U.S. system violates Manwaring's requirement for unity in managing the effort. To be successful in waging LIC, practically every department of the government will have to play a part. Ideally their efforts would be tightly interwoven or fused.

This applies equally to the military establishment, which traditionally has been so heavily weighted toward high- and mid-level conflict. The standard response has been that LIC capabilities are a lesser but included case inside of the "big war" structure. This conclusion overlooks the unique character of LIC and misleads policymakers. Although the military has made some significant steps to correct this bias, it has far to go, as General Galvin's chapter points out repeatedly. A "soft war" needs doctrine, tactics, training, and technology specifically tailored to its demands. On occasion, LIC has made a bid for increased priority in the Defense Department but never with sustained success.

In essence, turf considerations run deep in the U.S. bureaucracy; these instincts are reinforced by political interests and groupings identified with the various organizations. It is not merely a matter of rearranging organizational lines; there are heavy political costs associated with rearranging traditional authority—particularly for a president. As Corr and Miller point out, even the National Security Council has failed in forcing such a reorganization.

The main failure is not policy formulation, but the everyday "coordination of personnel and resources from an array of often competing agencies that frequently have predetermined agendas." I can speak from personal knowledge as to the serious difficulty of managing such challenges. A graphic example is the current effort to stop the flow of drugs into the country, which is plagued by interagency warfare. Believe me, reorienting civilian and military thinking—and ultimately decision-making structure—to ensure LIC receives a proper priority will be no mean achievement.

Grant points out that in addressing this problem we are victims of our country's size, history, and success—all of which divert our attention to problems other than LIC. He concludes that we must therefore be modest in estimating the chances for success in overcoming this challenge. In fact all the commentators exhibit a strong streak of pessimism in looking to the future.

I find these conclusions penetrating and persuasive, and they are well documented by our experiences with the Third World—Vietnam, the Philippines, El Salvador, Peru, Thailand, and the Middle East. What I find missing and what I believe to be more important are solutions and recommendations. Therefore, let me briefly address the future of LIC in U.S. strategy.[1]

The Future of LIC

Historically, the fortunes of LIC in U.S. strategy and national policy travel along a predictable cycle. First, small wars are recognized as significant, in spite of the intensity of violence or the amount of threat they directly pose to U.S. interests. Next, some strategists come to understand that most forms of LIC demand a qualitatively different approach to fighting. An uphill battle ensues, with the small war advocates struggling to make appropriate changes in doctrine and organization. Some progress occurs, but it is usually partial and temporary. The conventional mind set of the U.S. military then reasserts itself, and LIC returns to the wings of strategic thinking, waiting for a new crisis to invite it briefly to center stage again. This happened in the sixties with the Kennedy administration's abortive attempts to make the military rethink its approach to counterinsurgency. It occurred again in the early eighties with the rush of interest in LIC following the Iranian hostage crisis, the rise of international terrorism, the fall of Somoza and the shah, the small but significant wars in Angola and the Horn of Africa, and the belief within the Reagan administration that key battles in the cold war would be fought in the developing world.

The early nineties are seeing another resurgence of concern about little wars: the cold war may be over, but as Desert Storm demonstrated, the world is still a dangerous place. Academics and government officials alike are realizing that whatever the new world order becomes, organized violence within or between societies will be part of it; and LIC will remain the norm.

What will prevent this new cycle in thinking about LIC from becoming yet another fad that leaves the United States no better prepared for fighting small wars? The answer lies in using this time of flux to institutionalize some important aspects of LIC strategy.

I am not as pessimistic as some of our writers about the prospects for change. Of course, it will not occur smoothly or as quickly as LIC advocates would prefer. Each writer has highlighted the necessity for State and Defense to work together. The fact is these two organizations have had considerable experience with each other. If the policymakers raise the priority of LIC and sustain their interest (and that is an especially big if) State and Defense can and will overcome the organizational challenge. Arms control is a graphic example of the two departments doing exactly that. On the other hand, extending the net to bring in other involved departments (particularly submitting to one authority) multiplies the problem many times. That objective cannot be achieved easily—as the antidrug campaign has illustrated.

One encouraging note is that a full-fledged LIC effort should not be prohibitively expensive. General Paul Gorman in his Report by the Regional Conflict Working Group submitted to the Commission on Integrated Long-Term Strategy in 1988 estimated that an adequate LIC capability would entail outlays by departments and agencies of about $12 billion per year, which at that time was about 4 percent of the Department of Defense budget. This includes economic security assistance and civilian activities plus military forces and hardware. Most estimates fall in that general neighborhood. Given the prospective returns, this is hardly a significant expense.

In the end, the keystone will be a matter of high-level attention and determination. LIC must be assigned a high priority at the top, and the policy must not be merely proclaimed but followed up constantly. As Corr and Miller stress, "only at the White House do all the required players effectively come together." With time that could very well occur.

Bear in mind, we are entering a different global climate. This is the first time the U.S. government will seriously address the LIC threat without the specter of the USSR in the background; all the constituencies who concerned themselves with the possibility of a Soviet war are floundering and reaching for new interests. My own experience in the military has been that real change takes place when the competition wanes. Good people move to the "sound of the guns"; and when good people attach themselves to the new thinking, respectability ultimately follows.

Doctrine

The services finally must shed the belief that the techniques of conventional, mid- to high-intensity war are applicable to all forms of low-intensity conflict. Revolutionary political violence in the forms of guerrilla warfare and terrorism follows different rules, both in the definition of victory in and the choice of means.[2] Thinking in the military, as reflected in manuals, training, and the work of military colleges and academies, must reflect this.

The Army War College, the National War College, the Air Force University, and many other high-level teaching institutions within the military have made great progress toward this end. The curriculum at the Army War College, for example, now includes a substantial and substantive curriculum in revolutionary political violence and low-intensity conflict. This new recognition of LIC must diffuse down the ranks, eventually becoming a part of fundamental training at lower levels of the military. The presence of Jack Galvin's article in this collection is a positive sign. The flurry in the government heralding "peacetime engagement" is likewise an encouraging signal, no matter what criticisms may be leveled at the substance of the term.

Here, the services must make a critical and painful choice. The classic dilemma for militaries girding themselves for small wars surrounds the question of resources. Which is the better investment in human and material capital, adding special training in small war doctrine for everyone or creating special units for small wars? At a time of shrinking budgets, this dilemma is even more acute. Can the U.S. military afford to add to the training of what remains of the general purpose military? Or should it preserve and perhaps expand the cadre of special units (i.e., the Special Operations Forces or SOFs) best equipped for LIC?[3] Personnel costs consume the largest part of the Pentagon's budget, so the latter policy may be very difficult for the military to embrace. Nevertheless, I incline toward the latter as being the most effective alternative. The special operations community is also a bureaucratic midget compared to the regular services; its position should not be further weakened in the present budgetary struggles. Frankly, Congress may play a constructive role here.

The worst mistake the services could commit, however, is to dedicate the Special Operations Forces solely to direct action missions and declare that the SOFs are the new LIC force. Direct action missions include only a small part of the universe of LIC tasks, and direct action training does not transfer to these other missions. Deep reconnaissance experience does not help a special forces adviser teach foreign soldiers how to defeat guerrillas. An increasing emphasis on direct action would also put too much emphasis on the military components of LIC, when in fact low-intensity wars involve far more than simple military considerations. Galvin's comments strongly reinforce this thought.

LIC will remain an interagency problem, requiring more than simple coordination among the SOFs, or between the SOFs and the regular services. An emphasis on direct action would even further separate those who work on LIC in the military and the rest of the government because LIC will increasingly be defined incorrectly as a purely military concern.

Beyond the expensive solutions, however, there is a small and relatively cheap alteration the military can make: expand the basic manual for low-intensity conflict, FM 100–20. This document provides the barest sense of the strategic, operational, and tactical differences between conventional warfare and LIC. True, its present incarnation is a significant improvement over its predecessor, which included many marginally useful sections such as the proper layout of a truck convoy. The new manual included a better discussion of what makes LIC distinctive, but more needs to be said on the subject. If officers must learn a new kind of warfare to cope with the modern face of conflict, then a more thorough treatment of LIC should be available.

One further thought regarding force employments is that well-trained special forces personnel give the national authorities exceptional capabilities in the areas of counterinsurgency, terrorism, and unconventional combat. It would be a mistake, however, to assume that these individuals are the only ones the government can call on in carrying out the tasks included under the rubric of LIC. There may be tasks that can be handled very well by conventional units, such as gunboat diplomacy, peacekeeping, shows of force, and so forth. The choice would be at the option of the national authorities. I believe Galvin was saying something like this when he stressed "balance" in the armed forces. Some would argue that this policy weakens the call of LIC forces or the budget and their bureaucratic clout. In my view this consideration gets lost in the background noise. If LIC has proper support bureaucratically, it will not matter that conventional forces are called on occasionally. If that backing is missing, it will not matter one way or another. All of our military capability should be considered available, if it can contribute meaningfully to the LIC tasks at hand.

****

Clearly the contributors to this book are persuaded that LIC will be an increasingly important challenge for the U.S. government. At the same time they are rather pessimistic about the ability of the bureaucracy to accommodate the special demands of LIC. Too many times in our history such changes have been brought about not by foresight or prudence, but in response to suddenly emerging crises for which we have been ill prepared and which exacted a high cost in terms of treasure and lives. The thought processes and case studies explored in this book should assist our nation in developing a considered and forehanded response to the challenge of limited intensity conflict.

Notes

1. I am indebted to Tom Grant for much of the following on the future of LIC in U.S. strategy.

2. For an explanation of the operational differences between conventional and revolutionary warfare, see John Shy and Thomas W. Collier, "Revolutionary Warfare," in David Galula, *Counterinsurgency Warfare* (New York: Frederick A. Praeger, 1964) and scores of other treatises on the subject.

3. Douglas Blaufarb, *The Counterinsurgency Era* (New York: The Free Press, 1977), p. 158.

15

Final Reflections

Stephen Sloan

The contributors to this book have addressed the intellectual, operational, bureaucratic and legal aspects that have determined U.S. policies toward low-intensity conflict (LIC) over the last three decades. They have applied the insightful Manwaring paradigm as a framework for comparative analysis of trenchant case studies that are grounded in research, experience, and involvement in national security decision making. The paradigm proves to have value for both analytical and operational purposes. The studies provide a foundation for formulating new policies and bureaucratic structures to meet the challenges of LIC in a period of international instability and change. This chapter offers a few final reflections on selective critical elements of LIC that the political leadership, policymakers, and ultimately the U.S. public should consider in defending and promoting our national security interests.

First, those who formulate and conduct foreign policy must develop the vision necessary to move beyond their preoccupation with current bureaucratic competition and with the crisis of the day. Those who work inside the Beltway are constantly "putting out fires," but they must look beyond the immediate danger. They must develop broader insights, policies, and strategies to meet the complex long-term demands that LIC poses for the United States and its allies. The formulators and implementors of U.S. foreign policy can use the following insights and others presented by the contributors as a basis to deal effectively with chronic and long-term instability that cannot readily be addressed by short-term fixes and even the most sophisticated forms of crisis management.

At the outset, it is vital to recognize that low-intensity conflicts often develop slowly, are protracted, and may not be readily identifiable in their early phases. Therefore, policymakers must develop the capability to identify and take appropriate actions in the critical period before underlying causes of conflict are transformed through neglect or miscalculation into different forms of political violence and armed conflict that may require large-scale responses by Washington. As the contributors note, in all too many instances when a military action is considered or taken in a country or region facing a LIC the endangered government or social order has already died of dry rot.

Policymakers will not be able to make such long-term assessments or to identify key indicators and warnings before a LIC environment becomes critical unless they are advised and assisted by those within the intelligence and academic communities who have regional and functional expertise and can identify long-term trends in conflict. Analysts and scholars must refine their abilities to look beyond the massive flow of information on current affairs and identify longer term developments that can act as a triggering mechanism; they can thus make policymakers aware of potential LIC environments before such areas became critical to U.S. security.

In the past the preoccupation with the short-range assessment was further intensified by the intelligence community's fascination with and reliance on highly sophisticated technical means of data collection, which provided short-term tactical information but did not satisfactorily substitute for people with the background required for assessing the potential, slow emergence of low-intensity conflict in their area of expertise. This issue of focus fortunately is now being addressed in the profound discussions on the future responsibilities of the intelligence community. The need for more training and use of area and country specialists is now recognized, as is the need to have competent human intelligence (HUMINT) sources in the field.

Policymakers must be capable of formulating and implementing new courses of action to identify the gradual emergence of social movements, the underlying causes of instability and the other, often hidden factors that could lead to the erosion of legitimacy in a particular country or region. They must have the information and dedication to act before the damage is done and cannot be resolved except by sending in the troops.

Even if information is available on an impending LIC, appropriate policy alternatives will not be generated—much less implemented— unless we recognize that low-intensity conflicts, particularly in the early phases, are primarily political and diplomatic and that such factors will probably determine the outcome of the conflict. Recognition of the primacy of politics requires very close interaction between the State Department, the Department of Defense, and other agencies in suggesting appropriate courses of action that may be necessary from the initial phases to the full maturation of LIC. Therefore, the bureaucratic and legal restraints that make it difficult for the State Department to take the lead and act except in situations of peaceful competition and for the Defense Department only to act when there is a perceived or real threat of armed conflict must be overcome. Just as a government facing a low-intensity threat requires unity of action to meet the challenge, so must those who are fighting the bureaucratic battles in Washington break down the arbitrary dichotomy of war and peace and work together when appropriate in supporting in-country programs and operations. This need for unity of action in Washington may run against the respective bureaucratic culture of State and Defense and be complicated by the struggle for funding from an ever-decreasing financial pie, but the current disunity must give way to a unity of outlook and action in Washington and where the conflict is either emerging or taking place. Such unity will only be realized if there is a mutual recognition that low-intensity conflict is indeed an environment in which an arbitrary division between war and peace loses its meaning.

Third, because of the primacy of politics—especially in the earlier phases of a low-intensity conflict—unity of action must be further enhanced by the promotion and employment of a wide variety of nonmilitary instruments in support of U.S. policy objectives. The temptation to confuse quick strike and withdrawal operations and invasions with low-intensity operations must be avoided. Such tactics have their place but must be complemented by a wide variety of assistance programs and psychological operations that are far more useful in pursuing alternative policies in political orders that will be subject to heightened levels of instability. Because low-intensity conflicts are often long and in the formative stages not readily identifiable as a potential threat to either an affected government or a region, it is particularly difficult for policymakers to ascertain whether such threats have serious implications for U.S. national security unless appropriate actions are taken. Those responsible for meeting the demands of LIC must therefore recognize that they may have to deal with popular and attendant bureaucratic indifference based on the view that low-intensity conflicts are often a "remote" form of conflict, peripheral to the immediate national security concerns and therefore not amenable to what are essentially reactive forms of crisis management.

It is therefore vital that policymakers succinctly provide to the public the reasons why a particular LIC may be significant to national security. The rationale should be stated in terms as nonpartisan as possible. Ideological rhetoric should be avoided because such rhetoric often leads to fractious debates within Congress, and between Congress and the president, that generate more heat than light. A substantive, informed discussion of how a seemingly distant low-intensity conflict can create serious domestic and foreign problems may lead to consensus building instead of the partisan strife that has surrounded previous U.S. involvement in LIC.

In the final analysis the formulation and implementation of U.S. policies on LIC rest in the hands of the president. Despite competition between Congress and the executive and the attempted restraints on the preeminent presidential role, as perhaps best illustrated by the War Powers Act, the formulation and conduct of foreign policy are still the domain of the executive. Especially in international affairs, as President Harry Truman succinctly noted, "The buck stops here." Nonetheless, the ability of the president to dominate foreign affairs, to set the national security agenda, and to implement it may be increasingly tested because of the crucial role of low-intensity conflict in the coming decades.

As noted throughout this book, it will be difficult for the president to convince an ever-restive Congress and the public that political instability or outbreaks of various low-intensity conflicts in the form of ethnic conflict, separatist movements, and other types of particularly "dirty wars" may represent meaningful threats to U.S. national security. The president will be hard-pressed to justify either unilateral or multinational involvement in different forms of violence—however bloody—that seem distant to U.S. national security. Even if such violence moves beyond the formative stage and is so intensified that it threatens the integrity of a country or the stability of a region, the end of the Soviet-U.S. proxy warfare in the Third World, the reality of a shrinking defense budget, and the concern over domestic issues can fuel an invidious form of neo-isolationism. It will therefore be incumbent on political leaders to have the vision and courage to identify countries and regions that may be experiencing different degrees of LIC and to set guidelines on when the United States should become involved, based on potential or actual threats to national security.

It will be imperative that the president draw on both the national security bureaucracy and academia to identify and prioritize those types of LIC that may be significant in the conduct of foreign policy. The identification of potential LIC threats should not be based solely on the more obvious security military and economic dangers that a conflict may pose. Issues such as human rights that reflect basic U.S. values and strike a resonant chord in the public may be just as significant as the determination that a potential enemy may seek a base of operations through LIC against strategic choke points in U.S. trade and commerce.

By clearly outlining an agenda that goes beyond the immediate crisis of the day, the president can also encourage Congress to take a longer view. Having the vision to establish a new framework that addresses U.S. responsibilities and security concerns beyond the rhetoric of the cold war is a great challenge but provides equally great opportunities to present and future political leaders in the conduct of U.S. foreign policy. The challenges created by LIC are an excellent litmus test of Washington's ability to take the initiative in a transforming international order.

Ultimately, however, foreign policy will have to elicit broad public support. The protracted nature of LIC, the fact that it often involves unconventional conflicts that do not fit the U.S. ideal of waging war, the requirements for direct and indirect support—both overt and covert—all may act as impediments to such support. Nonetheless, such support should be forthcoming if an informed public recognizes the challenges to U.S. national security manifested by the demands of LIC and realizes that timely and appropriate action taken at the inception of such conflicts may be far more cost-effective than the U.S. heavy military involvement often used in the final phases. The public is more likely to be willing to engage in preventive diplomacy than to run the risk of bearing the immense costs accompanying even the "smallest" conventional war—which to the participants is never small.

Conclusion

The contributors to this book have fought in the bureaucratic, policy, legal and academic trenches of low-intensity conflict. The authors wanted to share with the readers the lessons they are still learning as our country's security situation undergoes reassessment in a new international order.

The contributors hope that their chapters will assist those who make and carry out national security to meet the challenges of low-intensity conflict. The book is not intended solely to be read, discussed, and then returned to the library after a seminar. Rather, the goal of the editors is to provide a mode of analysis and a range of substantive material that can assist those on both sides of the Beltway to develop a global vision and an agenda to guide us through fundamental political changes in the days ahead.

About the Book

The end of the cold war does not necessarily mean the end of the social and political instability that can lead to low-intensity conflicts. This book provides fresh insights into a difficult subject by bringing together knowledgeable contributors who have the academic expertise, operational experience, and strategic perspective essential to understanding this complex and challenging type of warfare.

Ambassador Edwin G. Corr holds the visiting Henry Bellmon Chair in Public Service at the University of Oklahoma. He was a career foreign service officer with assignments as ambassador to El Salvador, Bolivia, and Peru. **Stephen Sloan** is professor of political science at the University of Oklahoma and is the author of several books on terrorism.

About the Editors and Contributors

Sean K. Anderson is a Ph.D. candidate in the University of Oklahoma Political Science Department. He worked as chief editor of the International Department of the Pars News Agency in Tehran, Iran, from 1980 until 1982. He is fluent in modern Persian and speaks modern standard Arabic. Anderson has several publications, among which is an article, "Iranian State Sponsorship of Terrorism" in the Fall 1991 issue of *Conflict Quarterly*.

James Cheek is U.S. ambassador to the Republic of Sudan. He has been a career foreign service officer since 1961 and had assignments in Chile, Brazil, Ethiopia, Nepal, Uruguay, and Nicaragua. Cheek received his B.A. from Arkansas State Teachers College and holds a Master of International Service from American University in Washington, D.C. He taught in the Department of Political Science at Howard University and served as an associate of the Center for International Affairs at Harvard University and of the Fletcher School of Law and Diplomacy at Tufts University.

Edwin G. Corr is visiting Henry Bellmon Chair at the University of Oklahoma. He was a career foreign service officer with assignments as ambassador to El Salvador, ambassador to Bolivia, ambassador to Peru, and deputy assistant secretary of state for international narcotics matters. He served also in Thailand, Mexico, and Ecuador, as a Peace Corps Director in Colombia, and as an infantry officer in the U.S. Marine Corps. Corr received his B.S. and M.A. at the University of Oklahoma and spent a year at the Institute for Latin American Studies at the University of Texas. He has written articles and a book, *The Political Process in Colombia*.

William J. Crowe was appointed the eleventh chairman of the Joint Chiefs of Staff in 1985 and was reappointed to a second two-year term in 1987. He is now university professor of geopolitics at the University of Oklahoma. He is also councillor at the Center for Strategic and International Studies in Washington, D.C. Crowe graduated from the United States Naval Academy in 1946. He holds an M.A. in education from Stanford University and a Ph.D. in politics from Princeton. Some of Admiral Crowe's most important assignments included commander, Middle East Force; senior U.S. military adviser to the United Nations; and commander in chief, Allied Forces Southern Europe.

John R. Galvin is the supreme allied commander, Europe, and former commander in chief, United States Southern Command in Panama. He received his B.S. degree from the U.S. Military Academy, M.A. from Columbia University, and he is a graduate of the U.S. Army War College. Galvin has served in a variety of command and staff positions and as an instructor at the Colombian Military Academy and the *Escuela de Lanceros*. General Galvin has published articles and books including *The Minuteman, Three Men of Boston*, and *Air Assault*.

Thomas A. Grant is postdoctoral researcher and part-time administrator at the Center for Global Peace and Conflict Studies (GPACS), a part of the Institute for Global Conflict and Cooperation (IGCC) at the University of California, Irvine. His research interests include low-intensity conflict, strategic theory, the bureaucratic and political character of militaries, wars in the developing world, and international relations theory. Grant earned his Ph.D. at the University of California, Irvine. He is currently working on several articles on recent small wars and a book on the history of U.S. counterinsurgency efforts.

David C. Isby, a Washington-based attorney and consultant on national security issues, has been a legislative assistant in the U.S. House of Representatives. He has made frequent visits to South Asia during the war in Afghanistan and was in the field with the Afghan resistance. A member of the International Institute of Strategic Studies, Isby received his J.D. from New York University and his B.A. degree in history from Columbia University. His writings dealing with Afghanistan include *Weapons and Tactics of the Soviet Army, War in a Distant Country, Afghanistan: Invasion and Resistance,* and *Russia's War in Afghanistan*.

Max G. Manwaring is an associate with Booz-Allen & Hamilton, Inc. He received his Ph.D. from the University of Illinois at Urbana-Champaign and was a Fulbright fellow in Brazil. He has served in various academic and military positions, including the Army War College, the Defense Intelligence Agency, and the United States Southern Command's Small Wars Operations Research Directorate. Manwaring is the author of several articles dealing with low-intensity conflict and Latin America. He is also senior editor of *El Salvador At War: An Oral History* and editor of *Uncomfortable Wars: Toward A Paradigm of Low Intensity Conflict*.

David C. Miller, Jr., is senior vice president of The Investigative Group, Inc., and executive vice president of the American European Special Opportunities Fund, both in Washington, D.C. He was special assistant to the president for national security affairs with responsibilities for international counternarcotics strategy, counter-terrorism, low-intensity conflict, and African affairs from January 1989 to December 1990. Miller served as the U.S. ambassador to Tanzania from 1981 to 1984 and to Zimbabwe from 1984 to 1986. He graduated from Harvard University with honors and received his J.D. from Michigan Law School.

John Norton Moore is the Walter L. Brown Professor of Law and director of the Center for National Security Law at the University of Virginia Law School. He formerly served as the counselor on international law to the U.S. Department of State with the rank of ambassador. He has had five presidential appointments, including chairman of the board of the U.S. Institute for Peace, member of the U.S. delegation to the United Nations General Assembly, and consultant to the president's Intelligence Oversight Board. Among his publications are *The Secret War in Central America* and *Law and the Indo-China War*. Moore earned an A.B. in economics from Drew University and an L.L.B. from Duke University and did postgraduate studies at Yale University Law School.

David Scott Palmer is professor of international relations and political science at Boston University and is director of the Latin American Studies Program there. From 1976 to 1988 he served at the Foreign Service Institute of the Department of State as chairman for Latin American and Caribbean studies. Palmer has lived and studied in Chile, Uruguay, and Peru, and is author of *Peru: The Authoritarian Tradition* (1980) and editor of *The Shining Path of Peru* (1992). He holds a B.A. from Dartmouth College, an M.A. from Stanford University, and a Ph.D. from Cornell Univeristy in comparative government.

Courtney E. Prisk is a senior associate with Booz-Allen & Hamilton, Inc., in Panama. He received his B.S. from the U.S. Military Academy and M.A. from the University of Missouri at Kansas City, and he is a graduate of the Air War College. Colonel Prisk served in various posts, including the U.S. Army Command and Staff College and the Political-Military Affairs Division of the Office of the Joint Chiefs of Staff (JCS), and has served as executive officer for the JCS representative to the SALT II negotiations. Prisk is editor of *The Comandante Speaks: Memoirs of an El Salvadoran Guerrilla Leader*.

Caesar D. Sereseres is associate professor of political science at the University of California, Irvine. He worked for the Department of State as a staff member in the Bureau of Inter-American Affairs, and he was a consultant on national security at the Rand Corporation. Sereseres has served on the editorial board of *The Journal of Small Wars*, traveled throughout Latin America, and published many articles and books, including *U.S. Arms Transfers, Diplomacy, and Security in Latin America, The Central American Policy Conundrum,* and *U.S. Policy for Central America.* Sereseres received his B.A. from the University of California, Santa Barbara, and his M.A. and Ph.D. from the University of California, Riverside.

Stephen Sloan is professor of political science at the University of Oklahoma. He has served as consultant for military, police, and corporate officers dealing with the threat of terrorism. Sloan has served as a senior associate for Booz-Allen & Hamilton, Inc., and was a senior research fellow at the Center for Aerospace Doctrine Research and Education. He has lived in Indonesia and was a Fulbright professor in political science at Tribhuvan University in Kathmandu, Nepal. Sloan has published many articles and books, including, *The Pocket Guide to Safe Travel, Simulating Terrorism, Responding to the Terrorist Threat: Security and Crisis Management,* and *A Study in Political Violence: The Indonesian Experience.* He received his B.A. from Washington Square College of New York University and an M.A. and Ph.D. from New York University.

Robert F. Zimmerman is currently completing a book on the use of economic assistance to promote U.S. political objectives: *Dollars, Diplomacy and Dependency.* He has had more than twenty-three years of foreign service experience as a Peace Corps volunteer and an officer of the Agency for International Development, the U.S. State Department in Southeast Asia, the Near East, and the U.S. Mission to the United Nations. Zimmerman has published many articles on these topics and a monograph, *Reflections on the Collapse of Democracy in Thailand.* He received his B.A. degree from the University of Akron and an M.A. and Ph.D. from the American University in Washington, D.C.

Index